# The Gelug/Kagyü Tradition
## *of* Mahamudra

# The Gelug/Kagyü Tradition
# *of* Mahamudra

*by*
H.H. the Dalai Lama

*and*
Alexander Berzin

Snow Lion Publications
Ithaca, New York

Snow Lion Publications
P.O. Box 6483
Ithaca, New York 14851 USA
607-273-8519

Special thanks to Paul Hackett for supplying a Tibetan copy of the First Panchen Lama's root text.

Printed in Canada on acid-free recycled paper.

ISBN 1-55939-072-7

**Library of Congress Cataloging-in-Publication Data**

Bstan- 'dzin-rgya-mtsho, Dalai Lama XIV, 1935-
    The Gelug/Kagyü tradition of Mahamudra / by H.H. Tenzin Gyatso and Alexander Berzin. -- 1st ed.
        p.    cm.
    Translated from Tibetan.
    Includes the text of Blo-bzaṅ-chos-kyi-rgyal-mtshan's Dge-ldan bka' brgyud rin po che'i phyag chen rtsa ba rgyal ba'i gźuṅ lam.
    Includes index.
    ISBN 1-55939-072-7
    1. Blo-bzaṅ-chos-kyi-rgyal-mtshan, Panchen Lama I, 1567?-1662. Dge-ldan bka' brgyud rin po che'i phyag chen rtsa ba rgyal ba'i gźuṅ lam.   2. Mahāmudrā (Tantric rite)   3. Dge-lugs-pa (Sect)--Rituals.   4. Bka'-rgyud-pa (Sect)--Rituals.   I. Berzin, Alexander.   II. Blo-bzaṅ-chos-kyi-rgyal-mtshan, Panchen Lama I, 1567?-1662. Dge-ldan bka' brgyud rin po che'i phyag chen rtsa ba rgyal ba'i gźuṅ lam.   III. Title.
294.3'44--dc21                                                    96-48435
                                                                        CIP

# Table of Contents

# Preface

The present book has evolved through a long history. At the suggestion of His Holiness the Fourteenth Dalai Lama, I initially translated the First Panchen Lama's *A Root Text for the Precious Gelug/Kagyü Tradition of Mahamudra* in 1973, with the help of Sharpa Rinpochey, Khamlung Rinpochey and Jonathan Landaw, based on an explanation by Geshey Ngawang Dhargyay. Originally published as *A Root Text on Mahamudra: The Great Seal of Voidness* (Dharamsala: Library of Tibetan Works & Archives, 1974), it was reprinted in *Four Essential Texts* (Dharamsala: Library of Tibetan Works & Archives, 1982).

On June 10, 1978, His Holiness, at the request of the late Ven. Anne Ansermet, delivered a discourse on this text in Dharamsala, India, to a small private group of especially interested disciples. Subsequently, with the help of Ven. Lobsang Rabgyay, I translated these teachings from the tape cassettes into English, which then formed the basis for a French translation prepared by Madame Ansermet. This French version was published as *Meditation sur l'esprit*, par le 14ᵉ Dalai Lama (Paris: Dervy-Livre, Coll. mystique et religion série B, 1982).

From March 18 to 22, 1982, His Holiness, requested by the late Lama Thubten Yeshe, delivered in Dharamsala a public discourse on the First Panchen Lama's auto-commentary to his root text. I translated the lectures orally, with the occasional assistance of Ven. Georges Dreyfus. For years, cassettes of these teachings were unavailable to me. In 1995, however, Kaitlin Collins located a copy of them and prepared a transcription of the English translation. Encouraged by this,

I requested Ven. Thubten Chodron to key into the computer the hand-written version of my English translation of His Holiness's first discourse, to which she kindly consented.

At the request of Sidney Piburn of Snow Lion Publications, I have completely retranslated the First Panchen Lama's root text and His Holiness's two discourses and edited them for publication. I have incorporated into the flow of the discourses His Holiness's answers to questions asked at the end of each session, as well as elaboration and clarification of points, persons and texts mentioned in abbreviated form, drawing from other teachings by His Holiness and Tibetan reference works. The root text appears as Part Two of the present volume, while His Holiness's teaching on it as Part Three and his explication of the auto-commentary as Part Four. As an introduction to the subject matter, I have added, as Part One, an edited, expanded version of a set of lectures on mahamudra meditation I delivered from November 7 to 8, 1995, at the Aryatara Institute in Munich, Germany, at the request of Alnis Grants.

I have used a system of translation terminology initially developed under the guidance of my root guru, the late master debate partner of His Holiness, Tsenzhab Serkong Rinpochey, and which I have refined over the last seventeen years by experimentation and use. It is designed to help overcome obstacles to understanding due to jargon that has become meaningless. For ease of reading for non-specialists, I have used a simplified phonetic transliteration system for Sanskrit and Tibetan names and terms. Their standard transcription, as well as the Tibetan, and Sanskrit when available, for the titles of cited texts and major technical terms specific to the subject matter, occasionally along with their more common translation, are included in the indices.

Rajinder Kumar Dogra kindly provided me with the facilities in Bangkok, Thailand, for a two-month intensive work retreat during the rainy season, 1996, to prepare this book. I acknowledge his and my Snow Lion editor, Susan Kyser's, helpful suggestions for improving its style and language. I worked on the final draft during the autumn of 1996 at various places on an extensive lecture tour of the Middle East, the former Soviet Central Asian Republics and Mongolia, during which I was kindly given facilities to work by many universities and private individuals. Bakula Rinpochey, the Indian ambassador to Mongolia, generously offered me his time to clarify certain obscure points. In the end, the research staff of the Library of Tibetan Works & Archives, in Dharamsala, India, provided me with further textual resources and details for finalizing the text. The pre-publication process was initiated by donations made by Edith Erbacher and several other persons who attended the meditation courses I taught in Western Europe during the spring of 1996, and then funded by a grant from the Kapor Family Foundation. I gratefully acknowledge the support of all of them. This book thus exists by virtue of its having arisen dependently on the kindness of many. By the positive potential of the joint efforts and contributions of all these people, may everyone attain to enlightenment for the benefit of all.

Alexander Berzin
Dharamsala, India
December 5, 1996

# Part I

# AN INTRODUCTION TO MAHAMUDRA
# AND
# ITS PRACTICAL APPLICATION TO LIFE

# Chapter One
# THE BUDDHIST FRAMEWORK

## OVERVIEW OF THE TOPIC

"Mahamudra" is a Sanskrit word meaning "great seal" and refers to the nature of all phenomena. Just as a wax seal is stamped on legal documents to authenticate their signature, likewise the nature of reality is figuratively stamped upon everything as a guarantee that nothing exists in a fantasized, impossible way. The fact that everything is devoid of existing in any impossible manner thus validates that things actually exist.

Mahamudra also refers to sophisticated Buddhist systems of meditation and practice to realize this great sealing nature. The distinctive characteristic of these techniques is to see this nature by focusing on mind itself and discovering the relationship between mind and reality. When our mind confuses reality with fantasy, we produce problems for ourselves. Furthermore, when our mind gives rise to an appearance of others in a way that does not correspond to their reality, we are unable to be of help to them. Understanding the intimate relation between mind and reality, therefore, is essential for achieving both liberation and enlightenment, the goal of mahamudra practice.

The most commonly discussed fantasized and impossible manner of existence in Buddhism is literally called "true existence," referring to existence truly independent from a relation with mind. Since true existence is, paradoxically, false existence, referring to a manner of existence that is impossible and not at all real, we can perhaps avoid the confusion by using, instead, variations of the term "solid existence."

We can begin to appreciate the complex relation between mind and reality by examining it from various points of view. For example, if we approach the topic in a practical, down-to-earth manner and call the actual way in which we and the universe exist "reality," we live "in reality." On the basis of our everyday experience of reality, we can know and perhaps understand it. This process can only occur through the medium of mind.

If directly experiencing and knowing reality is not sufficient to be able to understand it clearly and we also need to think about it, we can only do so through a conceptual scheme, which is a construct of mind. Furthermore, if we need to formulate and express to ourselves or others what reality is, we can only do so through words or symbols, which are also a construct of mind. Reality exists, but it is a fantasy to imagine that we can experience, understand, prove or describe it independently from the relationship between reality and mind. If we may borrow a term from post-modernist philosophy, we must "deconstruct" reality from being some solid thing "out there."

If we ask how do phenomena exist, we have already involved mind in merely asking the question. Moreover, we can only answer this question by also involving mind. Suppose we reply, Yes, that is obvious, but on a theoretical level don't things exist separately from mind? We would have to say that a theoretical level does not exist by itself, independently from a mind that is either formulating or at least thinking about it. We cannot say anything further about how a theoretical level exists, because to say anything involves language, which is a construct of mind.

In fact, as soon as we raise the issue of how things exist, we have entered the realm of description which can only be carried out by mind. But that does not mean that everything exists only in the mind and that the earth did not exist before there was life on it. An object need not be experienced by a specific mind at this moment in order to exist. But if we are going to talk about how things exist, or try to understand, prove and know it, we can only do so in relation to mind. Mahamudra starts on this premise.

We can formulate the relationship between mind and how things exist in several ways. There are two major approaches in mahamudra. Let us characterize them in very general terms. The first presents what exists in terms of phenomena being either mind or objects of mind — in other words, experience or the contents of experience. Phenomena, including minds, exist merely by virtue of the fact that mind can simply give rise to an appearance or occurrence of them as an object of cognition. We can establish that our children and love for them exist simply because we can know and experience them. The other major approach discusses what exists in terms of mental labeling, which means things exist as what they are simply in relation to words and what words refer to or signify. Phenomena exist as what they are by virtue of being simply the meaning of the words, mental labels or conceptual formulations of them. We can establish that our children and love exist simply because we can give them names that refer to them.

In neither case is the existence of phenomena established from their own side by virtue, for example, of an inherent, findable self-nature rendering them truly what they are, independently from any relation with mind. Our children do not exist as our children because they have some defining characteristic somewhere inside them making them inherently "our children" even if we ourselves never existed. And love does not exist by itself somewhere in the sky with a defining internal force empowering its existence. These are impossible, fantasized manners of existing, and all phenomena are devoid of existing in those ways. The absence of any phenomenon's existing in impossible manners is called its voidness or "emptiness."

Each of these two approaches entails its own characteristic style of mahamudra meditation on the nature of reality. With the former, we focus on the mind that apprehends voidness as its object and come to realize that all appearances are the play of that mind. With the latter, we focus on voidness as an object of cognition, specifically on the voidness of mind, and come to realize that even mind itself exists merely by virtue of the fact that it can simply be labeled as "mind." With the former, then, we focus on a mind that apprehends a certain object, while with the latter, on an object apprehended by a certain mind.

The Kagyü, Sakya and Gelug traditions of Tibet each transmit lineages of mahamudra presented with a distinctive manner of explanation and with an individual style of meditation. All derive from common sources in India transmitted to Tibet during the early eleventh century. Kagyü and some schools of Sakya present mahamudra in terms of the inseparability of appearance and mind. Gelug presents it in terms of mental labeling, while other schools of Sakya combine the two by first seeing the relation between objects of mind and mind itself, and then realizing the nature of mind itself in terms of mental labeling. Kagyü and Gelug present mahamudra techniques involving both coarse and the most subtle levels of mind, whereas

Sakya approaches this only from the point of view of the subtlest level. Kagyü explains two styles of mahamudra practice — one for those who progress through graded stages and the other for those for whom everything happens at once. Sakya and Gelug describe paths of practice for only the former. The Gelug tradition of mahamudra is known as Gelug/Kagyü because it uses Kagyü-style techniques for recognizing the conventional nature of mind and then typically Gelug ones for recognizing its deepest nature. In the end, as the First Panchen Lama explains in *A Root Text for the Gelug/Kagyü Tradition of Mahamudra*, each approach comes to the same intended realization and result. Each leads, on the basis of mind itself, to the elimination of all confusion and the realization of all potentials, which enables us to be of fullest benefit to others.

## THE FOUR TRUE FACTS IN LIFE

In order to understand, appreciate and, if we are so inclined, eventually practice mahamudra techniques, we need to see them within their appropriate context. Let us begin by outlining this context briefly in terms of the four facts in life that Buddha realized and taught, and which all aryas, or highly realized beings — "noble ones" — see as true. They are usually called the "four noble truths."

Living in India two and a half thousand years ago, Buddha was a person who liberated himself from all confusion and thus became able to use all his potentials for the benefit of others. He achieved this state of enlightenment basically by understanding reality, namely what is true in life. First he saw the truth of suffering. The standard way of expressing this first true fact, however, that "life is suffering," sounds rather ominous and pessimistic. It does not quite convey the intention. He saw, in fact, that no one who looks at life truthfully could deny that it is difficult.

Nothing in life is ever easy. It is not easy to live in society, make a living or raise a family. As trying as these normal aspects of life may be, we tend to make them even more difficult than necessary. For example, we become so nervous, upset and worried about everything that we do not handle life's trials as well or as gracefully as we could. Always tense, we make not only ourselves, but everyone around us miserable.

Buddha explained that the deepest cause of our making life more difficult than need be is our unawareness, or "ignorance." This is the second true fact of life — the true cause of suffering. Unawareness can be about either behavioral cause and effect or reality, and we can be unaware of each by either simply not knowing about it or, in addition, apprehending it in an incorrect manner. "Apprehending," usually translated as "grasping," means to cognize an object in a certain way. Since apprehending reality in an incorrect manner is the root cause of our difficulties in life, we shall refer to unawareness in this context as "confusion about reality."

Being confused about reality, we naturally feel insecure and are nervous and tense. We tend to make such heavy ordeals out of everyday things in our life, such as driving to work or putting the children to bed, that we feel constantly stressed. Of course we need to be concerned about life and take care of our responsibilities, but there is never any need to handicap ourselves with compulsive worry and chronic anxiety. They only prevent us from effectively dealing with life. They certainly do not lead to happiness and peace of mind. To paraphrase the eighth-century Indian master Shantideva, "If there is something difficult in life that we can change, why be upset? Just change it. But if there is nothing that can be done, why be upset? It doesn't help."

When we are feeling tense, either about a specific situation like being caught in traffic, or in an unlocalized manner such as when in a bad mood, we tend to externalize our tension. We express it and perhaps spread it to others, but more importantly, on a deeper level, we misapprehend our tension as something solid and project it onto all situations we are in. Our mind gives rise to an appearance of the traffic jam, and even of our getting up in the morning, as if they were themselves solid, monstrous ordeals. It gives rise to an appearance of them as though their very natures made them truly and inherently stressful, regardless of who might experience them. In addition to our mind automatically and unconsciously giving rise to appearances of things in that way, we may also dwell on these appearances with morbid, uncontrollably recurring thoughts, reinforcing our belief that these appearances are true reality. Everything feels so tense and stressful, it seems as if life were a bear-trap, somewhere "out there," and we are caught tightly and inexorably in its cruel grip.

Buddha explained that this confusion about reality — our imagining that everything exists in the manner in which our mind gives rise to an appearance of it — is the root cause of our trouble. In this way we make difficult aspects of life even more difficult for ourselves. It does not appear to us that tension is merely an experience of a situation, but rather that it is truly and inherently part of the situation itself. If a situation were inherently stress-producing, there would be no way to avoid becoming stressed by it. As a personal experience of a situation, however, stress arises dependently on many psychological factors and is not inevitable. Unless we understand this well, we condemn ourselves to unremitting stress.

Certainly it is difficult to live in a crowded city and be caught in traffic, noise and pollution each day, not to mention being prey to possible crime. No one can deny that. But when we construct a concrete, fixed mental image of the city as some fearful, horrible, tense place "out there," impinging like a monster on poor me, the victim, "in here," we make living there even more difficult. The city in our head that we project onto the streets seems even more concrete and solid than the actual city made of cement. In this way, our belief that our image is the actual reality generates all our tension and stress. Sadly, many people view not only where they live, but all of life in that way.

Buddha taught that it is not inevitable that we experience such painful syndromes as this. It is possible for these syndromes and their causes to cease, not just temporarily, but forever. Their true stopping or ending, equivalent to their total removal, is the third true fact in life — the true "cessation" of suffering and its causes. If we eliminate the recurrence of the causes for suffering, we definitely experience the absence of the suffering that would have arisen as their results. Without a cause, a result cannot arise. Moreover, since the root cause of the recurrence of our problems is the confusion with which we imagine that things actually exist in the impossible manner in which our muddled mind deceptively makes them appear to exist, it is possible to eliminate the recurrence of this cause. This is because confusion cannot be verified. Based on fantasy, not fact, it lacks a stable foundation and cannot withstand close scrutiny. Therefore true endings can definitely occur.

In order to realize a true stopping of our problems and their causes, however, we must actively do something to bring it about. Otherwise, due to strong habit, we endlessly continue to make our life miserable — for instance by generating tension over and over again. Since the root cause of our suffering is a confused state of mind, we need to replace it permanently with an unconfused state so that it never arises again. Such unconfused states of mind with which we see reality are the fourth true fact in life — true pathways of mind, or true "paths." It is not sufficient, therefore, merely to mask over the problem of stress, for example, by taking a tranquilizer or having a drink. We must rid ourselves, or "abandon" the confusion with which we believe that somehow the tension exists "out there." We must replace confusion with correct understanding, for example with understanding that tension is a creation of mind.

Our attitudes of mind can be changed much more easily than the entire world. To paraphrase Shantideva once more in the context of his discussion of patience, "It is impossible to cover the entire rough surface of the world with leather. But, by covering the bottom of our feet with leather, we accomplish the same purpose." Therefore, to liberate ourselves from our problems in life and be of best benefit to others, it is crucial to understand the nature of the reality of the appearances we experience and to do so in terms of their relationship with our mind. The mahamudra teachings present effective, sophisticated techniques for accomplishing this aim.

## TAKING OURSELVES AND OUR LIFE SERIOUSLY

If the first true fact is that life in general is not easy, we should certainly not expect that seeing the nature of our mind will be simple. The actual nature of mind, on any level, is not very obvious. Even to identify and recognize correctly what is mind is extremely difficult. Just to start to try to see it, we need strong motivation. We need to be clear about why we would like to see the nature of our mind. Let us briefly review the Buddhist presentation of the graded stages of motivation through which we progress to gain optimum success in this undertaking.

The foundation for any level of spiritual motivation is to take ourselves and the quality of our life seriously. Most people get up in the morning and either have to go to work or school, or stay home and take care of the house and children. At the end of the day, they are tired and try to relax by maybe having a beer and watching television. Eventually they go to sleep, and the next day get up and repeat the sequence. They spend their whole lives trying to make money, raise a family and catch whatever fun and pleasure they can.

Although most people cannot alter the structure of their lives, they feel they also cannot change the quality of their experience of this structure. Life has its ups, but also lots of downs, and it is all very stressful. They feel they are a tiny part of some solid, giant mechanism they can do nothing about. They therefore go through life in a mechanical, passive manner, like a passenger on a life-long speeding roller coaster going up and down and round and round, assuming that not only the track, but also the tension and stress experienced while circling on it are an inevitable part of the never-ending ride.

Since such experience of one's life, despite its pleasures, can be very depressing, it is vitally essential to do something about it. Just drinking ourselves into oblivion each night, or seeking constant entertainment and distraction by having music or television on all the time or incessantly playing computer games so that we never have to think about our life, is not going to eliminate the problem. We must take ourselves seriously. This means to have respect for ourselves as human beings. We are not just pieces of machinery or helpless passengers on the fixed ride of life that is sometimes smooth, but all too often bumpy. We need, therefore, to look more closely at what we are experiencing each day. And if we see that we are stressed by the tension of our city, household or office, we should not just accept this as something inevitable.

Our living, work and home environments, including the attitudes and behavior of others in them, merely provide the circumstances in which we live out our lives. The quality of our life, however — what we ourselves, not anybody else, are experiencing right now — is the direct result of our own attitudes and the behavior they generate, not anybody else's. This is clear from the fact that not everyone in the same environment experiences it in the same manner.

Admittedly, some environments are more difficult than others, for instance living in a war zone, and we must be always alert to avoid real danger. But alertness is different from tension, and the latter does not necessarily need to accompany the former. If, however, we feel that our tension is inescapable, we will not even try to overcome it. We condemn ourselves to an extremely unpleasant experience of life. It does not have to be that way.

If we are feeling very nervous all the time, the first step toward doing something to remedy the situation, then, is to take ourselves and the quality of our life seriously. Suppose we are walking down the street and we step on a bug and partially crush but have not actually killed it. If we continue walking and ignore the bug's experience of its leg being crushed or severed, we do so because we do not take the insect and its life seriously. We have no respect for it. If we treat ourselves no better than we do a bug and ignore our innermost pains and anguish, that is most unfortunate.

Taking ourselves seriously means actually looking at how we are experiencing our life and, if there is something unsatisfactory about it, admitting it to ourselves. Our tension and stress do not go away by denying them or avoiding taking an honest look. And admitting that something is amiss is not the same as complaining about it and feeling sorry for ourselves. Nor does it imply that something is fundamentally wrong with us and we are guilty of being a bad person because we are nervous. Being objective, not melodramatic, and remaining non-judgmental are essential for any healing, spiritual process.

## SAFE DIRECTION AND BUDDHA-NATURE

Once we take ourselves and the quality of our life seriously, and acknowledge the difficulties we may be experiencing, the next step is to have confidence that (1) it is possible to overcome them, (2) there is a way to accomplish this, and (3) we are capable of achieving it. This bring us to the topics of refuge and Buddha-nature.

Taking refuge is not a passive act of placing ourselves in the hands of a higher power that will do everything for us, as the English word "refuge" might imply. It is an active process of putting a safe, reliable and positive direction in our life. That direction is indicated by the Buddhas, the Dharma and the Sangha — the Three Precious Gems. They are precious in the sense that they are both rare and valuable. Each has two levels of significance — interpretable and definitive — and a common representation. The interpretable level leads to the definitive one, while the representation serves as a focus for respect without providing an actual safe direction in and of itself.

The Buddhas are those who have eliminated all their confusion so that they are able to use their potentials fully to benefit others. On the definitive level, the safe direction of the Buddhas is provided by their *dharmakaya* or bodies encompassing everything — namely, their omniscient awareness and its nature, both of which encompass everything. The *rupakaya* or bodies of form that Buddhas manifest serve as the interpretable level, while Buddha statues and paintings are the representation of the first precious gem.

On the definitive level, the Dharma source of direction refers to the complete removal or total absence of obstacles, and the full attainment of good qualities the Buddhas have achieved. Its interpretable level is what they indicate that helps us achieve the same ourselves, namely their scriptural pronouncements and realizations. These are represented by Dharma texts.

The definitive level of the Sangha source of direction is the internal "community" of total removals or cessations of obstacles and attainments of good qualities within the mind. Specifically, it is the community of these gathered together by all aryas — those who have straightforwardly and non-conceptually seen reality — as they progress further along the spiritual path. Its interpretable level is the community of aryas, both lay and monastic, with some token of these true removals and attainments. The general community of monastics represents them.

In short, the definitive level of the Three Precious Gems of Buddha, Dharma and Sangha presents the goal we would like to achieve. Their interpretable level indicates what we rely on, externally, to bring ourselves there. But we also have internal factors that we need to rely on as well. These refer to our Buddha-nature.

We are capable of eliminating our problems and achieving the definitive Three Precious Gems because everyone has Buddha-nature, namely the various factors or working materials that make it possible. Of all our natural resources, the most important is mind. We all have a mind which, in its nature, is unhampered by anything from experiencing whatever exists. No matter what happens — no matter how confused, stressed or unhappy we may be — we experience it. Even death is something that we experience when it occurs. Therefore, because we have a mind that allows us to experience whatever exists, we have the basic resource that allows us to experience a total absence of confusion and a utilization of all possible good qualities for helping others — provided that such a total absence and utilization actually exist. In other words, if we can establish that it is possible for these two things to exist — and that they are not just objects of nice but totally unrealistic wishes — we can be confident that we are capable of attaining them, simply because we have a mind.

We can experience things without confusion and without being tense. Even the most disturbed, nervous person has moments of clarity and calmness — even if only when he or she is peacefully asleep and dreaming pleasant or innocuous dreams. This demonstrates that confusion and tension are not integral parts of the nature of mind. Thus confusion can be removed. Not only can it be removed, but since confusion cannot be validated and can be totally replaced by understanding, which can be verified, confusion can be eliminated forever. Thus it is possible for a total absence of confusion to exist. Furthermore, since confusion limits mind from using its full potentials, once confusion is gone, a utilization of all potentials can also exist. Therefore, since we all have a mind, and all minds have the same nature of being able to experience whatever exists, we can all realize and experience the definitive Three Precious Gems.

Thus, if we aim to remove our confusion and realize our potentials as indicated by the Buddhas, their achievement, their teachings, what they have built up along the path and those who are progressing along it, we are traveling through life with a safe, reliable and positive direction. Taking refuge, then, means to put this realistic, safe direction in our life. Without it, our practice of mahamudra either has no direction and leads nowhere, or an unsound direction leading to more confusion and trouble. In addition, the further we travel in this safe direction through the mahamudra techniques — in other words, the more we realize the nature of mind and its relation to reality — the more confident we become in the soundness of this direction and our ability to reach its goal. The stronger our confidence, the further we progress along the path.

BEHAVIORAL CAUSE AND EFFECT

To proceed in the safe direction of eliminating our confusion and realizing our potentials the way the Buddhas have done and the highly realized community is doing, we need to understand that all life's experiences arise through a complex process of cause and effect. What we are experiencing now has come about from causes and will produce effects. For example, we may discover that we are often unhappy and have little peace of mind. This may be because most of the time we feel nervous and stressed, and this is because we run around constantly and never relax or take time out for ourselves. We need to realize that if we continue to lead our life in this manner, we are going to experience the same unhappiness and tension, if not worse, in the future. Therefore, if we wish to avoid having a nervous breakdown, we take responsibility upon ourselves to modify our behavior. This is how we travel in a safe and positive direction in life. We need to pay closer attention to our state of mind and try to relax. We try to stop running constantly, for example, and take time each day to sit in a hot bath and calm down.

Thus, at this first stage of our development, our dread of our situation becoming worse motivates us to try to understand the nature of our mind. Taking ourselves seriously, we try to become increasingly aware of the state of our mind so that when it is tense we modify our behavior in order to affect what we feel. We do this because of our confidence in the laws of behavioral cause and effect. To experience something better in life, we realize we must enact their causes.

## RENUNCIATION

Although taking a hot bath may make us feel slightly better and our tension may subside for a little while, that does not really solve the problem. The next day we return to the same frantic pace, and our tension and unhappiness recur. We need to progress to a second level of motivation. We need to develop renunciation.

Since many people think of renunciation as a bit masochistic, as if it meant giving up all pleasure and comfort in life, we need to understand it properly. Renunciation has two aspects. The first is a strong determination to free ourselves totally from both our problems and their causes. It is important to stress here that we do not simply wish for someone else to free us, but that we are determined to free ourselves. Moreover, we are determined to rid ourselves not merely of our problems but of their causes as well, so that they never recur. That does not mean simply being willing to take some superficial measure, like swallowing a pill or taking a hot bath, so that we receive temporary relief. We are willing to probe very deeply to discover and root out the innermost cause of our difficulties in life.

It requires a great deal of courage to probe deeply to reach the actual source of our problems. We gain the strength of that courage, however, from being totally disgusted and bored with the poor quality of what we are experiencing in life — our constant unhappiness and tension, for example. With renunciation, we decide we have had enough of them. We must definitely break out of their grip.

The second aspect corresponds more closely to the Western notion of renunciation. We are determined not only to free ourselves, but in order to do so, we are willing to sacrifice something. This does not refer to forgoing something trivial, like television or ice cream, or even giving up something not at all trivial, like making love with our marriage partner, or ever relaxing and having fun. We need to let go of our problems and all levels of their causes.

We might be willing to give up the problem, for instance of being unhappy, because it is painful. But to let go of even the first levels of the causes of our problems is a different matter. The usual first level cause of our problems is our self-destructive personality traits. We must be willing to sacrifice these. We need to give up our attachments, anger, selfishness and, in this case, our nervousness, tension and constant worrying. If we are not totally willing to forgo these disturbing factors that are causing our problems, we can never be rid of our unhappiness. It is much more difficult to give up worrying than it is to stop smoking or watching television. But this is what we focus on when we try to develop renunciation.

Many people who approach the practice of Buddhism are willing to sacrifice one or two hours of their day in order to perform some ritual practice or engage in meditation. Time is relatively easy to give up, even though their life may be very busy. But, they are not willing to change anything of their personality — they are not willing to forgo anything of their negative character. With this type of approach to Buddhism, it hardly matters how much meditation we do, our practice remains merely a hobby or a sport. It does not touch our lives. In order actually to overcome our problems, we have to be willing to change — namely to change our personality. We need to renounce and rid ourselves of those negative aspects of it that are causing us so much trouble.

This requires even more courage — a tremendous amount of courage — to forge ahead into new territory in our life. But it definitely is possible to have such courage, even though it may be a bit frightening at first. For instance, the water in a pool might be very cold. But if, in the summer, we are sufficiently hot and sweaty, then because we are so disgusted with being uncomfortable, we have the courage to jump into the water. We are willing to give up, to renounce, not only being sweaty, but the cause of the discomfort, namely our being in the hot sun and not in the pool. When we first jump into the pool, of course it is cold. It is a great shock to our system, but we soon become used to the water. In fact, we discover that it is much more comfortable than standing on the side of the pool and sweating. So, it is quite possible to have this courage, this determination to be free of our negative qualities and this courage to be willing to give them up.

We must also have the courage to probe ever deeper into the sources of our problems. Being nervous, tense and worried, for example, is both a cause of unhappiness as well as the result of something deeper. With the first level motivation, we modify our behavior in order to prevent our problem becoming worse. We try to stop running around all the time and do something to relax as an initial measure to reduce and relieve our stress and tension. But now, in addition, we must discover the inner process behind the tension.

When we investigate more deeply, we realize that our running around is either the result of our tension or the circumstance in which our tension is manifesting. But it is not the actual cause of our tension. There is something deeper happening that is responsible for this state of mind we have while running around — we are constantly worried, for example. But we must also delve even deeper to discover why we are so anxious and worried all the time.

## ELIMINATING CONFUSION

The nature of reality is that the contents of what we experience, such as sights, sounds, thoughts and emotions, are all objects that arise dependently on a mind. They do not exist independently "out there," separately from the process of a mind experiencing them. Traffic is quite different from the sight of traffic reflected on the retinas of our eyes in connection with visual cognition. What we actually experience is the latter, the sight of the traffic, while the former, the traffic itself, is merely what we call, in Buddhist analysis, the objective condition for the experience of traffic. It is what the experience is aimed at, but not what actually appears to the mind experiencing it. Furthermore, our mind gives rise not simply to the appearance that constitutes the contents of our experience, but also to an appearance of a manner of existence of these contents that normally does not correspond to reality.

Normally, we fixate on the contents of our experience and imagine or misapprehend that they exist independently from their being merely what mind gives rise to as part of an experience. Fixated upon these contents and imagining they exist solidly "out there" — as they appear to — we become nervous and worried about them, which is the source of our tension and thus our unhappiness. This is because if we believe they are actually "out there," there is little we can do about them. So we feel helpless and hopeless.

With the mahamudra techniques, we shift our focus from the contents of our experience to the process of experience itself and, from that point of view, understand the relation between mind and the reality we experience. This allows us to deconstruct our experience and its contents from being solid and frightening to something fluid and manageable. To make this shift of perspective requires strong renunciation of our morbid fixation on the contents of our experience and the way in which we imagine them to exist. Thus there can be no practice of mahamudra without a proper development of renunciation.

## COMPASSION AND A DEDICATED HEART OF BODHICHITTA

To develop the most advanced level motivation, we consider how our nervousness and tension are adversely affecting others, for instance our children and friends. Our disturbed state of mind is not only preventing us from being able to help them effectively, it is making them as well feel nervous and tense. Only if we overcome all our confusion and realize all our potentials are we able to help them most effectively. In other words, to help them fully we must become an enlightened Buddha. In this manner, through our concern for others, we develop a dedicated heart of bodhichitta — a heart that is set on achieving enlightenment in order to benefit everyone.

Both overcoming confusion and realizing our potentials require seeing the nature of mind. Mind is the basis for all confusion, as well as the foundation for all good qualities. Thus, with a dedicated heart of bodhichitta as motivation, our concern for others causes us to feel we absolutely have to overcome all our problems and limitations, for example chronic worry and tension, and realize all our potentials by seeing the nature of mind. We have no alternative. We must do so urgently because we cannot bear our inability, otherwise, to be of benefit to anyone, not even ourselves.

Bodhichitta is not only the strongest motivation providing the greatest strength for mahamudra practice, but cultivating it as our state of mind helps in yet other ways to enhance this practice. Technically, bodhichitta is a heart or mind that takes enlightenment as its object and is accompanied by two strong intentions — to achieve that enlightenment and to benefit all beings by means of that achievement. Unless we are a Buddha, however, we cannot possibly know enlightenment directly and non-conceptually. We can only focus on enlightenment through the medium of an idea of it, or something that represents it such as the visualized image of a Buddha.

Before we become Buddhas ourselves, however, we can focus on and know directly and non-conceptually our Buddha-nature, namely the factors that allow us to attain enlightenment — specifically, the nature of our mind. The nature of mind is not stained by any disturbing emotions, confusion or even their instincts, and is the foundation for all good qualities for helping others, such as omniscient awareness and total concern for others. Thus the nature of mind can also serve as a representation of enlightenment for the purpose of meditation.

Focusing on the nature of our mind, then, with the strong intention to realize it and to benefit all beings by means of that realization, can serve as a way to meditate on bodhichitta. Such practice is known as cultivating the ultimate or deepest level bodhichitta, while focusing conceptually on enlightenment itself through any other image is the practice of relative or conventional bodhichitta. Thus the deepest level bodhichitta practice is, in fact, the practice of mahamudra.

Concern for others to be happy and compassion wishing them to be free from suffering are needed not only as the basis for a bodhichitta motivation for mahamudra practice, but also for keeping that practice on course to its intended goal. When we have changed our focus in life from the contents of our experience to the process of experience, there is great danger of becoming fixated on mind itself. This is because the direct experience of mind itself is totally blissful — in a calm and serene sense — and entails extraordinary clarity and starkness. Concern for others is one of the strongest forces that bring us back down to earth after having been up in the clouds. Although all appearances exist as a function of mind, other beings do not exist merely in our head. Their suffering is real and it hurts them just as much as ours hurts us.

Furthermore, to be concerned about someone does not mean to be frantically worried about this person. If we are fixated on our child's problems at school, for example, we lose sight that whatever appearance of the problems our mind gives rise to is a function of mind. Believing the appearance to be the solid reality "out there," we again feel hopeless to do anything and thus become extremely anxious and tense. We worry to the point of becoming sick and we over-react toward our child, which does not help. If we focus instead on the process of mind that gives rise to our perception of the problem as if it existed as some horrible monster "out there," we do not eliminate our concern for our child, only our worry. This allows us to take whatever clear and calm action is necessary to alleviate the problem. Thus not only is compassion necessary for successful practice of mahamudra, but mahamudra realization is necessary for successful practice of compassion.

# Chapter Two
# THE PRELIMINARY PRACTICES

RECOGNIZING OUR MENTAL BLOCKS

The mahamudra teachings also emphasize the importance and need for extensive preliminary practice. The point of such practice, for example making hundreds of thousands of prostrations, is to purify ourselves of the grossest levels of obstacles and build up positive potential so that our mahamudra meditation will be more effective for bringing us to enlightenment. In this context, obstacles do not refer to economic, social or other external hindrances, but to difficulties within ourselves. Positive potential, usually translated as "merit," refers to the conducive internal state that results from constructive, or "virtuous" actions of body, speech, mind and heart.

To appreciate how this process of purification works so that we can undertake it in the most effective manner, it is essential to understand what are internal obstacles. Shantideva has written, "If you have not come in contact with the object that is to be refuted, you cannot gain an understanding of its refutation." We cannot possibly eliminate the mental and emotional obstacles to our spiritual success unless we know what they are.

We can understand these obstacles on many levels. There are obstacles preventing liberation and those preventing omniscience. The former refer to disturbing emotions and attitudes, or "afflictions" such as pride and stubborn confusion, while the latter refer to the instincts of such confusion. Preliminary practices help to purify ourselves of the grossest levels of obstacles preventing liberation. Prostration, for example, helps weaken our pride. Within the context of mahamudra, however, we can perhaps best understand obstacles as mental blocks. Let us develop this theme by examining again the mechanism of tension.

If we are constantly tense, one of the main mental blocks causing this is that we are bogged down in the contents of what we are currently experiencing. For instance, we are filling out our tax forms — a task that we intensely dislike. Because we dislike it so much, we morbidly fixate and become stuck on each line of the form, feeling increasingly more tense and nervous. We start to complain in our mind, feel sorry for ourselves, doubt our ability to accomplish the task, worry if we shall ever finish it, wish we didn't have to do it at all, and fantasize about enjoying something else instead. We distract ourselves with a cigarette, a snack or a telephone call. It is as if the form is a quagmire of quicksand dragging us down. Such an attitude creates a serious obstacle to ever finishing the task. We likewise disable ourselves, through a similar mechanism, when we morbidly fixate with tension and worry on the contents of a future experience or task that we anticipate with dread.

Life, however, is an ongoing process that continues from each moment to the next without ever taking a pause. Each moment of life is the next moment of experience, and every experience has its own contents. There is always something different that we are experiencing each moment. Life always goes on, although, unfortunately, often entailing things we do not enjoy. The first true fact, after all, is that life is difficult.

When we are tense, however, we are stuck on the content aspect of a particular moment of our experience. It is as if we have frozen a moment of time and cannot go on. We are caught in the contents of what we are doing, or anticipate doing, as opposed to just doing the task and being finished with it. This fixation functions as a severe mental block — an obstacle preventing us from effectively doing anything, let alone liberating ourselves from all suffering.

My late mother, Rose, had a very wise and useful piece of advice. She always used to say, "Do things straight up and down, not sideways! Whatever you have to do, just do it and be finished." Thus if we have to wash the dishes or take out the garbage, just do the task, straight up and down, and be finished. If we make an ordeal out of it in our mind, we experience it as an ordeal.

Becoming caught up in and stuck on the contents of the experiences of daily life so that we feel tense and complain, not to mention becoming annoyed with them, is a serious mental block. It is an obstacle that prevents us from seeing the ongoing process of the nature of mind. As it is essential to see that process in order to overcome our confusion about reality, which generates our problems and our inability to help others effectively, we need to remove such obstacles. Preliminary practices, such as the repetition of a hundred thousand or more prostrations, are designed to weaken and thus to begin eliminating these blocks.

## PROSTRATION

Making prostration is not a punishment or penance, not some oppressive thing we have to do and get over with quickly so that we can go on to the good parts. Buddha is not like an overbearing parent insisting we do our homework before we can play any games. Rather, making prostration helps us loosen the mental block of being caught up in the contents of our experience. We just make prostration, "straight up and down," as Rose Berzin would say. This does not mean that we make them mechanically, but just directly. We just do it.

Of course, we accompany our prostration with an appropriate motivation, visualization and recitation of either a refuge formula or a short text helpful for purification such as *The Admission of Downfalls*. Doing so leaves little room in our mind for complaining, feeling sorry for ourselves or worrying if we shall ever complete the hundred thousand. But merely making prostrations itself can familiarize us with the approach to life of just doing things directly, straight up and down, without feeling tense. This helps us purify, to a certain extent, some of our mental blocks or obstacles and build up more positive potential to be able actually to see directly the nature of mind.

## VAJRASATTVA PRACTICE

Another important preliminary is the recitation of the hundred-syllable mantra of Vajrasattva, a hundred thousand times or more, for purification of negative potentials we have built up from previously committed destructive or "non-virtuous" actions. We accompany our recitation with an open admission to these negative actions and the acknowledgment that it was a mistake to have ever committed them. We feel regret, not guilt; offer our promise to try not to commit them again; reaffirm our safe direction of refuge and our commitment to achieving enlightenment to be able to benefit everyone; and graphically imagine a purification occurring with a complex visualization while we repeat the mantra.

The state of mind with which we engage in this preliminary, then, is the same with which we make prostration while reciting *The Admission of Downfalls*. In this way, Vajrasattva practice purifies us of negative potentials that, as karmic obstacles, would ripen into our experience of unhappiness or unpleasant situations that would prevent, respectively, our liberation or full ability to help others. In addition to its usual benefit, however, such practice also serves as an excellent preliminary specifically for mahamudra meditation.

One of the ways in which we experience having built up negative potentials is feeling guilt. Suppose we have foolishly spoken harsh words to our boss in a momentary fit of anger which has caused us to lose our job and may cause us future difficulty in finding other employment. If we become fixated on the contents of that experience, we solidify the event in our mind. We freeze it in time and then dwell on it over and again, identifying ourselves totally with what we did at that moment and judging ourselves to be a stupid, worthless, bad person. Such classic guilt is usually accompanied with a feeling of stress and anxiety, and considerable worry about what are we going to do now. So long as we do not let go of our stranglehold on the contents of that experience, we cripple ourselves from ever taking clear, self-confident action to remedy the situation by finding a new job.

Visualizing our negativities leaving us in a graphic form while we recite the hundred-syllable Vajrasattva mantra with the appropriate state of mind helps us let go of our fixation on the contents of our past experience of having acted destructively. Consequently, it helps us let go of our guilt. This helps train us to let go of our fixation on the contents of every moment of experience, which is the essence of the beginning levels of mahamudra practice. In this way, Vajrasattva serves as an excellent preliminary for mahamudra.

## GURU-YOGA

Guru-yoga is another preliminary always stressed as a method for gaining inspiration or "blessings." It is fairly easy to practice guru-yoga on a superficial level. We visualize before us our spiritual teacher in the appearance of either Shakyamuni Buddha, a Buddha-form like Avalokiteshvara, or a lineage master such as Tsongkapa or Karmapa. We then imagine lights of three colors emanating from this figure to us while we recite, a hundred thousand times or more, an appropriate mantra or verse while making fervent requests for inspiration to be able to see the nature of mind. It is very difficult, however, to understand on a deeper level what we are actually trying to do during and by means of such practice. What are we trying to cultivate on a psychological level? The answer revolves around one of the more difficult aspects of the Buddhist teachings — the proper relation with a spiritual teacher.

Almost every mahamudra text contains instructions like, "As an essential preliminary for mahamudra practice, diligently perform guru-yoga. Imagine that your body, speech and mind become one with those of your guru. Make fervent requests for inspiration to be able to see the nature of your mind." At first reading, it seems almost as if all we need do is perform such visualization and make such requests, and then we shall live happily ever after, as in a fairy-tale. We shall receive inspiration that, like magic, will act as the sole cause for our gaining realization, independently of our having to do anything else. Even in the Jodo Shinshu school of Japanese Buddhism in which we rely solely on the power of Amitabha to gain liberation and enlightenment, we implicitly understand from this formulation of the spiritual path that we must stop all ego-based efforts, which depends on realizing the deepest nature of "me" and mind. Thus we must obviously go deeper than just the superficial level of praying to our guru to inspire us to see the nature of our mind, and then leaving it at that, feeling that if we have enough faith and are truly sincere, we shall have our wish granted. All of a sudden, like having been touched on the head with a wizard's magic wand, we shall see and recognize the nature of our mind.

Mind has a two-leveled nature. Its conventional nature is mere clarity and awareness. It is what allows for anything to arise as an object of cognition and be known. Its deepest or "ultimate" nature is that it is devoid of existing in any fantasized, impossible ways, such as independently of the appearances that it gives rise to as the objects it knows. Guru-yoga is a profound though not mystical aid for seeing both. Let us examine the mechanism for each.

When we practice guru-yoga, request our guru for inspiration and then dissolve a replica of our guru into us, the stronger our fervent regard and respect for him or her, the more prominently we experience a blissful, vibrant state of mind as a result of this process. If our faith is mixed with attachment, the state of mind we gain is merely one of excitement — confused, distracted and not very clear. But if our fervent regard and respect are based on reason, this blissful, vibrant state of mind is founded on confident belief. Being emotionally stable, it is extremely conducive to utilize as both the mind that sees its own conventional nature and the mind having this nature upon which to focus.

To understand how the process of guru-yoga and requesting inspiration works to facilitate our seeing the deepest nature of mind, we need to understand how seeing our guru as a Buddha fits within the context of the teachings on voidness and dependent arising. Voidness means an absence — an absence of impossible ways of existing. When we imagine that a guru exists as a Buddha independently from his or her own side, for example, we are projecting an impossible way of existing onto that teacher. That mode of existence does not refer to anything real, because nobody exists as "this" or "that," or as anything from his or her own side. Someone exists as a spiritual mentor, a Buddha or both only in relation to a disciple. A "teacher" arises dependently not only on a mind to which someone appears as a teacher and not only on what the word or mental label "teacher" refers to, but also on the existence of students.

The role "teacher" cannot exist independently from the function of teaching. It is defined, in fact, as someone who teaches. The function of teaching could not possibly exist on its own if there were no such things as learning or learners. Thus, no one could be a teacher if there were no such thing as students. In other words, no one — not even Shakyamuni Buddha, Tsongkapa, Karmapa, or even our personal guru — could exist as a spiritual mentor if there did not also exist someone as a student. Even if someone is not teaching at this moment or has no students right now, that person could only exist as a teacher if he or she had been trained as a teacher, which could come about only if there were such a thing in the universe as students. Moreover, someone is functionally a teacher only when he or she is actually teaching, and that can only be in relation to a student.

The same line of reasoning applies to the interdependently arising existence of Buddhas and sentient beings. Sentient beings are those with limited awareness, while Buddhas are those with the fullest capacity to help such beings. No one could be a Buddha if sentient beings never existed. This is why it is said that the kindness of sentient beings far outweighs the kindness of the Buddhas in enabling us to attain enlightenment.

Since gurus and Buddhas do not exist independently from disciples or students, it follows that neither teachers nor disciples exist as totally independent entities, like two solid, concrete posts, either of which could exist on its own even if the other never had existed. We can therefore logically conclude that it is fantasy to imagine that a guru can produce an effect on a disciple as someone solid "out there" transmitting a solid effect, like tossing a ball, to someone solid "in here," namely "me." Effects, such as gaining realization of the nature of mind, can only arise by depending on many factors, among them the joint efforts of both a spiritual guide and a disciple. As Buddha has explained, "A bucket is not filled with water by the first or last drop of water. It is filled by a collection of a very large number of drops."

Realization of the conventional and deepest natures of mind is the result of a long and arduous process, over countless lifetimes, of collecting and cleansing. The former refers to building up two bountiful stores of positive potential and deep awareness — the "two collections of merit and insight" — while the latter means purifying ourselves of negative potentials and obstacles. In addition, we must listen to correct teachings on the two true levels of the nature of mind — conventional and deepest — ponder them until we gain a working level of understanding, and then meditate properly and intensively on them. By practicing in this way, we build up the causes for gaining realization and attainments. Inspiration from our guru cannot substitute for this process.

Inspiration from a spiritual mentor is, however, the most effective means for causing the seeds of potential for realization that we build up through these methods to ripen more quickly so as to produce their results more immediately. Inspiration, as a circumstance for the ripening of causes, cannot by itself bring about any results if there are either no causes or insufficient ones for it to ripen. Inspiration or "blessings" from a guru, a lineage founder, or even Shakyamuni himself, cannot function like magic to bring us realization and enlightenment. Therefore, we should not deceive ourselves into thinking that we can avoid the hard work necessary to overcome our problems so that we can gain everlasting, deep happiness and the ability to be of most benefit to others. Inspiration can definitely help us reap the effects of our efforts more quickly — and is widely praised as the most effective means for so doing — but it can never substitute for the sustained effort, over many lifetimes, to build up the causes for those effects.

In summary, for one to gain inspiration and then actually realize the nature of mind, it is crucial that not only the disciple but also the teacher understand how each of them exists and how the process of cause and effect can only function on the basis of voidness — an absence of impossible ways of existing. If either believes that self and other exist independently and concretely like cement posts, that inspiration and realization exist like a hard ball, and that the cause and effect process of gaining inspiration and realization works like tossing that ball from one post to the other, then no matter how skillful the spiritual mentor might be and how receptive and sincere the disciple may be, the effect will be blocked. If we believe that what we experience in relation to our guru, even as a Buddha, exists somewhere concretely "out there" and does not arise by depending on many factors — not the least of which is our mind — how can he or she send us either inspiration or the understanding of the nature of our mind, even if we request it nicely, with total sincerity and a proper motivation?

## THE RELATIONSHIP WITH A SPIRITUAL TEACHER

To understand guru-yoga more clearly, we need to examine more closely the topic of "guru-devotion." In order to avoid a possible misinterpretation, let us translate the technical term for this as a "wholehearted commitment to a spiritual teacher," namely the commitment to regard this person as a Buddha. Making this commitment is not dealing with the issue of whether or not our spiritual mentor exists "out there" as a Buddha. After all, we can only speak of our teacher in terms of our experience of him or her. The manner in which a spiritual mentor exists can only be formulated in terms of mind. Therefore we are committing ourselves to regard our *experience* of our teacher as we regard our *experience* of a Buddha.

This relationship with a spiritual teacher as a Buddha, then, is basically a very personal contract. If we speak from the point of view of a disciple, our contract with the spiritual teacher is, "It is of no concern to me now at this stage of my practice how you generate and experience your motivation for what you are doing. I want to be able to help others as fully as possible and reach the state of a Buddha in order to be best able to bring about that benefit. Therefore, having examined you and myself very carefully and having seen that both of us are suitable for entering into this type of relationship, I now intend to regard my experience of whatever you say or do as a personal teaching. I shall experience your actions and words as being motivated solely by the wish to help me develop so that I can overcome my problems and shortcomings and be of fuller benefit to others. A Buddha is someone whose every thought, word and action benefits others, in other words someone who always teaches. Therefore I am going to regard you as teaching me all the time.

"Neither our relationship nor the benefit I can derive from it exists as something coming just from your side or as some solid entity like a rope tied between us. Our relationship exists only in terms of our minds' experience of it, which is dependent on both of us. Since I can only experience our relationship in the way I conceive of and perceive it, I am going to experience it in such a manner as to maximize the benefit I can receive. It is for that purpose that I am going to regard my experience of you as an experience of a Buddha. And, in fact, if I regard it as such, for me it will be the same as experiencing a Buddha and will function as such. It is not self-deception carried out for a worthy, good purpose."

The main way in which our spiritual teacher or any Buddha can help us liberate ourselves from confusion and problems and use all our potentials effectively to help others is by training us to develop discriminating awareness, or "wisdom." We need to cultivate a mind that can discriminate between reality and fantasy and between what is helpful and harmful. Thus our relation with our guru is not that of a private in the army to his or her general. Whenever the general speaks, we jump to our feet, salute and shout, "Yes, sir!" and unquestioningly obey. It is not like that. When our spiritual mentor speaks, we are, of course, respectful, but we experience it as an opportunity to exercise our discriminating awareness.

Furthermore, in the army if we always obey and are a good soldier, our general may grant us a promotion. But it is totally different with a spiritual teacher. It is not that if we always obey our teacher unquestioningly, that makes us a good disciple. And if we sincerely request, our guru will grant us a promotion in rank to someone who sees the nature of mind. Seeing the nature of mind can only arise by directly depending on our development of discriminating awareness. The way in which we experience our teacher contributes to our success in an indirect manner, by helping us cultivate that discrimination.

The classic example of this process comes from an account of one of Buddha's previous lives. Once, in a former life, Buddha had a spiritual mentor who told him and all his other disciples to go through the village and steal for him. Everybody went out to steal, except Buddha, who stayed in his room. The guru came to Buddha's room and shouted with rage, "Why don't you go out and steal for me? Don't you want to please me?" Buddha calmly replied, "How can stealing make anyone happy?" The guru answered, "Ah, you are the only one who understood the point of the lesson."

Thus, if we regard and experience as a teaching whatever our spiritual mentor says or does, we can use it to help develop wisdom and discrimination. No matter what our teacher suggests we do, we examine to see if it makes sense. If it is in accord with Buddha's teachings and we are capable of doing it, we do it "straight up and down," as my mother would say. In the process, we have learned to think things over carefully before acting and then to act decisively with self-confidence. And if our teacher asks us to do something that we see is totally inappropriate, we politely explain why we cannot do it. Our spiritual guide has once more provided an opportunity to train and exercise discriminating wisdom.

The most beneficial relationship with a guru, then, certainly does not revolve around a personality cult. When we regard our teacher as a cult icon, we are caught up in and fixated upon the contents of our experience. We overinflate and solidify the object of our experience, in this case a guru, and almost literally set him or her up on a pedestal, like a solid gold statue, whenever we see or imagine this person on a teaching throne. With this state of mind, we abnegate ourselves and worship the contents of our experience, adding title after title to his or her name. We are neither aware of nor focused on the nature of mind itself and its relation to our experience of our spiritual mentor. With such a confused and naïve attitude, we open ourselves to serious abuse.

The other extreme we could go to when we become caught up in the object side of our experience of our teacher is that we criticize the guru with hostility and, perhaps, profound disappointment and dismay. He or she was supposed to have been perfect and we see serious ethical or judgmental flaws. Or, we keep our mouth shut out of fear, thinking that if we say no to our teacher, we are being a bad disciple and will be rejected. Or, we think that to say no is tantamount to an admission that we were stupid to have chosen this person as our spiritual guide, and rather than appearing stupid to ourselves and others, we blindly accept and agree to everything that our mentor says or does. In all these cases, we have lost sight of our contract to learn discriminating awareness from our interaction with the teacher, regardless of the contents of that interaction. To enter into such an agreement obviously requires not only a highly qualified spiritual master, but also a highly qualified disciple who is emotionally mature and not looking for a father or mother-substitute to make all his or her decisions.

Therefore, when we practice guru-yoga, even if we do not as yet have a personal mentor with whom we have such a contract, we try to follow the guidelines for how to gain the most benefit from such a relationship. We try to avoid becoming caught up in and infatuated with the contents of the visualizations. We do not become enraptured at how wonderful our guru or Buddha is in sending us blissful lights. Instead, we focus on the experiential side of what is happening — on the mind that is allowing for the interchange of lights and the inspiration that those lights symbolize. Just as we can develop discriminating awareness of what is appropriate or not by experiencing each and every action of our spiritual guide as a teaching, likewise we can also develop discriminating awareness of dependent arising and voidness from the practice of guru-yoga.

When we make requests to the guru, what are we doing? When we fervently request, "May I be able to see the nature of my mind," we are generating a very strong wish to see and understand the nature of mind through a proper interaction with a spiritual teacher. Just as tension does not exist "out there," but rather is dependent on mind, likewise stable realization or even a passing flash of insight into the nature of mind and reality, as well as inspiration to receive either of them, are not things "out there" that somebody can throw to us like a ball. They are things that arise dependently in relation to a mind as a result of a huge complex of causes.

## THE INSEPARABILITY OF OUR MIND AND OUR GURU

The early twelfth-century Tibetan master Gampopa said, "When I experienced the inseparability of my mind and my guru, I perceived mahamudra." We can understand Gampopa's guideline statement on many levels, such as concerning gaining inspiration from constant remembrance of our teacher; gaining a blissful, vibrant state of mind from fervent regard and respect for him or her; and so on. But, he certainly did not mean that when he had a mystical union with his guru, like with God or his beloved, he beheld mahamudra like a gift sent from heaven. Rather, he saw that the relationship with his spiritual mentor was an experience of mind that entailed learning from each moment of encounter. The resulting benefit was thus arising by depending on mind and could only exist by depending on mind. In that sense, he realized his guru and his mind were inseparable.

The implication of Gampopa's statement is not that the relationship with a spiritual master occurs only in the head of the disciple.

That is just as mistaken as saying that everything comes from the side of an all-mighty guru/Buddha. A relation between a teacher and disciple arises in dependence not only on the two persons, but also on a mind that experiences the interaction from moment to moment. When we understand this, we do not become caught up in the contents of the experience by fixating either on the object side of the "holy guru" or the subject side of "poor, helpless me." Rather, we remain focused on the experience and on the deepest nature of mind and reality that allows for the cause and effect relationship of inspiration and benefit to occur between the two persons involved. This is symbolized by a flow of transparent lights from guru to disciple, both of whom we visualize and thus experience as also made of clear light. There is no solid, concrete guru "out there" shining some solid glaring lights onto a solid, concrete me sitting independently "in here," in my head. Such practice of guru-yoga, then, is extremely helpful for training ourselves to focus with discriminating awareness on the deepest nature of mind in mahamudra meditation.

## GURU-MANTRAS

When we practice guru-yoga, we accompany our visualization with repeated recitation of a guru-mantra or verse that includes a request. In the Karma Kagyü tradition, for example, which developed from one of Gampopa's disciples, the First Karmapa, we recite the mantra, "Karmapa kyenno," which means, literally, "Karmapa, omnisciently know!" In the Gelug/Kagyü tradition of mahamudra, we substitute the visualization and mantra of Tsongkapa for those of Karmapa. Otherwise the procedure and process are exactly the same.

If our understanding remains at the level of the guru as someone external, then the recitation of the Karmapa mantra, for example, becomes an exercise in devotion alone, and nothing deeper. We are basically reciting the equivalent of "Karmapa, listen and know my troubles! Only you omnisciently know how to remove them." At best this leads to seeing Karmapa as a Buddha indicating the safe direction of refuge that we put in our life. At a less optimal level, this leads to feeling that only Karmapa can save us from all our problems.

But when we see the inseparability of our mind and our guru, we are in fact repeating "Mind, omnisciently know!" whenever we recite "Karmapa kyenno." With our fervent requests to the guru, then, we are directing our energies in a strong way toward mahamudra realization on the basis of confidence that our mind, as part of our Buddha-nature, has the resources for seeing reality. Even if we do not as yet have a personal guru to act as a conduit for the lineage coming from its founding figures, our Buddha-nature connects us with the lineage and thus can function as a source of inner inspiration. Thus not only do we rely on external gurus, we also have an inner guru — the nature of our mind. When we see the inseparability of our mind and our guru in this deepest sense, we gain the deepest level of inspiration.

The inner guru, then, is not some independently existing figure in our head from whom we can receive special messages that we must definitely follow. When thoughts, such as ideas to do this or that, or even realizations arise, they may be either good ideas or foolish ones, either correct realizations or false ones. Just because something new and unexpected arises in our mind all of a sudden does not at all mean that it is reliable. We must always examine its validity.

Furthermore, no little person in our head is sending thoughts to us purposely as a message. Thoughts and realizations, both valid and invalid, arise through a process of cause and effect as the ripening of some seed or potential. Seeds are planted by our previous habitual actions, which can be either constructive or destructive, well-informed or deluded. They ripen when the proper circumstances are present. Recognizing the nature of our mind as Buddha-nature and realizing the inseparability of our mind and our guru — more precisely, our mind and our Buddha-nature as our inner guru — act as circumstances for correct realizations to ripen from the seeds of potential we have built up through our previous practices of collecting and cleansing, as well as listening, pondering and meditating. Just as it is crucial not to romanticize our external guru into a worker of magic and miracles, the same is true of our inner guru.

## INVESTIGATING THE MEANING OF EVERY TEACHING

It is very important in the practice of Buddhism to look deeply at all the teachings, especially those that are repeated in almost every text on a particular topic, such as the statement that guru-yoga and requesting the guru for inspiration are the most important preliminaries for mahamudra practice. The early eleventh-century Indian master Atisha has said, "Take everything in the great texts as guideline instructions for personal practice." This does not mean, however, that we regard them simply as orders from our general that we must obey unthinkingly. We need to delve deeply to try to understand the significance and meaning of each instruction.

Buddha's teachings can be divided into interpretable and definitive ones — literally, those intended to lead us deeper and those concerning the deepest meaning to which we are led. The deepest point to which all Buddha's teachings lead is the realization of voidness. Therefore, in order to understand how, in Atisha's words, "all the teachings fit together without contradiction," we need to put the instructions about whatever we are practicing together with the teachings on everything else — particularly with those on voidness. The study of Buddhism is like being given pieces of an enormous jigsaw puzzle. It is up to us to gather all the pieces, such as guru-yoga and voidness, and fit them together. Even the process of thinking about how they fit together and working it out in more than just an intellectual manner acts as a preliminary for eliminating obstacles and building up bountiful stores of positive potential and deep awareness.

Thus preliminary practices are an essential prerequisite for achieving any success with the mahamudra techniques. Without them, we may sit and do what seems to be mahamudra meditation. It is not difficult to imagine we are focusing on the natural state of the mind. But, in fact, all we are doing is sitting there, either daydreaming or, at best, focusing on nothing, completely "spaced out" with our head in the clouds. We may become a bit more relaxed in the process, but our meditation will not be meaningful or profound.

## Chapter Three
# PREVENTING PRELIMINARY PRACTICES FROM BECOMING FLAT

WHY PRELIMINARIES LOSE MEANING

People engaged in preliminary practices sometimes find them becoming routine and lifeless. The primary fault lies with our motivation. The main measure to prevent this is continually reaffirming our reasons for engaging in the preliminaries. If, as Westerners, we perform them as if it were our duty to do so, like following orders in the army, then they will become meaningless. If we simply go through the motions mechanically, without any understanding or feeling for why we are doing them, they have already lost meaning. On the other hand, although there can be several different levels of spiritual motivation, if we sincerely try to develop a dedicated heart of bodhichitta, we always stay mindful of the difficulties others are experiencing and feel deeply the wish to be able to do something constructive to help them. This moves us to take action to develop ourselves fully; and the way to begin is through the preliminaries. Such an attitude, then, makes our preliminary practices vital and relevant to our goal.

Sometimes, however, even though we may have a proper and sincere motivation, we overinflate the preliminaries. We solidify them in our mind into something monstrous "out there." We may then fall to one of two extremes. The first is to regard the preliminaries with a distorted, antagonistic attitude, usually translated as a "wrong view." We denigrate and dismiss them, thinking they are a waste of time. We feel they are only for beginners, not for ourselves, and thus we should go straight to the main mahamudra practice itself.

The other extreme is to make a huge ordeal of the preliminaries, like something out of a Greek myth — Hercules cleaning the Augean stables of centuries of accumulated manure. Overwhelmed at the prospect of cleaning out all our accumulated mental filth and corruption, we feel we shall never get anywhere. Such an attitude makes the preliminaries into a horror-show, and of course they go flat because we become instantly discouraged, feeling we can never make any headway.

## BEING CREATIVE WITH PRELIMINARY PRACTICES

There are many different types of preliminary practices mentioned in the texts. Although there are lists and instructions for four, five, eight or nine standard ones, any type of repetitive positive action we do can function as a preliminary — if we have the right motivation. For example, once Buddha had a disciple who was extremely slow-minded and unable to understand or remember anything he was taught. But he had the sincere wish to learn and improve. What did Buddha do? He instructed the lad to sweep the temple, day in and day out, while repeating, "Dirt be gone; dirt be gone!" In addition, he arranged it so that the temple would always be filled with dust. That was the preliminary practice Buddha set for this disciple. Gradually, the dull-witted boy was able to understand that the dirt he was trying to sweep away was, in fact, the confusion in his own mind. Soon he was able to understand everything, and eventually became an arhat — a liberated being.

For nine years I had the privilege of being the translator and secretary for my late teacher, Tsenzhab Serkong Rinpochey. I often joked that my preliminary practice was to write a hundred thousand letters and make a hundred thousand telephone calls on his behalf, helping to arrange his teaching tours around the world. Although in one sense this might have been a joke, I also think that in another it was quite true. I happily carried out these tasks and translated for him as best as I could because I saw that this was the most effective way I could be of benefit to others, namely by helping my guru teach them. Surely such an attitude rendered those myriad letters and calls into a method for weakening obstacles and building up positive potentials for later becoming a teacher myself.

The important point of the preliminaries is not the form they take, but the process we are trying to undergo with them. It is not the contents or structure of the practices, but the state of mind experienced before, during and after them that is the most crucial factor. In this light, even changing the dirty diapers of our baby a hundred thousand times can be made into a very profound preliminary practice. We need to be practical and creative. Not everyone has the time to make a hundred thousand prostrations and, surely, being a mother responsibly caring for her baby should not be inherently an obstacle preventing spiritual practice and progress. We need to understand the essence.

What are we doing when we are changing the baby's diapers over and over again? If we look at it from the point of view of collecting and cleansing — a Tibetan synonym for preliminary practices — we are cleansing ourselves of certain negative attitudes. In particular, we are working to overcome the laziness and selfishness with which we might think, "I do not want to touch someone else's filth. I do not want to get my hands dirty." Lessening that attitude also helps us diminish the strength of the mental block with which we do not want to touch or become involved with other people's personal problems because, figuratively, we also do not want to get our hands dirty. Furthermore, we are building up positive potential. In the process of attending to our baby's needs, we are building up increasingly more ability and willingness to take care of others in the future.

## TRANSFORMING ALL ACTIVITIES INTO A SPIRITUAL PATH

The practice of preliminaries is not limited merely to the early stages of our spiritual path, after which they are finished. We need to continue to cleanse ourselves of obstacles and build up positive potential all along the path. We continue the process until we reach our goal of becoming totally purified and fully enabled to use all our potentials to benefit others. As this is such a long-term and central process, it is important to realize that, with a proper attitude and motivation, we can transform any repetitive positive or neutral act we do in our home or office into a preliminary effective for wearing away mental blocks and building up potentials.

We read in many standard Buddhist texts how we can transform even the most mundane activities into a spiritual path. For example, when we walk into a room, we may imagine that we are becoming liberated from samsara, or uncontrollably recurring rebirth, and entering into nirvana, a state of release and freedom from suffering. We can also imagine we are bringing along everyone with us. We need to be creative with the Dharma teachings and apply this principle to the circumstances of our personal life and transform everything we do into a preliminary.

For example, suppose we are working in an office typing papers all day. If we regard it merely as our job and find it boring, meaningless, and we hate it, we derive little from it other than some money, a headache and much frustration. The same thing can be true with making repeated prostrations. We do not derive much from them if we regard them as an unpleasant duty at work we are obliged to do. We just get a backache and not any money! But, if we regard typing all day with the attitude, "I am making things clear so that something can be communicated effectively to someone else," we find it makes no difference how trivial the contents are of what we are typing. It is the process that is important — we are making something clear and available for communicating to others. With such an attitude and motivation, our daily office routine functions effectively as a preliminary practice.

To be creative with the Buddhist teachings, we need to put everything together that we have learned. In this example of making our office work into a preliminary practice, we are combining the teachings on collecting and cleansing with the mahamudra guideline of not becoming caught up in the contents of our experience, but simply staying with the process. We are then fitting that together with *lojong* — the techniques for cleansing our attitudes, or "mind training," with which we transform negative situations into positive ones conducive for practice. When we put different pieces of the teachings together like this, we can figure out the answers ourselves of how to apply the Dharma to daily life. That is how we make our Buddhist practice come alive and sustain the freshness of our interest.

## BUILDING UP TWO BOUNTIFUL STORES

Another possible reason for our practice of preliminaries, and of Dharma in general, to go flat is because we are approaching the building up of the two stores of positive potential and deep awareness as if we were building up a collection of green stamps in an American supermarket. We accumulate more and more stamps with each purchase we make, which we paste in a book and keep in a drawer. In the end, when we have filled enough books, we can redeem them for a kitchen appliance. Thus when we spend time and energy on making repeated prostrations, we feel it is like spending money at the supermarket to get more stamps. They have no use or relevance to our life right now, but can be redeemed later for enlightenment as our prize.

We can eat what we purchase at the store, but, with the above attitude, we see no immediate effect from prostrations except sore knees and an aching back. However, when we transform each action of our day, particularly the repetitive ones, into preliminary practice, we also derive the immediate benefit of each moment of our day becoming meaningful. The quality of our life improves proportionately and we become happier, feeling that we are never wasting our time. This positive feeling of self-worth reinforces our enthusiasm for the standard preliminaries such as making prostrations. In this way, by putting all the teachings together so that we apply them to daily life, our practice of preliminaries does not go flat.

## FITTING TOGETHER THE DHARMA TEACHINGS

It is a very exciting and challenging process to try to fit together everything we have heard of the Dharma and discover further implications. One of the greatest benefits of having heard, read and studied Buddha's teachings extensively is that we obtain all the pieces of the "Dharma jigsaw puzzle." Now we can realistically put them together. The beauty of it is that the pieces do not go together merely in one static way, like a child's picture puzzle, but each piece fits into every other in myriad ways. The interconnection is far more multidimensional and dynamically expanding than those on the Internet's World-Wide Web.

The mahayana sutras give beautiful images of this interconnection of all facets of the Dharma. They describe scenes of billions of Buddha-fields in billions of Buddha-universes, with each field interpenetrating all the others and each containing billions of Buddhas. In each of the billion pores of each of these Buddhas there are a billion more Buddha-fields, in which every other field is also reflected. We read this and may feel embarrassed, if we are a Western Buddhist, that the scriptures contain such flowery, seemingly absurd sections. We may decide we do not want to read any more sutras.

But these sutras are, in fact, presenting a magnificent image of how all the teachings fit into and interpenetrate each other. In each teaching of each aspect of the Dharma we can see reflected every other aspect of the teachings. Just as billions of Buddha-universes can fit inside each tiny pore of a Buddha, likewise billions of Buddha's teachings can fit inside each word of the Dharma. Everything interrelates and fits together, like the image of Brahma's net in which each intersection of strands contains a mirror reflecting every other mirror of the net.

We cannot really appreciate these images simply by reading them. We can appreciate them only by fitting all the pieces of the Dharma puzzle together ourselves. Slowly, the image begins to emerge exactly as described in the mahayana sutras. This is the way to bring life back into our preliminaries. Try to see every aspect of the Dharma reflected in each tiny part of the preliminaries, while making everything in life a preliminary practice.

If we take our direction in life sincerely from the Dharma, we are confident that everything Buddha taught makes sense — not necessarily on a literal level, but as leading to a deeper, profound level of significance helpful for liberating ourselves from suffering and enabling us more effectively to help others accomplish the same. With this dynamic and pragmatic attitude toward the Dharma, we try to discover what Buddha meant in his teachings and see how they could be relevant for our own spiritual path. If Buddha taught something, he definitely intended it to be of benefit to others, including ourselves.

Let me paraphrase a guideline instruction of Tsenzhab Serkong Rinpochey. Occasionally, one of his Western students would complain to him about some of the so-called fantastic stories in the teachings on karma, such as the description of the man who was always followed by an elephant that defecated gold. As a result of his endless supply of wealth, he was constantly plagued by jealous people trying to steal the wondrous beast. But no matter how much the hassled man tried to give away or lose the elephant, it would disappear into the ground from wherever he left it and always re-emerge directly behind him. Serkong Rinpochey used to say, "If Buddha had wanted to write a good story, he could certainly have made up a much better tale than that! Buddha gave this example to teach us something. Don't just look at it literally. There is meaning behind it. Try to figure it out yourselves."

Rinpochey's response also indicates how a Buddhist teacher sets the appropriate tone for the most beneficial relationship with a disciple. A skillful master simply arranges the circumstances for us to grow. "Here are the pieces of the puzzle. You put it together. You figure it out yourselves." By teaching in this manner, a spiritual master helps the disciple not to become caught up with, fixated and dependent upon the teacher. The important point is for the disciple to focus on the process of putting together all the teachings and making sense out of them. The teacher provides the information, circumstances and perhaps inspiration for the disciple to gain insight and realization. The main focus is always on the disciple's spiritual growth.

## AVOIDING BECOMING INFATUATED WITH THE TEACHINGS

Fitting together the various pieces of the Dharma teachings and trying to understand the deeper significance of everything can be a very uplifting experience. But we must be cautious not to fall to an extreme of feeling overwhelmed with awe, "It's all so beautiful." If we become infatuated with the teachings, we can easily become set on a path towards what the mahayana sutras refer to as "hinayana arhatship." Arhats are liberated beings, those who have freed themselves from uncontrollably recurring rebirth filled with problems. Although living hinayana schools, such as modern Teravada, would not agree, the ancient mahayana sutras characterize such beings as so enraptured by their freedom that they lose all sight of the suffering of others and therefore remain in a blissful state of non-action, lost, as it were, in the bliss of nirvana. Teravadins would object that since an arhat is liberated from all disturbing emotions, such a person would certainly not have any attachment to the bliss of nirvana. Mahayanists would reply that attachment is not the issue. Arhats lack strong enough concern for others in order to overcome the inertia of simply remaining at rest.

In any case, regardless of how we label this extreme position and whether or not a Teravada arhat actually experiences it, we would all agree that infatuation with the beauty of how the teachings fit together is certainly not part of the path to Buddhahood. When our appreciation of the beauty of the Dharma leads us to feel, on the other hand, "How magnificent this is for being able to help others!" we are on a far more stable footing along the path. This is an important distinction to make.

It is very easy to become seduced into what we are calling here an arhat-style path. We start to see and understand so many profound things, and it is all so beautiful. Our mind becomes so serene and uplifted that we do not want to get up from our meditation seat. It is so enjoyable and rapturous merely to sit with our head in the clouds, it is similar to being under the influence of a narcotic drug. We lose all mindfulness of anything else. This is a great danger.

What can arouse us from that state of enrapture? If we answer, "A feeling of compassion, the thought of others," and then think that our familiarity with compassion from previous meditation is sufficient to cause a feeling of concern for others to arise, we may still have difficulties. Some meditators — for example, from the Zen tradition — experience compassion naturally arising as part of their Buddha-nature. But most practitioners need a circumstance to trigger the

arising of compassion in that state. If we think that simply recalling in
our imagination all suffering beings is sufficient for generating concern in that state, we might well be disappointed. Generating conceptually a thought of others seems so artificial in that enraptured state
that we lack sufficient energy to inspire ourselves to compassion
through a visualization. What acts as a far more effective circumstance
for generating compassion and what, in fact, rouses us from our comfortable meditation seat is actually seeing or hearing others — encountering others directly, not just conceptually in our imagination.

If we look at the classic stories of bodhisattvas and mahasiddhas —
those intent on attaining enlightenment to benefit others and those
with actual attainments — where did they meditate once they had
achieved a stable level of realization? They meditated at busy cross-
roads — in places where there were people. They did not just retire
and remain forever in an isolated cave. If we go off to a lofty mountain
retreat and decide to stay there until we complete our spiritual path,
we may never want to come back down. But if, once our meditation
becomes stable, we meditate further in a place filled with traffic, where
there are constantly people around us whom we can clearly see and
hear, we are more easily roused to help others directly.

We must be very careful, however, about how we understand being roused by compassion from our meditative state. It is not like being woken up from a delicious sleep and feeling resentment at our
rest having been disturbed. If we have been meditating properly, we
are not deeply attached to our meditative state, although we might
have become enraptured by it. Attachment to our own serenity and
insufficient mindfulness of others are two distinct obstacles that do
not necessarily accompany each other. If we have overcome the grossest levels of attachment, we experience no resentment or sense of loss
when we rise from our meditative absorption by a renewal of our mindfulness of others and the compassion that induces.

Furthermore, there is a subtle but extremely important distinction
between being blissfully uplifted and serene, on the one hand, and
being "spaced-out," with our head in the clouds, on the other. The
former is a clear, fresh and alert state of mind, while the latter is a
subtle form of dullness. The mind may be clear about how all the teachings fit together and have good understanding and stable focus, but if
it is enraptured by this realization, it is not fresh. Its lack of freshness
is due, again, to a deficiency in mindfulness. The mindfulness required

here is not mindfulness of others, it is mindfulness of the state of our mind and alertness that brings its focus back to the "here-and-now" if it has become stale.

A serene, uplifted, blissful state of mind, then, is not necessarily a hindrance to helping others. If it is fresh, it can respond to each moment of life's happenings. It does not necessarily translate into an idiot grin on our face despite others' suffering. A mind of "spaced-out" rapture, on the other hand, is dull and insensitive to both the world and its own state. It leads to indifference. We are just "up there in our heads" and we simply do not react to anything. Thus Tsongkapa stressed repeatedly that subtle mental dullness is the greatest danger to correct meditation because it is easy to mistake it for *shamata* — a serenely stilled and settled mind, sometimes translated as "mental quiescence" or "calm abiding."

The same danger of becoming enraptured can happen when we focus on the nature of mind in mahamudra meditation. We might just want to stay there, focused, and not get up. To avoid this hazard, the mahamudra teachings strongly emphasize the realization of the inseparability of appearance and mind. What is significant here is not the appearance of the wall before us, but the appearance of suffering people in front of our eyes. When we practice mahamudra correctly, we can meditate on the nature of mind and reality while still being involved in helping others. We do not simply remain focused on mind itself, but on its nature of being inseparable from appearance. Maintaining a balance, then, between mind and appearance in our practice is very delicate and totally crucial.

Thus, there are not only obstacles or mental blocks preventing us from entering into meditative states, but also obstacles that make us go too far and prevent us from combining our meditative states with ordinary life. This is another way of saying there are not only obstacles preventing our realization of the deepest level of reality, but also obstacles preventing us from seeing that level simultaneously with the conventional one. These are included among the obstacles preventing liberation and omniscience respectively. A proper relationship with a spiritual teacher can be very effective for helping us overcome both types of blocks. This is especially true if we are actually involved in taking care of our teacher. We cannot just sit and meditate, feeling, "How beautiful!" We must get up and make tea or answer the telephone.

The same is true, then, in our ordinary lives. Taking care of our family can serve the same beneficial purpose as taking care of our spiritual teacher. If, in our daily life, we are constantly being interrupted and asked, "Make supper! Get me a drink of water! Do this, do that!" we can transform it into something spiritually useful. We can make it into a preliminary practice helpful for overcoming an obstacle that may arise later on the spiritual path — the obstacle of wanting just to sit on our meditation cushion, feel so blissful and not get up.

Practicing this type of transformation of attitudes, we start to appreciate on yet another level how the kindness of other beings far exceeds the kindness of the Buddhas. Just seeing another suffering being brings us more progress in developing compassion and seeing simultaneously the deepest and conventional levels of reality than seeing all the Buddhas. The kindness of others to ask us to do something for them cannot be compared. As Shantideva has expressed it succinctly, "Nothing pleases bodhisattvas more than when others ask them to do something for them."

Chapter Four

# THE INITIAL LEVEL OF MAHAMUDRA MEDITATION

## THE DEFINITION OF MIND

Having discussed the preliminaries, let us now turn to the actual practice of mahamudra — meditation on the nature of mind. When we raise the topic of the nature of mind, we of course need to explore first what we mean by "mind." This is because if we are asked to focus and meditate on the nature of mind or on mind itself, we may find it not very obvious what we are intended to do.

To investigate this, we must look closely at the definition of "mind" in Buddhism. As soon as we look at the standard definition, we discover that Buddhism is talking about something quite different from what we mean by any of our corresponding Western words. Even in Western languages, there is no consensus on the meaning of "mind." If we speak just in terms of English and German, there is a great difference between the English word "mind" and the German word "Geist." "Geist" also has the connotation of "spirit," which is not included in the English concept of "mind." The classical Asian Buddhist languages of Sanskrit and Tibetan speak of something quite different from both, and the difference between what they refer to as "mind" and what the corresponding Western terms refer to is much greater than that between the referents of the equivalent English and German terms. The problem of how to translate the Buddhist concept into a Western word is, obviously, very challenging.

In Western languages we differentiate clearly between mind and heart, or intellect and feelings. We think of the intellectual, rational side as "mind" and the emotional, intuitive side as "heart," something quite different from mind. Many Westerners would say that although a dog has emotions, it has no mind. In Buddhism, however, we do not make such a large gap between intellect and emotions. We incorporate the functions of both under the rubric of one word — "chitta" in Sanskrit or "sem" in Tibetan — and include as well in the scope of its meaning all sense perception, such as seeing, hearing, smelling and so on. Thus, although we translate "chitta" or "sem" with the English word "mind" or the German word "Geist," the Sanskrit and Tibetan Buddhist terms encompass a much larger scope of meaning than that of either the English or German renderings of them.

The problem is not limited to Western languages. Mongolian also differentiates between the intellectual and emotional sides, but, unlike English, uses the term for the latter, "setgil," in Buddhist texts. The Chinese translators as well chose a word meaning heart, "xin," which the Japanese also accepted and used. The issue of what is mind brings to the surface many fundamental differences in cultural world views.

If we want to find a better synonym for the Indo-Tibetan terms in European languages, perhaps the closest equivalent is the word "experience," although this word, too, is not quite precise. We do not include in its meaning here experience in the sense of familiarity and expertise through repetition, as in: "This doctor has a great deal of experience." Furthermore, in Western languages, to experience something often implies to feel emotions about it, either positive or negative. We feel we have not really experienced something deeply unless we have consciously been moved by it on an emotional level. This is also not included in the Buddhist notion. Nor is there any connotation of evaluation, as in: "I learned a lot from that experience." In the Buddhist context, experience is merely whatever happens to us, whatever occurs.

In the Buddhist discussion of mind, then, we are not talking about some sort of "thing" or organ that is in our head, like the brain. Nor are we talking about a space, as is implied by the Western expression, "Imagine in your mind this or that" — as if mind were a stage or room in our head through which thoughts parade or in which memories are stored. Rather, we are talking about some sort of occurrence that is happening on the basis of the brain and nervous system.

What is happening when we see, hear or think something? Although we may be able to describe the occurrence biochemically or electro-chemically, we can also describe it subjectively. This latter is what we mean by "mind" in Buddhism. When we see, hear, think or emotion-ally feel something, there is an experience from moment to moment. This is what is happening. Furthermore, experience always has con-tents. An equivalent way of saying that is: "Mind always has an ob-ject." In fact, "mind" in Sanskrit and Tibetan is also called "that which has an object."

## THE NON-DUALITY OF SUBJECT AND OBJECT

Buddha taught the non-duality of that which has an object and its object — usually translated as the "non-duality of subject and object." We must understand this point correctly, otherwise we may mistak-enly think that Buddha contradicted himself when he also taught that mind always has an object. We may think this implies that since the two are different, they are dual. If we become angry with the table, the non-duality of subject and object, however, does not mean that my anger is the table. Non-duality does not render mind and its objects totally identical — one and the same thing.

Experience always has contents. We cannot have an experience without experiencing something. A thought does not exist without a thinking of the thought, and no one can think without thinking a thought. Non-dual, then, means that in any moment, these two things — mind and its object, or experience and its contents — always come together as one entity. Putting this in simple, everyday language, we can say they always come together in the same package. There cannot be one without the other. Therefore, in Buddhism "mind" always re-fers to experience and the contents of experience.

## CLARITY — THE ARISING OF THE CONTENTS OF AN EXPERIENCE

The standard Buddhist definition of mind or experience contains three words: "clarity," "awareness" and "merely." It is usually rendered as "mere clarity and awareness." As each word of the definition is sig-nificant, we need to explore carefully each of their meanings. Let us look first at the term "clarity."

The most crucial point to note is that this word needs to be taken as a verbal noun with an object, not as a quantitative noun referring to something that can be measured. Clarity is not some sort of light in our head that has varying intensity. Rather, it is the action, or occurrence of the action, of being clear about something or making something clear. Making something clear, however, does not imply a conscious act of will. It merely happens. Furthermore, the word "clear" itself is also misleading. Let us examine its meaning as well.

"Clarity" is glossed in Tibetan as "arising" — the same word used for the rising or dawning of the sun. "Being clear about something" or "making something clear," then, actually refer to the "arising of something" or the event of "making something arise," although, again, with no implication of passivity or lack of responsibility on the one hand, or conscious will on the other. The expression, "giving rise to something," perhaps minimizes the connotation of these two extremes.

What occurs when we experience something? There is the giving rise to something. For ease of expression, we need to say, "mind gives rise to something." This is preferable to saying, "something arises." "Something arises" puts too much emphasis on what is happening from the side of the object, whereas the accent needs to be more on the subjective side. The phrase, "mind gives rise to something," however, also has its shortcomings. It is just a convenient manner of expression. Mind is not an entity or "thing," so there is nothing that is actually an agent giving rise to anything. The word "mind" is simply a term mentally labeled onto the occurrence of the subjective event of the giving rise to something.

When we experience something, mind gives rise to a sight, a sound, a smell, a taste, a tactile or bodily sensation, a thought, a feeling, an emotion or a dream. Even when we are asleep with no dreams, mind gives rise to a darkness. Subjectively, there is always the arising of something. What arises, however, does not necessarily have to appear directly. When we hear that the fat lady does not eat during the day, we know that she must eat at night, because she is fat. Our mind does not give rise to the sight of her eating at night, however, although there is the arising of the understanding of that fact.

The major shortcoming of using the word "clarity" in this context is that "clarity" implies that whatever is clear is in focus if it is visual, or understood if it is conceptual. But that is not necessarily the case. When we take off our glasses and look at someone, our mind gives rise to a blur, and when we do not understand what someone says, it gives rise to confusion. In both cases, there is the arising of something. Conventionally, it would be awkward to say that a blur or confusion is clear.

## AWARENESS — AN ENGAGING WITH THE CONTENTS OF AN EXPERIENCE

Arisings, namely of images, also occur with mirrors, photographic plates and computer screens. Therefore, in order to differentiate mind from a mirror, the next word, "awareness," is added to the definition. Again, this a verbal noun with an object, not a quantitative one. It is "being aware of something" or "making something an object of awareness," but not necessarily as a conscious act of will.

The English term "awareness," however, is also misleading. The Tibetan term is explained as an engaging with or relating to an object. Unlike the English words "engagement" or "relation," however, the Tibetan carries no connotation of an emotional bond. Being detached about something is also a form of engagement with it or a way of relating to it. The Tibetan word translated here as "engagement" or "relation" literally means an "entering into something." It connotes doing something cognitive with an object. It can be, for example, seeing, hearing, thinking or feeling it. That is what is happening when we experience something. There is an arising of something and an engaging with it in a cognitive way. There is the arising of a sight and the seeing of it, the arising of a thought and the thinking of it, and so on. For ease of expression, and with all the previously mentioned qualifications, we would say that mind gives rise to something and apprehends it.

The English word "awareness" is misleading here in the sense that it implies that we understand something and are conscious of it. But that is not necessarily the case. Not understanding something is just as much a form of engaging with an object as is understanding it. Whether we are conscious or unconscious of something, we can still experience it. For instance, we can be talking to somebody with unconscious hostility. Even though our hostility is unconscious, it still exists. We still experience it and it produces an effect. Thus the scope of the Buddhist concept usually translated as "awareness" is much larger than that of the equivalent English word.

In every moment, then, there is an arising and a cognitive engagement with something. These two do not occur one after the other, however. It is not the case that first a thought arises and then we think it. The process is not of two events happening consecutively, but of two functions occurring simultaneously. Mind gives rise to a thought and thinks it simultaneously. This is going on each moment for every being with a mind. This is the experience not only of life, but even of death.

MERELY

The third word of the definition, "merely," sets the basic minimum that needs to occur for there to be experience. Mind needs merely to give rise to something and cognitively engage with it in some manner. "Merely," then, excludes the need for there to be any significant strength of attentiveness to the contents of an experience — in Western terminology, consciousness of them. It also excludes the need for there to be any significant level of understanding, emotion or evaluation. An experience is simply a cognitive event.

Thus deep sleep with no dreams is also an experience. We cannot say that when we are asleep with no dreams we do not have a mind anymore, or that the mind is no longer functioning. If the mind were turned off during sleep, how could it ever perceive the sound of the alarm clock so that it could turn back on again? The experience of deep sleep, then, entails mind giving rise to a darkness and engaging with it in the manner of being absorbed with only minimal attention to sensory perception.

Furthermore, the word "merely" also excludes there being (1) a solid, concrete "me" or "mind" inside our head that is experiencing or controlling experience as its agent, (2) a solid, concrete object as the content "out there" that is being experienced, and (3) a solid, concrete "experience" that is occurring between the two. Cognitive events merely occur. Conventionally we can say "I" am having "the experience" of "this" or "that," and subjectively it appears like that, but none of the items involved can exist independently of each other. In other words, the three spheres involved in an experience — a subject (either a person or a mind), a content and an experience itself — are all devoid of this impossible way of existing. "Merely," however, does not deny that experience actually occurs and is always individual. Just as Tsongkapa has emphasized in his presentation of voidness that we must be careful not to refute either too much or too little, likewise we must be cautious with the word "merely" also not to exclude either too much or too little.

SUMMARY OF THE BUDDHIST DEFINITION OF MIND

In summary, mind in Buddhism refers to experience, namely the mere arising and cognitive engaging with the contents of experience. The continuity of experience is known as the mind-stream, or "mental continuum." It is always individual, with each moment of experience following from previous moments of experience according to the karmic laws of behavioral cause and effect. There is order in the universe, and "my" experience is never "your" experience. If I experience eating a meal, I and not you will next experience the physical sensation of being full. Buddhism does not posit a universal or collective mind.

The never-ceasing, moment-to-moment event of arising and engaging that constitutes experience, then, refers to the arising of a sight and merely seeing it, the arising of a sound and merely hearing it, the arising of a thought and merely thinking it, the arising of an emotion and merely feeling it, and so on. This is the conventional nature of mind — it gives rise to things and apprehends them. Its deepest nature is its voidness, namely that it is devoid of existing in any impossible manner, from being a physical entity itself up to involving a solid, concrete subject, content or experience. Such a mind, then, with these two levels of true nature — or "two levels of truth" — is the topic of mahamudra meditation.

## THE NATURE OF MAHAMUDRA MEDITATION

In order to engage correctly in mahamudra meditation on the nature of mind, we need to understand clearly not only the meaning of mind, but also what it means to meditate on something. We do not mean meditating on something like meditating, literally, on a cushion. Nor do we mean, more abstractly, meditating on the basis of something. Mahamudra meditation is not conducted merely on the basis of mind's nature, it is meditation focused on that nature. In German we avoid this confusion because there are two different prepositions that can be used with the verb "to meditate," namely "über" and "auf," whereas in English there is only one, "on."

In general, meditation means to build up a beneficial state of mind or attitude through attentive repetition. Tibetan glosses it with the word "to familiarize or habituate oneself with something," while the connotation of the original Sanskrit term is simply "to make something be." There are two main varieties of meditation. When we meditate on a visualization of a Buddha, we are focusing on an object. When we meditate on love, on the other hand, we are not focusing on an object, but rather we remain focused while being in a certain state of mind. We can either consciously generate a state of mind that was not there before, as in the case of love, or focus attentively while being in a state of mind that is always there. Meditation on the nature of mind is an example of this latter case.

When we meditate on the nature of mind, then, the moment-to-moment experiential process of the mere arising and engaging with the contents of experience is not some static object that we are focusing on like a visualization of a Buddha, or even a moving object as with tantric sadhana practice when we visualize a flowing sequence of images while reciting a text or mantras. Nor is it the case that we are attentively focusing while being in a state of mind, like love, that we have created and generated in the sense of worked ourselves up to feeling by relying, either directly or through memory, on a line of reasoning such as "all beings have been my mother in previous lives and shown me kindness." We do not have to generate or fabricate artificially the nature of mind. It is always the case. Experience is always happening — we do not have to make it happen.

Thus with meditation on the mind, we are focusing attentively on something that is happening all the time and has always been the case. But this is not in the sense of observing the process. That is again making mind into an object, like a visualization, and is based on misconceiving, either consciously or unconsciously, a duality between an observer and the event that is happening. Rather, we are focusing attentively, but not self-consciously, on being in that process — just doing it "straight up and down," as my mother would say.

## THE ANALOGY OF A FLASHLIGHT

As it is very difficult to comprehend correctly what we are supposed to be doing with mahamudra meditation, let us look at it in terms of the analogy of a flashlight. If we are shining a flashlight on something, there are three points upon which we may focus attention — what is being illumined, the person holding the flashlight, or the flashlight itself. Focusing on what is being lit by this flashlight is how we normally go through life. We are caught up in the contents of our experience. We enter our child's room and see clothes and toys strewn everywhere. We become fixated on them and shout. We become so upset because we are caught up and stuck in the contents of our experience of seeing the untidy room. We are focusing only on what the flashlight is illuminating.

We can also look at life from the point of view of the person holding the flashlight. With such an outlook, we disengage from experience and, in a subjective sense, sit in the back of our head and just observe what is happening. This is a danger that can arise when we practice the vipassana style of mindfulness meditation in an unbalanced manner. In order to deconstruct our experience and become aware of moment-to-moment impermanence or change, in vipassana meditation we note — sometimes even with mental words — that now this sensation is arising, now it is passing, now another is arising and so on. Merely noting, "Now I am seeing this and now I am seeing that," however, could easily degenerate into the extreme of merely observing that our child's room is dirty and neither telling him or her to tidy it, nor cleaning it ourselves.

With mahamudra meditation, we are focusing neither on what the flashlight is illumining nor on being the person holding the flashlight. Instead, we are looking from the point of view of the flashlight itself. In a sense, we are focusing on being the flashlight. But what does it mean to focus on being the flashlight? It is not merely observing the process of giving rise to the appearance or occurrence of something — it is just doing it. It is not "doing it," however, in an active willful manner, nor merely passively letting it occur as if we could control it but are refraining from so doing. There is no factor of control, not even in the sense of the process being "out of control," which could precipitate anxiety and fear. Nor is it just doing it mindlessly like a cow looking at a barn wall. It is doing it with perfect clarity and awareness in the sense of the usual meaning of the two English words — with clear mental focus and attentive awareness. We try to focus with freshness, mindfulness, alertness and full attention on what is occurring with each moment of experience, without being self-conscious, not becoming caught up either in what we are experiencing or in being the one who is experiencing it.

## THE INITIAL STAGES OF MAHAMUDRA MEDITATION

Although mahamudra practice may seem simple — "Just settle into the natural state of the mind" — it is, in fact, extremely difficult to do properly. If it were so simple, there would be no need for preliminary practices to weaken mental blocks and build up positive potentials. However, even with a minimal amount of preliminary practice, we can begin practice on an initial level as explained, for example, in *Mahamudra Eliminating the Darkness of Ignorance*, by the Ninth Karmapa.

The first stage of practice is to work with the experience of seeing things. Mahamudra meditation is always done with eyes wide open. We look all around us, slowly, just being the flashlight, focusing attentively on the cognitive process that is occurring of the mere arising and engaging with a sight. Again, remember that "process" here does not mean a sequence of actions or events, but rather a single action or event entailing two simultaneous aspects, an arising and an engaging, without a conscious agent that is willing it to happen or making it happen. There is a great difference between, on the one hand, deciding to shift the focus of our attention so that we look at a different object and, on the other, when we focus on that object, consciously willing the sight of it to arise and the seeing of it to occur. They just happen, don't they?

Then we investigate, from the point of view of the flashlight, the difference between seeing the wall or the floor, or something blue or something yellow. What is the difference between seeing the vase of flowers on the table or the dirty dishes next to it with crumpled, stained napkins soaking in leftover food on top of them? From the point of view of there being an arising and an engaging with the contents of an experience — with a sight — is there any difference in terms of the cognitive process itself?

From the point of view of the flashlight, there is no difference. If we become caught up in the contents, we become emotionally involved in a disturbing manner. But if we experience them from the point of view of the flashlight itself, we do not become upset with either attraction and attachment, or repulsion and anger. We stop being so obsessed with the contents of our experience and focus instead on the mere process of experience itself.

We can then try the same experiment on more challenging examples. What is the difference between seeing a person or the adjacent wall, seeing a person or a photo of a person, seeing a man or a woman, seeing someone pretty or someone ugly, seeing a child sleeping or throwing a tantrum, seeing our best friend or our worst enemy, seeing a printed word or a blank piece of paper, seeing writing in a language we know or in one we do not, seeing writing in an alphabet we know or in one we do not, seeing something on television or something right next to it, and so on? We need to be creative with our meditation.

We have to be careful, however, when doing this. If we ignore the conventional point of view and become stuck on the experiential side of the seeing, we risk developing a state in which we do not react or respond to anything. From the point of view of the cognitive process, it is true that there is no difference between seeing a car coming down the street or seeing that nothing is coming. Nevertheless, that does not deny the fact that from the point of view of our wanting to cross the street, there is a very great difference. To believe that on all levels there is no difference and then not to react to the differences that in fact exist is going to the extreme of fixating on the experiential side of an experience as if it existed divorced from its contents. Thus we must try to avoid both extremes, either being too caught in the contents of an experience or too divorced from them.

After investigating seeing sights, we follow a similar procedure with hearing sounds. What is the difference between hearing the sound of birds or traffic, music or a child's haphazard banging on a drum, soft music or the dentist's drill, a song that we like or one that we hate, a voice or the wind, the voice of a loved one or of someone we cannot stand, words we can understand or those we cannot, a mosquito buzzing around our head or one on the other side of the screened window next to our ear, and so on? We then do the same with a variety of odors, such as those of scented talcum powder and the baby's dirty diaper; tastes, such as those of an orange and vinegar; and tactile sensations, such as tickling and scratching the palm of our hand very hard. We then go on to various thoughts, such as verbal and pictorial; various feelings, such as happiness and sadness; various emotions, both positive and disturbing, such as love and hatred; and various levels of concentrated meditative states with mental silence. Following that, we compare senses, such as seeing and hearing; and then the mind settled in concentration and the mind moving with thought. Finally we just sit and follow the same procedure with whatever experience occurs through any of the senses or with mind alone. We stay attentively with the process of mere arising and engaging, without becoming either caught in the contents or ignoring them completely. This is the first stage of mahamudra practice.

## BENEFITS OF THE INITIAL STAGE OF PRACTICE

Even if we proceed no further in our mahamudra practice, this initial stage itself is extremely useful and helpful. We go on vacation to the shore and take a hotel room. We walk into the room and there is a terrible view from the window. We can only see the side of the building next door and we become very upset. Then we do this type of meditation. What is the difference between seeing a pretty view or an ugly one? From the point of view of seeing, it is just seeing. Thinking like this helps us not to become so attached or angry. Then, in a calm state of mind, we apply Shantideva's advice to our situation, "If we can change our room, why get upset? Let's just change it. And if we cannot change our room, why get upset? It's not going to help. Besides, what difference does the view really make? If we want to see the ocean, we can go up to the roof restaurant or step outside."

Suppose we succeed in changing rooms and get one that is facing the beach. We walk into the room and hear the loud noise of traffic on the busy street in front of the hotel, and we become upset all over again. Once more we focus on the difference between listening to traffic or the sound of the waves. Then we either apply Shantideva's advice once more, or, if we decide not to bother trying to shift rooms again and just keep this one, remind ourselves of the first true fact in life — life is difficult! Without applying effective techniques for dealing with our situation, we are going to spoil our entire vacation.

Thus the initial level of mahamudra practice can be one of the most effective methods for coping with noise. By shifting the focus of our attention from dwelling morbidly on the noise itself, to the cognitive process that is occurring of merely the arising of a sound and the hearing of it, we realize that the arising of the noise of traffic is the arising of just another sound, and the hearing of it is just another experience of hearing. There is nothing more. With such shift of focus, we subjectively experience the same event of hearing the traffic in a totally different qualitative manner. Our experience of hearing the noise can now be accompanied with indifference, peace of mind or even happiness, instead of anger, unhappiness and self-pity.

Chapter Five

# THE DEEPER LEVELS OF MAHAMUDRA MEDITATION

## MAHAMUDRA MEDITATION ON THE CONVENTIONAL NATURE OF MIND

The mahamudra realization is never "Just live naturally like an animal. Just see and hear, and have no thoughts." That is not it at all. Furthermore, even if we are able, through the initial mahamudra techniques, to achieve the level of attainment at which we are not greatly disturbed by the contents of our experience, we should not fool ourselves into thinking that mahamudra practice is so simple, or that this initial level is all that there is. It is a step in the correct direction — a very big step — but it is not yet a profound understanding of mahamudra. To go deeper into mahamudra practice, we need to develop shamata, a serenely stilled and settled state of mind totally absorbed with single-pointed concentration on mind itself, first specifically on its conventional nature as mere arising and engaging. The First Panchen Lama, in *A Root Text for the Precious Gelug/Kagyü Tradition of Mahamudra*, begins his presentation of mahamudra meditation at this point.

There are two classic ways to describe the meditative procedure. One is that with mental consciousness we focus on the remembered experience of the mere arising and engaging of the immediately preceding moment of cognition. The other is that one aspect of mind focuses on the mere arising and engaging of its own moment of cognition. In either case, we use mindfulness to maintain the mental hold of our attention on mind itself and alertness to notice and correct any deviation from this focus due to flightiness of mind or mental dullness. When we have totally eliminated these faults from our meditation, we achieve *samadhi* — a state of absorbed concentration. We attain shamata when, in addition, we experience, accompanying samadhi, a serenely joyous sense of physical and mental suppleness and fitness at being able to concentrate perfectly on anything for as long as we wish.

Throughout the process of gaining shamata through mahamudra meditation, we focus only on mind itself, which is a way of being aware of something and not a physical phenomenon. Any moment of mind upon which we focus, however, has an object. Consider the case of sensory consciousness, in which the object apprehended by that consciousness is a form of physical phenomena such as a sight or a sound. During the early phases of this stage of mahamudra meditation, which is focused on the mere arising and engaging that constitute the conventional nature of sensory consciousness, our focus simply on sensory consciousness itself causes our sensory cognition to be an inattentive perception. In other words, the sensory consciousness still gives rise to its object, for instance a sight, but because that sensory consciousness is primarily the object upon which our meditating mental consciousness is focusing, it does not decisively apprehend its object, the sight. It is inattentive of it, and thus our meditating mental consciousness does not give rise to a clear appearance of the sight. Eventually, as our single-pointed placement of mind on mind becomes perfected, our meditating mental consciousness gives rise only to the mere arising and engaging that constitute the sensory consciousness upon which it is focused. It does not give rise at all to any appearance of the object of that sensory consciousness.

This meditative experience is reminiscent of how the mind of an *arya* focused in total absorption or "meditative equipoise" on the voidness of an object, for instance a sight, gives rise to an appearance of only the voidness of the sight and not the sight itself. Voidness, however, does not exist separately from its basis, for example the sight. It is only due to obstacles still affecting the mind of an arya in total absorption that his or her absorbed mind is unable to give rise simultaneously to both voidness and its basis as its objects of cognition. Similarly, sensory consciousness does not exist separately from its cognitive object, for example a sight. However, obstacles still affecting a mahamudra practitioner's mind when it is focused single-pointedly on the conventional nature of a sensory consciousness will prevent both that sensory consciousness and its sensory object from simultaneously arising as objects of cognition.

Next, consider the case of a mind, meditating on mahamudra, focusing on the mere arising and engaging of a mental consciousness, for example a verbal or pictorial thought. The apprehension that the contents of the thought are merely something the mind is giving rise to at first weakens the enticing power of the contents. Eventually, however, the contents of the thought cease to arise as soon as we focus on the mere arising and engaging of the mind that is thinking them. The same obstacles preventing a mind that is totally absorbed on a sensory consciousness from simultaneously giving rise to the object of that consciousness automatically block our mind from giving rise to the contents of a thought as soon as we focus on the mere arising and engaging that constitute that thought. Thus mind, focused single-pointedly on the conventional nature of mind, gives rise to the appearance — meaning the manifest occurrence, not a visual aspect — simply of mere arising and engaging, whether it focuses on the conventional nature of a moment of sensory or mental consciousness.

## THE NECESSITY FOR MEDITATING ON THE CONVENTIONAL AND DEEPEST NATURES OF "ME"

The Gelug/Kagyü tradition of mahamudra next prescribes meditation on the deepest nature of mind — its voidness or absence of existing in any fantasized, impossible manner. It precedes this with meditation on the deepest nature of "me." We need to see both with an exceptionally perceptive mind, *vipashyana*. We achieve such a mind when, on the basis of shamata focused on their voidness, we experience simultaneously an additional serenely joyous sense of physical and mental suppleness and fitness at being able to perceive and understand anything. Although we shall now explore these meditations on voidness in accordance with the Gelug/Kagyü explanation, let us look at them in a manner and context that allows for their application to all traditions of mahamudra — Gelug/Kagyü, purely Kagyü and Sakya.

Although a correct understanding of the voidness of both "me" and mind is necessary for ridding ourselves of unawareness of reality, the true cause of all our problems in life, it is also needed to overcome subtle faults that arise in any form of meditation. All Buddhist meditation, including mahamudra, involves (1) attention on an object or state of mind, (2) understanding it, (3) mindfulness to stay with both the object or state of mind and the understanding of it, and not to lose either of them because of flightiness of mind or mental dullness, and (4) alertness to detect these hindrances and correct them if and when they occur. But even with all these mental factors present, we must be able to focus on mere arising and engaging without conceiving of ourselves as being either the one who is observing their occurrence or the one who is making them happen and controlling them. Otherwise, we become self-conscious and therefore experience subtle forms of distraction. The only way to rid our meditation of such faults is to accompany it with an understanding of the conventional and devoid natures of "me."

Conventionally, "I" exist. "I" am thinking, "I" am experiencing, "I" am acting — not anybody else. This conventional "me," however, does not exist in any fantasized, impossible manner, for instance as a solid person, "me," inside our head who is the agent or controller of everything that happens, or the one who experiences it. Such a "me" is called the false "me," and does not refer to anything real. Thus the conventional "me" is devoid of existing as a false "me." Understanding this distinction is crucial for eliminating the obstacles preventing our liberation and enlightenment.

When we apprehend our mind to be something solid, we naturally imagine a solid "me" behind it who uses it to experience life. Such a view of ourselves generates self-preoccupation, self-importance and selfishness, which in turn give rise to all our difficulties in life and prevent us from being of fullest help to others. Thus the causes of our problems arise in this order: first we apprehend our mind and experience as existing solidly, and then we imagine a solid "me" existing behind them.

Even if we understand how our mind exists in relation to reality, in other words even if we understand the relation between experience and its contents, we could still imagine a solid, independent "me" behind such a process who is the agent or controller of the non-solid process, or the one who experiences it. Therefore the order of meditational practice to remove the causes of our problems is first to understand the deepest nature of "me" and then of mind or experience itself. The deepest nature of "me" is its voidness, namely the conventional "mes'" lack of existing in the manner of a false "me."

## THE CONVENTIONAL AND DEEPEST NATURES OF "ME"

The conventional and false "me"s in Buddhism differ from the healthy and inflated "ego"s discussed in Western psychology. The Western notion of these two sorts of ego is that they are types of awareness. The conventional "me," on the other hand, can only be an object of awareness. Being neither a way of being aware of something, nor a form of physical phenomenon, it is an existent variable that nevertheless affects our experience. The false "me" does not exist at all. Only an idea of one can exist. Thinking and acting on the basis of such an idea, however, also affects our experience.

Even though most people's healthy ego is normally mixed with an inflated one, for purposes of discussion we can differentiate the two. A healthy ego is an awareness or well-developed sense of "me" as an individual that allows us to organize and take responsibility for our life. Without a healthy ego, we would never get out of bed in the morning and dress ourselves. The "me" that is the object of focus of a healthy ego is analogous to the conventional "me" discussed in Buddhism. An inflated ego is an awareness or sense of "me" as the center of the universe, the most important person in the world who must always have his or her way. The "me" that is the object of focus of an inflated ego is analogous to the Buddhist false "me" in the sense that it is an idea of one projected onto and mixed with a conventional "me."

An inflated ego, then, is the closest Western equivalent for what we call in Buddhism "apprehending 'me' as existing solidly," which means apprehending or taking the conventional "me" to exist in the manner of a false "me." Inflated egos certainly exist, but the idea of a false "me" upon which such an ego is fixated does not refer to anything that actually exists. The understanding of the absence of a real referent for that idea of a false "me" is the understanding of the voidness of "me" — in other words, the understanding of the absence of the conventional "mes'" existing in the manner of a false "me."

But then if the conventional "me" does not exist in the manner of a false "me," how does it exist? When it appears to us that "I" am experiencing something — for instance "I" am thinking a thought, or feeling an emotion, or seeing a sight — what appears, or simply happens, is the experience of thinking, feeling or seeing, with its contents. On the basis of that experience, we use the word, mental label, convention or concept, "I" or "me," to organize, make intelligible and describe that experience. We can say or think, "'I' am experiencing this," although we do not have to do so in order actually to experience it in the Buddhist sense of the word "experience."

The "I" in this example is the conventional "me." It exists inasmuch as it can simply be mentally labeled or imputed onto any moment or series of moments of an individual's experience in order to organize, understand, describe and refer to that experience. The conventional "me" is not the word, label or concept "me," however. It is what that word, label or concept refers to when it is labeled onto and used to describe an appropriate basis, such as a moment of experience of a particular, individual mind-stream. The conventional "me" does not, however, exist as a solid "me" in our head as the controller or agent of our experience, or the one who experiences it. Such a solid "me" would be an example of a false "me," and does not refer to anything real.

Every moment of experience is accompanied with a certain level of the mental factors of motivation, intention and decisiveness, the combination of which is referred to by the Western notion of "will." The conventional "me" can be labeled onto any moment of experience accompanied by these factors such that we may say, "'I' decided to do that." However, that conventional "me" does not exist in the manner of a false "me," for instance as a solid agent who made that decision. The decision may have been accompanied by the mental factor of a sense of self-importance, but that does not imply a solid manipulator, "me," making that decision.

## APPLYING THE UNDERSTANDING OF THE NATURE OF "ME" TO MAHAMUDRA MEDITATION

The conventional "me" can be labeled onto our mahamudra meditation on the conventional nature of mind in order to organize, understand, describe and refer to that experience as "'I' am meditating," "'I' am experiencing the contents of each moment of experience," "'I' am attentive and understand what is happening." But we need to understand that this conventional "me" does not exist in the manner of a false "me," namely as a solid meditator behind the meditation or a solid person behind an experience experiencing it.

How does this understanding apply to the manner in which we meditate on the conventional nature of mind and experience? It applies in the sense that such an understanding allows us to meditate without being self-conscious. Our understanding allows us not only to meditate but also to live each moment of our life without even a subtly inflated ego with which we self-consciously feel there is a solid "me" who is observing, doing or controlling the experiencing. When we have eliminated this level of self-consciousness, we no longer feel "alienated" from our experience.

In order to sustain a motivation of renunciation or bodhichitta, however, not only for our meditation, but for every moment of our life, we need a healthy ego. Without a healthy ego, we could not organize our efforts in terms of "'I' wish to overcome my sufferings" or "'I' wish to achieve enlightenment in order to benefit all beings." We would be unable to take ourselves seriously or put any direction in our life. But, when we engage in mahamudra meditation, we are not manifestly self-conscious even in a healthy ego way. We can understand this through an analogy.

Total meditative absorption on voidness is not accompanied with a conscious bodhichitta motivation that we actively and directly focus upon at the same time as our absorption. It is merely held by the force of bodhichitta. This means it is apprehended by a mind that, having had some moments of bodhichitta as the immediately preceding condition for its arising, now has awareness of bodhichitta in either a latent or unconscious manner. The relation between meditation on mahamudra and a healthy ego is somewhat similar. When we are totally absorbed on either the conventional or deepest natures of experience, we are not self-conscious even in the sense of simultaneously being actively or directly focused on the fact that "I," in just the conventional sense, am experiencing this. But our meditation is, nevertheless, held by the force of a healthy ego. It is apprehended by a mind that has an understanding of the conventional "me" in either a latent or unconscious manner.

## THE RELATION BETWEEN THE CONVENTIONAL AND DEEPEST NATURES OF MIND

Having understood the manner of existence of "me" and applied it to our mahamudra meditation on the conventional nature of mind, we proceed to examine and understand the deepest nature of how mind itself exists. As the First Panchen Lama has stressed, we must not leave our mahamudra practice simply focused on the conventional nature of mind as mere arising and engaging. We must supplement it with meditation on the deepest nature of mind, and then meditate on the inseparability of the conventional and deepest level natures of mind.

It is preferable in our discussion not to use the terms "absolute truth" or the "ultimate level of reality." They give the impression that the conventional level is no good and must be rejected, abandoned and transcended. If we call it the "deepest level," we are less likely to conceive of it as something totally separate "up in the sky," the one we really want to reach and for which the conventional level was merely a stepping stone. Rather, there is a surface and a deeper level about everything, including mind, and both actually exist. But neither exists on its own. Just as there is no independently existing conventional level, likewise there is no independently existing deepest level. Although we can only focus on both levels simultaneously if we have first focused on each individually, one at a time, we must remember that it is incomplete to focus just on either of the two by itself. What is to be gone beyond, then, is not our seeing of the conventional nature of mind, but our seeing of that conventional nature divorced from seeing simultaneously mind's deepest nature. This is a crucial point.

## MAHAMUDRA MEDITATION ON THE DEEPEST NATURE OF MIND

For understanding the deepest level, we may examine a verbal thought — for example, "This is stupid." We think each word of it individually and slowly. What is the actual thought, "This is stupid"? Does it exist as something on its own, independently from a mind that is thinking it? What is its relation to the individual thoughts, "this," "is" and "stupid"? Is it simply equal to the sum of the three component thoughts? If it were, we should be able to think, "This is stupid," even if we think each of the component words with a month's interval in between. We should be able to think, "This is stupid," with those exact mental words even if we do not know the English language. On the other hand, is it something totally separate and different from each of its component words? If it were, we should be able to think, literally, "This is stupid," without thinking any of the three words. Furthermore, thinking the three words in sequence, one by one, could occur without being the equivalent of thinking, "This is stupid."

Although we might be able to think something is stupid without having to say so in our head, what is the relation between thinking words and thinking their meaning? Does something's being stupid exist independently from being the meaning of the words that express and formulate it? What is the relation between words and their meaning? What is the relation between the meaning of individual words and the meaning of a sentence made up of those words? We examine deeply all these issues. In this way, we approach the understanding of the voidness of our mind and experience — they do not exist in any impossible manner. We apply our understanding of the conventional and false "mes'" to discriminating between the conventional and false ways in which mind and experience could exist.

## UNDERSTANDING THAT THE CONVENTIONAL "ME" EXISTS LIKE AN ILLUSION

As a result of our mind's automatically making our experience of thinking a sentence appear in a manner that does not correspond to reality, we instinctively imagine — perhaps unconsciously — that there is a little "me" inside our head, or our mind, who is the author of our mental voice. This solid little "me" seems to take in, experience and evaluate the information that comes in through the sense channels to "control-headquarters" in our brain and then seems to comment on it, make the decisions, press the buttons and control what we do. As a result of such a conscious or unconscious fantasy, we become very self-centered and selfish, generating all our problems. But our fantasy is not referring to anything real. There is no such thing as a little being in our head who is controlling everything. That is a vision out of some science fiction horror movie.

Of course we exist. Conventionally we experience life as "'I' am thinking; 'I' am seeing; 'I' am deciding to do this or that." Conventionally we describe what is happening in this way, and it is a correct description. "I" am thinking and deciding, not anybody else. This is conventional truth. But, what is absent is an actual, findable "me" sitting in our head doing all this. We do not exist in the manner in which we appear to exist — in the manner of existence our mind gives rise to an appearance of when it gives rise to an appearance or feeling of "me." When we understand voidness, we understand the absence of this fantasized, impossible way of existing. We understand that this way of existing does not refer to anything real.

"I" exist, but not in this fantasized, impossible manner. What am "I" and how do "I" exist? The only thing we can say is that "I" am or exist simply as what the mental label or word "I" or "me" refers to when it is labeled onto an individual stream of continuity of experience as its basis. Such a "me" exists like an illusion in that "I" appear to be a solid, independent entity, but am not. However, "I" am not an illusion. "I" can experience happiness or pain, an illusion cannot. There is a big difference between saying "I" exist *like* an illusion and "I" *am* an illusion.

## UNDERSTANDING THE NATURE OF MIND IN TERMS OF MENTAL LABELING

Next we apply this understanding of voidness to mind itself. Experience, or the mere arising and engaging in contents of experience, does not exist in any fantasized, impossible way. It is not something absolute or transcendent that functions inside us, as either a solid or an abstract "thing." If it were, it should be able to exist on its own. But experience or mind has contents, and its continuity has sequence that arises dependently on previous moments of experience according to the principles of cause and effect. It cannot exist independently of these, all on its own.

How can we describe how it exists? We can only say that mind is or exists simply as what the mental label or word "mind" refers to when it is labeled onto a mere arising and engaging with contents of experience. Mind exists by virtue simply of mental labeling. The word "simply" does not imply that mind is merely the word "mind." A word signifies a meaning. It is not the same thing as its meaning. Mind can know something, the word "mind" cannot. Nor does "simply" imply that mind only exists when someone actively labels it and says or thinks "mind." If it did, we would hardly ever have a mind. "Simply" merely excludes there being anything solid or ultimately findable on the side of the mere arising and engaging that renders it "mind," independently existing on its own. We can say no more.

## UNDERSTANDING THE DEEPEST NATURE OF MIND TO BE LIKE SPACE AND ITS CONVENTIONAL NATURE TO BE LIKE ILLUSION

Next we focus on the voidness of mind that is *like* space, although not *the same as* space. The Buddhist notion of space does not refer to the space something occupies, its location, the space between objects, or even outer space. Rather, it is an unchanging fact about a material object that is the case about it so long as that object exists. This fact about it is that there is nothing tangible or physically obstructive on the side of the object — such as some eternal primal matter, as posited by certain non-Buddhist Indian schools of philosophy — that logically, if it were there, would necessarily impede that object from being manifest and existing in three dimensions. Likewise, there is nothing tangible or obstructive — in other words, findable — on the side of either objects or mind that logically, if it were there, would necessarily impede either of them from existing at all. This is the case about them, unalterably so long as they exist, whether we speak of their dependently arising existence in the sense of mental labeling — which entails the inseparability of words or concepts and their meanings — or in the sense of the inseparability of appearance and mind. Similarly, there is nothing from the side of objects impeding them from arising as objects of mind, and nothing on the side of mind impeding it from being able to give rise to an appearance of objects. Mind is not the same as space, however. Mind can know things, space cannot.

Finally, we focus once more on the conventional nature of mind with the understanding that it exists *like* an illusion, although it is not *the same as* an illusion. It only appears as though there are objects solidly "out there" and mind solidly "in here," with experience being the solid result of the interaction between these two solid things, and a solid "me" behind it all, controlling or experiencing the entire process. But none of these things involved in experience, or mind, exist in the manner our mind makes them appear to exist, as is the case with illusions. Our illusion-like mind, however, generates our problems and can realize liberation from them, whereas an actual illusion can do neither.

## FURTHER APPLICATIONS OF THE UNDERSTANDING OF VOIDNESS TO MAHAMUDRA MEDITATION

Not only must we gain an accurate understanding of the devoid nature of mind, we need to apply it to correct our meditation of faults. We have already seen how understanding the devoid nature of "me" is necessary for overcoming the fault of meditating on the conventional nature of mind — mere arising and engaging in contents of experience — from the point of view of the observer, agent or controller of the process, or the one who is experiencing it. Understanding the devoid nature of mind itself helps us overcome becoming infatuated with this process. The compassion we develop from seeing other beings, when not combined with this understanding, may momentarily rouse us to action, but is not enough to prevent the fault of infatuation recurring.

When we focus on the conventional nature of mind, even if we do so in a "non-self"-conscious manner, we inevitably, as a result of perfect concentration, gain what Karma Kagyü terminology calls "boon experiences." They are a boon in the sense of being like a bonus or extra gift. We become filled with a blissful experience of clarity or brilliance as well as starkness or bareness. This is a crisp, vibrant, serene type of bliss pervading the entire body and mind. It is uplifting, but never disturbing, nor even exciting in the sense of rousing us to express our joy.

In the terminology of the Indian Buddhist masters Asanga and Kamalashila, as explained in the Gelug tradition, the boon experience of clarity undoubtedly corresponds to the total elimination of all degrees of mental dullness, while that of starkness to the stilling of all levels of flightiness of mind. Starkness is equivalent to the bare absence of all distraction, such as thoughts. The boon of bliss undoubtedly corresponds to the serenely joyous sense of physical and mental suppleness and fitness, which comes from perfectly absorbed concentration free of dullness and flightiness, and which is a defining characteristic of shamata.

The great danger is that we become so infatuated with these boon experiences that we become overwhelmed and attached, and do not want to get up and leave them. They are very attractive and can therefore be seductive. Compassion that arises from actually seeing others and their suffering, not just visualizing them, provides us with the energy to get up and help them. But compassion alone will not dissolve our attachment to returning to the boon experiences once we have attended to the needs of others. We will want to climb back into the "warm, cozy bed," as it were, in our head. We need to apply the understanding of the devoid nature of mind and experience. Just as mind is inseparable from appearance, or experience from content, likewise mind is inseparable from bliss, clarity and starkness. Boon experiences do not exist separately from being a mere arising and engaging with contents; while focus, with understanding and absorbed concentration, on mere arising and engaging does not occur without its being blissful, clear and stark.

On one level, just as we could shift our focus from the contents of experience to the process of experience itself — the mere arising and engaging with the contents — likewise we could shift our focus from the contents of the boon experiences to the process of the experience of them. But this too may not be enough to overcome the danger of infatuation recurring. In order not to solidify or overinflate the boon experiences, we need to stop regarding them as existing in a fantasized, impossible manner — as if they existed all by themselves — as something so special that we become infatuated with them. If we see them as something that arises dependently on many factors, we deconstruct or "desolidify" them. We can then experience them without apprehending them to exist in a manner in which they do not, and thus without becoming distracted from our goal or lost in them.

It is not that we are striving to eliminate these boon experiences, just like we are not striving to eliminate the conventional level of reality. But we are trying to see and experience the conventional level of these boons as merely part of the experience of the nature of mind.

Thus we try to experience them with the understanding of their devoid nature so that we do not reify them and become attached.

## NON-CONCEPTUAL MEDITATION

One of the most advanced levels of mahamudra practice is meditating on the nature of mind in a non-conceptual manner. But what does this mean? Non-conceptual means direct, not through the medium of an idea. An idea of something is a semblance of it used in thought to represent it. The term is usually translated as "mental image," but a semblance of something need not have shape or color, especially in the case of a mental representation of mind. For non-conceptual perception of mind, then, we need to rid ourselves of reliance on an idea of what merely arising and engaging with the contents of experience is. We need to see and focus on the process directly.

Non-conceptual, bare mental perception of something, then, does not involve thinking, although of course mind is still functioning and there is mental cognition. The Western and Buddhist notions of "thinking," however, are quite different. The Western notion implies a sequence of conceptual, usually verbal thoughts, whereas the Buddhist notion of conceptual thinking is much broader. It includes not only mental processes involving non-verbal ideas such as mental images, but also merely mentally focusing on something through an idea of it. A non-conceptual mental cognition of something is free of thinking not only in the Western sense of the term, but also in the more extensive Buddhist sense.

Furthermore, non-conceptual does not mean without understanding. It means merely without relying on an idea of something — either a verbal formulation, a symbolic representation or even an abstract feeling. We can understand something without necessarily understanding it through an idea of it. But although we can understand something directly without mixing it with a verbal or pictorial idea, there is still understanding. This is the crucial point. We need to see not merely directly, but to see, both directly and with understanding, the conventional and deepest natures of mind — first one at a time and then both simultaneously.

To see something with our eyes is automatically non-conceptual. All sensory perception is non-conceptual. It does not, however, necessarily entail understanding what is seen, for instance seeing a foreign alphabet we do not understand. Mental seeing, however — and not in the sense of visualizing a Buddha — is something else. So far in our discussion we have been using the expression "to see something with the mind" to mean to understand it, and that is usually conceptual, namely through the medium of an idea. It is not at all easy to understand something non-conceptually.

We must be careful not to confuse a conceptual understanding of something with what Western languages refer to as an "intellectual understanding." An intellectual understanding can be one that is either derived consciously through logic or can be expressed in a logical manner. In this meaning, such an understanding is opposed to an intuitive one which is gained as a result of more unconscious processes. But not all conceptual understandings are intellectual in this sense. An infant's conceptual understanding of who is its mother is not intellectual. Furthermore, intuitive understandings can also be conceptual, such as a mechanic's intuitive understanding of what is wrong with our car. In fact, almost all intuitive understandings are conceptual.

Another connotation of the Western notion of an intellectual understanding is one that we do not apply to transforming our life. We can understand intellectually that smoking cigarettes is bad for our health, but we smoke anyway. The fault is usually our lack of sufficient motivation, but may also be a lack of sufficient instruction, for instance on how to stop smoking. The fault is not that our understanding is conceptual. Yet even when we understand something, for instance how to cook, and we cook every day, our understanding of how to do so is still conceptual. We need to explore what it means to understand something.

## THE RELATION BETWEEN IDEAS, UNDERSTANDING AND CONCEPTUAL MEDITATION

First we need an idea of something in order to understand it. If we have no idea of what something means, how can we possibly understand it? Moreover, that idea has to be accurate and precise, not distorted or vague. This is true regarding the nature of mind as well. How can we possibly understand mind, let alone focus on it in meditation, if we have no idea of what mind means or if our idea of it is fuzzy or mistaken? But then, once our understanding becomes very deep, we can focus on the nature of mind directly — and not through the medium of an idea of it — while still maintaining full understanding.

We begin mahamudra meditation, however, by first trying to stay with the conventional nature of mind — the mere arising and engaging with the contents of each moment of experience — by means of focusing on the process, as it occurs, from moment to moment, through some idea of it. That idea of it need not be a verbal formulation of the definition of mind that we say in our head over and again like a mantra. Nor does it need to be a mental picture of it or, in Western popular terminology, some sort of "intuitive feeling" about what it is.

There are two types of ideas with which we conceptually think about something. One is an idea that involves merely a sound — either the sound of a word or set of words, or any other type of sound such as music or static on the radio — of which we have no understanding of its meaning or significance. An example is thinking "mind" or the Tibetan word "sem" when we have only the idea of the sound of the word "mind" or "sem," but no idea whatsoever of what it means. To think about "mind" or "sem" with only such an idea of it would be, literally, meaningless thought.

The other type of idea is of the meaning or significance of something, such as of the word "mind." It may or may not be accompanied with a representation or indication of that meaning, such as a mental word, mental picture or an intuitive feeling, at the moment of actually thinking with this idea. It may be more abstract than that. But the idea of the meaning of the word "mind" obviously does not exist independently of the word "mind," nor independently of mind itself. Furthermore, ideas of the meaning of the word "mind" can have varying degrees of accuracy. Moreover, regardless of the accuracy of our idea, our focus on it can also have varying degrees of clarity.

The main difference between imagining our mother, which is a conceptual process, and either seeing her or dreaming about her, both of which are non-conceptual processes, is that imagining her is far less vivid than the other two. We can use this as a guideline for recognizing the stages through which we pass in order to focus non-conceptually on the nature of mind. Let us look at the stages for focusing, for example, on simply its conventional nature as the mere arising and engaging in the contents of experience.

## THE STAGES FOR GAINING A NON-CONCEPTUAL MAHAMUDRA MEDITATION

For any level of meditation on the nature of mind, we need, of course, concentration, attention, mindfulness and alertness, in the senses in which we have already defined them. We are not just sitting and doing nothing while the process of arising and engaging in the contents of experience is happening anyway. We are paying attention to it with concentration, but not as a separate observer or as the agent or controller making it happen. There is also understanding of what is happening, with whatever level of accuracy we might have, but without the mental distance of there being a solid "me" as a separate person who understands it.

In Buddhist technical terminology, we say that attention, concentration, mindfulness, alertness and discriminating awareness — what we have been calling "understanding" — are all mental factors that accompany mental consciousness focused on the mere arising and engaging with the contents of experience that is occurring each moment. Such a mental consciousness is, optimally, not accompanied by a mental factor of incorrect discriminating awareness that misunderstands this conventional nature to be some solid, concrete object existing separately from the mind.

To be able to focus on this nature with all these accompanying nondeluded mental factors, and without either any verbal thoughts about something extraneous or even the "mental itchiness" to think such thoughts, is one of the aims of eliminating mental wandering and both gross and subtle flightiness of mind. But, of course, we also need to stop our attention from flying off to any other object besides a verbal thought, such as a mental picture, or a sight, a sound or the physical sensation of an itch or a pain in our knees. Although the quieting of the mind of all extraneous mental chatter and images is necessary for any level of accomplishment, and is not, in itself, something easy to achieve, we should not think that its attainment is that of a non-conceptual understanding of mahamudra. It is simply an indication of an early stage in the attainment of concentration.

We may even be able to focus on this conventional nature of mind through an idea of what it means that is not accompanied with a verbal representation of that idea. In other words, we may be able to focus on the nature of mind without thinking verbally, "This is the nature of mind," or "mere arising and engaging." But, if our experience of the object is not vivid, our meditation is still conceptual.

What does it mean for our meditation to be vivid? We are not talking simply about our meditation being free of mental dullness. When we work to eliminate mental dullness, we are adjusting the state of mind with which we are concentrating by removing the mental factors of gross, middling and subtle mental dullness so that they do not accompany that concentration. We have eliminated gross mental dullness when our focus is clear, middling dullness when our focus is also sharp, and subtle dullness when our focus is, in addition, fresh in each moment. But even with all those factors removed, our meditation may still not be vivid.

Vividness is a quality of experience that is not attained by simply removing an accompanying mental factor that, by itself, is adversely affecting the quality of our concentration. Rather, it is attained by removing an accompanying level of mind that is giving rise to an idea of the object of engagement of our mental consciousness and causing that mental consciousness to focus on both the idea and the object mixed together. The result is that the object is veiled, although not totally obscured, to that mental consciousness, and therefore experienced in a non-vivid manner.

Ideas are static phenomena — usually translated as "permanent phenomena." This means they remain fixed so long as we think in terms of them, and do not undergo organic change from moment to moment. While we are thinking of our mother, for example, our idea of her does not become tired or hungry. We can imagine her walking, in which case our idea of her walking involves a semblance of movement. The sequence of images entailed, however, taken as a whole, constitutes a single idea. The mental pictures that compose this idea, like frames in a movie, are not actually walking.

Our idea of something, of course, may change, but this occurs in a special way. One idea is replaced by another. The latter version does not arise from the former through an organic process of depending on causes and circumstances, like a flower arising due to its dependence on a seed, soil, water, air and so on. Nor does an idea organically grow into a new one through a moment-to-moment process of transformation or change, like a flower aging and wilting.

We can now begin to understand why conceptual thoughts are not vivid. When we think of something that changes from moment to moment, such as our mother, through the medium of an idea of her, we are mixing our mother with an idea of her. Our mother changes from moment to moment, while our idea of her does not. The appearing object of our thought — the idea of our mother — and its object of engagement — our actual mother — are not in the same category of phenomena. Because the focal object of our thought — our mother through the filter of our idea of her — is a hybrid object, the conceptual mind with which we think of our mother cannot give rise to a vivid appearance.

We can perhaps understand this point better through the analogy of looking through the moving water of a stream at a stationary rock on the bottom. Although the analogy is not precise because our focal object in the example is something immobile mixed with the filter of something in motion — not something ever-changing mixed with the filter of something static — nevertheless we can appreciate from this analogy that a hybrid object cannot appear as vividly as one that is unmixed. But what about when we think of the nature of mind?

Unlike our mother, the nature of mind, either on the conventional or deepest level, does not change from moment to moment. Each moment of our experience has the same conventional nature of being a mere arising and engaging with the contents of that experience, and the same deepest nature of being devoid of existing in any impossible way. Although both levels of nature of our experience do not change from moment to moment, our experience having those natures does change from moment to moment. This is because the contents of experience are always changing, both in terms of focal objects and accompanying mental factors.

The nature of mind cannot exist separately from actual moment-to-moment experience. Each moment of experience and its nature come in the same package. Although that nature does not change, the basis for that nature — each moment of experience — changes each moment. When we focus on the unchanging nature of an ever-changing phenomenon through each moment of its change, we find it very difficult to keep up with each moment of change. Naturally we focus on that unchanging nature through a static idea of it.

Mind cannot exist in a different package from its nature. Its nature, however, can certainly exist in a different package from an idea of that nature. Therefore, although mind's nature and an idea of that nature are both static phenomena, they are still in different categories of phenomena. This is because the former is always freshly together with each changing moment of experience, while the latter may lapse. Thus the mixture of the nature of mind and an idea of it is a hybrid object. As a result, a conceptual mind focused on such a hybrid object, even with perfectly absorbed concentration, cannot be vivid.

In short, it is extremely difficult even to recognize the difference between perfect states of conceptual and non-conceptual meditations on the nature of mind, let alone to transform the former into the latter. No wonder it takes, according to the sutra teachings, zillions, or a "countless number" of eons of building up positive potential and cleansing obstacles in order to reach this stage!

## THE ANUTTARAYOGA TANTRA LEVEL OF MAHAMUDRA MEDITATION

There are, in general, three levels of mind. The coarse level is that of sensory consciousness. The subtle level is the gross levels of mental consciousness, both conceptual and non-conceptual. The subtlest level is that which is totally devoid of the grosser minds and which provides the basic continuity from moment to moment and life to life. Known as primordial clear light mind, it has no beginning and no end. It is what continues into Buddhahood, becoming the omniscient mind of a Buddha.

With the methods of the highest class of tantra, anuttarayoga, we engage in mahamudra meditation with the subtlest level of mind. We gain access and activate that level through an extremely difficult and complex series of meditations. On the first, or generation stage of practice, we simply imagine we are using the subtlest level of mind. We progress to the second, or complete stage — sometimes translated as "completion stage" — when all causes are complete for actually manifesting clear light mind. We accomplish this by focusing on specific, vital points in the subtle energy system of the body and, as a result of previously having imagined or visualized the process, manipulating those energies. Since clear light mind is more subtle than the three levels of conceptual mind — the conscious and personal, the preconscious and primitive, and the subtlest unconscious levels, often translated respectively as "conceptual thoughts," the "eighty indicative conceptual minds" and the "three conceptual minds of white, red and black appearance" — our realization of mind with it is automatically non-conceptual. It is also the only level of mind with which we can focus simultaneously and directly on both the conventional and deepest natures of mind. For these reasons, the great masters have praised the path of anuttarayoga tantra as the quickest, most efficient path to enlightenment.

### SUMMARY

In summary, it is very easy to practice what seems to be mahamudra, but is in fact a technique that does not penetrate deeply enough to root out our problems and their causes. The practice of mahamudra is certainly not simply to become like a cow that sits without moving, just seeing and hearing without thinking anything. But even if we just sit quietly and look and listen attentively to whatever is happening around us, and even if we are able to do this without judging or mentally commenting on anything and, in fact, without any mental chattering at all, we are still not practicing mahamudra meditation.

There is no question that quieting the mind of all mental chatter and noise is extremely beneficial. Such thought prevents us from being attentive to anything around us. But we must be careful not to quiet the mind of understanding when we quiet it of its chatter. There can be no level of mahamudra meditation without at least some accompanying level of understanding of the nature of mind.

It is very important to be humble and not to belittle mahamudra, dzogchen or any of the very advanced, difficult practices by thinking they are simple. For example, we learn an introductory practice that is extremely beneficial, such as quieting the mind of all judgments, comments and verbal thought, and staying with the "here-and-now." If we can accomplish this — which is certainly not easy by any means — we have the necessary foundation not only for mahamudra meditation, but for any type of meditation, as well as life itself. But, if we think this is all there is to mahamudra practice, we are belittling mahamudra, making it into something small and comparatively trivial.

If we think we are a great yogi or yogini because we are engaging in this initial level of practice, and if we do not even conceive that we can go deeper, we are suffering from the fault of weak motivation. We lack sufficient strength of renunciation and bodhichitta to go beyond the initial levels of practice and accomplishment so that we can be truly free of our problems and best able to help others. As the great masters have said, a combination of renunciation and bodhichitta is essential as the driving force not only for beginning the spiritual path, but for sustaining our efforts all along its course and, in the end, for reaching its goal. Thus, with proper and sufficient motivation and sustained effort, mahamudra practice can bring us to the attainment of Buddhahood for the benefit of all.

First we practice preliminaries such as prostration and, especially, guru-yoga and making heartfelt requests for inspiration. When done with proper understanding and motivation, these help weaken our fixation on the contents of our experience, such as the pain in our legs while prostrating or the guru as some omnipotent idol "out there." Thus they help weaken the mental blocks preventing our understanding the nature of mind, and help build up the positive potential to bring us success in this venture.

We begin our formal mahamudra meditation with initial exercises examining the various contents of our experience of each of the senses and of thoughts and emotional feelings. We realize that from the point of view of the conventional nature of experience, namely from the point of view of there occurring merely an arising and engaging in the contents of experience, there is no difference at all between seeing a pleasant or unpleasant sight. This allows us to not become so caught up in the contents of our experience that we become upset and cause problems for ourselves and others. We do not become so dissociated from the contents, however, that we fail to react to them in an appropriate manner, such as by moving out of the way of an oncoming truck that we see in front of us.

On this level, however, we deal with the problem of being caught up in the contents of our experience only when we are already caught up in them. When we are already upset about hearing traffic noise from our room, we compare it with hearing the chirping of birds and then disengage our obsession with the noise by switching our focus to the conventional nature of the experience itself. We need to go much deeper in meditation, however, to prevent that deviation of focus onto the contents from ever arising. We must develop absorbed concentration and a serenely stilled and settled mind.

We therefore focus next on the conventional nature of mind itself. We focus on the mere arising and engaging with the contents of experience that occur in each moment, but without making that process into a solid, concrete object or ourselves into a solid, concrete subject who is the observer, agent or controller of that process or the one experiencing it. By focusing freshly each moment, with perfectly absorbed concentration, we weaken even further our tendency to lose sight of this conventional nature and, consequently, to become caught up in and upset by the contents of our experience.

In order to avoid the dangers of apprehending or taking ourselves to be a solid "me" — either during meditation or, in general, while living our life — we next focus on the conventional and deepest natures of ourselves as "me." We need to see that although conventionally "I" am meditating and experiencing the contents of every moment of experience of my life, that conventional "me" does not exist in the manner of a false "me." Its deepest nature is that it is devoid of existing as some solid, concrete observer, agent or controller of the experiences of life, or the one experiencing them, either in meditation or at any other time. Such realization enables us not only to meditate more properly on the conventional nature of mind and experience, but also eventually to free ourselves from self-preoccupation and selfishness, which cause us to create all our problems for ourselves and prevent us from effectively helping others.

Once we have understood the deepest nature of how "I" exist, we need to apply that understanding to how mind and experience exist. If we no longer become caught up in the contents of our experience, yet apprehend our mind itself to exist as some solid, concrete "thing," we again cause problems for ourselves and prevent ourselves from being best able to help others. We become infatuated, for example, with the boon experiences of blissful clarity and starkness that come with perfectly absorbed concentration on the conventional nature of mind. We need to see that mind itself is devoid of existing in any fantasized, impossible manner.

At first we focus on the conventional and deepest natures of mind conceptually, through an accurate idea of them. But eventually, when we are able to focus on each of them directly and barely, we achieve a mahamudra meditation that is non-conceptual and vivid. Our meditation then becomes potent enough, in combination with the force of our joint motivation of renunciation and bodhichitta, to actually eliminate forever, step by step, the various grades of our apprehending impossible ways of existing with respect to our mind, experience, its contents and "me."

Finally, when we have eliminated the obstacles that have been preventing our mind from being able to give rise, directly and simultaneously, to both the conventional and deepest natures of each moment's experience, we directly and fully engage them both at once. Our mind thus becomes the omniscient, totally compassionate awareness of a Buddha. Our body and form of communication likewise transform so that as an enlightened being we are best equipped to benefit others.

This full ability to benefit others is the result of the elimination of all obstacles preventing liberation and omniscience, namely confusion about the nature of mind and experience, and the instincts of that confusion. We eliminate these by realizing and focusing, first conceptually, then non-conceptually, on the conventional and deepest natures of mind, one at a time. To do so properly, we need to work on eliminating our apprehension of "me" as existing solidly. We approach that task more effectively if we have disengaged ourselves from being so caught up in the contents of experience that we become upset by everything that occurs in life.

We build up the ability to shift our focus from the contents of our experience to the experience itself, and weaken our mental blocks that would prevent us from so doing, by engaging in preliminary practices. We transform every aspect of our life into a preliminary practice by living our life "straight up and down, not sideways" — not complaining and not making an ordeal out of anything. We gain the strength to do this when we become so concerned about the welfare of others that we decide we definitely must overcome all our problems and shortcomings and realize all our potentials so that we can be of best help to them all.

We are able to develop this dedicated heart of bodhichitta as our motivation only if we have become sufficiently disgusted with our problems that we decide we must definitely free ourselves from them. We can only conceive of doing this if we acknowledge our problems, recognize their causes and gain the confidence that if we eliminate these causes, our problems will never recur. As the deepest cause of our problems is confusion about the moment-to-moment experiences of life and their contents, it is essential to understand the nature of mind. The path of mahamudra is one of the most effective methods for accomplishing this goal for the benefit of all.

# Part II

# THE ROOT TEXT

*A ROOT TEXT FOR THE PRECIOUS GELUG/KAGYÜ TRADITION OF MAHAMUDRA:*
*The Main Road of the Triumphant Ones*

*by*
The First Panchen Lama

# A Root Text for the Precious Gelug/Kagyü Tradition of Mahamudra:
## The Main Road of the Triumphant Ones

by The First Panchen Lama, Lozang-chökyi-gyeltsen

*Namo mahamudraya*: Homage to mahamudra, the great seal of reality.
I respectfully bow at the feet of my peerless guru, lord of that which pervades everywhere, master of those with actual attainment, who expounds the all-pervasive nature of everything, the great seal of reality, mahamudra, inseparable from the diamond-strong sphere of mind that is beyond speech. Gathering together the essence of the sutras and tantras and condensing oceans of guideline instructions, I shall write some advice concerning mahamudra from the Gelug/Kagyü tradition, deriving from the pioneering fatherly Dharmavajra, a mahasiddha with supreme actual attainment, and his spiritual offspring.

For this there are preparatory practices, actual techniques and concluding procedures. As for the first, in order to have a gateway for entering the teachings and a central tent pole for erecting a mahayana mind, earnestly take the safe direction of refuge and develop a dedicated heart of bodhichitta. Do not let these merely be words from your mouth. Since seeing the actual nature of mind is dependent upon building up bountiful stores and purifying yourself of mental obstacles, direct [toward your root guru] at least a hundred thousand repetitions of the hundred-syllable mantra and as many hundreds of prostrations as possible, made while reciting *The Admission of Downfalls*. In addition, make repeated heartfelt requests to your root guru inseparable from all Buddhas of the three times.

As for the actual basic techniques, although there are many ways of asserting mahamudra, there are two when divided according to the sutras and tantras. The latter is a greatly blissful clear light mind manifested by such skillful methods as penetrating vital points of the subtle vajra-body and so forth. The mahamudra of the traditions of Saraha, Nagarjuna, Naropa and Maitripa, it is the quintessence of the anuttarayoga class of tantra as taught in *The [Seven Texts of the] Mahasiddhas* and *The [Three] Core Volumes.* The former refers to the ways of meditating on voidness as directly indicated in the expanded, intermediate and brief [Prajnaparamita sutras]. The supremely realized Arya Nagarjuna has said, "Except for this, there is no other pathway of mind leading to liberation." Here I shall give instruction on mahamudra in accordance with his intentions and discuss the methods that lead you to recognize mind in keeping with the exposition of the lineage masters.

From the point of view of individually ascribed names, there are numerous traditions, such as those of the simultaneously arising as merged, the amulet box, possessing five, the six spheres of equal taste, the four syllables, the pacifier, the object to be cut off, dzogchen, the discursive madhyamaka view, and so on. Nevertheless, when scrutinized by a yogi learned in scripture and logic and experienced [in meditation], their definitive meanings are all seen to come to the same intended point.

Of the two main techniques of the sutra tradition of mahamudra, namely seeking to meditate on mind on top of having gained a correct view of reality and seeking a correct view on top of having meditated on mind, [I shall explain] here in accordance with the latter technique. On a seat conducive for mental stability, assume the sevenfold bodily posture and clear yourself purely with a round of the nine tastes of breath. Thoroughly cleanse your state of awareness, and then, with a purely positive mind, direct [toward your practice] your taking of refuge and the reaffirmation of your dedicated heart of bodhichitta. Meditate next on a profound path of guru-yoga and, after making hundreds of very strong, fervent requests, dissolve your visualized guru into yourself.

Absorb for a while unwaveringly in this state in which all haphazard appearance-making and appearances have been contracted until they have disappeared. Do not contrive anything with thoughts such as expectations or worries. This does not mean, however, that you cease all attention as if you had fainted or fallen asleep. Rather, you must tie [your attention] to the post of mindfulness in order not to wander, and station alertness to be aware of any mental movement.

Firmly tighten the hold of your mindfulness on that which has the nature of clarity and awareness and behold it starkly. Should your mind give rise to any thoughts, simply recognize them. Or, like your opponent in a duel, cut thoughts immediately as soon as they occur. Once you have completely cut these off and have settled your mind, then, without losing mindfulness, loosen and relax its tightness. As has been said, "Loosen and relax its firm tightness and there is the settled state of mind." And elsewhere, "When mind ensnared in a tangle is relaxed, it frees itself without a doubt." Like these statements, relax but without any wandering.

When you look at the nature of any thought that arises, it automatically disappears by itself and a bare absence dawns. Likewise, when you inspect mind's nature when it is settled, a non-obstructive bare absence and clarity is vivid. You see that the settled and moving minds are mixed together. Thus, no matter what thought arises, when you recognize that it is a movement of mind and, without blocking it, have settled on its nature, [you find] it is like the example of a bird confined on a boat. As is said, "Just as a crow having flown from a ship after circling the directions must re-alight on it...."

From cultivating such methods as these, you experience the nature of the totally absorbed mind to be a non-obstructive lucidity and clarity. Not established as any form of physical phenomenon, it is a bare absence which, like space, allows anything to dawn and be vivid. Such nature of mind must in fact be seen straightforwardly with exceptional perception and cannot be verbally indicated or apprehended as a "this." Therefore, without such apprehension, settle in a fluid and flowing manner on whatever cognitive dawning arises.

The great meditators of the snow mountains are practically of a single opinion in proclaiming that this is a guideline indicating how to forge a state of Buddhahood. Be that as it may, I, Chökyi-gyeltsen, say that this is a wondrous skillful means for beginners to accomplish the settling of their mind and is a way that leads you to recognize [merely] the conventional nature of mind that conceals something deeper.

As for the methods that can lead you to recognize the actual [deepest] nature of mind, I shall now record the personal instructions of my root guru, Sanggyay-yeshey, who [as his name literally means] is the embodiment of the Buddhas' deep awareness. Assuming the guise of a monk clad in saffron, he has eliminated the darkness enshrouding my mind.

While in a state of total absorption as before, and like a tiny fish flashing about in a lucid pond and not disturbing it, intelligently inspect the self-nature of the person who is meditating. It is just as our source of direction, the highly realized Arya Nagarjuna, has said, "A person is not earth, not water, nor fire, nor wind, not space, not consciousness. Nor is he or she all of them. Yet what person is there separate from these? And just as a person is not perfectly solid because he or she is what can be labeled on the collection of these six constituents, likewise none of the constituents are perfectly solid because each is what can be labeled on a collection of parts." When you search and, as has been said, cannot find even a mere atom of a total absorption, someone totally absorbed and so on, then cultivate absorbed concentration on voidness which is like space, and do so single-pointedly without any wandering.

Furthermore, while in a state of total absorption, [scrutinize] mind. Not established as any form of physical phenomenon, it is a non-obstructive bareness that gives rise to the cognitive dawning and emanation of anything, and which endures as an unhindered clarity and awareness, engaging [with objects] without discontinuity. It appears not to depend on anything else. But as for the implied object of the mind that apprehends it [to exist as it appears], our guiding light, Shantideva, has said, "Such things as a continuum or collection are not as they seem. They are false, as in the case of a rosary, an army and so on." By means of scriptural authority and lines of reasoning such as this, totally absorb yourself on everything's lack of existing as it appears.

In short, as my spiritual mentor, Sanggyay-yeshey, omniscient in the true sense, has said, "When, no matter what dawns in your mind, you are fully aware that what it is an appearance of exists simply as what can be apprehended by conceptual thought, you experience the deepest sphere of reality dawning without need to rely on anything else. While this is dawning, to immerse your awareness in it and totally absorb, my goodness!" Similarly, fatherly Pa Dampa-sanggyay has said, "Within a state of voidness, the lance of awareness twirls around. A correct view of reality cannot be impeded by anything [ultimately] tangible or obstructive, O people of Dingri." All such statements come to the same intended point.

At the conclusion of your meditation session, dedicate whatever ennobling, positive potential has accrued from meditating on mahamudra, the great seal of reality, as well as your ocean-like store of positive potential of the three times, toward your attainment of the peerless state of enlightenment.

Having accustomed yourself like this [to seeing with a correct view], when you subsequently inspect how your mind makes the objects of any of your six collections of consciousness appear, [you experience] their bare mode of existence dawning in an exposed, resplendent manner. This is called the essential point of a correct view — recognizing whatever dawns in your mind.

In short, always cultivate your realization by not apprehending things, such as your mind and so forth, [to exist in the manner in which] your mind gives rise to an appearance of [them]. Do this by keeping firm to their actual mode of existence. When you cognize [one thing] like this, [you see] the nature of all phenomena of samsara or nirvana as being uniformly the same. Aryadeva has confirmed this point, "As has been explained, the way in which [mind] becomes the seer of one functional phenomenon is the way it becomes the seer of everything. The voidness of one thing [suffices for] the voidness of all things."

Before the face of proper, total absorption on the actual nature of reality, there is just the severance of fantasized, impossible extremes — namely, inherent, findable existence or total non-existence — with respect to everything of samsara and nirvana. Yet after you arise, when you inspect, you see that your mind still gives rise to the appearance of things that dependently arise, which do function and can only exist as simply what can be labeled by names. It is unmistakable that such things still naturally dawn, yet they are like dreams, mirages, reflections of the moon in water and illusions.

When the time comes that you can perceive simultaneously the appearance of things without this causing their voidness to be obscured to your mind, and their voidness without your mind ceasing to make their appearance dawn, you have directly manifested the excellent pathway mind that perceives everything from the single, integrated point of voidness and dependent arising being synonymous. The attainment of the resultant two unified Buddha-bodies comes from the unified practice of wisdom and method. This follows from the fact that all objects have both voidness and appearance [levels of truth].

These words have been written by the renounced meditator Lozang-chökyi-gyeltsen, who has heard many teachings. By its positive merit, may all beings quickly become triumphant Buddhas through this pathway of mind, apart from which there is no second gateway to a state of serenity.

I have compiled these techniques that lead you to recognize the great seal of reality, mahamudra, at the repeated request of Gedün-gyeltsen, who holds the monastic degree of Infinitely Learned Scholar of the Ten Fields of Knowledge, and of Sherab-senggey from Hatong, who holds the monastic degree of Master of the Ten Difficult Texts. They have seen all concerns for the eight worldly emotional states to be dramas of madness and now live in remote solitude, following a sagely way of life and taking this pathway of mind as their essential practice. Many other of my disciples who truly wish to practice mahamudra at its definitive level have also requested such a text.

I have especially composed this text now since the triumphant Ensapa, the omniscient lord of masters with actual attainment, himself has said in one of his songs of experience to instruct himself and others, "I have written explanations of *lamrim* — the graded stages of the path from the Kadam tradition — all the way from whole-hearted commitment to a spiritual teacher up through shamata and vipashyana. But I have not committed to paper the ultimate guideline instructions for mahamudra, which are not included among these aforementioned pathways of mind and which are not well known at present to those of the Land of Snows."

Thus, what was not set down in writing at that time due to need for restriction was intended for a later period. Scriptural sources establish as much — for example, from *The Lotus Sutra*, "Because it is to be realized completely by the Buddhas' deep awareness [Sanggyay-yeshey], you could never say to those who would prematurely write about this method of their own accord that you are enlightened. If you ask why, it is because those who are sources of safe direction have regard for the times."

Therefore, also in order for such prophesies as this to be fulfilled, I, the renounced meditator Lozang-chökyi-gyeltsen, who have not let degenerate the lineage of inspiration from those who have practiced straightforwardly this pathway of mind from the peerless universal teacher, the king of the Shakyas, down through my root guru, the omniscient Sanggyay-yeshey, and who myself have become a member of this lineage, not letting the close bond of its practice be lost, and who uphold the guideline instructions of the sutras and tantras, have compiled this at Gaden Monastery.

# Part III

# A DISCOURSE ON
# *A ROOT TEXT FOR THE PRECIOUS GELUG/KAGYÜ TRADITION OF MAHAMUDRA*

*by*
*H.H. the Dalai Lama*

**Chapter One**
# INTRODUCTION AND PRELIMINARIES

## INTRODUCTORY REMARKS

Everyone wishes to be happy and not to suffer. Whether we are rich or poor, young or old, highly educated or illiterate, we all have this same hope and aspiration. A religious person uses spiritual means to attain this goal, while someone who does not accept religion uses whatever techniques he or she can find. Whether our suffering is great or small and whether the happiness we strive for is deep or shallow, we each work in our own way, trying to apply the most profound methods we can. In a spiritual context, we strive to eliminate our problems and unhappiness not just temporarily, but completely; and we work to achieve not merely a fleeting happiness, but a solid and lasting one. Our intention is not limited. We seek methods that can eliminate all suffering completely and bring about total, everlasting joy.

Why have we come here today? We do not seek food or clothing. We are not seriously lacking any material necessities for this life. Despite language difficulties, we have come because of our keen interest in attaining mental happiness in this spiritual context. Such happiness, however, cannot be gained through receiving blessings or inspiration from a lama or by the grace of the Three Jewels of Refuge. If that were possible, happiness would be very easy to achieve. But, as the Buddhist teachings explain, our happiness depends on our karma, namely our impulsive or intentional actions. Thus karma depends on mind and whether or not we have controlled or tamed our mind. Therefore, in the end, our happiness or suffering depend on us.

There are many different pathways or methods for taming the mind. Regardless of which we follow, the process entails many stages. Furthermore, in accordance with the means employed, the nature of the tamed state we achieve varies. The nature of the ultimate level of tamed mind is one in which the disturbing emotions and attitudes, their instincts and all obstacles preventing omniscience have been overcome completely and definitely. Only an ultimate or complete path that is a unity of method and wisdom, inseparable by nature, can lead us to such an ultimate state of tamed mind. Mahamudra offers one such unified path.

In general, method and wisdom inseparable by nature means the two being inseparably together at all times. We can accomplish this, for example, by always having a method held by wisdom and a wisdom held by method. This means always apprehending method within the context of wisdom and wisdom within the context of method, without either of the two ever being absent.

But, not only do we need both method and wisdom always present, we need both to be complete in the same entity or package, namely in one moment of mind with a single manner of apprehending its object. Practicing in this way is a special feature of tantra and entails many stages. Although practicing with this ultimate type of inseparability is the principal aim, our root text on mahamudra discusses this topic mainly from the sutra perspective. There we utilize a method and wisdom that are different entities — in other words, that have different manners of apprehending their object. Consequently, they must be cultivated separately and then combined into one. This is the main point the text discusses.

What is method within the sutra context of a unity of method and wisdom? It is a dedicated heart of bodhichitta, based on love and compassion. It apprehends its object, enlightenment, with the intention to achieve it in order to benefit others. Compassion, as its basis, apprehends its object, the suffering of others, with the wish to remove it. Wisdom, on the other hand, is a correct view that understands voidness — the absence of fantasized, impossible ways of existing. Even if it is aimed at the same object as method, it apprehends that object as not existing in an impossible way. The ways wisdom and compassion each apprehend their object are not at all the same. Therefore, we need to actualize these two, as method and wisdom, first separately and then together. Even if we speak about the mahamudra that is method and wisdom inseparable by nature in the ultimate tantric sense, the first stage for its realization is understanding the abiding nature of reality, just as in the practice of sutra. As this is the case, we must gain decisive understanding of the correct view of voidness before we can possibly practice tantric level mahamudra.

Although the voidness that is to be ascertained on the sutra and tantra paths is exactly the same, the methods for meditating on it can differ widely. For this reason, the great masters of old in Tibet have explained several distinct techniques for gaining decisive understanding of voidness. Among them, even the works of Tsongkapa contain varied methods for ascertaining the nature of reality. The present work by the First Panchen Lama, entitled *A Root Text for the Precious Gelug/ Kagyü Tradition of Mahamudra: The Main Road of the Triumphant Ones*, explains a special, uncommon way to gain decisive understanding of a correct view and meditate on voidness. Although these teachings come specifically from Tsongkapa, the First Panchen Lama composed this text to clarify them since several slightly different ways of explaining arose as their oral teachings were transmitted down the lineage.

The Fifth Dalai Lama has said we can do without the name "Kagyü" in the title and just call it the "Gelug tradition of mahamudra." Yongdzin Yeshey-gyeltsen, Gungtangzang and others have followed his advice. I wonder what his reason might have been? But, then again, it is not necessary for me to come up with an explanation for everything. Let us therefore proceed directly to the text.

## OPENING HOMAGE, PRAISE AND PROMISE TO COMPOSE

In order to establish instincts for a connection with the Sanskrit language through the process of dependent arising, the text begins with the Sanskrit praise,

> *Namo mahamudraya:* Homage to mahamudra, the great seal of reality.

The text then continues,

> I respectfully bow at the feet of my peerless guru, lord of that which pervades everywhere, master of those with actual attainment, who expounds the all-pervasive nature of everything, the great seal of reality, mahamudra, inseparable from the diamond-strong sphere of mind that is beyond speech.

The "all-pervasive nature of everything, the great seal of reality" refers to voidness as an object of mind. This object, voidness, and that which takes or apprehends this as its object, namely a mind with a

correct view understanding voidness — referred to here as the "diamond-strong sphere of mind" — are inseparable. Not tainted by even
the slightest trace of discordant appearance-making, or "dual appearances," the two are totally of one taste, like water mixed with water.

If we explain on a level common to sutra and tantra, the "diamond-
strong sphere of mind" refers to mind as mere clarity and awareness.
If we explain in connection exclusively with tantra, it refers to simultaneously arising primordial clear light mind — in other words, the
subtlest level of mind, which arises simultaneously with each moment
of experience. Mahamudra discusses voidness as an object which is
inseparably in the same package as one of these two levels of mind
understanding a correct view of voidness. Furthermore, just as the
nature of all phenomena that exist, and which mind can thus produce
an appearance of, is that they are devoid of existing in a truly inherent
manner, likewise the nature of inseparable voidness and the mind understanding it is that it too is devoid of existing truly and inherently.
Inseparable voidness and the mind understanding it, therefore, is always in the same package as the voidness of that inseparability.

Not only is there an inseparability of voidness and the mind understanding it — with that inseparability likewise being devoid by nature — there is an additional aspect of inseparability. In mahamudra
meditation, mind is taken inseparably as both the object apprehended
by mind as being devoid by nature and the mind that is apprehending it as such. Thus when we say that mahamudra entails, on the tantra
level, simultaneously arising clear light mind and, on the sutra level,
deep awareness realizing voidness, we must understand each within
the context of all these types of inseparability. The author offers prostration respectfully at the feet of the guru who expounds the methods
for actualizing all this.

Of the body, speech, mind, enlightening influence and good qualities of the guru, the author offers prostration specifically to the speech
of the guru. From among all the activities of the guru's speech explaining extensive pathway minds, the reference here is specifically
to the speech that explains deep awareness understanding voidness,
the all-pervasive nature of everything.

Next comes the author's promise to compose:

> Gathering together the essence of the sutras and tantras and con-
> densing oceans of guideline instructions, I shall write some ad-
> vice concerning mahamudra from the Gelug/Kagyü tradition, de-
> riving from the pioneering fatherly Dharmavajra, a mahasiddha
> with supreme actual attainment, and his spiritual offspring.

Voidness as an object of mind is the same in both sutra and tantra; however, the mind taking voidness as its object is different in each. Although this text occasionally refers to the mind that ascertains voidness in accordance with the tantra teachings, it mostly explains the sutra approach to this topic. It does so, however, with the purpose of leading up to the tantra presentation of the mind that meditates on voidness.

The sutras here refer to the Prajnaparamita sutras, concerning far-reaching discriminating awareness, or the "perfection of wisdom" — specifically the hundred thousand, twenty thousand and eight thousand stanza recensions. The tantras refer primarily to *The Guhyasamaja Tantra*, concerning the assembly of hidden factors that bring us to enlightenment. There are also guideline texts written by greatly learned and highly realized Indian masters that can help us understand the meanings of these sutras and tantras. The most outstanding of these for understanding the Prajnaparamita sutras is *A Filigree of Clear Realizations* by Maitreya, while for *The Guhyasamaja Tantra*, there are the works of Nagarjuna, for instance *The Five Stages [of the Guhyasamaja Complete Stage]*, and so forth. The author has gathered together and condensed the essence of all these guideline texts and composed this work.

Although the Gelug/Kagyü lineage of mahamudra explanation comes from Togden Jampel-gyatso, a direct disciple of Tsongkapa, the First Panchen Lama specifically mentions fatherly Dharmavajra and his spiritual offspring. This is because Dharmavajra was a very highly realized master who not only attained a single-pointed state of unity, but also received a clear vision of Tsongkapa and composed *The Guru-yoga of the Foremost Three-part Composite Being*.

## THE COMMON PRELIMINARIES

The actual body of the text begins,

> For this there are preparatory practices, actual techniques and concluding procedures. As for the first, in order to have a gateway for entering the teachings and a central tent pole for erecting a mahayana mind, earnestly take the safe direction of refuge and develop a dedicated heart of bodhichitta. Do not let these merely be words from your mouth.

Mahamudra meditation entails preparatory practices, actual techniques and concluding procedures. As preparation, we first take refuge, or safe direction in life, in order to distinguish our practice from non-Buddhist paths. Then, to differentiate what we are doing from more modest vehicle, or hinayana, paths, we regenerate and enhance our dedicated heart of bodhichitta.

Without taking refuge, we cannot be considered a Buddhist. Thus we take safe direction in life from the Buddhas, Dharma and Sangha, not just merely with words, but from the depths of our heart. We do this with a profound sincerity gained by understanding the good qualities of the Three Jewels of Refuge which are all based on reason. In this way, we ensure our confident belief in this source of safe, sound and positive direction.

Primarily we take refuge in the attainment of the Three Precious Gems that we shall manifest in the future and that we commit ourselves now to attaining. In other words, we actively put the safe direction in our life of working to achieve this goal. Specifically, we put the vast vehicle or mahayana safe direction in our life — a direction in which all the vast qualities are complete in addition to, above and beyond the more modest direction of hinayana.

Furthermore, to differentiate our practice from more modest paths, we regenerate and enhance our bodhichitta motivation — we re-dedicate our heart to achieving enlightenment in order to benefit all beings to the fullest extent. Without developing bodhichitta in addition to taking mahayana refuge, we might consider attaining arhatship as our supreme goal — in other words, becoming a liberated being rather than a fully enlightened Buddha. Consequently, we would be working merely for that more limited achievement. Even if we practice tantra, if we do so without bodhichitta motivation, we are practicing what can only be counted as a more modest, or hinayana, path. Therefore bodhichitta is the distinguishing feature of all pathway minds that lead fully to enlightenment.

Bodhichitta is essential not only in the context of mahayana, but is like a central tent pole for structuring and supporting all Buddha's teachings. As Tsongkapa has explained in *A Grand Presentation of the Graded Stages of the Path*, "Hinayana practices are a necessary preliminary for developing a dedicated heart of bodhichitta. Training yourself with extensive mahayana actions of generosity and so forth is the commitment from generating bodhichitta and bonds you closely to it. Bodhichitta motivation makes you keenly interested in developing shamata and vipashyana. It moves you to achieve all states of samadhi, absorbed concentration, explained in the tantras."

This precious bodhichitta is rare to find in the three realms of compulsive existence. It is the root that has given rise to all Buddhas' teachings.

Any amount of meditation on it is always beneficial. It is constructive for beginning, maintaining and completing our spiritual path to enlightenment. Its cause is excellent; its result is excellent and it is excellent by nature. It gives us both temporary happiness and lasting benefit. In all ways, it is like a wish-granting gem. As soon as we develop this bodhichitta on our mind-stream, we quickly and easily finish building up the bountiful stores of positive potential and deep awareness necessary for attaining Buddhahood. With that attainment, we are able, automatically and spontaneously, to fulfill, in the ultimate sense, the spiritual aims of ourselves and others.

Therefore we must adopt the safe direction in life of refuge and then dedicate ourselves with bodhichitta — and both not merely with words, but sincerely from our heart. We must certainly not seek merely an intellectual understanding of refuge and bodhichitta. Knowing what both of them specifically mean, we need to approach the two with the full intention of making them an integral, characteristic feature of our mind and heart — in other words, with the full intention of transforming the state of our mind so that it has them as its combined nature. Thus, by keeping in focus the goal of the safe direction we commit ourselves to attain, we must strive to achieve a state of mind that has a combined nature of both refuge in that direction and the intention to attain Buddhahood through it for the benefit of all beings.

We are only able to transform the nature of our everyday mental state into one of combined refuge and bodhichitta when we have completely habituated ourselves to the way of thinking and feeling of each of them. This is not something we can accomplish in a day. As beginners, we need to make a concerted and sustained effort to work ourselves up to this goal consciously, becoming familiar with it in stages. To strive in this way is the meaning of having refuge and bodhichitta not merely as words, but from the depths of our heart. This is the preliminary for mahamudra shared in common with all other mahayana practices.

## THE UNCOMMON PRELIMINARIES

As for the uncommon preliminaries, the text continues,

> Since seeing the actual nature of mind is dependent upon building up bountiful stores and purifying yourself of mental obstacles, direct [toward your root guru] at least a hundred thousand repetitions of the hundred-syllable mantra and as many hundreds of prostrations as possible, made while reciting *The Admission of Downfalls*. In addition, make repeated heartfelt requests to your root guru inseparable from all Buddhas of the three times.

"Seeing the actual nature of mind" here refers to directly understanding voidness itself. The text later discusses the conventional and deepest natures of mind. Although we also need to build up positive potential and eliminate obstacles in order to see the conventional nature of mind, we have a special, stronger need to do so in order to see mind's deepest nature of voidness. We cannot possibly realize it otherwise. Therefore, to purify ourselves of the negative potentials accumulated by our previously committed destructive actions and the downfalls from having transgressed our vows, we build up a bountiful store of a hundred thousand repetitions of the hundred-syllable mantra of Vajrasattva and prostrations offered while reciting *The Admission of Downfalls*, also known as *The Confession Sutra Before the Thirty-five Buddhas*. These are the major methods for cleansing away obstacles.

In general, the "field" or focus upon which to direct our energy for building up this positive potential is the Three Jewels of Refuge. Because the guru is the condensation or synthesis of these Three Precious Gems, we offer seven-part practice — prostrating, presenting offerings, openly admitting to mistakes, rejoicing in positive deeds, requesting teachings, beseeching not to depart and dedicating positive potential — not only to the field of the Three Jewels, but especially to the field of our supreme root guru who has the nature of all Buddhas of the three times. In addition to building up positive potential and eliminating obstacles in this way, we also repeatedly make heartfelt requests to our own individual gurus for inspiration to develop a correct view understanding mahamudra according to its definition.

## Chapter Two
# THE TANTRA AND SUTRA TRADITIONS OF MAHAMUDRA

### THE TANTRA TRADITION OF MAHAMUDRA

The text continues,

> As for the actual basic techniques, although there are many ways of asserting mahamudra, there are two when divided according to the sutras and tantras.

On the basis of our efforts to eliminate obstacles and build up positive potential, we now proceed with the actual meditations on mahamudra. Although there are many ways of explaining them according to different mahamudra lineages, we can condense them all into two — the sutra and tantra traditions of mahamudra. This division does not refer to a difference in the mahamudra that is realized, but to a difference in the level of mind used to realize it.

The text goes on,

> The latter is a greatly blissful clear light mind manifested by such skillful methods as penetrating vital points of the subtle vajra-body and so forth.

The latter tradition of mahamudra, that of the highest class of tantra, anuttarayoga, entails harnessing and utilizing clear light mind for understanding and realizing mahamudra. There are various methods for reaching, manifesting and then activating this subtlest level of mind. One involves working with the subtle vajra-body.

As humans, we are born with a body having various levels of components that we can use as inner circumstances for supporting meditational practice. On one level, our body has six constituents, namely the constituent spheres of the elements of earth, water, fire, wind and space, as well as consciousness. On a more subtle level, we have, in addition, a vajra or diamond-strong body consisting of energy-channels as what abides, energy-winds as what courses through them, and energy-drops as what can be led by the latter through the former.

This subtle vajra-body is the gateway for reaching to subtlest, primordial clear light mind which arises simultaneously with each moment of experience. But, in our present, ordinary situation, the swarm of our conceptual thoughts — both conscious and personal, as well as preconscious and primitive — denies us access to that subtle body and, through it, that subtlest level of mind. Therefore we need to silence and eventually rid ourselves of the swarm of our coarse and subtle conceptual minds in order to penetrate vital points of the vajra-body so as then to be able to use the constituents of that body to make manifest primordial clear light mind. As this is rather difficult to accomplish, we need a forceful method.

One such method for activating the vajra-body is to take as our object of meditation the stages of progressive dissolution of our external and internal circumstances. This refers to dissolving, which means withdrawing, our mind from our environment, the beings within it, and the elements of our body. We do this by focusing on certain vital points of our subtle vajra-body and gathering into them and dissolving there, through progressive, sequential stages, the energy-winds that carry with them the levels of mind that give rise to appearances of the environment and so forth as objects of our cognition.

In *A Lamp for Further Clarifying the Five Stages [of Guhyasamaja]*, a commentary on Tsongkapa's *"The Pure Stages of the Yoga of Guhyasamaja,"* Kaydrub Norzang-gyatso has explained that there are basically two methods for manifesting clear light mind through the gateway of triggering, in meditation, the stages of progressive dissolution. The Chakrasamvara system uses the generation of the inner flame, or tummo, and the four levels of joyous awareness it induces, while the Guhyasamaja system employs certain sophisticated practices with the energy-winds, such as vajra-recitation. Moreover, there is also the Nyingma method of dzogchen meditation that accomplishes the same, but without inciting experience of these progressive stages.

Basically, there are two ways to manifest simultaneously arising primordial clear light mind. One is through stopping the deceptiveness of the conscious and preconscious levels of conceptual mind through a pathway of manipulating various aspects of the subtle vajrabody. This is accomplished by means of either the Guhyasamaja or Chakrasamvara techniques. The other major method, the Nyingma technique, stops the deceptiveness of these two coarser levels of mind by taking thoughts themselves as the object of focus, without conscious manipulation of any aspects of the subtle vajra-body. Although these two major approaches are very different, they each lead to the same accomplishment.

The various tantric traditions of mahamudra, then, employ such diverse and skillful means as these to manifest the clear light mind that is simultaneous not only with each moment, but also, through other techniques, simultaneous with a greatly blissful awareness, or "great bliss." They then utilize this simultaneously arising clear light mind for understanding voidness itself.

The text goes on,

> The mahamudra of the traditions of Saraha, Nagarjuna, Naropa and Maitripa, it is the quintessence of the anuttarayoga class of tantra as taught in *The [Seven Texts of the] Mahasiddhas* and *The [Three] Core Volumes.*

The above explanation of the tantra level of mahamudra practice is in accordance with the works of such greatly accomplished mahasiddha masters as Saraha, Mahasukha, Nagarjuna, Naropa and Maitripa, especially concerning the complete stage practices of anuttarayoga tantra. This level of mahamudra meditation is, in fact, the quintessential practice of this highest class of tantra.

## THE SUTRA TRADITION OF MAHAMUDRA

The text continues,

> The former refers to the ways of meditating on voidness as directly indicated in the expanded, intermediate and brief [Prajnaparamita sutras]. The supremely realized Arya Nagarjuna has said, "Except for this, there is no other pathway of mind leading to liberation."

The sutra tradition of mahamudra refers to the methods for meditating on voidness as explained in *The Three Mothers* — the hundred thousand, twenty thousand and eight thousand stanza recensions of the Prajnaparamita sutras. As Nagarjuna has said, there is no other pathway of mind to liberation except through this. So long as we are not aware of and do not eliminate our apprehending everything to exist truly and independently, we wander through uncontrollably recurring rebirths by a mechanism of twelve factors that dependently arise — unawareness, affecting impulses, consciousness, nameable mental faculties with or without form, stimulators of cognition, contacting awareness, feeling a level of happiness or suffering, craving, grasping, the compulsive impulse to continue living, conception, ageing and dying — the "twelve links of dependent arising."

The two major divisions of madhyamaka, the "middle way" Indian Buddhist tenet systems that follow from Nagarjuna, provide progressively more subtle understandings of true, independent existence. Svatantrika uses the term to mean unimputed existence — existence truly independent of being what mind can produce an appearance of, and impute or mentally label as "this" or "that," on an appropriate basis. Such a basis is one having an inherent, findable self-nature or defining characteristic mark making it not only existent, but what it is. Prasangika takes true, independent existence as a synonym for inherently findable existence — in other words, existence truly independent of being simply what mind can impute or mentally label on an appropriate basis, without that basis having such a self-nature or mark. For the former, then, true, independent existence means true, unimputed existence, while for the latter, it means true, inherent existence.

The beginningless lack of awareness of the total absence of true, inherent existence, responsible for our samsaric existence, can be explained in two ways. We are unaware of the actual nature of how things actually exist in the sense of either (1) being clouded about it, or (2) projecting and apprehending that nature to be a manner of existence contrary to that which is actually the case. Fatherly Nagarjuna and his spiritual offspring take the second position. They assert that (a) projecting that things exist in a manner contrary to the way in which they actually exist, and (b) apprehending things to exist in this fantasized, impossible manner, are both within the sphere of the lack of awareness that apprehends true, inherent existence. Since such ignorance causes and perpetuates our samsaric existence, bringing us all our problems and suffering, we must definitely eliminate our lack of awareness of how everything actually exists.

To extinguish our ignorance, we must realize that our lack of awareness is due to the confused and disturbing way in which we apprehend the appearance of everything that arises in our mind. That, in turn, is due to the obstacles preventing our omniscience that cause our mind to make everything appear as if it existed truly and inherently. A scriptural quotation indicates the solution, "The mind that craves for uncontrollably recurring rebirth is distorted with respect to its objects. Its understanding, however, of the voidness of its objects causes its craving for such rebirth to cease."

Awareness that understands voidness — the lack of true, inherent existence — has a manner of apprehending its object that focuses on there being no such thing as true and inherent existence. It apprehends such existence not only to be totally absent, but never to have existed at all. The force of this manner of apprehension, then, is the exact opposite of the manner in which apprehending true, inherent existence takes its object — namely by implying that this impossible manner of existence is actually real. Therefore the understanding of voidness causes direct harm to and undermines the ignorance that entails this mistaken apprehension. The former has the support of valid cognition, while the latter lacks such support. The former is a mind that apprehends what corresponds to reality, while the latter is a mind that apprehends what does not correspond to anything real.

Furthermore, in addition to the difference in validity between the former mind that causes direct harm and the latter one that can be harmed by it, the former is such that completely accustoming ourselves to it brings us a habit that has no end. The latter, on the other hand, is such that even our beginningless familiarity with it does not bring us an unending habit because that mind can be harmed or undermined. This being the case, if we become accustomed to a mind that understands the lack of true, inherent existence, we gradually eliminate, in stages, our apprehending true, inherent existence together with all seeds or traces of such apprehension.

Thus, as the root of samsara is the unawareness that apprehends true, inherent existence, what neutralizes, pacifies or eliminates this root and makes manifest a peaceful state of non-discordant liberation is a correct view understanding voidness. Therefore Nagarjuna has said that except for this method, there is no other path to liberation.

The texts continues,

Here I shall give instruction on mahamudra in accordance with his intentions and discuss the methods that lead you to recognize mind in keeping with the exposition of the lineage masters.

The intention of Nagarjuna and his spiritual offspring, in the context of our text, is that we must first come to a decisive understanding of voidness, or the abiding nature of reality, in accordance with the sutra tradition of mahamudra. Therefore we need to have more than just keen interest in understanding voidness in general. We need to meditate on and realize the devoid nature of our mind and make this our top priority.

## Chapter Three
# MAHAMUDRA WITHIN THE CONTEXT OF VARIOUS BUDDHIST TRADITIONS

### THE DIFFERENT LINEAGES OF MAHAMUDRA

In general, we could gain a decisive understanding of voidness with respect to any basis characterized by voidness or having voidness as its nature, such as a vase. There is no difference in the abiding devoid nature itself of a vase or our mind. There is, however, a great difference between a vase and our mind as things having voidness as their nature. Since our wandering in samsara is determined by whether or not we see the voidness of our mind, its abiding nature is especially important to see decisively. Therefore Aryadeva has stated in *A Lamp for the Compendium of Practices, A Commentary on the Meaning of the Five Stages [of the Guhyasamaja Complete Stage]*, "The discussion of how to attain mahamudra entails methods for meditating on mind itself as something having voidness as its nature."

These methods for meditating on the abiding nature of mind — specifically, on the abiding nature of the subtlest level of mind — undertaken in order to recognize what mind actually is, have several different lineages of explanation. Each was founded by a learned and experienced master and expounded in accordance with his or her individual conventions. The text continues,

> From the point of view of individually ascribed names, there are numerous traditions, such as those of the simultaneously arising as merged, the amulet box, possessing five, the six spheres of equal taste, the four syllables, the pacifier, the object to be cut off, dzogchen, the discursive madhyamaka view, and so on.

According to the First Panchen Lama's auto-commentary to this root text, the simultaneously arising as merged tradition "was founded by the venerable Gampopa who trained disciples with the six practices, or 'yogas,' of Naropa. It deals primarily with meditation on simultaneously arising and merged deep awareness" — in other words the deep awareness of primordial clear light that arises simultaneously with each moment of experience. The tradition of the amulet box, "was founded by Kaydrub Kyungpo. It teaches that the preliminary basis is [mind's] automatically coming to its own level in its three aspects. The actual method is [mind's] automatically releasing into itself the three faults. The result is [mind's] automatically giving rise to the three bodies of a Buddha. The actual method is also called 'recognizing the thieves.' The main guideline instruction of the Shangpa Kagyü line is that of the six practices, or 'yogas,' of Niguma."

Kaydrub Kyungpo, from whom the Shangpa Kagyü tradition traces, has written, "May everything be auspicious for the mahamudra of great bliss — the sphere of voidness, clarity and appearance — [seen] when purified down to the depths. Any appearance to which mind gives rise, of anything that exists, automatically emanates like a dream or illusion — a tone of uninterrupted great bliss."

Gurus from various traditions, such as those mentioned in our text, have understood the points raised in this verse in slightly different ways in accordance with their personal meditative experience. More precisely, they have described their experience in different manners, although their ultimate understanding has been the same. They each have ascertained the total absence or voidness of true, inherent existence and the play of simultaneously arising primordial clear light mind of deep awareness. Any phenomenon that mind makes appear as if truly and inherently existent, which yet has the nature of being devoid of existing in the way in which mind gives rise to an appearance of it, does exist. It exists simply as the play of its devoid nature. Not only that, the appearance of it, to which mind gives rise, is the play of simultaneously arising primordial clear light mind, which likewise is something having this very same nature. Each of these masters has understood both these points.

When the great gurus of the past came to a decisive understanding of the correct view having both these points, they explained it in two ways. Some have spoken of a correct view in terms of devoid nature itself, while others of a correct view in terms of what has voidness as its nature. We must keep these two correct views in mind when we consider the line, "Any appearance to which mind gives rise, of anything that exists, automatically emanates like a dream or illusion." We can also read it, "Any phenomenon that exists, and to which mind gives rise to an appearance of, automatically emanates like a dream or illusion."

How are we to understand the meaning of "automatically emanates"? From the viewpoint of a correct view presented in terms of devoid nature itself, it means that no matter what object, having voidness as its nature, that mind makes appear, its appearing arises out of the basis of that object's having voidness as its nature. Its nature does not block its appearance or the appearance-making of it, because its nature is that it is devoid of true and inherent existence. Thus the fact that, by nature, something is dissociated from true and inherent existence allows for an appearance of it automatically to emanate or arise as an object of cognition.

Also, in another way, we can say that ultimately any appearance of anything that exists originates from, or is the play of, primordial mind as something having this devoid nature. Just as any mass of clouds that appears in the sky both originates from and dissolves back into the sky, likewise all appearances of anything that exists both originate from and dissolve back into subtlest clear light mind. From the point of view of its cause, or root, or mental labeling, any appearance is ultimately like a wave of clear light mind itself, or its play. Because it originates from this diamond-strong sphere, it is an automatic or reflexive emanation in the sense of being the reflexive luster of clear light mind.

Thus we can understand "automatically emanates" in terms of both devoid nature and something having this devoid nature, namely clear light mind. Moreover, we can take this in both a sutra and a tantra sense, depending on the level of subtlety of mind we discuss. On the sutra level, we speak of the correct view only in terms of devoid nature itself. From the tantra point of view, however, we can explain the fact that all play of clear light deep awareness is like illusion in the context of either of these two correct views. Thus mind gives rise to an appearance of everything as if truly and inherently existent, although everything it makes appear in this way is devoid of existing in that impossible manner. In this sense, "Any appearance to which mind gives rise, of anything that exists ... [is] like a dream or illusion."

As for "uninterrupted great bliss," there are two types of bliss. One is an apprehension of a physical or mental feeling of bliss, while the other is the bliss of being free from all mental fabricating — specifically, mentally fabricating totally contrived, imaginary modes of existence such as true, inherent existence. This latter state is sometimes called the "youth of the mind" which, innocent of contriving fabrications, is blissful. According to the Sakya tradition of *lamdray* — the paths and their result — which speaks from the point of view of the path, primordial clear light mind arises simultaneously each moment as a blissful awareness in this latter sense of bliss. The term "uninterrupted great bliss" may refer to this.

Furthermore, when our present coarse levels of mind apprehend sensory objects, or think about anything, they do so incorrectly, in the manner of taking a striped rope to be a snake. They do not have the ability to understand, in a bare manner, the stark, actual nature of things. To understand something in a bare manner means to apprehend something with an understanding stripped of all coarse levels of mind, both conceptual and non-conceptual. Thus the actual nature of things is stark in the sense of being not only uncontrived, but also beyond conventional thought. Therefore, it can only be seen from our own deep, non-conceptual meditative experience. As it cannot be apprehended by the coarse levels of mind, it can only be seen "when purified down to the depths." Meditation on the "mahamudra of great bliss — the sphere of voidness, clarity and appearance," characterized like this, is the amulet box tradition of Kaydrub Kyungpo.

As I do not have realization of the salient features of all the traditions the author cites next, I can only explain what comes to my mind. The possessing five tradition, as the auto-commentary states, "asserts in songs of meditational experience that the enlightening influence of the Dagpo Kagyü lineage masters is great and that of Jigten-gönpo is the root." The six spheres of equal taste is likewise another lineage.

The four syllables tradition elaborates on the four syllables "a-ma-na-si," a Sanskrit word that means "not to take to mind." The auto-commentary explains the four syllables as follows, "The first means cutting down to the foundational root state of mind. The second shows the methods for settling mind. The third means to cut off mind from points where it can deviate. The fourth demonstrates how to take mind as a pathway." The author does not elaborate further on any of these points.

Next is the pacifier tradition of fatherly Pa Dampa-sanggyay, deriving from the scriptural line, "The pure view pacifies all suffering." There is also the object to be cut off tradition of the One Mother of All,

Machig Labkyi-drölma, dealing with *chöd*, the cutting-off rite. There is, in addition, the dzogchen or great completeness tradition of the Nyingma tantras of the old translation period and, finally, the madhyamaka or middle way tradition of the old and new Kadam, the latter being the Gelug tradition.

## THE HARMONY OF THE TWO CORRECT VIEWS OF REALITY

The text continues,

> Nevertheless, when scrutinized by a yogi learned in scripture and logic and experienced [in meditation], their definitive meanings are all seen to come to the same intended point.

If we explain according to the Shangpa Kagyü tradition of Kaydrub Kyungpo, for instance, we can meditate on a correct view presented in terms of either devoid nature itself or something having this devoid nature, namely clear light mind. The latter is similar to Tsongkapa's explanation in *Precious Sprout, Deciding the Difficult Points of [Chandrakirti's] "An Illuminating Lamp [for 'The Guhyasamaja Root Tantra']."* In the prologue section, commenting on a quotation from Nagarjuna's *The Five Stages [of the Guhyasamaja Complete Stage]*, Tsongkapa has mentioned that the inanimate environment and the animate beings within it are all the play or emanation of subtlest consciousness and subtlest energy-wind — in other words, simultaneously arising primordial clear light mind and the subtlest level of energy-wind upon which it rides. This is the same understanding as explained before concerning the correct view presented in terms of objects having a devoid nature.

As for the correct view presented in terms of devoid nature itself, Tsongkapa has written in *A Treasury of Commentaries on the Five Stages [of the Guhyasamaja Complete Stage]* and *A Lamp for Clarifying the Five Stages [of the Guhyasamaja Complete Stage]*, "Many possess one taste and one taste is possessed by many." This refers to the fact that all objects emanated, in a cognitive sense, from primordial clear light mind have the same taste of voidness as their deepest nature. This explanation from tantra literature corresponds to the main madhyamaka assertion of the sutra presentation of the correct view presented in terms of devoid nature itself.

Although there are many traditions of explanation, the definitive meaning of voidness to which they all lead is exactly the same. Many erudite masters have explained voidness through logical lines of reasoning concerning the conventional and deepest levels of truth. But many other realized masters whose meditational experience did not accord exactly with these lines of reasoning have explained voidness by taking their innermost meditational experience as more significant than logic. If we examine the words of such masters strictly from the point of view of logic, they may seem to have faults. But if we examine them from the point of view of meditation, we see they are flawless. Thus despite there having been so many famous masters in Tibet with different traditions of meditation on a correct view, they all come to the same point in deep meditation.

Some learned scholars have said that the assertion of the First Panchen Lama that all these traditions come to the same point of realization must be understood as a teaching that needs interpretation and cannot be accepted literally. The Third Panchen Lama, for example, has said this when giving a mahamudra discourse at Kumbum Monastery: "Except for when the First Panchen Lama was alive and could explain what he meant himself, how can we understand now that a view based on an affirming nullification and one based on a non-affirming nullification come to the same point in meditation? This must not be what the First Panchen Lama had literally in mind."

Despite the Third Panchen Lama's opinion, we cannot decide this issue for sure. Many other learned scholars have said that these teachings were definitive and, having thought myself about this for a long time, I concur with their conclusion. The First Panchen Lama was a monk upholding the vinaya vows of monastic discipline and the three higher trainings in ethical self-discipline, concentration and discriminating awareness. Concerning such a crucial point, which if we understand properly we gain liberation and if we misunderstand we remain caught in the uncontrollably recurring cycle of rebirth, how could he not have spoken forthrightly?

The fact that if something was so, he said it was so, and if something was not so, he said it was not so, is demonstrated clearly later in the text where coming to a decisive understanding of the conventional nature of mind is explained. There the First Panchen Lama has written, "The great meditators of the snow mountains are practically of a single opinion in proclaiming this as a guideline indicating how to forge a state of Buddhahood. Be that as it may, I, Chökyi-gyeltsen, say that this is a wondrous skillful means for beginners to accomplish the settling of their mind and is a way that leads you to recognize [merely] the conventional nature of mind that conceals something deeper."

From such manner of expression, we can see that the First Panchen Lama spoke straightforwardly exactly what he thought. He unabashedly stated that it is not an amazing feat to accomplish this much and it is not at all the same type of realization that is gained on the complete stage of anuttarayoga tantra. We have only recognized the conventional nature of mind, not the voidness of mind. With only this much realization, we cannot gain liberation from samsara and it cannot be considered a state combining shamata and vipashyana. If the First Panchen Lama were not someone who spoke directly and straightforwardly, he would not have written such words. Thus it seems appropriate to take what he has said about a correct view as a definitive teaching to be understood literally.

## CONFIRMATION FROM THE DZOGCHEN SYSTEM

As for the Third Panchen Lama's objection that a view of voidness that entails an affirming nullification and one that entails a non-affirming nullification cannot be harmonious, it is pertinent to consider what great meditational masters have explained about the Nyingma dzogchen tradition. For example, the Gelug master from Mongolia, Kelka Damtsig-dorjey, a disciple of Gungtangzang, who in turn was a disciple of the Third Panchen Lama's disciple Yongdzin Yeshey-gyeltsen, has written in several of his texts on the Nyingma form of Hayagriva practiced within the Gelug tradition, "When you meditate on a correct view according to the dzogchen tradition, you deal with it in terms of both devoid nature itself and objects having this devoid nature. This is the key for unlocking realization." His statement becomes easy to understand in light of our previous discussion of these two views in the context of the Shangpa Kagyü tradition of Kaydrub Kyungpo.

The dzogchen system emphasizes two main points in connection with the hidden path of tantra: (1) meditation on a correct view presented in terms of what has a devoid nature — namely, meditation on primordial clear light mind, known in dzogchen terminology as rigpa, pure awareness — and (2) understanding all appearances as the play of clear light. Let us examine how these two fit together in order to shed further light on the harmony of the two correct views of reality.

In general, we can speak of clear light as an object of mind and clear light as a mind that takes or apprehends objects. Here we must explain according to the latter type of clear light. Through the dzogchen meditational techniques, we come decisively to and habituate

ourselves with this subtlest level of mind. Totally absorbed meditation on clear light mind, then, is the main implication of a correct view
presented in terms of what has a devoid nature.

Dzogchen meditation focuses on clear light mind as being devoid
of such characteristics as being produced, abiding and passing, or arising, remaining and ceasing. Such meditation is on an affirming nullification. An affirming nullification affirms or leaves a phenomenon
with leftover qualities remaining as the focus of concentration when
the meditating mind apprehends that phenomenon in the manner of
nullifying that it has other qualities. In other words, this manner of
meditation focuses on a basis and, in understanding that it is devoid
of certain qualities that are absent, indirectly affirms that it is in possession of other qualities. It affirms this fact because the meditating
mind still gives rise to an appearance of that basis as the focal object of
its concentration or, in the Buddhist technical vocabulary, it still gives
rise to an appearance of that basis before the face of its absorbed concentration. Thus, meditation that (1) focuses on a clear light mind that
is dissociated from being produced, abiding and passing, or that is
devoid of these characteristics, and (2) also understands this clear light
mind to be the basis supporting the appearance-making and appearance of all phenomena — as in the Shangpa Kagyü and dzogchen systems — is clearly meditation on an affirming nullification. Nevertheless, although when we meditate on clear light mind, we directly meditate on an affirming nullification, yet on the side, we indirectly understand that all phenomena lack true, inherent existence as the
madhyamaka teachings explain.

The total absence of true, inherent existence, on the other hand, is a
non-affirming nullification. Meditation on such a nullification merely
focuses on the total absence of something — in this case, the total absence of a fantasized, impossible manner of existence. It does not affirm anything else. It does not focus on an appearance of the basis that
is characterized by that absence. The meditating mind does not even
give rise to an appearance of the basis of that absence before the face
of its total absorption.

When we meditate on the correct view presented in terms of something having a devoid nature, we focus primarily on clear light mind
that is free from arising, abiding and ceasing. Secondarily, however,
as Kaydrub Kyungpo has explained, as we meditate on clear light
mind, we gain decisive understanding that all appearance-making and
appearances of conventional existence are the play of this very mind,

or are the appearance of the sport of this very mind. If it is the case that the appearances of all pure or impure phenomena arise as the play of clear light mind, this means that all phenomena arise as objects of cognition dependently on clear light mind.

From another point of view, we can also consider clear light mind as a basis for labeling or a basis for affixing a name. In that case, all phenomena are not only that which this basis can give rise to an appearance of as its play, but also their appearances are that which can be mentally labeled or named onto that basis. Thinking in this way, we can understand the interdependence between phenomena and mind — described as the former being the play of the latter — also in the context of the assertion that the existence of all phenomena is established by virtue simply of names or mental labeling. In other words, the fact that mind gives rise to appearances of all phenomena of samsara or nirvana as the play of the clear light mind of deep awareness serves as the ultimate reason for understanding that the existence of all phenomena is established by virtue simply of factors other than themselves — and, specifically, by virtue simply of names. Thus when we come to a decisive understanding of a correct view presented in terms of what has a devoid nature — clear light mind — we indirectly understand that all phenomena exist by virtue simply of the fact that they can be mentally labeled, without their existence being established by something inherently findable from their own side. We understand this only indirectly, however, because our meditating mind does not give rise to an appearance of the total absence of this fantasized, impossible manner of existence while focusing on clear light mind.

## CORROBORATION FROM THE CHITTAMATRA PRACTICE OF TANTRA

Someone once asked the Third Panchen Lama, "At what stage does a yogi practicing anuttarayoga tantra with belief in the chittamatra philosophical tenets gain complete conviction in the uncommon prasangika-madhyamaka view of reality?" This master replied, as recorded in his *Answers to Questions*, "One comes to a decisive understanding of this correct view at the mind isolation stage of anuttarayoga tantra's complete stage of practice." Let us examine why this is so.

According to the chittamatra or "mind-only" tenets, also known as *vijnanavada* or *yogachara*, objects of sensory cognition are devoid of being substantially different from the sensory consciousness of them

— both derive from the same seed of karma on the *alayavijnana*, foundational mind or "storehouse consciousness." Although such objects and consciousness of them are dependent, or "other-powered" phenomena, they nevertheless have inherently findable self-natures making them what they individually are. They do not exist as what they are by virtue of imputation or mental labeling on the basis of their appearance. Only objects of conceptual cognition have imputed existence. As imputed, or "totally imaginary"objects, they are, however, devoid of having an actual basis to which they refer and upon which their name can be affixed. Nevertheless, they too have inherently findable self-natures making them what they are.

On the mind isolation stage of anuttarayoga complete stage practice, we actually manifest subtlest primordial mind through the power of gathering in and dissolving in stages at our heart chakra all coarse and subtle levels of sensory and conceptual consciousness. Even if we hold a chittamatra view of reality, we become convinced through this experience that the existence of all phenomena, particularly dependent and imputed ones, is established by virtue simply of imputation or names, which is the prasangika view of mental labeling. We directly experience that nothing has an inherently findable self-nature establishing its existence, because everything exists by virtue simply of the fact that it can be mentally labeled on the basis of clear light mind as its source.

The Third Panchen Lama's assertion arrives at the same conclusion as the dzogchen position. According to the latter, when we arrive at a definite activation and understanding of clear light mind — which occurs on the dzogchen path at a point corresponding to the mind isolation stage in the Gelug presentation of anuttarayoga tantra's complete stage — we also come to understand that the existence of all phenomena is established by virtue simply of imputation or names. In the case of dzogchen, we realize this through the experience of all vivid appearances of existence arising as the play of primordial mind, whereas the chittamatra practitioner of anuttarayoga techniques arrives at the same realization through the experience of all coarse and subtle levels of consciousness, together with the appearances to which they give rise, dissolving into subtlest clear light mind.

In *An Ornament for "The Stainless Light"* [*Commentary on "The Abbreviated Kalachakra Tantra"*], Kaydrub Norzang-gyatso has hinted at something quite similar. This great master has asserted that at the time of the clear light of death, primordial mind directly gives rise to an appearance of voidness in the same manner as it does through the force of meditation. We cannot gain a decisive understanding of voidness at that time, however, unless we have previously built up the powers of listening, pondering and meditating on voidness. The implication is that all clear light minds manifested by pathway methods — whatever those methods might be — likewise give rise to an appearance of voidness and thus allow for a prasangika-madhyamaka understanding of that voidness.

In short, when we look superficially and quickly at the dzogchen method of meditating on a correct view, it seems to be a way of meditating solely on an affirming nullification and nothing more. When we look superficially and quickly, on the other hand, at the prasangika-madhyamaka method of meditating on voidness in the anuttarayoga tantra context, it appears to be something totally different. It appears to be meditation merely on a non-affirming nullification — a total absence with which, when whatever is to be refuted is completely negated, there is no further manner of apprehension of the basis for the refutation left over. But if we look at both of these meditational methods deeply, we see there is no contradiction in what is attained by each of the two.

Dzogchen, as an example of meditation on a correct view presented in terms of something having a devoid nature, is a method of meditating by focusing single-pointedly on a mind that understands voidness, specifically a primordial clear light mind having such an understanding. This meditation also brings about the realization that the existence of all phenomena is established by virtue simply of names or mental labeling. The dzogchen method, then, has a direct means of realizing a specific type of mind and, in addition, an indirect means of realizing that which that mind understands. Meditation according to the prasangika-madhyamaka approach to anuttarayoga tantra as transmitted by the Gelug tradition, on the other hand, as an example of meditation on a correct view presented in terms of devoid nature itself, focuses directly on the abiding nature or voidness itself. It can only do this, however, on the basis of realizing a mind that understands that abiding nature of voidness — specifically, in this context, a primordial clear light mind. Thus the meditational approaches of the two correct views each bring the sincere practitioner to the same end point.

## Chapter Four

# MEDITATION ON THE CONVENTIONAL NATURE OF MIND

PRELIMINARIES FOR SHAMATA MEDITATION

The text continues with a full discussion of the sutra tradition of mahamudra,

> Of the two main techniques of the sutra tradition of mahamudra,
> namely seeking to meditate on mind on top of having gained a
> correct view of reality and seeking a correct view on top of having
> meditated on mind, [I shall explain] here in accordance with the
> latter technique.

All phenomena are devoid of true, inherent existence. To gain a
decisive understanding of this and then to focus single-pointedly on
this understanding is the tradition of first understanding the view and
then meditating on it. The second tradition, on the other hand, is to
focus single-pointedly on mind first and then to gain a decisive understanding of the correct view on this basis. This is the tradition of
mahamudra that the First Panchen Lama now explains.

The text continues,

> On a seat conducive for mental stability, assume the sevenfold
> bodily posture and clear yourself purely with a round of the nine
> tastes of breath.

On a seat or cushion that is slightly raised in the back, sit, with your
back perfectly straight, in either the full vajra, half-vajra or the ordinary cross-legged position, whichever you can, and begin by clearing
your mind with a round of the nine tastes of breath. Breathe slowly

and evenly, first in the right nostril and out the left three times, then reverse the order of the nostrils for the next three rounds, and finally in and out both nostrils simultaneously for the last three rounds.

Because we often feel compelling attractions and aversions as well as oppressive confusion, we have great need to practice these nine rounds of breathing. We must quiet our mind of longing, angry and confused thoughts that take strong interest in and fixate, respectively, on pleasurable objects that we find desirable, displeasing ones that we find undesirable, and any object that we find confusing. By shifting the focus of our attention to our breath through these nine rounds, we temporarily stop all extraneous, disturbing thought and thus achieve an unspecified or neutral state of mind. We try to stay for a reasonably long time in this neutral state, temporarily free from attraction to certain objects, aversion from others and confusion about yet others.

As this is a meditation on mind, we need both a clear state of mind upon which to focus and a clear state of mind that does the focusing. Therefore we must first make the mind as clear as possible with such preliminary methods as these nine rounds of breathing in order to make it the most suitable for the task. Then, as there is great need to build up positive potential for gaining success in our practice, we next generate this neutral state of mind into a positive one. The root text says,

> Thoroughly cleanse your state of awareness, and then, with a purely positive mind, direct [toward your practice] your taking of refuge and the reaffirmation of your dedicated heart of bodhichitta.

By thinking about the precious human life, impermanence, death, the suffering of the worst states of rebirth and so forth, we turn our mind toward the Dharma. On this basis, we then reaffirm the safe direction we are putting in our life by taking refuge once more, and re-enhance our motivation by re-dedicating ourselves with bodhichitta. We direct the energy of the positive state of mind that we generate in this way toward building up the positive potential that will contribute to future success in our mahamudra practice.

The text continues,

> Meditate next on a profound path of guru-yoga....

As a preliminary guru-yoga for this tradition of mahamudra, we practice either *The Hundreds of Deities of Tushita* or any other appropriate form of guru-yoga.

The text continues,

> ... and, after making hundreds of very strong, fervent requests, dissolve your visualized guru into yourself.
>
> Absorb for a while unwaveringly in this state in which all haphazard appearance-making and appearances have been contracted until they have disappeared. Do not contrive anything with thoughts such as expectations or worries.

Making sincere requests for inspiration to our guru with great faith and then dissolving into ourselves whatever visualized form we have been imagining to represent him or her helps produce the state of mind that is most conducive for beginning the mahamudra practice of focusing on mind itself. This is because such preliminary practice renders the mind blissful and energizes it so that it apprehends its object with great strength of brilliance.

In such a state, we try to remove anything artificial, such as conceptual thoughts. Any conceptual thought is deceptive and disturbs our state of mind, causing it to waver. Thus we try not to think any thoughts at all, particularly those that hope for success in attaining something through this practice, or that fear or worry about possible failure. We try not to let any such thoughts that have already arisen continue and not to let any such thoughts newly arise. In this way, we settle our mind single-pointedly into an unwavering, vivid state.

## FOCUSING ON THE CONVENTIONAL NATURE OF MIND

In his auto-commentary to the root text, the First Panchen Lama lists various objects we can use to develop a serenely stilled and settled state of mind. He explains that any of them will do for attaining this goal of shamata, yet taking mind itself as the object of focus for achieving that state has special significance. In the long term, such focus is extremely meaningful for our eventual practice of anuttarayoga tantra's complete stage. More immediately, there are other benefits as well.

Of the five aggregate factors making up each moment of everyone's experience, the aggregate of consciousness is primary. On another level, between body and mind, mind is principal. Normally, however, we are not much aware of our mind. We must change this so that our awareness of our mind is as acute and constant as that of meditators. Usually our mind is so strongly and compulsively drawn to and caught up in external objects of sight, sound, smell, taste and tactile or physical sensation that the consciousness within does not appear at all. Although mind is obviously present in our continuum, yet since we are so preoccupied it seems as though we are nothing but body. This is a completely tainted and distorted appearance.

By focusing on mind, however, and by paying attention to and scrutinizing or analyzing the mind that controls the actions of our body and speech that cause us to experience happiness or suffering, we come to understand what mind is. This helps us become aware of our apprehending true, inherent existence, which causes us to act out of confusion. It also helps us think about past and future lives, in terms of not only what continues through them, but also what causes them to continue. When we recognize that, loosely speaking, we are not only our body but also our mind, and we think about how mind continues from moment to moment following a course of cause and effect, we establish for ourselves that mind and this process obtain through past and future lives. Since focusing on mind itself has these more immediate benefits, we settle on mind as our object of meditation.

When we look superficially and quickly at the mahamudra practice of mind focusing on mind, we are reminded of Shantideva's argument in *Engaging in a Bodhisattva's Deeds*, "The Guiding Light of the World has said, 'Mind cannot see mind.' It is like the edge of a sword not being able to cut itself. How could it?" But here we are speaking in a totally different context, one in which Shantideva's analogy of the mind to a sword does not pertain. We are not speaking of a separate, truly and inherently existent faculty, reflexive awareness, with which we are focusing on a truly and inherently existent mind. Since neither of them exists at all, mind conceived as existing in an impossible manner cannot focus on itself. Rather, in mahamudra meditation, we use either a later moment of consciousness to focus on the remembered experience of a preceding moment of mind, or one part of consciousness to focus on another, with both possibilities carried out within the context of understanding that consciousness or mind has a nature of being totally devoid of true, inherent existence.

We can understand this by analogy. When we focus on ourselves, we make a conventional, though not an absolute, difference in our mind between the "me" that is focused upon and the "me" that is focusing on it. Likewise, when mind focuses on mind, we have either one portion or a later moment of consciousness aimed at another portion or a former moment of consciousness differentiated conventionally, though not absolutely, as its object of mindful focus. In this way, we experience a focusing mind single-pointedly secured to a mind upon which it is focusing.

## EMPLOYING MINDFULNESS AND ALERTNESS

The text continues,

> This does not mean, however, that you cease all attention as if you had fainted or fallen asleep. Rather you must tie [your attention] to the post of mindfulness in order not to wander, and station alertness to be aware of any mental movement.

In general when we meditate, we must not forget about or lose the object upon which we are focusing. If we continually forget about or lose our object, we can never gain familiarity with it. How do we keep the mind on an object in a sustained fashion? We do so with mindfulness. As the First Panchen Lama says in the text, we must "tie our attention to the post of mindfulness in order not to wander."

Mindfulness, which can also be translated as the mental factor of remembering or keeping something in mind, has three characteristic functions. The first is to maintain a continuity of familiarity with what has been previously seen or known. The second is to prevent the mind from forgetting about or losing its object, and the third is to hold the mind on its object with endurance. We must tie our attention to such mindfulness in order not to wander and to sustain meditation.

Here, in mahamudra meditation, we have mind as both an object of focus and that which is focusing single-pointedly. It is very difficult, however, to have mind contact mind as its object. Although we can easily mouth the definition of mind as "mere clarity and awareness," actually to have a notion of what is mere clarity and awareness is very difficult. Whatever appearance of an object dawns or arises as something experienced, "mind" refers to that which merely allows for (1) the arising of that aspect of the object that appears, and (2) a cognitive engagement with that aspect. It is what accounts for or describes the mere experience of objects. We can only recognize it from personal experience.

When we experience mind as mere clarity and awareness, we focus and hold our attention on the aspect of what we experience to which our mind gives rise. We do this by applying mindfulness, the mental faculty of remembering this aspect or keeping it in mind. We must not let ourselves forget about or lose this object — the mind — which is the object of our mindfulness.

In addition, to check whether or not the way in which our mindfulness is holding this object is correct according to definition, we need alertness. Alertness is the mental factor that checks if the attention on an object of focus is wavering or becoming dull, or if the mind is moving away from its object, such as when it comes under the influence of the deceptiveness of thought. Thus alertness is like a policeman. While mindfulness keeps our mental hold or attention on the object, alertness keeps a careful watch, acting as a policeman to check if there is mental abiding on this object, and, if there is abiding, to make sure it is correct and proper.

The text continues,

> Firmly tighten the hold of your mindfulness on that which has the nature of clarity and awareness and behold it starkly.

When we experience the mind giving rise to and apprehending as its object of attention an aspect that is the conventional nature of mind as mere clarity and awareness, then, in addition to mindfulness and alertness, we need to tighten our focus on it. In other words, we need to single-pointedly focus on this nature with a firm manner of holding it as an object of attention such that our mind gives rise to a stark appearance of it.

The object upon which our mind is focused is mind itself. The way in which mind is aimed at mind is with tightened, single-pointed concentration. This is the function of mindfulness, namely to hold this object tightly in this way. In addition, on the side, the mental factor of alertness accompanies this mind and keeps watch to see if mind is remaining on this object or not, and if it is remaining, if it is doing so properly. "Properly" means not only with single-pointed placement on mind as the object of focus, but also with perfect mental clarity and sharpness.

In general, there are two types of interruptions to concentration — flightiness of mind and mental dullness. Flightiness affects whether or not mind stays fixed on its object. It can be divided into gross and subtle flightiness of mind. Mental dullness has gross, middling and subtle levels.

If we speak roughly, distraction is an interruption to placement of mind on an object, while dullness is an interruption to clarity. There can be many factors causing mind to be distracted, but the longing desire that causes mind to fly off to some other, extraneous, pleasing object is what is included under flightiness of mind. We single out distraction due to longing desire because it is the most compelling. Distraction due to annoyance, jealousy, pride, self-consciousness, doubt, boredom, weakness of mental hold on an object of focus, and so on is called mental wandering. With gross flightiness of mind, the mind actually loses its mental hold on its object of focus. With subtle flightiness, on the other hand, the mind maintains its hold on its object, but because the accompanying attention is weak, there is either an underlying current of thought or, even more subtly, a restlessness or "mental itchiness" to leave that object and focus on something else that we find more attractive.

Mental dullness concerns the quality of appearance-making — in other words, the quality of mind's giving rise to and apprehending an appearance of its object of focus and attention. In simple words, it concerns the quality of mind's seeing of its object — but "seeing" in a figurative sense, and not necessarily in a visual or even a mentally visual one. When we focus on the sound of a mantra or on the nature of mind, we are not focusing on a sight or a pictorial mental image, yet we must still deal with the issue of clarity of such an object of focus. Seeing the appearance of an object of focus primarily means giving rise to a manifest and, if manifest, clear appearance of the object, such that we focus upon and apprehend it. This occurs as a function not of clarity from the side of the object, but clarity from the side of the mind that is directed at the object.

With gross mental dullness, we lose placement on our object of focus, not because of losing the hold of our mindfulness, as is the case with gross flightiness of mind, but because of our mind's lack of sufficient clarity to give rise to an appearance of it. With middling mental dullness, our mind gives rise to a clear appearance of the object, but without sharpness of focus. With subtle dullness, although our mind has sharpness of focus, it is slightly too loose. Thus it is not fresh in each moment. It has become stale. Mental dullness, then, concerns the issues of whether mind gives rise to an appearance of its object lucidly, forcefully and directly, or whether with a tired boredom. Even in colloquial Tibetan, when we say "dull," the connotation is tired boredom. Mind is not alert and fresh, not clear and lucid.

Foggy-mindedness is slightly different from mental dullness. Once dullness develops, it can degenerate into foggy-mindedness, with which mind becomes totally dark and both mind and body become heavy. This can further degenerate into sleep.

Mental dullness and flightiness of mind are the main interruptions and interferences to accomplishing a settling of mind, and each has several degrees of subtlety. Therefore we need to station mental alertness single-pointedly to become aware of any degree of dullness or flightiness. In order to do so, we must be able to recognize correctly mental wandering, flightiness, dullness and foggy-mindedness. We can only do this from personal meditative experience.

## TECHNIQUES TO EMPLOY WHEN MIND GIVES RISE TO A THOUGHT

As for the actual meditative technique, the text says,

> Should your mind give rise to any thoughts, simply recognize them. Or, like your opponent in a duel, cut thoughts immediately as soon as they occur.

When we are meditating single-pointedly, with nothing artificial, in other words, with no thoughts, and mind is very vivid, we may experience a new thought arising on occasion. If, all of a sudden, our mind wanders by giving rise to such a thought, we have strayed from our principal endeavor which is to settle single-pointedly on the mere clarity and awareness that is mind. We must immediately take hold of our meditation with mindfulness and alertness and not let ourselves be distracted by this newly arisen thought. We must come to its cessation. The text mentions two techniques for reaching this end.

As soon as our mind gives rise to a thought, we must immediately become aware of it. This is necessary for either technique. To do this, we need the power of alertness. The auto-commentary says, "When mind is tightened and looking starkly, if it deviates from this state and gives rise to a thought, you must recognize that this has happened. For this, you need alertness."

With alertness, then, we recognize any thought to which the mind gives rise as indicative of a loss of mindfulness. Then, by the force of the original intention we had set — which was to settle the mind in a state of vividness that is not made artificial with any thought and is not construed — any new thought that arises automatically ceases. This is the first technique. The other method is a more active approach. As soon as we notice the mind giving rise to any thought, we immediately cut it off and cause it to cease. The analogy for this is like cutting down an opponent with a sword in a duel.

The text continues,

> Once you have completely cut these off and have settled your mind, then, without losing mindfulness, loosen and relax its tightness.

As we progress through the nine stages of settling the mind, our mahamudra meditation on mind itself gradually improves. If, whenever our mind has given rise to a thought, we have either simply recognized it so that it disappeared automatically, or cut it off immediately with force, then, as a result of our familiarity in applying these techniques, we experience a steady decrease in the mind giving rise to thoughts distracting our meditation. This is helped by the power of mindfulness and alertness having become ever stronger.

Throughout this process of bringing our thoughts to a halt, our alertness has been remaining aware of whether or not our mind has been giving rise to thoughts. When we no longer experience the faults of dullness or flightiness, however, and we have good placement of mind on its object, we can let this forceful alertness be more at ease. Its work is basically finished.

We must do the same with the mindfulness with which we have been maintaining our hold on the object, and loosen it slightly. When mind is single-pointedly focused on mere clarity and awareness, without any faults of dullness or flightiness, continuing to maintain our mindfulness very tightly causes our mind to tremble. To avoid this, we relax our tightness and remain settled in a more relaxed manner. But, we must not let go of our mindfulness completely. That would be a great mistake. We need to remain focused and clear.

In short, through study and actual meditative experience, we become clear about the nine stages of settling the mind as explained in the teachings of the graded stages of the path. Then, at the appropriate stage, if our mind is too tight, we need to relax it.

The text continues,

> As has been said, "Loosen and relax its firm tightness and there is the settled state of mind." And elsewhere, "When the mind ensnared in a tangle is relaxed, it frees itself without a doubt." Like these statements, relax but without any wandering.

Thus, when we no longer experience the faults of dullness or flightiness in our meditation, we remain in a relaxed state of equanimity.

The text continues,

> When you look at the nature of any thought that arises, it automatically disappears by itself and a bare absence dawns. Likewise, when you inspect mind's nature when it is settled, a non-obstructive bare absence and clarity is vivid.

Some learned masters of the past have pointed out that whenever the mind gives rise to a thought, if we look nakedly or barely at its nature, we do not need to "stuff the thought back into the mind." It automatically disappears. We are left with the vacuum that is its bare absence. Likewise, if our mind is not giving rise to any thoughts, but rather is settled, and we scrutinize the settled mind, as it says in the text, "a non-obstructive bare absence and clarity is vivid."

Mind has no form. It has neither shape nor color, cannot be touched, does not obstruct anything and cannot itself be obstructed. In this regard, it is a bare absence of these qualities, like an open space or vacuum. Yet it can give rise to a clear appearance of anything, in the sense that it allows for anything to dawn clearly as an object of experience. Its nature, in fact, is mere clarity and awareness. If we recognize it properly, we can figuratively "see" this bare absence that is a mere clarity and awareness vividly in our meditation.

Whenever the mind gives rise to a thought, if we look at its nature, it automatically disappears. Just as waves disappear into water because they are of the nature of water, likewise thoughts naturally subside since they are of the nature of mind. They do not go beyond having a nature of mere clarity and awareness. Therefore when we scrutinize the nature of thoughts, we see that they automatically dissolve. Thus we come to the foundation of thought — mere clarity and awareness itself.

The root text says,

> You see that the settled and moving minds are mixed together.

Whether our mind is totally absorbed on its focus without any thoughts or is moving, giving rise to thoughts from moment to moment, if we scrutinize the nature of thoughts, we see they do not go beyond being mere clarity and awareness. They have the same nature as that of the settled mind. Thus we reach the same conclusion whether our mind is settled or moving. We come to mere clarity and awareness.

Since this conclusion is based on meditative experience, it is well known. The Kagyü tradition, for example, speaks about not consciously blocking thoughts or trying to "stuff them back in." When the mind gives rise to thoughts, one tries to see them as waves of play of dharmakaya — omniscient awareness encompassing everything. This is one version of "seeing that the settled and moving minds are mixed together."

The text continues,

> Thus, no matter what thought arises, when you recognize that it is a movement of mind and, without blocking it, have settled on its nature, [you find] it is like the example of a bird confined on a boat. As is said, "Just as a crow having flown from a ship after circling the directions must re-alight on it...."

When the mind emanates a thought, no matter how far it goes, where can it go? When we focus on the nature of the thought, we experience the thought automatically disappearing. In other words, when we look at the nature of any thought, we realize that it arises in the nature of mere clarity and awareness and subsides also in this very same nature. When we experience this nature, we also "see that the settled and moving minds are mixed together."

The text continues,

> From cultivating such methods as these....

By cultivating single-pointed placement of mind on mind, we experience a steady decrease in wandering with thoughts and a steady strengthening of absorbed concentration on mere clarity and awareness. As our mind becomes increasingly free from faults of dullness or flightiness, the nature of mind as mere clarity and awareness becomes increasingly manifest and clear from personal experience.

## THE ATTAINMENT OF SHAMATA FOCUSED ON THE CONVENTIONAL NATURE OF MIND

What comes from this? The text continues,

> ...you experience the nature of the totally absorbed mind to be a non-obstructive lucidity and clarity.

The nature of the settled, totally absorbed mind is free from all faults of dullness or flightiness. How it is to be experienced? This nature is a "non-obstructive lucidity and clarity." It is a cognitive lucidity and clarity that can be set on any object and used for any purpose. In other words, no matter at what object mind directs its attention, it can focus on and engage with that object single-pointedly such that it gives rise to an aspect of it by virtue of its cognitive clarity and lucidity. Its functioning is not obstructed by any disturbing emotions or attitudes, not even their instincts. It obstructs neither liberation nor enlightenment. In fact, it is the main factor that allows us to achieve either. Thus it is a "non-obstructive lucidity and clarity."

The text continues,

> Not established as any form of physical phenomenon, it is a bare absence which, like space, allows anything to dawn and be vivid.

Mind, by nature, cannot be established as having any form, shape or color. Yet, no matter what object it encounters at the moment, it produces an aspect or appearance of it as the object with which it engages in a cognitive manner. It allows for or gives rise to the cognitive dawning of anything, precisely because its nature is mere clarity and awareness. As Tsongkapa has said in *Totally Clarifying the Intentions [of Chandrakirti's "A Supplement to (Nagarjuna's 'Stanzas on) the Middle Way'"]*, "Mind is what allows for this or that aspect of this or that object to arise."

Since we can only realize and be aware of this nature from our personal meditative experience, the text continues,

> Such nature of mind must in fact be seen straightforwardly with exceptional perception and cannot be verbally indicated or apprehended as a "this." Therefore, without such apprehension, settle in a fluid and flowing manner on whatever cognitive dawning arises.

The conventional nature, abiding condition, or defining characteristic of this phenomenon called "mind" — its lack of form and its ability to allow for an appearance of anything to arise as a cognitive object — is not something to be known through logical reasoning. Rather, we can know it only from the impression we build up through the repeated habit of having our mind be focused on mind — in other words, from direct personal experience. To do this, we need to develop, in addition to shamata, an exceptionally perceptive state of mind known as vipashyana. Furthermore, although we may see straightforwardly this mere clarity and awareness — this mere experience, this mere awareness of experience — because mind has the nature it does, we are not easily able to capture it with a mental picture in terms of form or color, or pinpoint it with words. That is why the text says it "cannot be verbally indicated or apprehended as a 'this.'"

The text continues,

> The great meditators of the snow mountains are practically of a single opinion in proclaiming that this is a guideline indicating how to forge a state of Buddhahood. Be that as it may, I, Chökyi-gyeltsen, say that this is a wondrous skillful means for beginners to accomplish the settling of their mind and is a way that leads you to recognize [merely] the conventional nature of mind that conceals something deeper.

The conventional nature of mind is that it is a mere clarity and awareness that can allow for anything to arise as an object of cognition and, not being a physical phenomenon, cannot be blocked or impeded by any form of material object. The realization of the deepest nature of mind, however, is a realization of inseparable clarity and voidness, or, in terms of anuttarayoga tantra, the attainment of the deep awareness of inseparable bliss and voidness. Such realizations are what we must gain in order to achieve liberation or enlightenment. Therefore, to confuse a single-pointed seeing of the conventional nature of mind with a realization of its deepest nature is a reversed or contrary way of understanding and is a serious mistake. What the text has described so far is the attainment of shamata, a serenely stilled state of mind, settled on mind itself. Although the attainment of such a meditational state focused on mind is the foundation for developing the highest attainments and is, of course, very excellent, by itself it is insufficient for reaching those goals.

When we achieve a mind focused on mind with the perfect placement of absorbed concentration, free from all faults of dullness or flightiness, we increasingly experience an element of bliss accompanying our meditation. When we experience serene joy, on both a physical and mental level, brought on by the force of total absorption of mind on mind, we achieve a meditational state that fulfills the definition of shamata.

Our ordinary mind is like raw iron ore that needs to be made into a steel sword. Progressing through the stages for attaining shamata is like forging the iron into steel. All the materials are there at our disposal. But since the mind wanders after external objects, then although it is the material for attaining shamata, it cannot yet be used as this product. We have to forge our mind through a meditational process. It is like putting the iron ore into fire. To fashion the steel into a sword, or in this analogy to fashion the mind into an instrument that understands voidness, our serenely stilled and settled mind needs to come to decisive realization of voidness as its object. Without such a weapon of mind, we have no opponent with which to destroy the disturbing emotions and attitudes.

What has been explained so far in the text, then, is an effective and wondrous method for accomplishing the settling of mind for attaining a state of shamata. In terms of the sutra mahamudra technique of gaining first a meditative state and then, on top of that, an understanding of the correct view, just this much is the meditative state.

## Chapter Five
# MEDITATION ON THE DEEPEST NATURE OF THE CONVENTIONAL "ME" AND ALL PHENOMENA, INCLUDING MIND

### PROMISE TO COMPOSE
The text continues,

> As for the methods that can lead you to recognize the actual [deepest] nature of mind, I shall now record the personal instructions of my root guru, Sanggyay-yeshey, who [as his name literally means] is the embodiment of the Buddhas' deep awareness. Assuming the guise of a monk clad in saffron, he has eliminated the darkness enshrouding my mind.

This is the author's promise to explain how to reach a decisive understanding of the deepest nature of mind.

### SCRUTINIZING THE MANNER OF APPEARANCE AND MANNER OF EXISTENCE OF "ME"
The text continues,

> While in a state of total absorption as before, and like a tiny fish flashing about in a lucid pond and not disturbing it, intelligently inspect the self-nature of the person who is meditating.

How do we meditate here? While in a state of mind that is totally absorbed on mind, we employ a small part of that mind to inspect and scrutinize, intelligently, learnedly and discerningly, the nature of ourselves as the person or individual who is conventionally "me" and who is focusing with absorbed concentration on mere clarity and awareness. In other words, we supplement our serenely stilled and settled mind with the additional accompanying mental factors of inspection and scrutiny.

As we say about the nature of what dependently arises, "All phenomena are devoid of truly and inherently existent identities." This we must see and know with deep conviction. We must come to a decisive understanding of identitylessness, or "selflessness" — the total lack or absence of a truly and inherently existent identity with respect to anything. The way to gain such an understanding is by realizing the deepest nature of both phenomena and individual animate or "sentient" beings — persons. A person or conventional "me," regardless of current rebirth state, is the one who feels happy or sad and utilizes things, while phenomena refer to what that person feels or utilizes — be it among the five aggregates of the individual's experience, or whatever. Since understanding the identitylessness of the conventional "me" is easier to gain than that of other phenomena, we come first to a decisive understanding of the identitylessness of the conventional "me."

How shall we understand the manner of appearance of our conventional "me" — in other words, the usual way in which our mind makes it appear within the context of the aggregate factors of our everyday, moment-to-moment experience? How does its mode of actual existence compare with its mode of appearance? We begin by inspecting and scrutinizing each of them, discerning the differences.

Whenever the mind gives rise to an object of cognition, it makes that object appear as if it existed as something we could point our finger at as being truly and inherently "this" or "that." This is the case whether we speak of "me" as the one who feels things, or the things this "me" feels — such as pleasure or pain — or utilizes — such as aggregates, cognitive sources and so forth. No matter what we think of as being "this" or "that," the mind makes it appear as if the existence of this thing as a "this" or a "that" were established by something findable at the place where it understands the object to be located.

On a conventional level, there is a valid distinction between the person or "me" who utilizes things and the utilized body and mind controlled by this "me." There is what directs and what is directed. For the reason that my body is sick, we say, "'I' am sick." For the reason that my mind sees or knows, we say, "'I' see or know." Our mind, however, makes this "me" that is the knower, or the one to whom things appear, seem to be something the existence of which is inherently established from its own side. Our mind gives rise to an appearance, feeling or impression of a concrete "me" as if there were something independently existing there through its own power, by virtue of itself.

Sometimes when our body is in pain, we develop anger directed at our body. When we forget something important, we develop anger at our mind. The object of our anger is our body or our mind. That which is angry is "me." Our mind makes it appear as if there were something distinct, standing on its own, sending out anger, and something separate from it, also standing on it own, as the object or place to which anger is being directed. This is the manner in which we develop anger toward our body or mind.

For example, if we hurt our hand, we grab it as if it were an object, like a poison dagger, and regard the pain of it as an enemy to us. We develop anger or repulsion at this painful hand that is hurting us. Our mind makes it appear as if the hand and "me" were individual, totally separate things. It produces an appearance or feeling of a "me" who seems independent and unrelated to our body or mind. But what kind of nature does this "me" have? With a corner of our sharp intelligence, we inspect and scrutinize it while still in a state of unwavering absorbed concentration on the conventional nature of mind.

## REFUTATION OF THE "ME" TO BE REFUTED

The text continues,

> It is just as our source of direction, the highly realized Arya Nagarjuna, has said, "A person is not earth, not water, nor fire, nor wind, not space, not consciousness. Nor is he or she all of them....

If we examine what a person or a "me" who feels happy or sad and who utilizes things relies upon in order to be imputed, we could say the bodily elements of earth, water, fire, air and space — in other words, the solid, liquid, heat, gas and cavity constituents of the body. Although a person, such as "me," does rely on these things, if we evaluate each of them through a process of elimination and ask, Am "I" this body's solid constituents? Am "I" its fluids, or its temperature and acidity? and so on, we cannot find or identify this "me." But, from another perspective, we can conventionally say that the location or place in which "I" exist is in a body and mind. This body and mind as a basis or location is where "I" exist. "I" cannot be established as existing in some other location where the body and mind are not, such as in the table. Therefore where "I" exist is definitely somewhere in the body and mind.

Although this is the case, yet if we scrutinize our aggregates, by a process of elimination, examining those factors upon which "I" am imputed, asking, Am "I" this? Am "I" that? Am "I" the four bodily elements together with its cavities? Or if not, am "I" my body at all? Am "I" my mind? a basis with a defining characteristic making it "me" is not in the slightest bit findable there as any of the parts of the body. Nor is it findable there as their collection or continuity. Likewise, in terms of being based on the mind, a basis with a defining characteristic making it "me" is not in the slightest bit findable there as mind's continuity, collection or parts. This is why Nagarjuna has said, "A person is not earth, not water, nor fire, nor wind, not space and not consciousness. Nor is he or she all of them."

The quotation of Nagarjuna cited in the text continues,

"Yet what person is there separate from these?"

Although "I" am not the aggregates, yet there is not in the slightest bit a basis with a defining characteristic making it "me" that exists as a separate entity, in a different package from the body and mind, in the manner, for example, of the aggregates being possessions — either individually or taken all together — and "me" being their possesser. A "me" cannot be found totally apart from these aggregates, nor can a "me" be found as something distinct from them yet located in one of them, for instance in the mind and so forth. Where else could "I" be found?

Furthermore, it is not that there is no "me" at all. There definitely is a "me" who is helped and harmed, who collects karma and experiences its results. If, for the reason that a "me" cannot be ultimately found, we say there is no "me" at all, this is contradicted by straightforward perception. From straightforward perception and direct experience, it is well known in the world that there is a "me." From our own personal experience, we say, "'I' am happy. 'I' am sad." No one has to ask someone else for affirmation of this. Although we do not know clearly where this "me" ultimately is, the existence of a "me" is established from our own experience.

That being so, and there being no findable basis with a defining characteristic making it "me," then what is called "me" is simply what can be labeled or imputed upon the basis of the collected bodily elements and so forth. Because of that, a "me" is not something the existence of which is established by its own power, by virtue of itself, without relying on such a basis. It is not something the existence of which is established by virtue of an inherent self-nature. There is no inherent self-nature findable on the side of "me" that establishes, proves or empowers my existence and makes me "me." In this sense, a "me" is not something truly and inherently existent. That being the case, except for a "me" as an individual person who feels happy or sad and who utilizes things being simply that to which a mental label refers on the foundation of a basis for labeling, a "me" cannot at all be established as existing independently by its own accord.

The quotation from Nagarjuna concludes,

> "And just as a person is not perfectly solid because he or she is what can be labeled on the collection of these six constituents, likewise, none of the constituents are perfectly solid because each is what can be labeled on a collection of parts."

The "me" that is the collector of karma for happiness or suffering, the one that experiences its results and feels happy or sad, is simply what can be labeled on the basis of a collection of causes and circumstances. Do the aggregates, stimulators of cognition and cognitive spheres upon which "I" am labeled exist independently, by virtue of themselves? No, they do not establish their own existence. Just as with the manner of existence of "me," these lack inherently established existence. Why? Because each constituent is a collection.

Just as a "me" is what can be labeled by depending on the basis of a collection of six constituents of earth and so forth, likewise each of these six constituents depends for its existence  upon the basis of its parts and what is collected under its rubric, such as everything solid being included in the constituent element of earth. The earth element has parts, and what has parts entails both what a mental label refers to and a basis for labeling. Thus its existence can only be established by relying on, or depending upon factors other than itself. The existence and identity of these or those things, as what can be mentally labeled "this" or "that," cannot be established by anything ultimately findable on their own side in the place where they are referred to, or at the place where they are mentally labeled to be.

## THE CONVENTIONAL EXISTENCE OF PHENOMENA THAT IS NOT TO BE REFUTED

If we conclude that since phenomena cannot ultimately be found as establishing their existence from their own side, or at the place where they are mentally labeled to be, they do not exist at all, we are incorrect. They do exist. They should exist. But when we cannot ultimately find them establishing their existence from the side of the place where they seem to exist, what does this mean? It merely means that there is nothing ultimately findable on their side establishing their existence from the place where we would expect them to solidly exist, implied by the ordinary appearance of them our mind produces.

But when the issue of how do ultimately unfindable things actually exist becomes unbearable and we have to say something, the bottom line is that their existence is established by virtue simply of names. In other words, the existence of these things is established and proven by virtue simply of the fact that they can be named within the context of mental labeling. There is no additional need for an inherent, findable, defining characteristic on the side of the basis for labeling rendering things existent and giving them their identity. Thus the existence of ultimately unfindable things is merely conventional. This is the implication of it being unreasonable to consider them truly and inherently existent.

Nagarjuna has attested to this in *Root Stanzas on the Middle Way*, as has Tsongkapa in *The Essence of Excellent Explanation of Interpretable and Definitive Meanings*. If the existence and identity of things as "this" or "that" were established through their own power, by virtue of an inherent, ultimately findable self-nature — some defining, characteristic feature existing as something findable we could point to with our finger somewhere inside the crevices of the things that arise as our objects of cognition — their existence and identity would not be established by virtue simply of the conventions of the mind that can take them as its object of cognition. Their existence and identity would be established by virtue of their own defining characteristic making them "this" or "that" from their own side. But this is not so, because when we scrutinize closely and look for a defining characteristic on the side of the objects of our cognition, we cannot find even the slightest example of a defining characteristic that could render them "this" or "that" which exists from the side of their basis for labeling.

This being the case, then it is just as is said, things exist as "this" or "that" by virtue simply of the conventions of the mind that can apprehend them as "this" or "that." This means that things are established as unsuitable for being considered truly and inherently "this" or "that" from their own side, being made "this" or "that" by virtue of some inherent self-nature or defining characteristic. Thus the existence and identity of things are established by virtue simply of what can take them as its object, or by virtue simply of mind, by virtue simply of convention, by virtue simply of mental labeling. That being so, nothing exists independently, by virtue of itself, even in conjunction with mental labeling. Nothing has true, inherent existence.

The same is true with respect to each of the six constituents of an individual — in short, the body and mind of any animate, sentient being. Consider a body as something having parts. A body is simply what can be labeled a "body" on the basis of a collection of such things as a head, legs and so forth. This is because when we dismember the individual parts, a basis with the defining characteristic making it a body cannot ultimately be found. Likewise, a mind is simply what can be labeled as a mere clarity and awareness on the basis of the collection of many things, such as a continuity of former and later moments and the act of taking various aspects as objects of cognition. Except for being like this, none of these items exist as their basis for labeling having an ultimately findable defining characteristic — even the most minute or subtle one — rendering them existent and giving them their identity as "this" or "that" from their own side, separate from their being a collection of many things. What a label conventionally refers to can never be identical with its basis for labeling.

Thus each of the six constituents is merely something that can be labeled dependently. Each can be labeled in relation to a collection of causes and circumstances as its basis for labeling, and, as in the case of an individual or a conventional "me," therefore does not have true, inherent existence established by virtue of an intrinsic, findable self-nature or defining characteristic. Thus Nagarjuna has said in the quotation cited in our text, "None of the constituents is perfectly solid because each is what can be labeled on a collection of parts."

## TOTAL ABSORPTION ON VOIDNESS WHICH IS LIKE SPACE
The text continues,

> When you search and, as has been said, cannot find even a mere atom of a total absorption, someone totally absorbed and so on, then cultivate absorbed concentration on voidness which is like space, and do so single-pointedly without any wandering.

When we scrutinize closely like this, we cannot find even an atom of an agent who is totally absorbed in concentration, a state or act of total absorption, or an object upon which we are totally absorbed that exists independently — in other words, the existence of which is established by virtue of itself. Because the existence of anything cannot be established in any way other than by simply depending on mental labeling from this side, nothing can have its existence also established by something ultimately findable on its own side too. With the understanding that decisively knows that there is no such thing as independently established existence — existence established without depending simply on mental labeling — we strongly focus our mind very piercingly on just this mere nullification or refutation of what is to be refuted. We totally absorb our mind on voidness, the total absence or non-existence of independently established existence.

A mind that apprehends voidness does not apprehend it in an affirming manner. There are no such thoughts as "This is the voidness I have ascertained," or "Now I am meditating on voidness." There is nothing like this, but just the mere absence of what is to be refuted. Such a mind decisively understands that even though mind gives rise to cognitive objects, making them appear as if truly and inherently existent, and even though mind implies the actual existence of these truly and inherently existent things, yet the existence of such things is not in the slightest bit established by something truly and inherently there at the place where they appear to exist, as it seemed before. Therefore our decisiveness is a clear cutting off of a fantasy and what it implies, like the cutting of a taut rope. This means that our mind comes to be completely absorbed into a total absence or voidness that is the mere nullification of the object to be refuted — this fantasized, impossible manner of existence.

Dependent arising means the arising of something dependently on factors other than itself. We can understand this on four levels. All phenomena of samsara arise dependently on unawareness. With this meaning, we have the presentation of the twelve factors that dependently arise. From another point of view, all functional, non-static phenomena arise dependently on causes and circumstances. On another level, both non-static and static phenomena arise — in the sense of "exist" — dependently on parts. The prasangika-madhyamaka school, however, uses dependent arising to mean that the existence of all phenomena — of samsara or nirvana, non-static or static — arises or is established dependently by virtue simply of mental labeling.

At this stage, our understanding of the conventional existence of things is our understanding of dependent arising in the prasangika-madhyamaka usage of the term. Because things are objects whose existence arises or is established dependently on mental labeling, things conventionally have functions making them usable as what dependently arises as "this" or "that." Their dependently arising functioning is due to their being things that do exist — their existence arises dependently, established by virtue simply of factors other than themselves, specifically their names. Their functioning and causing benefit or harm is due simply to their having the full characteristics of existing by virtue simply of the fact that they dependently arise. And it is precisely because the existence and identity of things as "this" or "that" are established simply by their arising as such, dependently on mental labeling, that they do not have true, inherent existence.

What is a mind that has voidness as its object? It is a mind that, on the basis of conventionally existing objects, in other words a basis that does exist in the above sense of dependent arising — but without giving rise to an appearance of that basis as its object of focus — completely and cleanly cuts off true, inherent existence, being totally convinced that there is no such thing. What kind of absence or voidness does such a mind have or take as its object? It is merely the nullification of what is to be refuted. Since voidness merely nullifies or negates what is to be refuted, and does not leave over or cast anything else to the mind as an object of cognition, then, between affirming and non-affirming nullifications, voidness is explained as belonging to the latter. It is an absence that is a non-affirming nullification.

In this sense, voidness is like space, for space, too, is a non-affirming nullification. The space of any physical object is the absence of anything tangible or physically obstructive on the side of that object that would prevent it from existing three-dimensionally. Space is different from voidness, however, in that the object it nullifies — anything tangible or physically obstructive — does exist, whereas what voidness negates — true and inherent existence — does not exist at all.

If the mind that has voidness as its object thinks intellectually, "This is 'non-inherent existence.' I have found 'non-inherent existence.' This absence that is the nullification of what is to be refuted is 'voidness,'" this is referred to as "setting voidness out at a distance." This will not do. The mind that has voidness properly as its object is a decisive piercing of the mere nullification itself. In other words, with the understanding, from the depths of our heart, that things do not exist at all like they appeared a while back, the mind taking voidness as its object completely pierces the sphere of this mere nullification like a spear piercing a target. A mind that does that is totally absorbed on voidness which is like space.

Such a mind understands madhyamaka, the middle way from which the two extremes have been eliminated. What are the two extremes? They are the extreme of true, inherent existence and the extreme of total non-existence. When our mind stays within the sphere of the mere nullification of the object to be refuted, decisively under-standing that things actually do not exist at all in the manner in which they had appeared to exist, that very mind of understanding elimi-nates the extreme of true, inherent existence. Furthermore, when we understand that the objects upon which we affirm the absence of true, inherent existence arise and exist as what they are dependently, by virtue simply of mental labeling — in other words, when we under-stand that their existence is established and proven relative to condi-tions and factors other than themselves — we realize that their depen-dently arising existence eliminates their total non-existence.

In short, because things exist as "this" or "that" relative to condi-tions and factors, they have no way to exist independently as what they are. Understanding this exactly eliminates both extremes — ex-istence or non-existence. Furthermore, when our understanding that all objects are non-inherently existent induces conviction that all things can only exist and have the ability to function as "this" or "that" by virtue simply of conditions and factors, our understanding has also eliminated the two extremes.

## VOIDNESS OF MIND ITSELF

The text continues,

> Furthermore, while in a state of total absorption, [scrutinize] mind. Not established as any form of physical phenomenon, it is a non-obstructive bareness that gives rise to the cognitive dawning and emanation of anything, and which endures as an unhindered clar-ity and awareness, engaging [with objects] without discontinuity. It appears not to depend on anything else. But as for the implied object of the mind that apprehends it [to exist as it appears], our guiding light, Shantideva, has said, "Such things as a continuum or collection are not as they seem. They are false, as in the case of a rosary, an army and so on." By means of scriptural authority and lines of reasoning such as this, totally absorb yourself on everything's lack of existing as it appears.

Now we take mind specifically as our topic for scrutiny and use the same reasons as before to establish its being devoid of true, inher-ent existence. The quote by Shantideva that "such things as a con-tinuum or collection are not as they seem" means that what is called "mind" is, in general, simply what can be labeled dependently on the collection of a continuity of former and later moments of cognition. Thus we continue our shamata meditation in which our mind is se-renely stilled and settled on its own conventional nature as before. But, in addition, if we scrutinize — in the context of this quotation —

the abiding, deepest nature of mind itself as mere clarity and aware-ness, we see that its existence is established by virtue simply of the fact that it can be mentally labeled dependently upon a collection of many parts. Except for that, its existence is not established by any-thing else. This is the specific meditation on voidness with mind as the basis for that voidness.

## UNDERSTANDING VOIDNESS IN TERMS OF DEPENDENT ARISING

The text continues,

> In short, as my spiritual mentor, Sanggyay-yeshey, omniscient in the true sense, has said, "When, no matter what dawns in your mind, you are fully aware that what it is an appearance of exists simply as what can be apprehended by conceptual thought, you experience the deepest sphere of reality dawning without need to rely on anything else. While this is dawning, to immerse your awareness in it and totally absorb, my goodness!"

In everyday life, our mind gives rise to an appearance of so many things — mountains, fences and pastures, houses, towns and so on, sights, sounds, smells, tastes, tactile or bodily sensations, and mental objects or events. When we have gained an understanding of void-ness to some extent, according to our capacity — in other words, when we have gained some understanding of existence established by vir-tue of dependent arising — then no matter what our mind gives rise to an appearance of right now, we think that it exists as what it is simply relative to conditions and factors. It exists as what it is by vir-tue simply of mental labeling — by virtue simply of the conventions or labels that can label it as "this" or "that." It exists relative to condi-tions and factors other than itself. Since it exists simply as what can be apprehended as a cognitive object by conceptual thought, then any-thing mind gives rise to an appearance of as its object of cognition exists simply as what can be labeled by a conceptual thought that la-bels or ascribes a name to it. It exists simply as what can be appre-hended as an object of cognition by the conceptual thought that can conceive of it.

We are now aware of the non-inherent existence of everything our mind gives rise to an appearance of, including our mind itself. We are aware of the deepest nature of these things, namely that, because their existence is established by virtue simply of conceptual thought, everything is devoid of all impossible ways of existing, such as inde-pendent existence established by virtue of an inherent, findable self-nature or defining characteristic. When we are completely certain of this, we scrutinize the nature of this devoid nature or the deepest truth itself. We look closely to see if there is such a thing as a devoid nature that is immune from being itself devoid of existing inherently. Is there a devoid nature, existing truly and inherently on the side of either itself or the basis of the object having it as its nature, that establishes its own existence without simply depending on what can be mentally labeled? Can there be such a thing as a devoid nature that exists through its own power, by virtue of itself, without being dependent upon, or without existing simply as something we can be led to understand through a line of reasoning such as "all things are devoid of inherent existence because they and their identity do not inherently exist as one or many"?

When we examine these points, it dawns on us — through the power of our understanding existence by virtue simply of conditions — that devoid nature, or deepest truth, is itself devoid of true, inherent existence. As Sanggyay-yeshey has said, "You experience the deepest sphere of reality dawning" — the voidness of voidness — "without need to rely on anything else."

When we understand existence by virtue simply of mental labeling or dependently arising existence — in other words, when we understand that all things mind gives rise to an appearance of, even voidness itself, cannot exist without being something that simply arises dependently, relative to conditions and factors other than itself, specifically names — then, as the quotation continues, "While this is dawning, to immerse your awareness in it and totally absorb, my goodness!" When, without need to rely on anything other than the fact that everything arises dependently on mental labeling, we understand there is no such thing as true, inherent existence — even with respect to voidness itself — we immerse our awareness in our understanding of this deepest sphere of reality.

Then we reason from another point of view. Conventional or relative things lack true, inherent existence because it is not a fraud that mind dependently gives rise to appearances of them. This second angle on dependent arising causes our mind to become even further immersed in the deepest, ultimate nature — the total absence of true, inherent existence.

In summary, when our understanding of the unimpeded arising of dependently arising mere appearance becomes advanced, we see voidness in terms of dependent arising. We look at everything that arises in our mind. Relying on the reason that all appearances of things dependently arise, we understand that nothing arises as what it is with its identity established by virtue of itself. Nothing exists as what it is without depending simply on factors other than itself. In other words, when the mind that apprehends the dependently arising appearance of things makes something appear as its object of cognition, it understands that what this is merely an appearance of — be it an appearance of "this" or "that" — arises dependently, by virtue simply of mental labeling. This realization induces conviction in the understanding or meaning of its non-existence as something existing as what it is through its own power, independently of anything else. Thus as the root text quotes, "While this is dawning, to immerse your awareness in it and totally absorb, my goodness!"

When we do this, then the more our mind gives rise to the appearance of things, the more strongly the conviction is induced that whatever they are appearances of is devoid of true, inherent existence. That being so, as we say, quoting Tsongkapa's *The Three Principal Aspects of the Path*, "Appearance eliminates the extreme of true, inherent existence and voidness eliminates the extreme of total non-existence." Because things are devoid of true, inherent existence, mind gives rise to an appearance of them as "this" or "that" relative to circumstances, arising dependently on factors other than themselves, namely mental labeling. Thus understanding this line of reasoning effectively induces conviction in both existence and identity established by virtue simply of circumstances. Furthermore, conviction in existence and identity established by virtue simply of circumstances, induced in this way, invokes reciprocal conviction in the total absence of true, inherent existence and true, inherent identity. Appearance does not impede voidness and voidness does not impede appearance.

Some people think that because things appear, they could not possibly be devoid of true, inherent existence; and if things were devoid of true, inherent existence, they could not possibly be able to function. But their conclusions are the opposite of what is actually the case. When we understand correctly, then the strength of our understanding of things being devoid of inherent existence, far from annulling, exceptionally induces conviction in the reasonability of their functioning. And the fact that our mind gives rise to various appearances of things performing functions that wax and wane, start and stop, far from annulling, exceptionally induces conviction in their voidness of true, inherent existence. It seems as though this is what Sanggyay-yeshey meant in saying, "my goodness!"

The text continues,

> Similarly, fatherly Pa Dampa-sanggyay has said, "Within a state
> of voidness, the lance of awareness twirls around. A correct view
> of reality cannot be impeded by anything [ultimately] tangible or
> obstructive, O people of Dingri." All such statements come to the
> same intended point.

No matter what arises now in our mind, we understand, simply
because of the fact of its appearing as "this" or "that", that it exists as
such by virtue simply of circumstances. Thus no matter how many
appearances our mind produces, they induce conviction in their voidness. In other words, whatever our mind makes appear, the fact that
its cognitive appearance as "this" or "that" is something that dependently arises, and the fact that it is unmistakably appearing, grant cred-
ibility to its lack of true, inherent existence. When this happens, then,
while remaining focused on the sphere of voidness, the lance of our
awareness of non-inherent existence twirls around. A correct view cannot be impeded. It applies to everything.

This has been the actual meditation on the correct view, with total
absorption on voidness which is like space.

## DEDICATION

The text continues,

> At the conclusion of your meditation session, dedicate whatever
> ennobling, positive potential has accrued from meditating on
> mahamudra, the great seal of reality, as well as your ocean-like
> store of positive potential of the three times, toward your
> attainment of the peerless state of enlightenment.

It is important to dedicate very strongly whatever positive potential or merit we have accrued from this mahamudra meditation toward our peerless enlightenment. We must not let it become a cause
for something inferior or something just lost in a moment.

## Chapter Six
# THE DEEP AWARENESS SUBSEQUENTLY ATTAINED

## RECOGNIZING ANYTHING TO WHICH MIND GIVES RISE

The First Panchen Lama next explains how to cultivate seeing everything to be like illusion with the deep awareness we attain after we arise from total absorption on voidness. We cultivate this during the so-called post-meditation period, when we are either engaged in other meditation or conducting our ordinary affairs of life. Mainly, our understanding is as before. We simply re-affirm and thus reinforce our strong conviction in the lack of true and inherent existence.

The text continues,

> Having accustomed yourself like this [to seeing with a correct view], when you subsequently inspect how your mind makes the objects of any of your six collections of consciousness appear, [you experience] their bare mode of existence dawning in an exposed, resplendent manner.

No matter what our mind makes appear as an object of one of our six collections of consciousness — sights, sounds, smells, tastes, tactile or bodily sensations, or mental objects or events — we thoroughly scrutinize its mode of appearance. Our mind is making it appear as though its existence were established by virtue of itself, empowered by some truly and inherently existent self-nature — and not by virtue simply of mental labeling establishing its existence as what can be labeled as "this" or "that" from this side. We thoroughly scrutinize this mode of appearance and the mode of existence it implies. There does appear to be something solidly there, not existing as what it is by virtue simply of mental labeling, but by virtue of itself, independently of anything else. But, by reminding ourselves that it does not exist as it appears to exist — by being mindful that its existence and identity are not established through its own power — we automatically reconfirm and become even stronger in our conviction in its bare mode of existence. In other words, as the text says, "[You experience] their bare mode of existence dawning in an exposed, resplendent manner."

The text continues,

> This is called the essential point of a correct view — recognizing whatever dawns in your mind.

In short, no matter what arises in our mind, we do not apprehend it actually to exist in the manner in which it appears to exist. As is explained, "When our mind gives rise to an appearance of something as if it existed solidly on its own, our mind does so because it is obscured." Therefore we must not apprehend what appears to be solidly existent as actually existing in the manner in which it appears. Our mind gives rise to an appearance of it as if its existence were established under its own power, in the foreground before us, as its appearance implies. Our mind makes it appear as if it were something that did not exist as what is impossible ultimately to find as being inherently itself. But, in fact, it is merely the obscuring obstacles preventing omniscience — the instincts of unawareness — that are causing our mind to give rise to an appearance of it as though, from the beginning, it had a inherently findable self-nature establishing its existence from its own side. Nothing, however, actually exists in the manner in which the obscured mind makes it appear to exist.

The text continues,

> In short, always cultivate your realization by not apprehending things, such as your mind and so forth, [to exist in the manner in which] your mind gives rise to an appearance of [them]. Do this by keeping firm to their actual mode of existence.

We keep firm to the actual mode of existence of phenomena by remaining mindful of what we have previously realized upon close inspection. In other words, no matter what our mind gives rise to, appearing to have true and inherent existence as its mode of existence, we remain ever mindful of its total lack of this impossible mode of existence. We do not apprehend it actually to exist in the fantasized manner in which our mind makes it appear. In this way, our mind eventually gives rise only to an appearance of it as existing as "this" or "that" relative to circumstances, by virtue simply of mental labeling — existing in the manner of arising, abiding and passing without being ultimately findable as what it is. In short, by remaining always mindful that the mode of existence of anything that arises in our mind is actually that it exists as what it is by virtue simply of circumstances, we further our subsequent deep awareness, gaining ever stronger conviction in voidness.

## APPLYING OUR UNDERSTANDING TO ALL PHENOMENA

The text continues,

> When you cognize [one thing] like this, [you see] the nature of all phenomena of samsara and nirvana as being uniformly the same.

We induce conviction in non-inherent existence first on the basis of one phenomenon. We do so by relying on the reason that its appearance as "this" or "that" arises dependently, simply on the fact that it can be mentally labeled as "this" or "that." We understand, in this way, that its voidness does not impede its appearance and its appearance does not impede its voidness. In fact, its voidness and appearance establish each other. Consequently, voidness dawns to us in the sense of dependent arising and dependent arising dawns in the sense of voidness. When such an understanding occurs on the basis of one phenomenon, the nature of all phenomena becomes clear to us in the same way. We realize that the same understanding applies to the devoid nature of all phenomena of samsara and nirvana, "uniformly the same."

The text continues,

> Aryadeva has confirmed this point, "As has been explained, the way in which [mind] becomes the seer of one functional phenomenon is the way it becomes the seer of everything. The voidness of one thing [suffices for] the voidness of all things."

When we apply our understanding of voidness to all phenomena, there is no need to rely on various and sundry reasons to prove the voidness of each one of them. There is no need to proceed in the same manner as when we first come to a decisive understanding of the voidness of one thing. Once we are able to gain conviction in the total lack of true and inherent existence, in the full definition, on the basis of one phenomenon — in other words, once we are able to induce conviction in non-inherent existence by reason of dependent arising with respect to one phenomenon — we are able to gain strong conviction in non-inherent existence on the basis of all other phenomena as well. We accomplish this by merely recalling that they too are things that dependently arise as what they are. This is the way in which we gain strong conviction in the voidness of everything.

## ALTERNATING TOTAL ABSORPTION AND SUBSEQUENTLY ATTAINED DEEP AWARENESS

Furthermore, although the two levels of truth — conventional and deepest — concerning any phenomenon are of a singly cognizable nature, at this point in our practice, our mind can make voidness dawn only intermittently, and only by itself, in a meditative state of single-pointed concentration focused on the deepest level of truth. This is because we have not as yet eliminated the obstacles preventing omniscience. Until we have removed this final set of obstacles regarding all knowables, we cannot experience a deepest level truth — the devoid nature of a phenomenon — as the object of our mind simultaneously with our mind giving rise to the conventional level truth of that phenomenon — its conventional appearance as something arising, remaining, and ceasing. Because we cannot as yet have the two levels of truth of a phenomenon as the object of one moment of awareness, simultaneously and starkly, with bare, straightforward perception, the root text continues,

> Before the face of proper, total absorption on the actual nature of reality, there is just the severance of fantasized, impossible extremes — namely, inherent, findable existence or total non-existence — with respect to everything of samsara and nirvana.

In the state of total absorption on voidness, our only object of cognition is an absence and our only way of apprehending it is as the mere refutation and nullification of what is to be refuted and nullified. We experience everything other than this — namely all appearances of what can be established as conventionally existing — to have set, like the setting sun. This being the case, the text continues,

> Yet after you arise, when you inspect, you see that your mind still gives rise to the appearance of things that dependently arise, which do function and can only exist as simply what can be labeled by

names. It is unmistakable that such things still naturally dawn, yet they are like dreams, mirages, reflections of the moon in water and illusions.

When we arise from total absorption on voidness and scrutinize closely with subsequently attained deep awareness, we find that our mind still gives rise to an appearance of this or that phenomenon as if its existence were established through its own power, by virtue of its own inherent self-nature. There can be no mistaking that our mind still gives rise to this type of discordant appearance of things. When our mind gives rise to this appearance of something as if it were truly and inherently existent by nature — or, more fully, when our mind gives rise to a discordant appearance of it because of being under the influence of obstacles preventing omniscience — we recall our previous ascertainment of non-inherent existence. We recall our certainty that while being non-inherently existent, everything appears as if inherently existent. Despite our mind giving rise to a deceptive appearance of something as if inherently existent, our discordant appearance-making mind does not establish it as actually being inherently existent.

What happens as a result of this understanding? From our scrutiny and reliance on reason, we are totally convinced that even though our mind gives rise to an appearance of something as if it were truly and inherently existent, it does not exist in that impossible way. In other words, we are convinced of the fact that when our mind ordinarily gives rise to an appearance of something, it makes it merely appear as if it were existing under its own power, but does not establish or prove that it actually exists in that way, because, in fact, nothing does. Consequently, by simply recalling our twofold conviction in the appearance of true, inherent existence and yet the total absence of true, inherent existence, we experience our mind now making everything dawn like an illusion, a dream, a reflection of the moon in water and so on.

Therefore, the deep awareness which we attain subsequently to arising from total absorption on voidness is that we see things, as the author says, to be "like dreams, mirages, reflections of the moon in water and illusions." In other words, we see that although our mind gives rise to a discordant appearance of things, they do not exist in the way they appear. Conventional phenomena, however, are not illusions. Conventionally existent food can produce an effect — it can fill our stomach — an illusion of food cannot. We cultivate our practice during post-absorption periods by seeing appearances in this manner.

## SIMULTANEOUS PERCEPTION OF THE TWO LEVELS OF TRUTH

The text continues,

> When the time comes that you can perceive simultaneously the appearance of things without this causing their voidness to be obscured to your mind, and their voidness without your mind ceasing to make their appearance dawn, you have directly manifested the excellent pathway mind that perceives everything from the single, integrated point of voidness and dependent arising being synonymous.

Practicing like this, we realize that voidness and dependent arising are completely synonymous. They become yoked together as equals. When we look from the point of view of understanding the meaning of the voidness of anything, we understand that it dependently arises as "this" or "that" by virtue simply of mental labeling, and vice versa. On the basis of our mind giving rise to dependently arising things as a foundation, our mind also gives rise to their voidness. Through the gateway of a foundation of voidness, our mind simultaneously gives rise to the appearance of things existing as what dependently arises. Thus on a single foundation, looking from the point of view of voidness, we build up a bountiful store of deep awareness and, on the same foundation, looking from the point of view of dependent arising, we build up a bountiful store of positive potential.

Proceeding like this, the text continues,

> The attainment of the resultant two unified Buddha-bodies comes from the unified practice of wisdom and method. This follows from the fact that all objects have both voidness and appearance [levels of truth].

We must investigate on a specific basis, for instance our mind, and on this foundation come to a decisive understanding of its two levels of truth. On a single foundation, we come to a decisive understanding of both dependent arising and voidness, or the conventional and deepest levels of truth — the two levels of truth about anything. A mind that gives rise, with decisive understanding, to these two levels of truth simultaneously is a pathway mind of inseparable method and wisdom. Practicing in the way the author describes, we eventually experience our mind giving rise to this pathway mind of method and wisdom. On the basis of this ultimate pathway mind as immediate cause, we directly manifest the two sets of resultant bodies of a Buddha: two bodies of forms, or rupakaya — namely, a body of forms with full use, *sambhogakaya*, and a body of their emanations, *nirmana-kaya* — as well as two bodies that encompass everything, or dharma-kaya — namely, a body of deep awareness, *jnana-dharmakaya*, refer-ring to an omniscient mind, and a body of self-nature, *svabhavakaya*.

## CLOSING DEDICATION AND COLOPHON

The text concludes with the author's dedication and the colophon.

> These words have been written by the renounced meditator Lozang-chökyi-gyeltsen, who has heard many teachings. By its positive merit, may all beings quickly become triumphant Bud-dhas through this pathway of mind, apart from which there is no second gateway to a state of serenity.
>
> I have compiled these techniques that lead you to recognize the great seal of reality, mahamudra, at the repeated request of Gedün-gyeltsen, who holds the monastic degree of Infinitely Learned Scholar of the Ten Fields of Knowledge, and of Sherab-senggey from Hatong, who holds the monastic degree of Master of the Ten Difficult Texts. They have seen all concerns for the eight worldly emotional states to be dramas of madness and now live in remote solitude, following a sagely way of life and taking this pathway of mind as their essential practice. Many other of my disciples who truly wish to practice mahamudra at its definitive level have also requested such a text.
>
> I have especially composed this text now since the triumphant Ensapa, the omniscient lord of masters with actual attainment, him-self has said in one of his songs of experience to instruct himself and others, "I have written explanations of *lamrim* — the graded stages of the path from the Kadam tradition — all the way from whole-hearted commitment to a spiritual teacher up through shamata and vipashyana. But I have not committed to paper the ultimate guideline instructions for mahamudra, which are not in-cluded among these aforementioned pathways of mind and which are not well known at present to those of the Land of Snows."
>
> Thus, what was not set down in writing at that time due to need for restriction was intended for a later period. Scriptural sources establish as much — for example, from *The Lotus Sutra*, "Because it is to be realized completely by the Buddhas' deep awareness [Sanggyay-yeshey], you could never say to those who would prematurely write about this method of their own accord that you are enlightened. If you ask why, it is because those who are sources of safe direction have regard for the times."
>
> Therefore, also in order for such prophesies as this to be ful-filled, I, the renounced meditator Lozang-chökyi-gyeltsen, who have not let degenerate the lineage of inspiration from those who have practiced straightforwardly this pathway of mind from the

peerless universal teacher, the king of the Shakyas, down through
my root guru, the omniscient Sanggyay-yeshey, and who myself
have become a member of this lineage, not letting the close bond
of its practice be lost, and who uphold the guideline instructions
of the sutras and tantras, have compiled this at Gaden Monastery.

These apparently were restricted teachings, which means they were
not written down in the eighteen volumes of Tsongkapa's works.
Changkya Rölpay-dorjey has confirmed this in his *Answers to Questions*. Someone from Amdo had asked, "These days in Ü, central Tibet, there is a discourse tradition among the Gelugpa known as
mahamudra. But I do not see this in the works of Tsongkapa. How is
this? Are they correct?" Changkya Rinpochey has answered that it
was a special, uncommon discourse tradition and, as such, it was very
good.

Thus, the term "Gelug/Kagyü tradition" in the title of the text seems
to refer to some specific lineage. I believe that it does. The manner of
exposition in it is slightly different from the general way Tsongkapa
has spoken about the madhyamika tradition, as seen in *An Ocean of
Reason [Commentary on Nagarjuna's "Root Stanzas on the Middle Way"]*,
*Totally Clarifying the Intentions [of Chandrakirti's "Supplement to
(Nagarjuna's 'Root Stanzas on) the Middle Way'"]*, *A Grand* and *A Short
Presentation of an Exceptionally Perceptive State of Mind* and *The Essence
of Excellent Explanation of Interpretable and Definitive Meanings*. Also in
our text there are a large number of quotations from works by previous Kagyü masters. Even in *A Ritual to Honor the Spiritual Master*, concerning guru-yoga in connection with mahamudra, the First Panchen
Lama uses technical terms such as "primordial Buddhahood" and
"Samantabhadra, the totally excellent state." Especially the words of
the ceremony, praises and requests in connection with the fourth empowerment, are a bit eclectic. They have a shared basis with the terminology of the dzogchen view.

That being so, we can conclude that among the lineages transmitted by the Gelug gesheys, there was one of inner, hidden, personal
instructions, the explanation of which did not appear publicly. Thus
this was a previously restricted guideline teaching that was not well
known and that was passed down orally from mouth to ear up to
Sanggyay-yeshey, which the First Panchen Lama, Lozang-chökyi-
gyeltsen, has set down here in words. As Tsongkapa has said in *A
Lamp for Clarifying the Five Stages [of the Guhyasamaja Complete Stage]*,

"Do not just pass down the texts wrapped up on the shelves by poking them [as a blessing] from one nose to the next." In other words, these are guideline teachings to be put into practice.

## CONCLUDING ADVICE

This concludes an explanation of *A Root Text for Mahamudra*. It is an excellent, very clear and beneficial text that is extremely meaningful and purposeful for the mind. It has a close connection with the practice of anuttarayoga tantra's complete stage. In order to give those who are intensely interested in its practice far-reaching and unshakable inspiration, I have delivered, as requested, this discourse on mahamudra on the basis of inspiration from the entire line of lineage masters.

After listening to merely one discourse, we cannot gain a complete understanding and full realization of everything. And to try to understand it on the basis of merely listening to an explanation is of little benefit. Only on the basis of personal experience are we able to settle into a conviction that comes from pondering and meditating.

This being so, then, on the one hand, we need to scrutinize with intelligence. We must think about the subject matter — investigate and understand it — then practice it in meditation. On the other hand, as was said, we must have the backing support of collecting and cleansing. If we have this backing support, then with the slightest circumstances, we are able to realize the total absence of true, inherent existence. But if we lack the backing support of collecting and cleansing, then even if we are learned and practice meditation on the basis of other qualifications as well, we experience great difficulty in decisively apprehending with a correct view that is not the contrary of what it should be. Therefore, in order to gain certainty about voidness, the abiding nature of all phenomena, we must practice on the basis of both listening, pondering and meditating, as well as collecting and cleansing. This is what all the holy masters have said. Have you understood?

# Part IV

# A DISCOURSE ON
## *THE AUTO-COMMENTARY TO A ROOT TEXT FOR MAHAMUDRA*

*by*
*H.H. the Dalai Lama*

# Session One

## THE SOURCE OF THE TEACHINGS

Today many people have come, both Western and Tibetan, both laypersons and monastics, to listen to an explanation of mahamudra, the great seal of reality. For many of us, just hearing this word "mahamudra" causes our ears to perk up. We think that through mahamudra we can instantly become a Buddha. But, in fact, it takes much time and effort to meditate on and actualize mahamudra. We must approach the topic realistically.

The mahamudra teachings derive from India, ultimately from Shakyamuni Buddha himself, and contain both sutra and tantra presentations. They include all points for reaching enlightenment. In Tibet, the most well-known mahamudra traditions are those of the various Kagyü lineages. What we shall be discussing during these next few days, however, will be the mahamudra tradition that traces from the great Tsongkapa.

Some people say that since this particular lineage of mahamudra derives from Tsongkapa, the title of the root text need only have referred to it as the Gelug tradition of mahamudra, not the Gelug/Kagyü tradition. But the author, the First Panchen Lama, has clearly explained the reason for his choice of titles. The mahamudra lineage derives from India through the line of Tilopa and Naropa, and was transmitted to Tibet by the great translator Marpa. This lineage of masters that forms the backbone of the Kagyü traditions also transmitted to Tibet *The Guhyasamaja Tantra*. When we add to the presentation of Guhyasamaja coming from this Kagyü lineage the explanation of the lineage of the correct view of reality transmitted through Tsongkapa, we arrive at the combined Gelug/Kagyü tradition of mahamudra.

If we ask more specifically about the lineage of this mahamudra tradition, there is a distant one that derives from the universal teacher, Buddha Shakyamuni, and traces down through the lineage masters of the profound correct view of reality. Alongside this, and as part of it, is the lineage of inspiration from the practice of the correct view. Combined with these lineages is an uncommon near lineage deriving from the Buddha-form or "deity" Manjushri, bestowed on Tsongkapa in a pure vision due to his purification of karma and transmitted to his close disciple Togden Jampel-gyatso. From him, the lineage passed to the great Baso Chökyi-gyeltsen and then on to the Three Dorjey Brothers, his three uncommonly close heart disciples. From among them, the great mahasiddha Dharmavajra, known in Tibetan as Chökyi-dorjey, who reached the supreme actual attainment of enlightenment during his lifetime, passed it down to Ensapa. He transmitted it, in turn, to Sanggyay-yeshey, who passed it to the First Panchen Lama, Lozang-chökyi-gyeltsen.

Tsongkapa is commonly and widely known for his teachings on voidness meditation that explain the correct view of reality following the prasangika-madhyamaka position. He presents this explanation in various texts from his collected works, such as *A Grand* and *A Short Presentation of the Graded Stages of the Path*, *An Ocean of Reason [Commentary on Nagarjuna's "Root Stanzas on the Middle Way"]*, *Totally Clarifying the Intentions [of Chandrakirti's "Supplement to (Nagarjuna's 'Root Stanzas on) the Middle Way'"]* and *The Essence of Excellent Explanation of Interpretable and Definitive Meanings*. Tsongkapa also gave a restricted discourse on mahamudra to special disciples such as Gungru Gyeltsen-zangpo. Although Gungru took notes on it, they remained unpublicized.

The widely known Gelug/Kagyü mahamudra tradition derives from this complex of lineages through the First Panchen Lama. He wrote *A Root Text for the Precious Gelug/Kagyü Tradition of Mahamudra: The Main Road of the Triumphant Ones* and likewise an auto-commentary to it, *An Extensive Explanation of "A Root Text for the Gelug/Kagyü Lineage of Mahamudra": A Lamp for Further Illumination*. The lineage passed down from the First Panchen Lama through many great lamas. I received it from my root guru, Kyabjey Trijang Rinpochey. The lineage of teachings that I received on this from him included a practice-oriented discourse based on the root text and an explanation-oriented discourse based on the auto-commentary. On this occasion,

I shall explain the topic as presented in the auto-commentary, covering the essence of the text without giving a line-by-line, word-for-word explication.

The Gelug/Kagyü tradition of mahamudra includes both sutra and tantra levels of explanation. The sutra level contains the more extensive explanation of the actual ways to meditate on a correct view of voidness. To receive the tantra level requires receiving an empowerment or initiation into the highest class of tantra, anuttarayoga. The normal sequence, if we had time, would be, after conferring empowerment, to deliver a discourse explaining the First Panchen Lama's *A Ritual to Honor the Spiritual Master*. This would provide the context for the requests for inspiration to the gurus of the mahamudra lineage that we recite before each day's first session. After this, we would explain this text. On this occasion, however, we must abbreviate this procedure.

SPECIAL FEATURES OF THE TEACHINGS

If we explain in terms of the madhyamaka tradition of a correct view of reality, the usual method for gaining correct understanding is to realize the voidness of a person — a conventional "me." For this, we analyze the mode of existence of a person in terms of five aggregate factors of experience as the basis for labeling one — namely, the forms of physical phenomena, feelings of a level of happiness or suffering, distinguishing, other affecting variables, and types of consciousness experienced by or connected with the person. In the mahamudra tradition, however, although we still take the five aggregates as the basis for labeling a person, we focus primarily on the aggregate of consciousness as serving this function. Thus the mahamudra tradition presents a correct view of reality in terms of the voidness of mind. The Guhyasamaja literature, particularly that which concerns the five stages of its complete stage — body isolation, speech isolation, illusory body attained subsequent to mind isolation, clear light, and the unity of illusory body and clear light — also stresses the importance of gaining a correct view of voidness in terms of understanding the voidness of mind.

Many other traditions make a similar assertion. The Nyingma, or old translation school of Tibet, explains the meditational method of dzogchen, the great completeness. Among the Sarma, or new translation schools, Sakya transmits the meditational method of the view of clarity and voidness not apprehended apart, also known as the causal everlasting stream of the alaya, the all-encompassing foundation, and the inseparability of samsara and nirvana. Likewise among these Sarma schools, Kagyü transmits various lineages of mahamudra. All these meditational traditions are based on the highest class of tantra, anuttarayoga, and all come to an understanding of a correct view of voidness presented in terms of the voidness of mind. As the First Panchen Lama asserts in our root text, they all come to the same intended point.

## SETTING THE APPROPRIATE MOTIVATION

It is very important before receiving any Dharma teaching to set a proper motivation, or reaffirm and enhance that motivation if we already basically have it. This is important not only for those who are listening to a spiritual discourse, but also for the person delivering it. If a discourse or explanation is given with an attitude of pride, competitiveness or jealousy, it will not do as a Dharma teaching. A Buddhist teaching must be given with the sincere wish to benefit all beings by means of it.

Likewise, the listeners to a Buddhist teaching must have a proper motivation, always thinking, "What new point can I learn from this that will help me be of more benefit to others?" If we sit here with the notion to learn something about mahamudra so that we can make a display of ourselves and proudly talk to others about mahamudra so that they will consider us an erudite, spiritual person, we have a completely wrong motivation. Rather, we need to listen, thinking, "My mind-stream is filled with disturbing emotions and attitudes, causing me personal problems and preventing me from being of any help to others. It must be purified. I need the most profound and perfect method to do this, and mahamudra is indeed the most profound method. Therefore I shall listen to these teachings with the motivation of learning as much as possible from them in order to be able to reach a state at which I can most effectively benefit all beings." Thus, as I explain this teaching, I shall try to do so using examples that are easily understandable and relevant to all of us. Likewise, you should listen relating what I explain to your own experience.

## HOMAGE AND PRAISE TO THE GURUS

The First Panchen Lama provides an outline to his auto-commentary. He divides it into (1) a preliminary discussion, in which he explains the excellent features of the various texts and sources from which this material derives, (2) the actual explanation of these constructive teachings, and (3) the dedication of the positive potential or "merit" from having explained them.

Although there are many noble objects to which the traditional salutary praise can be made at the opening of a text, here the author offers homage and praise to the guru. Since the text includes a discussion of the methods for generating a correct view of reality through anuttarayoga tantra techniques, the guru is especially important. This is because during empowerments conferred by a guru, we receive the various seeds of potential on our mind-stream that allow us to gain flash experiences and stable realizations of the practices.

Buddhism presents three sources of safe direction or refuge — the Buddhas, the Dharma and the Sangha. There are no true sources of safe, sound and positive direction in life that cannot be included in these three. We can present the Dharma refuge as the preventive measures or teachings that the Buddha realized and imparted to others. But by merely reading a Dharma text, we cannot gain on our mind-stream the definitive Dharma refuge — a true stopping or cessation of our suffering and its causes, and a true pathway mind or realization of all good qualities by means of the Dharma techniques. A definitive Dharma refuge can only arise on our mind-stream from these methods if we receive the inspiration from our gurus that has come down through the unbroken lineage of masters from Shakyamuni Buddha himself. Such inspiration uplifts the mind and causes the seeds of potential planted there by our practice of Dharma methods to ripen into the deep experience of their realization. Therefore the author offers prostration and praise at the beginning of his text to the guru.

What are the good qualities of a guru? In general, there are the positive qualities of body, speech and mind, and here the most important are the qualities of speech. Thus the First Panchen Lama offers prostration and praise to the guru for his speech that expounds the methods of mahamudra based on personal experience. What is mahamudra? It is something having three levels of significance — basis, pathway and result. Both the sutra and anuttarayoga presentations of mahamudra entail these three levels.

In the sutra system, basis mahamudra is, as the first line of the root text indicates, "the all-pervasive nature of everything, the great seal of reality." This refers to the devoid nature of all things of samsara and nirvana — the total absence of their existing in any fantasized, impossible manner. This devoid nature pertains to everything, impure or pure, that arises to both unaware, samsaric minds and nirvanic ones that are purified of unawareness — including, in both cases, what can be affected by other phenomena and what cannot, in other words both "conditioned" and "unconditioned" phenomena. Nothing exceeds or goes beyond the bounds of this set.

First we listen to or read an explanation of this basis level maha-mudra, which is the devoid nature of all things, and gain an under-standing of it based on listening. Then we ponder or think about the meaning of this and slowly gain a presumptive understanding of void-ness. The deep awareness that is the non-conceptual, straightforward perception of voidness gained by meditating on this presumptive understanding is undoubtedly the pathway level mahamudra. The resultant jnana-dharmakaya, a Buddha's body of deep awareness en-compassing everything and endowed with all positive qualities, that we attain as the ultimate endpoint of familiarizing ourselves with the deep awareness that is the non-conceptual, straightforward percep-tion of voidness, is the resultant level mahamudra.

In the anuttarayoga tantra system, we can also say that voidness as an object is the basis mahamudra, but we have a further explanation as well. All impure and pure phenomena, both external and internal, are rooted in the mind and energy-winds. Of the various levels of subtlety of mind and energy-winds, they are specifically rooted in the subtlest levels of both. Thus several masters assert basis mahamudra to be the subtlest level of mind and energy-wind that are the basis for all appearance-making and appearances of samsara and nirvana. More specifically, they assert basis mahamudra to be the mother clear light primordial mind, in other words the subtlest level of mind that mani-fests once the three unconscious, most subtle conceptual appearance-making minds have ceased. These are the appearance-congealment, light-diffusion and threshold conceptual minds, often translated as "white appearance," "red increase" and "black near-attainment." The mother clear light primordial mind, as the source of all impure and pure appearance-making of samsara and nirvana is the basis level mahamudra according to anuttarayoga tantra. The karmamudra or sealing physical partner who can act as a circumstance or basis for bringing about the realization of this basis mahamudra on the anuttarayoga path is the pathway mahamudra in this context.

Resultant mahamudra is the resulting state of the five types of deep awareness, or "Buddha-wisdoms," as the foundation for everything, that possesses the seven facets endowing enlightenment. The five types of deep awareness of a Buddha are the mirror-like awareness to know the extent of everyone and everything that exists, the awareness of the equality of everyone as objects of compassion and everything as devoid in nature, the awareness of the individuality of everyone and everything, the awareness of how to accomplish the temporary and ultimate aims of everyone, and the awareness of the sphere of reality — the two levels of truth about everyone and everything. The seven facets endowing enlightenment are features of sambhogakaya, the body of forms with full use that we attain as a Buddha. These facets are having full use of the mahayana teachings; being always in union; having blissful awareness, full compassion, and deep awareness of voidness; never passing away; and manifesting a body of emanations, or nirmanakaya, without any break. We attain both with Buddhahood on the basis of relying on the pathway mahamudra.

Thus all the various points of the mahamudra teachings can be included within the categories of basis, pathway and resultant mahamudras presented in the sutra and anuttarayoga tantra systems. Thus we need to know and gain a decisive understanding of basis mahamudra. We then need to meditate single-pointedly on pathway mahamudra. By relying on that as a cause, we finally attain resultant mahamudra. The author offers homage and praise to the guru who expounds all this, making every point clear.

## PROMISE TO COMPOSE AND GENERAL PRESENTATION OF THE PRELIMINARIES

In his promise to compose, the First Panchen Lama states that he will gather together the essence of the subject matter discussed in the sutras and tantras, and, condensing oceans of guideline instructions concerning mahamudra, will write the text that follows. He then divides the actual body of the text into discussions of the preparations, actual techniques and concluding procedures.

What are the preparations? In general, there are nine, eight or four preliminaries that lead us forward on the path. The nine forward-leading preliminaries are taking the safe direction of refuge and dedicating our heart with bodhichitta, making prostration, offering a mandala, reciting the hundred-syllable Vajrasattva mantra, performing guru-yoga, making offerings to Vajradaka into a fire, reciting the Samayavajra mantra, offering water bowls and making *tsatsa*, or clay votive tablets. When we list eight preliminaries, we count the first two from this list as one and perform them at the same time. Here we have a presentation of four preliminary practices.

Since the gateway for entering the Buddhist teachings in general is putting a safe direction in our life, or taking refuge, we need to take safe direction very purely. Likewise, as the gateway for entering the mahayana path is developing a dedicated heart of bodhichitta — a heart that is dedicated to attaining enlightenment in order to benefit all beings — we need that as well. Since taking safe direction leads us on to dedicating our heart with bodhichitta, taking safe direction is the first forward-leading preliminary practice. Second is making mandala offerings, a preliminary practice that leads us forward through its building up of a bountiful store of positive potential. Meditating on and reciting the mantra of Vajrasattva is the third preliminary. It leads us forward through its purification of our negative potentials and mental blocks. Finally, we have the preliminary practice of guru-yoga which leads us forward by bringing inspiration to our mind-stream. These are the four preliminaries that prepare us for advancing to the main practice.

## SAFE DIRECTION AND THE FOUR TRUE FACTS IN LIFE

We can include within the first of these preliminaries — safe direction and bodhichitta — all the points of *lamrim*, the graded stages of the path to enlightenment, and *lojong*, the techniques for cleansing our attitudes or "training our mind." The way in which we do this is to include all the teachings of the initial and intermediate scopes of spiritual motivation under the topic of safe direction and all those concerning the advanced scope under the topic of bodhichitta. The initial spiritual motivation is to seek better rebirth because of dread of experiencing a worse one, the intermediate one is to strive for liberation from samsara because of total disgust with the problems of uncontrollably recurring rebirth, while the advanced motivation is to work to become a Buddha in order to benefit all suffering beings.

We cannot consider the actual preliminary practice of taking safe direction to be the mere repetition of the formula, "I take safe direction from the Buddhas, I take safe direction from the Dharma, I take safe direction from the Sangha," that comes only from the mouth, without any feeling. Otherwise, as our preliminary practice, we could play a tape recording of our voice repeating the refuge formula endlessly, "blah, blah, blah." Obviously this would bring us no benefit. We must have sincere feeling behind our recitation of the refuge formula, and we can only develop this if we have some understanding of the three sources of safe direction. We must understand what are the Three Jewels of Refuge — the Buddhas, the Dharma and the Sangha.

In the expanded refuge formula, we refer to the Buddhas as the "foremost of all those with two legs" — in other words, the foremost of all humans. This is just a manner of expression, since we could also speak of a Buddha as the best of all four-legged beings and the best of all hundred-legged beings as well! The main factor that establishes a Buddha, such as Shakyamuni, as the foremost of all humans is that he has explained the universal truths that he recognized, having been requested always to impart them by those who wished to follow in his footsteps. This shows that above, the Buddhas who indicate the safe direction are very precious, and below, the Sangha or community of helpful friends who actualize their teachings exactly as they are intended to be are also very precious. But the main factor that renders them both precious is the Dharma itself, the preventive measures that the one teaches and the other realizes.

The Dharma is indeed that which brings benefit. It is really something excellent. The more we understand and realize the Dharma ourselves, the more strongly we see that the Buddhas who realized it fully and taught it widely are a true source of safe direction in life. We see that not only are the Buddhas totally suitable for providing a safe direction in life, but the Sangha community of helpful friends who are realizing what the Buddhas have taught are also suitable for providing us safe direction. All Three Precious Gems are valid sources of safe direction, and foremost among them is the precious Dharma. Therefore we must gain certainty in what actually constitutes the pure Dharma.

In the expanded refuge formula, the Dharma is called "that which frees and is free from attachment." We can understand this from the explanation given in Maitreya's *The Furthest Everlasting Stream*, a hidden treasure text discovered and revealed in India by Maitripa at about the same time the first treasure texts of the Nyingma and Bön traditions were found in Tibet and Bhutan. In this fundamental text, Maitreya presents the Dharma, or preventive measures, as freedoms from attachment and that which free us from attachment. All suffering and problems, as the first true fact in life or "noble truth," have as their root longing desire or attachment, an example of the second true fact. What actually frees us from this attachment is the fourth true fact, true pathways of mind. The actual separations or freedoms from attachment achieved through them are the third true fact, true stoppings or cessations. These four true facts in life constitute two sets related by cause and effect — one on the side of total delusion and the other on the side of total purification. The causal and resultant facts on the side of total delusion are the first two facts, while the causal and resultant ones on the side of total purification are the second two. In terms of the four true facts in life, the Dharma encompasses the side of total purification "which frees and is free from" the side of total delusion.

To understand the Dharma fully, then, we need to understand the four facts seen as true by all aryas ("noble ones") or highly realized beings — namely the Sangha. Thus if we have not molded our mind with the teachings of the initial and intermediate scopes of spiritual motivation, which cover the subject matter of the four true facts, we are unable to put a safe direction in our life properly. Therefore we say that all the teachings of these first two levels of motivation must be included in taking refuge.

## THE WISH FOR HAPPINESS

We all want happiness and do not wish for any suffering, don't we? That wish naturally arises in everyone. Happiness is something perfectly appropriate to wish to have, while it is totally fitting to wish not to have suffering and unhappiness. But what is it that can bring the happiness we wish for and remove the unhappiness that we wish not to have? We soon realize that our wish by itself is unable to bring about those ends. No matter how strong our wish grows — no matter how much we wish to be happy — that still does not make us happy. In fact, when our wish does not come true, we become frustrated and angry. Thus our desire for happiness brings us nothing but unhappiness!

What is the root of this dilemma? If we examine the situation, we discover that the source of the problem is our craving and attachment. Since the basis for our wish to be happy is longing desire, craving and attachment, when our wish is frustrated even to the slightest degree, we become disappointed, frustrated, upset and angry. And even if we gain a little bit of happiness, because of our underlying discontent we gain no satisfaction, only further unhappiness. It seems, then, that the wish for happiness in the minds of almost all of us has arisen by the force of selfish craving for our own self-interest. Although such wishes have brought us the material progress of the twentieth century, they have certainly not brought us satisfaction or peace of mind.

The happiness we wish for is something that by itself is perfectly all right. But we must differentiate two distinct manners of wishing for or desiring it. One involves reliance on causality, while the other does not. The manner of wishing in which we rely on the actual process of cause and effect is one that brings a fulfillment that accords with what we desire. This is because it leads us to a perfectly appropriate pathway of action that can and does fulfill its wish. The manner of wishing in which we do not rely on the actual process of cause and effect, on the other hand, is doomed to failure.

For example, we might wish for a particular material object that we hope will make us happy. If we go about obtaining the object of our desire through destructive and harmful behavior, for instance by stealing it, we may well procure the object and gain a small amount of immediate pleasure and satisfaction from it. Nevertheless, the manner in which we tried to fulfill the aim of our desire for happiness was not one that was based on a proper understanding of cause and effect. Stealing, or any other mode of behavior that harms others, can never be a cause for stable happiness. Rather, it inevitably causes the opposite of the happiness we wish for, namely unhappiness and suffering that we experience in the future.

On the other hand, if we go about obtaining that same object through methods that are beneficial to ourselves and others, or that at least do no harm to others, such as by earning the money to buy it through honest work, then we are basing our method for fulfilling our wish on a proper understanding of cause and effect. We are able to experience a more lasting happiness from obtaining the object, and our manner of obtaining it does not act as a cause for experiencing unhappiness.

Furthermore, we can wish to have happiness and not to have suffering just temporarily for a particular occasion, or deeply and permanently. The main point, in terms of cause and effect, for obtaining happiness and avoiding suffering on a temporary basis is to use means that do not harm others. Such means are totally appropriate for bringing about what we wish. But, if we wish to obtain happiness and eliminate problems on the deepest level, forever, we must consider another factor.

There are two types of mind upon which we could rely in our quest to obtain everlasting happiness and the total elimination of suffering. One is a mind that apprehends everything as existing truly and inherently. If we act on the basis of such a mind, we come under the influence of disturbing emotions and attitudes, such as attachment, anger or confusion, which can only cause us problems and unhappiness in the long term. Nothing we do with a mind apprehending things as truly and inherently existing can act as a pure cause for everlasting happiness and total liberation from suffering. If, on the other hand, we use a mind that apprehends things as being devoid of existing truly and inherently, we are relying on a proper understanding of cause and effect and thus can achieve our goal.

The totally deluded side of the four true facts in life entails attachment, anger and confusion as the true causes that bring about true problems and suffering. If we wish to rid ourselves of these forever, we need to rely on mental states that can oppose these three poisonous, disturbing emotions and attitudes that bring us unhappiness and problems. The opposite states of mind to these true causes of our problems are the constructive emotions and attitudes that totally lack attachment, anger and confusion. These we can attain only on the basis of a realization of the total absence of fantasized, impossible ways of existing, such as true and inherent existence. If we take these constructive emotions and attitudes as true pathways of mind, from the totally purifying side of the four true facts in life, they eliminate the problems and suffering brought on by our attachment and so on. In other words, they bring about true stoppings of these, and lead us to a true and everlasting happiness.

To develop on our mind-stream the Dharma or preventive measures that can eliminate our problems and bring us triumph over our fears, we need to rely on the Buddha who imparted these measures and on the Sangha as helpful friends who are correctly realizing them. In other words, we need to develop on our mind-stream the realized preventive measures that are the Dharma refuge by relying on the Buddha refuge and the Sangha refuge as contributing circumstances. Thus, to eliminate the suffering that we do not wish, we need to take safe direction in the Precious Gems of the Buddha, Dharma and Sangha by relying on cause and effect to remove our problems.

In order to make a more vivid impression on our mind, then, in connection with tantra practice, we visualize or imagine the objects of refuge, or sources of safe direction, before us when we wish to reaffirm our taking of direction from them. We can visualize them in the form, for example, of the tree of assembled gurus from *A Ritual to Honor the Spiritual Master* as our field for building up positive potential. Focusing on this visualization, we take safe direction and purify ourselves of negative potentials and mental obstacles. This is the preliminary practice of taking safe direction that leads us forward. Furthermore, we put this safe direction in our life and continually reaffirm it on the basis of dread and confidence — the dread with which we do not wish to experience any suffering or unhappiness, and the confident belief that the Three Jewels of Refuge have the power and ability to help us fulfill this aim.

## BODHICHITTA

For developing a dedicated heart of bodhichitta, or reaffirming it, we visualize all motherly beings in the form of humans sitting around us, and then follow the various methods taught in the graded stages of the path. For instance, we apply the seven-part cause and effect technique — on the basis of developing equanimity towards all beings — namely, recognizing everyone as having been our mother, remembering the kindness of motherly love, wishing to repay that kindness, developing the love with which we wish others to be happy, compassion for them to be free of their problems, exceptional resolve to bring this about, and dedicating our heart to achieving that goal by becoming a Buddha. Or we follow the methods outlined by Shantideva in *Engaging in a Bodhisattva's Deeds* for equalizing and exchanging our attitudes about self and others.

In either case, we consider how all motherly beings around us wish to have ultimate happiness and ultimate separation from all their suffering and problems. Firmly deciding to take responsibility to bring this about, we realize that the only way we shall be able to help them fulfill their wishes is by eliminating all our shortcomings and realizing all our potentials — in other words, by becoming a Buddha ourselves. In this way, we develop strong resolve, from the depths of our heart, to achieve enlightenment for their sake. This is the way we develop and reaffirm our dedicated heart of bodhichitta.

After we have meditated in this way on taking safe direction and dedicating our heart with bodhichitta, we visualize a replica of the field for positive potential, our objects of safe direction, dissolving into us. We imagine, thereby, that we transform into a Buddha Shakyamuni. This is called "taking as a pathway the result of dedicating our heart with bodhichitta."

## MANDALA OFFERING

Next, for building up positive potential, we offer a mandala, a round symbol of the universe. The intention here is to bring to mind as many splendid objects as possible, both those that we own and those not belonging to us in the public domain. We then let pour out, from the depths of our heart, our admiration, respect and fervent regard for the objects of safe direction. If, motivated by this fervent regard, we then offer an external object that represents these splendid objects we have brought to mind, we build up positive potential proportionate to the strength of our fervent regard. Moreover, if we think on a very vast scale, and bring to mind and offer the thousand, million, billion world systems that have arisen as the comprehensive result of collective karma, we reap proportionate benefit.

In short, the main thing we need for building up positive potential and strengthening our resolve is to bring to mind and offer the most splendid environment and beings within it that we can. We therefore offer a mandala to accomplish that aim. Mandala-offering, then, is not an exercise in creating a map with Mount Meru in the center and arranging the four continent-worlds around its perimeter!

## VAJRASATTVA PRACTICE

Next, for openly admitting to our previously committed mistaken actions and purifying ourselves of their negative potentials, we practice meditation and mantra-recitation of Vajrasattva. There are several ways in which we can visualize, either generating ourselves as Vajrasattva or merely visualizing Vajrasattva on the crown of our head. In any case, while visualizing Vajrasattva in one of these ways, we recite his hundred-syllable mantra.

There are many Buddha-forms, or *yidams*, and each has his or her own special features. For example, Tsongkapa, as the Buddha-form called "The Spiritual Leader of the Three Buddha-family Traits," represents the combination of compassion, discriminating awareness and enlightening abilities — three Buddha-family traits, or aspects of Buddha-nature. Meditational practice of this Buddha-form, with recitation of the appropriate mantra, is a method to bond ourselves closely with and develop these qualities of enlightenment. Thus different Buddha-forms, such as Guhyasamaja, Vajrabhairava, Chakrasamvara, Hayagriva, Vajrakilaya and so forth, each have their close-bonding practice — their *samaya*, usually translated as "commitment." Likewise, Vajrasattva is the Buddha-form to bond us closely with and help us attain the aspect of enlightenment that is the total purification of all negative potentials and mental obstacles — in other words, the true stoppings associated with the omniscient mind of a Buddha, or, from another point of view, their total absence or voidness. This is the reason why we visualize and invoke Vajrasattva for this practice of purification.

For openly admitting and purifying ourselves, we can also make prostrations while reciting the *The Admission of Downfalls*. With either this practice or that of Vajrasattva, however, we accompany our open admission with the four opponent forces of sincere regret, the promise not to repeat these negativities, reaffirmation of our safe direction and dedicated heart together as our foundation, and application of remedial measures. The more complete these four opponent forces, the greater our purification of negative potentials. Signs that we repeatedly receive in dreams indicate the extent of our purification. For example, frequently recurring dreams of washing ourselves, or of various impure substances such as pus, blood, excrement, even insects or snakes leaving our body, or of drinking milk or light of emanating from our body, are signs of having purified ourselves.

## GURU-YOGA

Next, as a portal for inspiration to cascade upon us, we practice guru-yoga. In general, in order to gain realization and actualize any constructive pathways of mind, we need the strong inspiration on our mind-stream that can only come from our spiritual teacher, our guru. And, particularly for gaining realization of mahamudra, the guru's inspiration is especially important. I know several Kagyü and dzogchen practitioners who have attested to this from their personal experience. They had received discourses on mahamudra or dzogchen from their gurus and had everything assembled to enable them to meditate. But only when they had brought to consciousness their extraordinary respect and incomparable faith in their guru was their mind exhilarated and stimulated enough so that they were able to see, in that state, the nature of their mind. They told me that their fervent regard for their guru brought to their practice very special experiences and strong conviction. Thus, we can conclude that for gaining realization of constructive states of mind in general, and especially for gaining special realizations on our mind-stream in connection with practice of anuttarayoga tantra, it is definite that we need special inspiration from our gurus to fill our mind-stream. Guru-yoga is explained as the portal for that inspiration to cascade upon us.

## THE QUALIFICATIONS OF A GURU

As for the guru, not just anyone will do. It should not be someone who merely has the name "Lama" or "Rinpochey,"or someone who simply explains the Dharma. We must examine someone very thoroughly to see if he or she has all the qualifications of a spiritual master according to the vinaya rules of discipline, according to the sutras, according to the lower classes of tantra, and all the qualifications according to the highest class of tantra, anuttarayoga. We should not be in a hurry when we examine a potential guru, but examine slowly and carefully over many months and years. And if this person does not have all the qualifications complete, he or she must at least have the principal ones. Only on these as a minimum basis can we identify and accept this teacher as our guru.

In general, the qualifications of a proper guru according to the vinaya are, first of all, that he or she must be someone who keeps one of the classes of vows for individual liberation — one of the sets of *pratimoksha* vows. A guru who is a householder must keep the five vows of a lay person correctly and impeccably — namely, to refrain from killing, stealing, lying, engaging in inappropriate sexual behavior and taking alcohol or other intoxicants. One who is a monastic must follow the complete rules of discipline of either a novice or fully ordained monk or nun, depending on the gender of the guru. The most important qualification from this presentation, in addition to having pure ethical self-discipline, is having a heart that sincerely wishes to benefit others.

According to sutra, there are ten qualifications of a guru. He or she must have a mind that is well tamed by higher training in ethical self-discipline, stilled of flightiness of mind and mental dullness through higher training in concentration, and totally stilled of disturbing emotions and attitudes through higher training in discriminating awareness or wisdom. Moreover, a guru must have thorough knowledge of the scriptures and deep realization of their meaning through extensive meditational experience. Furthermore, a guru must have no motivation other than the pure concern of wishing to benefit his or her disciples. If we wish to summarize the qualities of a guru according to sutra, particularly a mahayana guru, we would say that he or she must have more concern for future lives than this life, as demonstrated by scrupulous regard for behavioral cause and effect — otherwise, that teacher has not even entered the sphere of being a spiritual person in the Buddhist sense — and more concern for others than self.

A guru of the lower classes of tantra, in addition to the above qualifications, must have the ability to actualize the *mandalas*, the symbolic universes of the Buddha-forms, of those classes and confer the appropriate empowerments, be skilled in all the rituals of these classes, and so forth. A guru of anuttarayoga tantra must also have the realizations of the generation and complete stages of its practice, having done all the full meditational retreats, be skilled in the various ritual procedures of this class, be able to lead disciples on its pathways of practice, and so forth.

Often it is difficult to know the qualities of a potential guru. We might think that we need the heightened awareness of extra-sensory perception. But in fact, unless we are an omniscient Buddha, we can never know all the qualities of another person in full detail. A scriptural quotation gives an analogy for dealing with this dilemma, "Just as we cannot see a fish swimming in the depths of the ocean, but we can sense its presence from ripples on the water's surface..." Thus, although we might not be able to be aware of all the deep qualities of a potential guru, nevertheless we can see the qualities that appear on the surface, like the ripples that appear from a fish beneath the water. We therefore look to the person's general behavior, his or her general mode of conduct, to give us an indication. Thus we follow the same procedure as we would for recognizing a bodhisattva. Likewise we can examine our dreams since sometimes signs of a karmic connection with this person appear there.

In general it is not necessary to identify and accept someone as our guru before we listen to a discourse from him or her explaining the Dharma. We could listen to it simply in the manner of going to a lecture, without identifying the person delivering it as our guru and ourselves as his or her disciple. As we have not yet really examined this teacher, if we simply leave it on the level of merely listening to a lecture, we are on more stable, safer ground. It is appropriate to identify a spiritual teacher as our guru and establish a guru-disciple relationship only if we have let a long time pass during which we have examined this person very thoroughly, while attending his or her lectures, and then found the person to be properly and suitably qualified. In receiving a tantric empowerment from someone, however, we must examine the person very thoroughly before, not after, receiving the empowerment. This is much more difficult. But for merely receiving explanatory discourses on Dharma from a teacher, the above procedure is best.

Sometimes we differentiate a root guru from our other gurus and focus particularly on him or her for our practice of guru-yoga. Our root guru is usually described in the context of tantra as the one who is kind to us in three ways. There are several manners of explaining these three types of kindness. One, for example, is the kindness to confer upon us empowerments, explanatory discourses on the tantric practices and special guideline instructions for them. If we have received empowerments and discourses from many gurus, we consider as our root guru the one among them who has had the most beneficial effect upon us. For deciding this, we do not examine in terms of the actual qualifications of the guru from his or her own side, but rather in terms of our own side and the benefit we have gained in our personal development and the state of mind this guru elicits in us. We consider the rest of our gurus as emanations or manifestations of that root guru. Or, when we practice guru-yoga, we think of all our gurus in the analogy of the eleven-faced Avalokiteshvara. Our root guru is the main face, while the rest of our gurus are the other ten faces. All share the same body and together comprise a single Buddha-form.

PRACTICE BEFORE FINDING A GURU
Often in countries that are not traditionally Buddhist, such as in the West, students do not have great access to many spiritual teachers. The Buddhist masters who visit may come only once a year, at the most. Thus it is difficult to find a sufficient variety of gurus to investigate in order to select a proper one, and there are insufficient opportunities to examine the qualifications of any of them. But this does not mean that before you have found a teacher who can serve as your guru, or even as your root guru, you cannot begin Dharma practice and at least engage in some of the forward-leading preliminaries.

First of all, you can certainly receive teachings from the various spiritual instructors who visit your countries, and do so in the manner of simply attending a lecture. As for engaging in meditational practices, even without a root guru you can proceed, on the basis of receiving instructions in a lecture or reading a book, to practice, for example, the placement of the four types of close mindfulness — on the bodily sensations, the feelings of a level of happiness or unhappiness, the mind, and all phenomena. You can also begin, without a root guru, to practice the meditational methods for developing a dedicated heart of bodhichitta and a correct understanding of the nature of reality, or voidness, on the basis of reading such texts as Shantideva's *Engaging in a Bodhisattva's Deeds*. Of course, however, before engaging in any meditational practice, you must first ponder and think over carefully what you have heard or read so that you understand it correctly.

# Session Two

## TAMING THE MIND

All of us wish for happiness and none of us wishes to have any suffering. This is true of everybody, but it is very difficult to come upon all the circumstances that will bring this about. If we look merely at external circumstances, we find it nearly impossible to eliminate all nonconducive conditions and bring about all conducive ones. But, if we think in terms of internal circumstances, if we can bring about all the causes for happiness and for eliminating suffering within our own mind, then, regardless of what the external circumstances might be, we will not be adversely affected by them. Even if we are in difficult external situations that might not normally be conducive for bringing about happiness, nevertheless, if we have the proper causes for happiness within our mind-stream, we are able to experience joy and not distress.

If our mind is tamed, then whatever type of external situation we encounter, we experience it in a way that causes us neither problems nor unhappiness. Conversely, if our mind is untamed, the same external situation will appear as threatening as if we were encountering a fearsome enemy, causing us to become unhappy and suffer. Thus we can see that for any given external situation, our experience of either happiness or fear and suffering in response to it are based on whether or not our mind is tamed or under our control. Thus the factor of whether or not we have tamed our mind shapes the appearances to which mind gives rise as our experience of what we encounter in life.

If the mind is not tamed, not under control, then even the tiniest external circumstance can make us extremely upset. We become angry and completely out of control, which creates a very unpleasant atmosphere for everyone around us, our family and so forth. If, on the other hand, our mind is at peace, serene and tranquil, then even the most disturbing external circumstances are unable to harm us — they will not touch us to the core. We remain ever calm, serene and happy. We can all see this if we reflect on our experience.

If we are Dharma practitioners, or religious persons, and we spend our entire lives helping others, trying to be of service and benefit to everyone around us, we provide ourselves with the most conducive circumstance to live happy and fruitful lives. It does not matter, then, how difficult the circumstances are that we encounter in life. They never adversely affect us because of our dedication and courage of heart with which we wish to be of benefit to all beings around us, no matter what the circumstances may be.

We can see the truth of this if we consider the situation of the Tibetans in Tibet. They have been facing extremely difficult circumstances and many have been thrown into prison or concentration camps. Nevertheless, if they have turned their minds to the Dharma, then even after remaining for a long time in prison they do not become depressed or overcome by their dire conditions. While staying in prison, they practice Dharma by thinking about the karmic laws of cause and effect to understand how their previous behavior has brought about their experience of this result. They also practice *tonglen*, taking on and giving — mentally taking on the suffering of all others and sending out happiness to them. In this way, regardless of how difficult their circumstances and conditions might be, they are not overwhelmed by them. This same process can occur whether we are Buddhists, Christians or followers of any other religious or spiritual path. If we tame our mind with a religious or spiritual practice, training ourselves to the best of our ability, and if we do this with a pragmatic, down-to-earth attitude and a practical approach, we gain from it great peace of mind to deal with the trials of life.

Regardless of who we might be, we all must face the basic problems and sufferings of life, such as becoming sick, growing old, and dying. It is merely a matter of time until the problems and suffering of death come to us, but inevitably they must come to everyone. If we have tamed our minds, for instance by having practiced the Dharma methods, then even though we might experience great physical pain as we approach death, our minds will not be affected by this. We will not be overcome by fear, panic or depression, but will be able to handle the situation with peace of mind, grace and dignity.

In general, if the mind is under the control of disturbing emotions and attitudes, such as attachment, greed, jealousy, competitiveness, arrogance and so forth, this brings a great deal of unhappiness and dissatisfaction. Consider longing desire or greed. Greed is something that can never be satisfied. Even if we devote our entire life to trying to satisfy our greed, we might be able to accumulate a great deal of material possessions and money, but merely having "stuff" around us or a large figure in our bankbook will not bring us lasting happiness.

This is true on the level of society as well. The stronger the greed, hostility and confusion of the public in general, the more pervasive is social unrest and unhappiness in that place. If the people of a society are tame, if their minds are under control, the society in general is happy and peaceful. But if people's minds are out of control, totally untamed and wild, their society has so many troubles and so much unhappiness. We see this clearly in the world today.

If we look at the attitude of wishing to benefit others and compare it with the attitude of wishing to cause harm, evaluating which is better, which is more beneficial, it is a hundred percent certain that we will conclude that helpfulness is the superior attitude and malice is not any good at all. Even those who are not practicing Dharma — who are not religious or spiritually inclined at all — will agree with this conclusion. The crucial issue is whether or not we have the ability to develop an attitude of wishing to help others. But it is completely certain that such an attitude of helpfulness has no faults at all.

The important question, then, is how can we actually go about generating such a beneficial attitude? We must think in terms of our personal experience and approach the challenge in a practical, down-to-earth manner. The most crucial requirement for developing an attitude of helpfulness is to rid ourselves of all disturbing emotions and attitudes that would prevent it, such as selfishness, greed, hostility, foolish confusion and so on. Since we will be unable to overcome these mental obstacles all at once, we must tackle them in progressive stages. First, we reach the point at which we do not become completely out of control and under the sway of our disturbing emotions and attitudes. Next, we rid ourselves of them completely. Finally, we eliminate their instincts so that our mind does not even give rise to an appearance of things in the deceptive manner that had previously caused these troublemakers to arise. In order to rid ourselves of disturbing emotions and attitudes, together with their instincts, we must rely on a profound method. This brings us to the topic of mahamudra.

When listening to a discourse on mahamudra, we must cultivate a proper motivation. We think of all beings spread out through the universe as extensively as space and generate the sincere wish to benefit them all. In order to be able to do that as fully as possible, we must attain the enlightened state of a Buddha. Therefore, with a dedicated heart of bodhichitta as our motivation, we now listen to further instructions on mahamudra, which we fully intend to put into practice and realize in order to reach that state of maximum benefit to all.

## VISUALIZATION OF THE SOURCES OF SAFE DIRECTION

The actual body of this text concerning mahamudra is divided into three sections: the preparation, actual techniques and concluding procedures. The preparation is presented within the context of tantra and, specifically, in terms of the four forward-leading preliminary practices. These are taking safe direction to lead us to dedicating our heart with bodhichitta, offering a mandala to lead us to building up a bountiful store of positive potential, practicing Vajrasattva meditation and mantra recitation to lead us to purifying ourselves of negative potentials and mental obstacles, and practicing guru-yoga to lead us to having inspiration cascade upon our mind-stream.

For taking safe direction, we visualize the three sources of safe direction, the Three Precious Gems, before us as a field for positive potential in the form of the tree of assembled gurus from *A Ritual to Honor the Spiritual Master*. The central figure of this visualization is Lama Lozang Tubwang Dorjeychang, namely Tsongkapa with Shakyamuni Buddha in his heart and Buddha Vajradhara in the heart of Shakyamuni. In this way, the central figure not only represents all levels of practice, but, like a Buddha-form for anuttarayoga tantric practice, is complete with beings for bonding ourselves closely, for deep awareness and for absorbed concentration. If we were to visualize ourselves in such a composite form, the outermost figure bonds us closely to the practice of a specific tantra, the figure in his or her heart helps us gather the energy-winds of deep awareness at our heart chakra, while absorbed concentration on the innermost figure helps us to dissolve those winds so as to manifest primordial clear light mind. These three figures are usually translated as "commitment beings," "wisdom beings" and "concentration beings." All the other sources of safe direction are arranged around this central figure in an appropriate manner.

Every Tibetan tradition of Buddhism agrees that when we practice Dharma, we need externally to uphold some level of pratimoksha or individual liberation vow as presented in the body of hinayana teachings, internally to realize all mahayana practices of bodhichitta, and hiddenly or secretly to actualize the methods of tantra. Upholding vows for individual liberation establishes a stable foundation. On this basis, the mahayana practices of the six far-reaching attitudes, or perfections — generosity, ethical self-discipline, patient tolerance, positive enthusiasm, mental stability and discriminating awareness — coupled with a unification of a serenely stilled and settled mind, or shamata, with an exceptionally perceptive one, or vipashyana, provide the life-force for our subsequent practice of tantra. Thus each Tibetan tradition presents a spiritual path that combines into the practice for one individual the essence of the three vehicles of hinayana, mahayana and tantrayana.

The composite figure Lama Lozang Tubwang Dorjeychang symbolizes this threefold practice complete in one individual. His external form as a fully ordained monk represents the hinayana practice of ethical self-discipline. Shakyamuni Buddha in his heart and Buddha Vajradhara in Shakyamuni's heart, as the original teachers respectively of mahayana and tantrayana, represent the practices of these second two vehicles. Thus visualizing this central figure as our source of safe direction has special significance.

All four traditions of Tibetan Buddhism — Nyingma, Sakya, Kagyü and Gelug — have both householder or lay as well as monastic practitioners. Regardless of which category we fall into, the common tradition of Tibet is to uphold one of the levels of pratimoksha vow — either the five vowed restraints for a lay person or the vowed restraints appropriate to our particular class of monastic ordination as a full or novice monk or nun. Thus no matter who we are, we uphold the threefold teachings of the complete path of hinayana, mahayana and tantrayana.

Moreover, the tree of assembled gurus contains representations of all three sources of safe direction. The central figure and the community of those around him represent the Buddhas and Sangha. The actual Dharma source of direction is the true stoppings and true pathway minds on the Buddhas' mind-streams. As these true stoppings and true pathways are quite difficult to imagine, we represent them by visualized Dharma texts in front of these figures.

Furthermore, it is important to take safe direction in the state of mind in which all causes are complete for so doing. Thus we need to feel dread of falling to a worse state of rebirth and have confidence that the Three Precious Gems can provide a safe and sound direction for avoiding that suffering. In addition, we need to supplement these causes with a mahayana motivation of compassion. Wishing for all beings to be free of not only worse rebirths but all possible types of suffering, we put a safe direction in our life. The ultimate endpoint of that safe direction is to become Buddhas ourselves through following the stages of progress of the Sangha of aryas, the highly realized ones, so that we can fully help all beings through the Dharma. Thus taking safe direction naturally leads to dedicating our heart with bodhichitta. To symbolize putting this safe direction in our life, we imagine a cascade of lights and nectars flowing to us from the visualized figures and texts before us, confirming our safe direction and dedicated heart.

## THE FOUR LEVELS OF MANDALA OFFERING

Next we offer a mandala, a round symbol of a universe. There are four levels of mandala that we offer — external, internal, hidden or secret, and that of the very nature of reality. Each can be explained in several ways. An external mandala consists of all the external phenomena of the universe, both the inanimate environment and all animate beings in it, usually imagined in the form of Mount Meru surrounded by four continent-worlds. An internal mandala is constructed of the limbs of our body, dissected in our imagination and arranged like four continents around our trunk and head, imagined in the center like a Mount Meru. A hidden or secret mandala is made of the subtlest level of mind generated into a blissful consciousness and used as the mind that understands voidness — in other words, a subtlest mind that is inseparably both a blissful awareness and an understanding of voidness. A mandala of the very nature of reality is constructed of the inseparable unity of that blissful, subtlest mind that understands voidness and all appearances that come spontaneously and simultaneously with it as its emanation.

Aku Sherab-gyatso has explained that these last two types of mandala offering have as the basis for their actualization, respectively, the deep awareness of indivisible bliss and voidness, and the state of unity of the two levels of truth. This means that we offer a hidden or secret mandala by offering, with a symbol, our understanding that the three spheres of the mandala offering — the person making it, the object to whom it is offered and the mandala offering itself — are all equally the play or emanation of the subtlest primordial mind that is inseparably both a blissful awareness and an understanding of voidness. They do not go beyond this as their nature. Likewise, we offer a mandala of the very nature of reality by offering, with a symbol, our understanding that these three spheres of the mandala offering are the play of the unity of the two levels of truth. We can take the two levels of truth in this context in several ways, such as inseparable voidness and conventional appearance, inseparable primordial mind of indivisible bliss and voidness and its play of appearances, and so on.

We can also understand these four levels of mandala in terms of Gungtangzang's explanation of the four types of offering. Gungtangzang was the teacher of two of Aku Sherab-gyatso's teachers. External offerings are of all external objects of desire — sights, sounds, fragrances, tastes and tactile or bodily sensations. Internal offerings are of purified transformations of substances connected with the mindstream of animate beings, such as the five types of flesh — of cattle, dogs, elephants, horses and humans — and five kinds of nectar-like bodily fluids — feces, blood, semen, marrow and urine. These ten are symbolic of either the aggregates and bodily elements, the disturbing emotions and attitudes, or the energy-winds of the subtle vajra-body. The hidden or secret offering is of the play of deep awareness of inseparable bliss and voidness, while the offering of the very nature of reality is of the play of the unity of the two levels of truth. Gungtangzang then correlates the two levels of truth with the unity of the object to whom the offering is made, namely the Buddhas, and the enlightening activities of that object. He admits that this is very difficult to understand.

His special manner of explanation of the last two types of offering is different from the usual way in which they are taken. Within the context of inseparable bliss and voidness — meaning a blissful subtlest consciousness used as the mind that understands voidness — the hidden or secret offering is commonly of the blissful consciousness of this inseparable unity of a pair, while the offering of the very nature of reality is commonly of the voidness it understands. Thus we make the last two offerings by realizing that the person making the offering, the objects to whom the offerings are made and the offering itself are all the play, respectively, of the blissful primordial mind that understands voidness and the voidness understood by that blissful primordial mind.

Gungtangzang explains the four offerings in the special manner he does because he asserts that we must connect them with the four empowerments of anuttarayoga tantra. The external offering is connected with the vase empowerments, which are conferred with an external object, a vase. The internal offering is associated with the hidden or secret empowerment, conferred with secret substances connected with the mind-stream. The hidden or secret offering is suggested by the deep awareness empowerment, conferred with the experience of the deep awareness that is inseparably a blissful primordial mind and an understanding of voidness. The offering of the very nature of reality is connected with the fourth or word empowerment, conferred by words that indicate the state of unity of the two levels of truth. I think we can adopt this presentation of the four types of general offering and apply it to the four types of mandala offering as well. This is suggested by the similarity between Gungtangzang's explanation of the last two types of offering in general and Aku Sherab-gyatso's presentation of the last two types of mandala offering.

Concerning the mandala of the very nature of reality, however, it is very difficult for us to focus on a unity of the two levels of truth. Only the omniscient mind of a Buddha can have straightforward non-conceptual perception of the two levels of truth simultaneously. In the context of the Guhyasamaja system of anuttarayoga tantra, however, we take the illusory body and clear light as representing the two levels of truth. On the final steps of the complete stage path, we have an inseparable state of unity of a blissful mind of clear light understanding voidness and also the appearance of an illusory body. Neither blocks the other and the two are thus inseparable.

On a basis level, subtlest mind and subtlest energy-wind are also inseparable. Subtlest mind is what we transform on the path into the primordial clear light mind that is a blissful awareness of voidness, while subtlest energy-wind is the material cause for an illusory body, as well as materially responsible for all pure and impure appearances as the play of primordial mind. I therefore think, when we offer a mandala of the very nature of reality, we can offer, with a symbol, our understanding that the person making the offering, the objects to whom the offering is made and the offering itself are all the play of inseparable subtlest mind and subtlest energy-wind.

## ALL APPEARANCE-MAKING AND APPEARANCES AS REFLEXIVE PLAY

In order to be able to properly offer a hidden or secret mandala and a mandala of the very nature of reality, we need to understand what we mean by all appearance-making and appearances of phenomena being the play of voidness, or of the primordial mind of great bliss, or of the inseparable unity of the two levels of truth, or of the inseparable unity of subtlest mind and subtlest energy-wind. As this topic of appearance-making and appearances being the reflexive play or emanation of primordial mind will arise repeatedly in our later discussions, let us examine this topic now, although it is quite difficult.

Because tantric practitioners meditate on primordial deep awareness generated as inseparable blissful awareness and discriminating awareness of voidness, the tantra teachings show high regard for both greatly blissful deep awareness and voidness as its object, the two of which become of one taste, like water poured into water. It is commonly accepted that all phenomena are the play or appearances of voidness. The devoid nature of sights, for example, is that which allows for and makes possible their arising. Sights do arise. They arise dependently on factors other than themselves, and it is perfectly reasonable that they arise because they are devoid of existing in impossible ways. In this sense, all phenomena as things having a devoid nature are like the play of their devoid nature. That being the case, then as a consequence of tantra's high regard for a greatly blissful deep awareness and voidness as its object becoming inseparable by nature, the appearances of everything categorized as the play of voidness can also be presented, in terms of the appearance-making of them, as the play of a greatly blissful awareness. This is one point.

Furthermore, we can speak of appearance-making and appearances as the play or emanation of simultaneously arising primordial clear light mind. "Simultaneously arising" refers to the fact that the clear light mind of each individual has no beginning and will have no end, even after each of us becomes a Buddha. It has always existed and always will — there is no time when it was non-existent or when it will cease to be. Therefore primordial clear light mind arises simultaneously with each moment of experience, with an everlasting, constant nature. On the path, through various methods, we cause that clear light mind to arise as a blissful awareness simultaneously with each moment.

The cognitive arising of all phenomena can be presented within the sphere of clear light in the sense that the appearances, to which mind gives rise, of anything that exists are the emanated luster or effulgence of simultaneously arising clear light. In the context of cognition, all emanations of the appearance of things arise, or literally "dawn" from clear light and, ultimately, dissolve or "set" into the sphere of clear light mind. Thus the nature of emanations, in this context, comes down to clear light mind. Our experience of all phenomena, then, is the result of both the appearance-making and appearances of this ever-present mind. In this cognitive and not substantial, chittamatra sense, then, all phenomena are the play of clear light mind arising simultaneously with each moment.

Let us look at this point more deeply. In *The Furthest Everlasting Stream*, Maitreya has explained that the elements withdraw or disintegrate progressively, one into the other, starting from earth, water, fire and wind up to space. They also emerge or arise progressively from each other, but in the reverse sequence, starting from space, wind, fire and water down to earth. Thus on the external level , at the end of a universe, the elements of earth, water, fire and wind — in other words, matter in solid, liquid, heat and gaseous forms — dissolve in a progressive order, one melting into the next, ultimately ending with empty space. Then with the emergence of a new universe, the elements of wind, fire, water and earth arise once more from empty space.

The growth and decay of the form of the elements on the external level parallels and is thus related to their growth and decay on an internal level concerning the body. Thus, in the formation and development of a human embryo, for example, the five forms of the constituent elements grow or emerge progressively out of each other. Emerging from empty space, the body grows from a gaseous form through heat and liquid stages to, finally, a solid one. With death, it decays in the reverse order of these stages from a solid form back into empty space.

When we speak of the growth and decay of elements into and out of space on an internal level, however, we are referring not only to a material level and some sort of empty space like the ether, but also to a cognitive level and simultaneously arising primordial clear light mind. All coarse and subtle levels of mind and energy-wind withdraw, contract or dissolve into internal, all-void, subtlest clear light mind, and then slowly emerge as well from this all-void clear light mind, becoming increasingly more gross or coarse in stages. These coarser levels of mind are the ones that give rise to the appearance of the elements. Thus it is in this sense that we can understand that the place from which the luster or effulgence of emanations arises and into which it sets is clear light mind of deep awareness.

## THE RELATION BETWEEN APPEARANCES, CLEAR LIGHT MIND, DEATH AND REBIRTH

We can understand further how subtlest clear light mind is the source of all that is pure or impure by considering the anuttarayoga tantra explanation, from the Guhyasamaja system, of the relationship between clear light mind and impure appearances. Mind, as mere clarity and awareness, must have a physical basis for its functioning. It is always supported on energy-wind as its "mount." The two abide in the same package and, in this sense, mind always "rides" on energy-winds. At the time of death, mind withdraws progressively from the elements of earth, water, fire and wind as its basis. This means that mind is supported by progressively less coarse levels of energy-wind and there is less movement of these winds in the subtle vajra-body. As a result of this process, all coarse levels of mind cease to function — in other words, the five types of sensory consciousness cease to function since mind no longer gives rise to the coarse appearance of the five elements. It no longer gives rise to the appearance of any sights, sounds, smells, tastes or tactile or bodily sensations.

The process of the strongest movement of energy-winds ceasing occurs in four stages, and is usually described as earth dissolving into water, water into fire, fire into wind and wind into space or consciousness. Through this four-stage process, the coarse levels of mind, with their attendant mental factors, likewise dissolve or cease. At the first stage, we no longer see anything. At the second, we no longer hear or feel any level of physical pleasure or pain. At the third, we no longer smell or distinguish any remaining sensory object. At the fourth, we no longer taste or feel any bodily sensation, such as hot or cold, or have any remaining mental factors regarding sensory objects, such as the intention to move. Simultaneously with this process, our conscious, personal level of conceptual mind gives rise to four stages of appearance that resemble progressively less congealed forms of light — namely, a mirage, a mist or smoke, sparks of light and a dim flame at the bottom of a well.

Although the process of falling asleep progresses through similar stages as the process of dying, sleep is different from death. With sleep, sense perception does not totally cease, but is merely accompanied by increasingly thicker inattention the deeper we sleep. The fact that sleeping persons can be awakened by a tickle on the foot indicates clearly that their coarse levels of mind have not completely ceased to function.

At this stage in the dissolution process of death, mind is supported only on the more subtle levels of energy-wind, and their movement through the subtle vajra-body is only slight. Consequently, mind can only give rise to more subtle appearances, namely the appearances cognizable by subtle conceptual levels of mind. As the dissolution process continues and the energy-winds enter and abide in the central channel, mind gradually withdraws from those winds as well. There is even less movement of winds, and mind is supported only on even more subtle energy-winds at the center of the heart chakra. This is described as the energy-winds dissolving at the center of the heart chakra.

As the energy-wind basis for mind becomes more and more subtle, and its movement continues to decrease, the level of mind that can be supported also becomes proportionately more subtle. First we reach the level of the eighty preconscious, primitive conceptual minds — sometimes translated as "indicative conceptual minds" — in three groupings of progressive subtlety indicative of the next three levels of mind also being progressively more subtle. The first group of thirty-three include such primitive conceptual minds, or preconscious thoughts, as those of repulsion, sorrow, fear, hunger, thirst and pro-tectiveness. The next group of forty include more subtle preconscious thoughts of longing, satisfaction and wishing to suckle, kiss, hug or be unruly; while the last group of seven include even more subtle thoughts of boredom, indifference and laziness. Even animals have these subtle, preconscious conceptual minds, perhaps called "feelings" in Western schemes of psychology. According to the explanation of most Gelug masters, this level of eighty preconscious, primitive con-ceptual minds ceases all at once, whereas most Sakya masters, on the basis of their personal meditational experience, assert that these minds cease in three stages.

Mind is now supported on even more subtle levels of energy-wind at the center of the heart chakra. As it continues to withdraw from these as its basis, the three most subtle levels of conceptual mind cease in the order of their decreasing coarseness. These are the usually un-conscious conceptual appearance-making minds called appearance-congealment, light-diffusion and threshold, which give rise, respec-tively, to appearances of white moonlit snow, the red glow of sunset or sunrise, and pitch-black darkness.

Finally, mind is based only on the subtlest level of energy-wind. The mind that is left, devoid of all coarser ones, is the subtlest level of mind, known as clear light. In fact, the Guhyasamaja literature refers to the three subtlest conceptual appearance-making minds and clear light as the four voids — void, very void, greatly void and all-void — since each is progressively more devoid of coarser levels of mind. The all-void clear light mind is always inseparable from — in the same entity or package as — subtlest energy-wind. As clear light mind, individual in each being, has neither beginning nor end, it is called primordial, arising simultaneously with each moment of experience of life, death, samsara, nirvana or enlightenment. On the basis level, at the time of death, it gives rise to an appearance of clear light which, according to Kaydrub Norzang-gyatso — a disciple of two of Tsong-kapa's disciples, Sherab-senggey and the First Dalai Lama, Gedündrub — in *An Ornament for "The Stainless Light" [Commentary on "The Abbreviated Kalachakra Tantra"]*, is the appearance of voidness. It does not, however, normally apprehend it as voidness.

As it is ordinarily impossible for mind to remain in the state of clear light devoid of coarser levels of mind, continuing to experience the death phase of uncontrollably recurring existence, it soon begins to deviate from this state. This occurs with movement of the subtlest energy-wind upon which clear light mind is supported and heralds the re-emergent sequence of the coarser levels of mind and body. It quickly passes, in order, through the stages of the threshold, light-diffusion and appearance-congealment unconscious conceptual minds and reaches the level of the eighty preconscious, primitive conceptual minds. At each of these levels, mind gives rise to the appearances associated with each of these states.

Starting with the experience of these stages of re-emergence, the mind-stream continues through *bardo*, the samsaric state of existence in between death and conception in a new rebirth. The mind in bardo, being on the level of coarseness of the eighty primitive conceptual minds, gives rise to various appearances, pleasant or frightening, depending on the instincts and habits built up in previous lives. At the end of an appropriate period of time, up to a maximum of seven days, mind again withdraws to clear light with what is called a "small death." This emergence and dissolution sequence may recur a maximum of seven times, lasting over a maximum period of forty-nine days.

Finally, the coarser levels of mind re-emerge once more through these same four stages, heralding conception at the start of a new rebirth. At this point, if the mind-stream takes as its physical basis a human or animal embryo, mind becomes increasingly coarse as it is progressively supported by the increasingly coarse form of the constituent elements of this basis — energy-wind, fire, water and then earth. Correspondingly, mind gives rise to appearances of these elements in the form of sights, sounds, smells, tastes and tactile sensations. The specific forms of these appearances are shaped by the instincts built up by the effects of previous actions and transmitted with the continuity of clear light mind. Thus, we can understand clear light mind as the source of all impure appearances within the context of this process of dissolution and re-emergence. It is through this process that we can explain, on the anuttarayoga tantra level, how impure appearances rise out of and set into clear light mind, in a manner reminiscent of the rising and setting of the sun.

These are the points we need to ponder in order to understand that all appearance-making and all appearances — in other words, all phenomena — are the emanation or play of the clear light mind of deep awareness of inseparable bliss and voidness. We offer the hidden mandala and the mandala of the very nature of reality with this understanding.

## THE RELATION BETWEEN MIND, KARMA AND ENVIRONMENT

We can say that the three realms of existence — the realms of desirable sensory objects, ethereal forms and formless beings — are the creations of karmic impulses on yet another level. The instincts, habits or propensities built up from our previous actions ripen not only into our experiences of happiness or suffering, but also into the external conditions that provide the circumstances for those experiences. We can understand this in terms of our discussion of the dissolution and re-emergence of the elements not only on an internal level, but also on an external one. The internal progressive re-emergence of the elements from primordial clear light mind is not only parallel to the external process of emergence from empty space, but in some intimate way is causally related to it.

For example, these days in Dharamsala it is especially cold. As a result of the habits and propensities built up by their previous actions, some people experience the cold with happiness, others with unhappiness and suffering. If we investigate the cause of the cold weather itself that is acting as the circumstance for the ripening of people's karma into their experience of delight or discomfort, we would have to say that the immediate cause is the movement of weather systems or, more deeply, the movement of the elements, in the world in general and, in particular, in the Arabian Sea and Himalayan plateau. If we trace the causes for the movement of the elements in our local region back ever further, we come eventually to the causal relation between the emergence of the internal and external elements.

The most important factor regarding karma or impulses is mind. Although the vaibhashika and prasangika theories assert some types of karma to be subtle forms of physical phenomena, in general we can say that karmic impulses always involve mind. When the impulse of a karmic action ceases, it builds up a habit, instinct or propensity that can be labeled onto the mind-stream of the person, or onto the person himself or herself, as the basis for its labeling. The problem is how does such an instinct on a mind-stream — specifically on a mind-stream of primordial clear light — bring about any immediate change in the external world, for instance this cold spell in Dharamsala? Since the scriptures are not clear on this point, we need to analyze it ourselves.

My own thinking is that there definitely is some kind of relation between internal and external elements. On one level, we can say that now our internal elements are totally under the power or influence of the external elements. But when we reach an extremely advanced state of meditational realization, we gain control over our internal elements. At such a time, through meditational techniques, our internal elements can affect the external ones, for example in starting and stopping rain. Because of this relationship, on the level of the spiritual path, of actions involving the internal elements effecting changes in external ones, I believe there must also be some similar relationship on the basis level as well.

If we investigate the causes for changes in the external environment, for example the changes in the external elements that cause the daily variations in weather, we could say that it is the work of God. But if we conceive of God as a supreme, omnipotent creator, an individual whose actions arise without being affected by anything, we would have to conclude, on the basis of logic, that this is an impossible mode of existence. Actions can only arise dependently, affected by causes and conditions. Therefore Buddhism does not assert the existence of such a God. This is not intended as a criticism of other religions, nor does it deny that other religions that speak of God assert many levels of understanding God that go deeper than the superficial, popular one. But since we all assert that there is order in the universe, we must find a cause for external changes in it. Buddhism asserts that this cause is karma. And, since the impulses of karma arise from mind — and ultimately from primordial clear light mind — and set back into that mind, building up instincts and propensities, we can say that the deepest cause is mind.

In *A Supplement to [Nagarjuna's "Root Stanzas on] the Middle Way,"* Chandrakirti has discussed two types of karma, common and uncommon — in other words shared or collective karma and individual karma. The instincts or propensities from shared karmic actions on the mind-streams of many beings ripen into their common experience of the same event, while propensities from their individual karmic actions ripen into their individual experiences. My own idea is that there are similarly two levels of cause for changes in the elements of the external environment.

The propensities from shared karmic actions on the mind-streams of many beings ripen not only into their common experience of the same event, but also into external circumstances that provide the conditions for those events. When we speak on the level of the comprehensive results of shared karma, the ripening is in the form of the environment. Thus we could say that the universe and this world in general are the result of the shared karma of the enormous number of animate beings — in other words, "sentient" beings, those with a mind affected by karma — who live in and experience it. But it would be very difficult to assert that individual karma is responsible for the minor changes in the environment once it has arisen, although of course there can be man-made changes in the environment such as global warming and degradation through pollution and abuse.

For example, it is very problematic to try to explain, on the basis of karma, why one leaf on a certain tree is bigger than another, or why two leaves on the same tree fall from it at different times. It seems better to say that these minor happenings occur as the result of physical factors from the power of the external elements themselves. Thus shared karma shapes the formation of the elements of the universe and world in general and, although man-made actions also affect the environment, the play of physical factors associated with the elements themselves brings about minor daily changes in the weather.

In short, although we can understand voidness on the basis of logic and reason, we cannot do so with respect to karma and the full mechanics of cause and effect. The workings of karma, and how all phenomena are the play of mind in the sense of being the result of karma, are extremely obscure points that are very profound and difficult to understand.

## THE TWO LEVELS OF VAJRASATTVA PRACTICE

The next forward-leading preliminary practice for mahamudra is Vajrasattva meditation with recitation of his hundred-syllable mantra. We can practice this in conjunction with either the generation or complete stage of anuttarayoga tantra. On the generation stage, we work primarily with the imagination and complex visualizations. We focus on overcoming our mind's ordinary manner of producing an appearance of things in general, and especially of our own body, as if they were truly and inherently existent, and then implying that they exist in the manner in which it makes them appear. Thus when we practice Vajrasattva purification in conjunction with generation stage practice, we imagine the flow of purifying nectars from Vajrasattva flushing our entire body, purifying it completely of the way in which our mind ordinarily makes it appear and implies that it exists.

On the complete stage, when all causes are complete for bringing about actual changes on the more subtle levels of body and mind, we work with the subtle energy-body, particularly the central energy-channel, to gain access to subtlest mind and energy-wind so that we can actualize what we have only imagined on the former stage. When we practice Vajrasattva meditation in conjunction with the complete stage, we imagine the flow of purifying nectars from Vajrasattva penetrating vital points of our central channel and  .shing that channel of all its knots and other obstacles that would prev ent our realizations of the attainments of this stage. Although these two levels of Vajrasattva practice have these differences in focus, their general meaning and procedures — openly admitting to our negative actions, invoking the four opponent forces and so forth — are the same.

## GURU-YOGA — EXTERNAL AND INNER GURUS

The last of the four forward-leading preliminaries, guru-yoga, also has two levels of practice. These are in conjunction with the two levels of guru, the definitive one to which we are led and the interpretable one who can lead us there. We sometimes refer to these as the inner and external gurus. We can understand them in analogy with the definitive and interpretable levels of the Buddha source of safe direction. The definitive level Precious Gem of a Buddha is his or her dharmakaya, or bodies encompassing everything — both omniscient deep awareness and its nature. The interpretable level Buddha Gem is a Buddha's rupakaya, or bodies of form in which an enlightened being appears. A Buddha's external bodies of form lead us to the attainment of a Buddha's more inner aspects, the bodies that encompass everything.

On the anuttarayoga tantra level of mahamudra, we use various methods to make manifest subtlest primordial mind and use it to realize its own nature. The subtlest primordial mind that we all have within is the definitive level guru to which we are led — our inner guru. The external guru is the interpretable level one who can lead us to it. Therefore, with guru-yoga, we make requests to our external guru for inspiration to manifest the inner guru. We also receive inspiration from our inner guru, as our Buddha-nature, to complete this endeavor.

## PARTING FROM THE FOUR FORMS OF CLINGING — THE COMMON PRELIMINARIES

The auto-commentary now cites several great Kagyü and Sakya masters of the past as examples of highly realized gurus who have taught the general stages for training the mind that we too must follow as a preliminary for mahamudra practice that is common to all sutra and tantra mahayana paths. These masters have expressed these stages in terms of the tradition known as "parting ourselves from the four forms of clinging."

First we part from clinging to this life. Instead of total involvement with affairs of this life, we involve ourselves with future lives. We accomplish this by thinking about our precious human life with all its freedoms and endowments for spiritual growth, how we lose it because of death and impermanence, and then the karmic laws of behavioral cause and effect that shape our future lives. Next we part from clinging to future lives and involve ourselves, instead, in the quest for liberation. By thinking about all the suffering of uncontrollably recurring rebirth, or samsara, we generate sincere renunciation of it — the strong determination to be free and attain the total liberation that is nirvana.

In addition, we part from clinging to our own selfish concern and involve ourselves fully, instead, with the welfare of others. We dedicate our heart with bodhichitta and, not merely leaving it at that, actually involve ourselves in the practices that benefit others. Therefore we train ourselves with the six far-reaching attitudes of generosity and so forth. Finally, we part from clinging to our apprehension of true, inherent existence and involve ourselves totally, instead, in the understanding of voidness, the absence of this fantasized, impossible manner of existence. For this we develop the state of mind that is both serenely stilled and settled as well as exceptionally perceptive — a state of joint shamata and vipashyana.

Each of the Tibetan Buddhist traditions presents these four points as the common preliminary for all mahayana sutra and tantra paths. The only differences are the order and emphasis, as well as the name given to the presentation. The Gelug tradition organizes these points into the lamrim, or graded stages of the path, and arranges them according to three levels of motivation — aiming for better rebirth, liberation from samsara, or enlightenment — as presented by the Indian master Atisha in *A Lamp for the Path to Enlightenment* and transmitted to Tsongkapa through the Kadam lineage. Tsongkapa has presented the teachings for persons of these three levels as all being rooted in a wholehearted commitment to a spiritual master. The Kagyü tradition mostly organizes the stages of the path in terms of parting from the four forms of clinging. Its most famous textual presentation of this is *A Jewel Ornament for the Path to Liberation* by Gampopa. Following the teachings of Milarepa, it presents the stages of the path as all being possible because of Buddha-nature, the factors in everyone that allow for their liberation and enlightenment.

The Sakya tradition's unique presentation of the stages of the path — lamdray, the paths and their result — derives from the Indian mahasiddha Virupa. It organizes these stages around an initial discussion of suffering, as Buddha had done with the four true facts in life, and elaborates in terms of three stages of appearance-making — the impure one of sentient beings, the pathway one of those who strive, and the pure one of the Buddhas — and the three everlasting streams — the causal one of the alaya, the all-encompassing foundation for all; the pathway one of methods concerning the body; and the resultant one of mahamudra. The Nyingma tradition organizes the graded paths in terms of the teachings of the nine vehicles — three sutra ones of the shravakas or listeners to the teachings, pratyekabuddhas or self-evolving practitioners, and bodhisattvas or dedicated beings; three lower tantra ones of kriya, charya and yoga tantra; and maha-, anu- and atiyoga. Its classic text for this is Longchenpa's *A Treasury of Deep Awareness*, which presents all these commonly shared preliminaries, beginning with recognizing and appreciating the precious human life.

## THE IMPORTANCE OF PRELIMINARIES

Our success in Dharma practice, whether of mahamudra or any of its other multitude of facets, totally depends on the efforts we make in these preliminary practices, especially the commonly shared preliminary of training our mind through the graded stages of the path. Therefore we should never trivialize or dismiss these preliminaries, or devote only minimal effort to them. Even if we spend our entire life developing and strengthening these preliminary realizations, it will only serve to further support and strengthen our success with the actual advanced practices. Thus we devote as much effort to the preliminaries as we do to the actual techniques such as mahamudra.

All the texts of the great mahayana masters stress the importance of practicing with a proper motivation, namely with a dedicated heart of bodhichitta. This is a heart set on achieving enlightenment, through the various practices, in order to benefit all beings fully. Practicing the advanced Buddhist techniques without such motivation can be very dangerous and disastrous. For example, if we devote our efforts to visualizing ourselves as a multi-faced, multi-armed, multi-legged Buddha-form and reciting the appropriate mantras, but without a bodhichitta motivation of doing so in order to reach enlightenment to benefit all, we certainly cannot achieve enlightenment as a result of that practice. On the contrary, if we have a worldly motivation, indicative of our lack of understanding voidness, we experience a downfall as the result of our repeated visualization and are reborn as a ghost or spirit in the shape of this Buddha-form. As there are many accounts of such things happening, it is crucial to practice with a proper motivation. Since none of us would wish to be reborn as a ghost with a bizarre form, we must sincerely dedicate our heart with bodhichitta as the foundation for our mahamudra practice.

In general, in order to see the nature of mind, we need to build up a bountiful store of positive potential. But let us be more specific than that. When we discuss the nature of mind, we can differentiate its conventional and deepest natures. We need to recognize and see both with certainty, parallel to how, during a tantric empowerment, we need to recognize and see both the conventional and deepest natures of a particular Buddha-form's mandala, or symbolic universe. To be able to recognize and see, with straightforward, non-conceptual perception, not only mind's nature in general, but specifically mind's conventional and deepest natures simultaneously, we need an especially vast store of positive potential. We also need to purify ourselves of the mental obstacles that would prevent this, namely the obstacles preventing both our liberation and omniscience. Thus the preliminary practices of collecting and cleansing, namely building up positive potential and purifying ourselves of mental blocks, are especially essential for mahamudra practice.

## PAYING ATTENTION TO DEFINITIONS OF TECHNICAL TERMS

When we discuss the nature of mind, it is important not only to differentiate its conventional and deepest natures, but also to note the difference between speaking in terms of the nature itself and that which has this nature. This differentiation is prominent in Kagyü and Nyingma texts and affects their presentations of the two levels of truth.

Various traditions and texts define differently the two levels of truth — conventional and deepest. For example, the Nyingma master Longchenpa, in the eighteenth chapter of *A Treasury of Deep Awareness*, presents the two levels of truth in the context of that which has the nature of reality. If we look at his presentation in light of the usual Gelug definitions of the two levels presented in terms of the nature of reality itself, and are unaware that we can make other distinctions, we are likely to miss the point and become confused. Therefore it is important to know that there is a wide variety of definition and usage of technical terms.

For example, Maitreya's *Differentiating the Middle from Extremes* presents three deepest or ultimate things — the deepest, ultimate meaning; the deepest, ultimate attainment; and the deepest, ultimate practice for realization. Likewise, the literature of the stages of Guhyasamaja practice speaks of conventional and deepest levels of its complete stage. Here, the terms "conventional" and "deepest," or "ultimate," levels have a specific meaning in the context of the steps into which we divide the Guhyasamaja complete stage.

Thus, whenever we read and study a Dharma text, it is essential that we pay particular attention to such crucial terms as "conventional" and "deepest" truths, "nature" and "things having this nature," and so on. We must know the precise significance and meaning these have within the context of that text. If we are clear about how the author is defining and using his or her technical terms in a particular text, we find that everything in that text makes sense. Otherwise, if we take the meaning and usage of technical terms that we have learned from the context of one text and try to apply them to another text — even, sometimes, to another book by the same author — we may see many contradictions and become very confused. Thus it is important to understand the use of terminology within the context of each specific text we study.

Consider, for example, the term "dual appearances." It does not refer to the appearance of two things, but rather to discordant appearances — appearances that do not accord with reality. Furthermore, it not only refers to the side of the discordant appearances themselves as objects of mind, but to the action of mind giving rise to them. Although we need to refute that the appearance of something in a manner discordant with reality refers to something real, the main focus of our practice is to eliminate the true causes of our problems. The true causes are our mind's discordant appearance-making and its apprehension of the discordant appearances it fabricates as referring to something real.

Within this context, then, there are many kinds of discordant appearance-making. For example, as soon as we see something, our mind usually gives rise to the discordant appearance of an idea of the object, which it projects onto and mixes with the mere appearance of that object itself to which it also gives rise. Then there is the discordant appearance-making of conventional phenomena whereby our mind gives rise to an appearance of them as if they existed truly and inherently. Furthermore, there is the discordant appearance-making of objects of mind and minds having these objects as being two separate, unrelated phenomena existing independently. We need to be aware of which type of discordant appearance-making is meant in any specific passage of any particular text we study.

Furthermore, we sometimes have different names for a very similar type of practice in various traditions. For example, our text mentions that some of the Kagyü traditions speak of "actualizing through the guru." Various Nyingma texts speak of "actualizing through the descendents of the *vidyadharas*, those apprehending pure awareness" and "actualizing through the mind of the vidyadharas." The Gelug tradition uses the term "guru-yoga," while Sakya lineages present "guru-yoga of three rounds of inspirations." Despite the difference in names and slight variations in mode of practice, in essence they all come to the same intended point of preliminary practice.

## CONFIDENT BELIEF IN THE GURU

The most important point in the practice of guru-yoga is to have respect and confident belief in our guru or spiritual master. As a result of this respectful faith, we receive a steady flow of inspiration from our guru, filling our mind-stream and serving as the basis for gaining insight and realization. At the beginning, do we start our practice of Buddha's teachings simply on the basis of faith alone? Definitely no, we do not. It is not that way at all. Between faith and wisdom, wisdom or discriminating awareness is the more important.

Buddha's scriptural texts stress the four reliances. Concerning a teacher, do not rely simply on the person, but on the Dharma measures he or she imparts. Concerning those measures, do not rely simply on the words, but on their meaning. Concerning that meaning, do not rely simply on the interpretable meaning that leads deeper, but on the definitive meaning to which it leads. For understanding that definitive level of meaning, do not rely on an ordinary consciousness, but on deep awareness. Thus, discriminating deep awareness is extremely important for Buddhist practice. We must examine every point of the Dharma teachings with logic and reason. We only accept what accords with reason and makes sense, and never accept anything that is illogical or makes no sense. Thus reason and understanding are essential.

This is particularly true when it comes to establishing a guru/disciple relationship with a spiritual teacher. We must base our choice of someone as our guru on reasons. We must first thoroughly investigate this teacher on the basis of reason and examine all his or her qualifications. On this basis of discrimination and reason, once we are totally convinced that this person is properly qualified and personally suited for us, then, and only then, do we regard this teacher as our guru. Following this, on the basis of confident belief in our guru's qualifications, we may receive tantric empowerments and guideline instructions from him or her when we are fully prepared and the appropriate opportunity arises. Only then does meditation with absorbed concentration on confidence in the guru lead to stable progress. If we follow the proper procedures in this way for bonding ourselves to a guru who can provide us with inspiration for gaining realization, we are not on shaky grounds.

Thus entering into tantric practice requires a great deal of examination beforehand. This is extremely important. In short, confident belief in a guru — the essential point in meditation on guru-yoga — is one that we develop in conformity with the order of priorities indicated in the four reliances.

## PREMATURE COMMITMENT TO AN UNSUITABLE GURU

In some cases it happens that disciples do not examine a spiritual teacher very carefully before accepting him or her as their guru and committing themselves to a guru/disciple relationship. They may even have received tantric empowerments from this teacher. But then they find they were wrong. They see many flaws in this teacher and discover many serious mistakes he or she has made. They find that this teacher does not really suit them. Their minds are uneasy regarding this person and they are filled with doubts and possibly regret. What to do in such a circumstance?

The mistake, of course, is that originally the disciples did not examine this teacher very carefully before committing themselves to him or her. But this is something of the past that has already happened. No one can change that. In the future, of course, they must examine any potential guru much more thoroughly. But, as for what to do now in this particular situation with this particular guru, it is not productive or helpful to continue investigating and scrutinizing him or her in terms of suspicions or doubts. Rather, as *The Kalachakra Tantra* recommends, it is best to keep a respectful distance. They should just forget about him or her and not have anything further to do with this person.

It is not healthy, of course, for disciples to deny serious ethical flaws in their guru, if they are in fact true, or his or her involvement in Buddhist power-politics, if this is the case. To do so would be a total loss of discriminating awareness. But for disciples to dwell on these points with disrespect, self-recrimination, regret or other negative attitudes is not only unnecessary, unhelpful and unproductive, it is also improper. They distance themselves even further from achieving a peaceful state of mind and may seriously jeopardize their future spiritual progress. I think it best in this circumstance just to forget about this teacher.

## PREMATURE COMMITMENT TO TANTRA AND DAILY RECITATION PRACTICES

It may also occur that disciples have taken tantric empowerments prematurely, thinking that since tantra is famous as being so high, it must be beneficial to take this initiation. They feel they are ready for this step and take the empowerment, thereby committing themselves to the master conferring it as now being their tantric guru. Moreover, they commit themselves as well to various sets of vows and a daily recitation meditation practice. Then later these disciples realize that this style of practice does not suit them at all, and again they are filled with doubts, regrets and possibly fear. Again, what to do?

We can understand this with an analogy. Suppose, for instance, we go to a store, see some useful but exotic item that strikes our fancy and just buy it on impulse, even though it is costly. When we bring it home, we find, after examining the item more soberly now that we are out of the exciting, seductive atmosphere of the marketplace, that we have no particular use for it at the moment. In such situation, it is best not to throw the thing out in the garbage, but rather to put it aside. Later we might find it, in fact, very useful.

The same conclusion applies to the commitments disciples have taken prematurely at a tantric empowerment without sufficient examination to determine if they were ready for them. In such situations, rather than deciding that they are never going to use it at all and throwing the whole thing away, such disciples would do better to establish a neutral attitude toward it, putting tantra and their commitments aside and leaving it like that. This is because they may come back to them later and find them very precious and useful.

Suppose, however, disciples have taken an empowerment and have accepted the commitment to practice the meditations of a particular Buddha-form by reciting a sadhana, a method of actualization, to guide them through a complex sequence of visualization and mantra repetition. Although they still have faith in tantra, they find that their recitation commitment is too long and it has become a great burden and strain to maintain it as a daily practice. What to do then? Such disciples should abbreviate their practice. This is very different from the previous case in which certain disciples find that tantric practice in general does not suit them at the present stage of their spiritual life. Everyone has time each day to eat and to sleep. Likewise, no matter how busy they are, no matter how many family and business responsibilities they may have, such disciples can at least find a few minutes to maintain the daily continuity of generating themselves in their imagination in the aspect of a Buddha-form and reciting the appropriate mantra. They must make some effort. Disciples can never progress anywhere on the spiritual path if they do not make at least a minimal amount of effort.

## VISUALIZING OURSELVES AS A BUDDHA-FORM

If, for whatever reason — lack of time, sickness, travel and so forth — we need to abbreviate our practice, we must be careful not to omit fulfilling the main purpose in tantra of visualizing ourselves in the aspect of a Buddha-form. In general, that purpose is to stop the mind from making things appear in their ordinary fashion and implying that they exist in the ordinary manner in which they appear to exist. The ordinary manner in which our mind makes things appear is as if they existed truly and inherently, findable at the place where they appear to be. Therefore, no matter how abbreviated our practice may be, we visualize ourselves in the aspect of a Buddha-form by first withdrawing the mind from ordinary appearances.

This does not mean that ordinary appearances of true and inherent existence actually exist in the place where they appear to be existing independently of the mind that is fabricating an appearance of them, and that we simply withdraw our attention from them in the manner of becoming inattentive of or ignoring them. Neither does it mean to realize that ordinary appearances of true and inherent existence do not occur or exist at all and to withdraw from them in the manner of denying their conventional existence. Rather, we withdraw our mind from its usual activity of producing these ordinary appearances. We do not literally collect ordinary appearances back into our mind like collecting trash back into a garbage pail from which it has spilled. We stop the mind from its ordinary appearance-making — from its giving rise to an appearance of things as if they existed truly and inherently — by focusing on their voidness, the total absence of their existing in this fantasized, impossible manner.

If, after ascertaining voidness, we were to leave this understanding aside and, forgetting about it, let our mind resume giving rise to an appearance of ourselves as truly and inherently existent, but now in the aspect of a Buddha-form, and let it resume apprehending ourselves to exist in the way we appear to exist, but now in this new shape and form, this would not do. There would have been no purpose in doing the voidness meditation. Rather, having dissolved our ordinary appearance-making and withdrawn our mind into a state of focus on voidness, we try to gain a stable understanding of the voidness of true, inherent existence as deeply as we can. Then, without losing awareness, we have one part of this mind that understands voidness create an appearance of the aspect of a Buddha-form. In this way, the arising of this Buddha-form is the play or emanation of the mind that understands voidness.

Let us explore this process more deeply. Ordinarily, our mind has two levels of appearance-making that occur simultaneously, mixed together like milk and water. One is ordinary, impure appearance-making — the mind's making conventional phenomena appear as if they were truly and inherently existent. This is the work of the contriving mind that mentally fabricates and projects appearances of totally fantasized, impossible modes of existence. The other is pure appearance-making — mind's simply giving rise to an appearance of conventional phenomena as what they are, dependently arising phenomena. When mind is accompanied by unawareness of voidness, it apprehends the impure appearances it makes arise as truly existing in the manner in which they appear to exist.

Although the pure and impure appearances of anything are ordinarily mixed together like milk and water, they are not of the same entity — they do not always come, by nature, in the same package. They can be separated in the sense that when we stop impure appearance-making by removing the instincts of unawareness of voidness that cause our mind to fabricate them, we are left simply with our mind giving rise to conventional phenomena purely in the way that they actually exist. The conventional and deepest levels of truth about all phenomena, on the other hand — their pure or accurate conventional appearance as something that dependently arises and their lack of existing in any fantasized and impossible way — are of the same entity. They always come in the same package in the sense that they are always both valid with respect to everything. They cannot be cognized simultaneously in one moment of mind, however, until we have removed the obstacles preventing this, which again are the instincts of unawareness of voidness. These instincts constitute, then, the obstacles with respect to knowable phenomena. They prevent omniscient awareness.

Just as mind itself has two levels of truth that are both valid about it, it also has two aspects for validly knowing what is true. One aspect is valid for apprehending what is conventionally true, while the other is valid for what is true on the deepest level. Each of these two aspects of mind can only validly cognize its respective level of truth about something specific to its aim. The obstacles preventing omniscience block these two aspects of mind from functioning in the same moment of awareness.

Here, in our practice of tantra, when we stop our mind's ordinary appearance-making, we focus on voidness with that aspect of mind that is valid for apprehending phenomena of the deepest level of truth — namely the voidnesses of all phenomena. On this level, our apprehension of voidness is not with straightforward, non-conceptual perception with which, in addition merely to achieving, we have thoroughly familiarized ourselves over a long course of repeated meditation. Although, because of that, we are unable to have our mind focus directly on both the conventional and ultimate levels of truth in the same moment of awareness and, when our mind gives rise to conventional appearances, stop its impure appearance-making from occurring mixed with its pure appearance-making, nevertheless we try to do both, at least in our imagination. As an aid, we have the aspect of our mind that cognizes conventional phenomena make ourselves appear not in our usual form, but in the form of a Buddha. At the same time, we try to remain aware, at least indirectly, of the voidness of that pure appearance by accompanying our appearance-making mind with the discriminating awareness of all appearances to be like illusion. We refer to this as having the mind that understands voidness give rise to an appearance of a Buddha-form, or appear as a Buddha-form.

## ESTABLISHING THE DIGNITY OF BEING A FORM OF THE BUDDHA

Just as previously we took as a basis for labeling "me" our aggregates appearing in their ordinary fashion, likewise here, once we have gained a certain stability in visualizing the pure appearance of this Buddha-form, we take this appearance as the basis for labeling "me." The mental labeling of "me" on the basis of an appearance of a Buddha-form that our mind creates, accompanied by discriminating awareness of its voidness, is what we call "setting the pride" or "establishing the dignity" of being a form of the Buddha.

This entire procedure of withdrawing the mind from its ordinary appearance-making, focusing on voidness, with that understanding of voidness creating a pure appearance, and taking that pure appearance as the basis for mentally labeling "me" is exactly the same whether we practice tantra as a male or a female. Furthermore, as the mind realizing voidness understands that all appearances, whether ordinary or pure, are equally devoid of existing truly and inherently as male or female, the gender of the practitioner doing the visualization and the gender of the Buddha-form visualized make no difference on the deepest level. Therefore, both male and female practitioners of tantra can visualize the appearance of either a male or female Buddha-form and equally take either as the basis for labeling "me." Visualizing ourselves in this manner, while reciting the appropriate mantras, then, are the main points on which to focus in our tantric practice no matter how much we abbreviate it.

## SIX-SESSION GURU-YOGA

Furthermore, if we have received an empowerment into the anuttara-yoga class of tantra within the Gelug tradition, it will not do to break the continuity of our daily recitation and practice of the six-session guru-yoga, at least in its abbreviated form, three times during the day and three times at night. Regardless of what might happen to us, we must at least remember to do this each day and night. This is extremely important.

Just as the alarm on our wristwatch can remind us of our important appointments during the day, Buddha Vajradhara himself has designed the six-session guru-yoga to remind us each day and night of the essential practices that will bring us to our goal of enlightenment — the practices of bodhichitta, meditation on voidness and the nineteen practices that bond us closely to the five Buddha-family traits. Therefore, even though we might not be able to practice many sessions each day and night of single-pointed meditation, focusing on ourselves in the aspect of a Buddha-form so as to gain shamata, we must at least maintain this six-session practice so that slowly our mind progresses toward our goals in that direction.

# Session Three

## DIFFERENT PRESENTATIONS OF THE FOUR TYPES OF SEALS

The text continues now with the next point in the outline, the actual techniques of mahamudra. Although mahamudra practice can be explained in many ways, this text divides it into two: the sutra and tantra levels of mahamudra techniques. As subdivisions within these two, Drigungpa Jigten-gönpo, the founder of the Drigung Kagyü tradition, elaborating on the intentions of Drogön Rinpochey, has explained four types of mudras or seals with respect to each of the three vehicles. This refers to the hinayana vehicle of the shravakas, the mahayana vehicle of the bodhisattvas and the tantrayana vehicle of hidden measures. Let me read his words, filling in here and there what needs to be expanded in order to be clear.

In the context of the shravakas' mode of practice, never separating the actions of their body, speech and mind from the behavior shaped by the vinaya rules of ethical discipline is karmamudra, the seal of their behavior. The realization of the lack of any true, unimputed identity of a person, specifically the total absence or voidness of a person existing as a substantial entity able to stand on its own — the coarse identitylessness of a person according to the prasangika-madhyamaka presentation — is dharmamudra, the seal of their preventive measures. The state of separation from disturbing emotions and attitudes, on the basis of the abiding nature of purity, attained through meditation on the identitylessness of a person is samayamudra, the seal of their close bond. The nirvana or total release to which they attain without any remainder of aggregates is mahamudra, their great seal.

As for the four seals presented in terms of the bodhisattvas' practices, never separating the actions of their body, speech and mind from behavior based on practice of the six far-reaching attitudes is the seal of their behavior. Based on their practice of the six far-reaching attitudes in general, and particularly of the joint path of shamata yoked with vipashyana, their meditation on voidness, free from all mental fabrication, seeing that all phenomena appear but without true, inherent existence, like illusion, is the seal of their preventive measures. Through the ethical self-discipline of a bodhisattva, restraining themselves from all selfish thought or action so that they are never tainted by any stain of working for their own purposes is the seal of their close bond. As they follow a path that has as its essence the combination of compassion and the understanding of voidness, on which they have practiced method and discriminating awareness without one having ever been missing, but rather with method always apprehended within the context of wisdom and wisdom within the context of method, their single taste of compassion and voidness is their great seal. Since the great seal of the listeners' mode of practice refers to the resultant state they attain, the great seal of the bodhisattvas' practice undoubtedly refers to their resultant state as well. At that point, their ultimate combined vision of both the full extent of what exists and how it all exists, being of a single taste of compassion and wisdom, totally pacifies the extreme of remaining passively in a nirvanic state of total release from all suffering.

As for the four seals formulated in terms of tantra, specifically its anuttarayoga class in general, tantric practitioners' relying on a transferring partner, or "messenger" — someone to help them transfer themselves to higher states of insight and realization — as an external method to bring life-force to their practice is the seal of their behavior. By relying on external and internal methods, joining their mind and energy-winds together at the center of their chakras — primarily, their heart chakra — without ever separating the two, is the seal of their preventive measures. Never letting the vows and close bonds that they receive at empowerments degenerate is the seal of their close bond. Taking as foundation their keeping of all their vows and close bonds and then, by relying on external and internal methods such as gathering their mind and energy-winds at the center of their heart chakra, manifesting the deep awareness that is a discrimination of voidness arising inseparably from being a blissful awareness, in other words manifesting simultaneously arising deep awareness, is their great seal.

Drigungpa has also explained the four seals in the exclusive context of practitioners of anuttarayoga tantra's complete stage. Their many pathways of practice, such as of the oral instructions for developing tummo, the inner flame, and likewise the physical exercises explained in the six practices or "yogas" of Naropa, the various branches of energy-wind practice such as holding the vase-breath, vajra-recitation and so forth, are the seal of their behavior. By relying on these types of method, the deep awareness that arises as a blissful consciousness is the seal of their preventive measures. At the time when they manifest a simultaneously arising blissful awareness, their lack of attachment to it is the seal of their close bond. In other words, the root of attachment is apprehending things as existing truly and inherently. The opponent for such apprehension is the discriminating awareness of the lack of true, inherent identities. Thus generating a greatly blissful deep awareness and a discriminating awareness of voidness running together as one, without either of them ever quitting, is, more specifically, the seal of their close bond. Having familiarized themselves with this deep awareness that is also a blissful awareness and a discrimination of voidness, then when, without having to rely on any other external or internal circumstances, their merely focusing on voidness as an object induces by itself a greatly blissful deep awareness, its spontaneous arising is their great seal.

These then are the various presentations of the four seals gathered together by Drigungpa based on the intentions of Drogön Rinpochey. In addition, our text mentions that the great translator Gö Lotsawa Zhönnupel, a contemporary of Drigungpa's teacher Pagmo-drupa, had taken mahamudra, the great seal, to be the non-conceptual deep awareness that realizes voidness.

## PENETRATING VITAL POINTS OF THE VAJRA-BODY

In general, however, we can classify all mahamudra practices into either the sutra or tantra categories. Concerning the tantra tradition of mahamudra, the First Panchen Lama states in the root text, that it entails "a greatly blissful clear light mind that has been brought about by such skillful methods as penetrating vital points of the subtle vajra-body and so forth."

As human beings of this world, we have a coarse body made of six constituent elements of earth, water, fire, wind, space and consciousness, and a subtle vajra-body of energy-winds, energy-channels and energy-drops. Consequently, through various methods, such as penetrating vital points of the subtle vajra-body and so forth, we can manifest the subtlest clear light mind and generate it into a deep awareness that is simultaneously a blissful awareness and a non-conceptual discriminating awareness of voidness. The techniques that involve penetrating these vital points succeed in making subtlest clear light manifest by stopping the coarser levels of mind. To stop those levels of mind, we must stop the energy-winds upon which they ride from coursing wildly through the energy-channels. We must cause those energy-winds to enter and abide in the central energy-channel, and dissolve there either at the center of the heart chakra, according to the new translation anuttarayoga tantras other than Kalachakra, or at the center of all six major chakras, according to the Kalachakra system.

The vital points of the subtle vajra-body are those points at either the top or bottom end of the central energy-channel at which the energy-winds can be made to enter that channel, or the center of the various chakras where the energy-winds can be made to dissolve. To penetrate these points means to gather there the energy-winds and the subtle minds that ride on them, basically by means of different types of absorbed concentration focused on these spots. Such practices as Guhyasamaja, Chakrasamvara, Hevajra and, within the body of Kalachakra teachings, Vajravega, provide various methods for penetrating these vital points, such as causing tummo to flare, joining the energy-winds together at the upper or lower gateway to the central energy-channel, holding to the non-dissipating energy-drop at the center of the heart chakra, and so forth. For example, in *A Lamp for Further Clarifying the Five Stages [of Guhyasamaja]*, a commentary on Tsongkapa's *The Pure Stages of the Yoga of Guhyasamaja*, in the discussion of the level of practicing with elaboration at which we take the supreme mind of death as a pathway for actualizing the bodies of a Buddha, Kaydrub Norzang-gyatso has mentioned two methods for manifesting clear light mind through stages similar to what happens at the time of death. These are penetrating vital points of the vajra-body through focusing there either energy-winds or blissful states of awareness.

The subtle vajra-body in all people, whether male or female, is exactly the same. Thus there is no difference in technique between a man or a woman penetrating vital points of the vajra-body, and no difference in the primordial clear light mind that he or she manifests. On the basis of this lack of gender difference, anuttarayoga tantra asserts the attainment of enlightenment on the foundation of either a male or female body, whereas sutra and the three lower classes of tantra assert that we can only attain enlightenment or liberation as an arhat during rebirth as a human male.

In the auto-commentary, the First Panchen Lama goes on to explain the expression, "and so forth," in the above-quoted line from his root text. It refers to the fact that there are other methods as well for manifesting clear light mind. Those who practice the Nyingma system of meditation, for example, do not rely on actions for penetrating vital points of the vajra-body. They follow, instead, a guideline instruction for manifesting clear light mind by relying solely on meditation on a non-conceptual state. Thus, making manifest simultaneously arising greatly blissful clear light mind of deep awareness, either by relying on methods for penetrating vital points of the vajra-body or, for those of especially sharp faculties, by not having to do so, is the tantra tradition of mahamudra as explained in the texts of Saraha, Nagarjuna, Naropa and Maitripa.

## THOSE WHO PROGRESS THROUGH GRADED STAGES AND THOSE FOR WHOM EVERYTHING HAPPENS AT ONCE

The Kagyü system refers to those who manifest clear light mind by relying on the methods for penetrating vital points of the external and internal body as those who progress through graded stages of methods. Such practitioners manifest clear light mind by progressing through stages. Those with sharp faculties, however, may be practitioners for whom everything happens at once. The Nyingma tradition of dzogchen also distinguishes between these two types of practitioners. Those who manifest *rigpa*, pure awareness, by training through stages involving various practices with the energy-winds, tummo, and so forth are those who progress through graded stages, while those for whom everything happens at once achieve the same by relying solely on meditation on a non-conceptual state of mental consciousness without the practices of the energy-channels and energy-winds.

According to Maitreya's *A Filigree of Clear Realizations*, there are five pathway minds that we progressively develop during the course of attaining enlightenment — accumulating, applying, seeing and accustoming pathways of mind and, finally, such a mind needing no further training. These are often translated as the "paths of accumulation, preparation, seeing, meditation and no more learning." Practicing as a bodhisattva, we achieve an accumulating pathway of mind when we have bodhichitta as our motivation day and night. With an accumulating mind, we build up and add shamata and vipashyana to this bodhichitta foundation. When we have accomplished that, we have an applying pathway of mind we can effectively apply to removing the obstacles preventing our liberation — namely our disturbing emotions and attitudes, and particularly our unawareness of voidness, together with its seeds. When we gain straightforward, nonconceptual realization of voidness with our mind that already has bodhichitta, shamata and vipashyana, we achieve a seeing pathway of mind and become an arya.

Disturbing emotions and attitudes, including unawareness, have two levels — one based on preconceptions from an ideology and the other that automatically arises, even in animals. If, with sutra methods, we make our subtle — not subtlest — mental consciousness into a seeing pathway of mind, we find that its non-conceptual seeing of voidness rids our mind of disturbing emotions and attitudes based on preconception. Once we have accomplished this, we achieve an accustoming pathway of mind free from these obstacles, with which we now accustom ourselves to seeing voidness. In this way, we gradually rid our mind of its more subtle obstacles.

There are ten *bhumi* or bodhisattva levels of mind, with the first corresponding to a seeing pathway of mind and the other nine to graded levels of an accustoming mind. When we achieve these levels of mind with subtle mental consciousness on the sutra path, we remove the automatically arising disturbing attitudes and emotions, together with their seeds, in stages as we progressively attain the first seven bodhisattva minds. These are the seven impure levels, since they are not yet fully purified of all the obstacles preventing liberation. The last three levels are purified of them, and as we progressively attain them, we remove the obstacles preventing omniscient awareness. These obstacles are the instincts of unawareness, which cause our mind to give rise to discordant appearances and prevent it from cognizing the two levels of truth about anything simultaneously. When we rid our mind of this subtlest level of obstacles, our mind becomes an omniscient awareness. We become a Buddha, with a pathway of mind needing no further training.

According to Tsongkapa's *A Grand Presentation of the Graded Stages of the Secret Mantra Path*, if we progressively develop these pathway minds through the practice of anuttarayoga tantra, we achieve a seeing mind with primordial, subtlest clear light mind that is inseparably a blissful awareness and a non-conceptual deep awareness of voidness. Because of the special features of such an intense, subtle mind, we rid ourselves at that point of all obstacles preventing liberation — both the preconceptual ones based on ideology and those that automatically arise. With an accustoming pathway of mind, we work exclusively on removing the obstacles preventing omniscience as we progressively attain the various bodhisattva levels of mind. This is the mode of practice of those who progress through stages. For those for whom everything happens at once, straightforward non-conceptual realization of voidness with clear light mind, as a seeing pathway of mind, removes all obstacles at once — both those preventing liberation and those preventing omniscience. As Indrabhuti has said, "Realization and liberation [with enlightenment] come simultaneously."

According to one Kagyü text, the method of practice of those for whom everything happens at once is powerful medicine. But it is deadly poison for those who progress through graded stages. In other words, the method of meditating solely on the non-conceptual state of the mind is suited only for those of sharpest faculties. For those who are not of their level, such practice brings only harm, no benefit. For them the medicine acts like a poison.

Kaydrub Norzang-gyatso, in *A Lamp for Clarifying Mahamudra to Establish the Single Intention of the Kagyü and Gelug Traditions*, has explained that those for whom everything happens at once are persons who have trained extensively through stages either in previous lives or earlier in this life. As a result, meditation on the non-conceptual state of the mind, without need to rely on any further meditation on penetrating vital points of the vajra-body, alone causes clear light mind to manifest so that everything happens at once. Such meditation does this by acting as a circumstance for triggering the ripening of potentials built up from previous practice with energy-winds and so forth, so that they automatically enter, abide and dissolve in the central energy-channel. If a practitioner has not built up these potentials, then no matter how intensively he or she may focus in a non-conceptual state of mind, clear light mind or pure awareness will not manifest. The practitioner lacks sufficient causes.

Before Milarepa studied with the great translator Marpa, he studied with a master of the dzogchen tradition. This lama told him of the guideline instruction that without need to study, meditate or even do any practice, one can instantly become a Buddha. When Milarepa heard this, he just lay down and went to sleep, thinking, "Wonderful, now I do not have to do any practice any more!" He did not even have a good dream. When he awoke in the morning, this master scolded him for his pretension and laziness. He told him these instructions certainly did not pertain to him and that, in fact, his mental obstacles were so thick he could not help tame him any further. He mentioned that there was, however, another guru, a translator who had studied and trained in India with the great master Naropa, who could be of great help.

At merely hearing the name of the great translator Marpa, Milarepa developed extraordinary faith and respect in him, convinced that he was the appropriate guru for him. When he went to study with the translator, however, Marpa gave him a very hard time, didn't he? Milarepa had to endure tremendous difficulties and make incredible efforts to practice in stages over many years. But, as a result of his efforts, he was able to reach total enlightenment in this graded manner. Therefore, we should not imagine that practitioners who progress through stages are stupid or inferior, or that they do not attain the same result as those for whom everything happens at once. Also, we should not be pretentious and think we are more advanced and well prepared than in fact we are.

## DZOGCHEN IN COMPARISON TO MAHAMUDRA

Although both the Kagyü tradition of mahamudra and the Nyingma tradition of dzogchen present methods of practice for those who progress through stages and those for whom everything happens at once, there are subtle differences in their styles of practice. Although these differences are difficult to appreciate and understand without personal experience, let us look briefly at some of them and compare them both to the Gelug/Kagyü tradition of mahamudra, which transmits only a path for those who progress through stages.

The main point in the Gelug/Kagyü tradition of mahamudra is meditation on voidness as the object clear light — in other words, as an object realized by primordial clear light mind. In the purely Kagyü tradition of mahamudra, the main emphasis is, on the other hand, meditation on clear light mind itself. Unlike either of these two mahamudra traditions, however, dzogchen asserts that all impure and pure phenomena — in other words, all phenomena of samsara and nirvana — have a foundation for their being a phenomenon, in the sense of a foundation for their appearing. This is the creator of all samsara or nirvana in the sense of being the foundation for the arising and disappearing of all impure or pure appearances and all impure or pure appearance-making minds. Dzogchen meditation focuses on this foundation.

The dzogchen teachings differentiate two types of *alaya*, or all-encompassing foundations — one that is primordially there from the depths and one that is for various instincts or propensities of karma. The former is the foundation for all impure and pure appearances — the foundation for the appearance-making of all impure and pure phenomena. As the root of all samsara and nirvana is like a foundation, then all conventional phenomena of samsara and nirvana — everything that emanates, in the context of cognition, as conventional phenomena — arise out of and pass into this sphere. That being the case, we must come to know this point which is the ultimate, final way in which things exist, the foundational situation, the way in which everything abides. This is because when we do not recognize the alaya that is primordially there from the depths, that alaya functions as a foundation for the instincts of karma that bring us all our problems.

Once we have come to know the way in which this ultimate point functions, we need to focus single-mindedly on this point. We need to see the correct view of reality single-pointedly with it and hold to that view with mindfulness. This mindfulness is not the intermittent one that we ordinarily employ on coarser levels of mind and which can be lost due to flightiness or dullness, but rather is a special, uncommon type of mindfulness that arises spontaneously and is simultaneous with this foundational level. We meditate, holding to this point and this view with this special mindfulness. When all our actions are held by the force of this type of meditation and view, then everything we do, whether conventionally good or bad, arises without any action being better or worse than any other.

The dzogchen tradition differentiates between *sem* or limited awareness, and *rigpa* or pure awareness. Limited awareness is the level of mind that is fleeting. Adulterated with conceptual thinking, it contrives and mentally fabricates totally fantasized and impossible manners of existence. A sentient being is, literally, an animate being with such type of limited awareness. Because of this, a Buddha is not a sentient being. Pure awareness, on the other hand, is the level of mind that has been there forever, with no beginning, primordially pure from its depths, unadulterated by any stains. The Kalachakra system calls it the holder of the diamond-strong scepter of space, pervasive with space, or simply the diamond-strong scepter of mind.

We must come to recognize this pure awareness. When we recognize and know it through seeing and experiencing its nature, we can cultivate this pure awareness that is far removed from all variety of minds that contrive and mentally fabricate. Then, it is explained, we come figuratively to that which abides with great spaciousness.

This is slightly different, then, from the mahamudra systems, which have no equivalent to this differentiation of limited awareness and, as its underlying foundation, pure awareness. If we speak from the point of view of dzogchen, when we have divided our pure awareness from our limited awareness, seeing them as two distinct levels of mind, and have compared that level of mind to which we have come in meditation with those states of mind that are adulterated by conceptual thinking and that contrive and mentally fabricate, we clearly see that the latter is far inferior to the former. The profundity and extensiveness of the dzogchen system derives from this point.

On the basis of having recognized pure awareness like this, we then cultivate the ultimate of correct views with respect to the nature of all phenomena that exist and which mind can thus produce an appearance of that emanates out of and dissolves back into pure awareness. We do this by gaining, through meditative experience, a decisive understanding of pure awareness itself being primally pure of concrete reality — in other words, its being devoid of an inherent, findable nature. We must fully experience and thus know the meaning of being primally pure and then, on that basis, proceed with meditation on the meaning of spontaneous establishment.

In dzogchen we speak, on the one hand, of pure awareness being primally pure of concrete reality. Equivalent expressions for this in the madhyamaka system are that all phenomena are totally devoid of fantasized and impossible ways of existing, such as true inherent existence or existing as concrete reality. Primordially and from their depths, all phenomena are totally devoid of an inherently findable nature that can establish them as being something concrete and real. In dzogchen, we say that the clear light diamond-strong scepter of mind — which is like a foundation for everything that exists, impure and pure, which can thus appear — is primally pure of concrete reality.

In dzogchen, we also speak, on the other hand, of pure awareness by nature spontaneously establishing everything. This means that all phenomena abide as the play of this deep awareness in the sense that all appearances of phenomena are its effulgence. Pure awareness, by nature, spontaneously establishes the existence of all phenomena in that all appearances mind produces of what exists are its effulgent play. Seeing this point is extraordinarily profound for bringing us even more conviction in the fact that all phenomena can only be established simply as what their names refer to.

This is very significant because there are certain persons who are unable to gain a decisive understanding of the prasangika-madhyamaka view of reality based on reasoning alone. When such persons, however, experience in meditational practice the manifestation of primordial clear light mind — by either penetrating vital points of their vajra-body or other means — they are able to understand, based on personal meditative experience of clear light mind, that the existence of things can only be established dependently upon names. In this way, they come to a decisive and correct understanding of the prasangika-madhyamaka view of reality.

In the Gelug/Kagyü style of tantra level mahamudra meditation, as we advance in our practice, we achieve a unification of bliss and voidness, which is not merely a mind with conviction in the voidness of mind, but has a special feature from the point of view of the mind that has this conviction — that mind is a clear light mind generated simultaneously as a blissful awareness. Thus the unification of bliss and voidness is a clear light mind having the special feature of being a blissful awareness that understands voidness. When, through mahamudra meditation, we realize the unification of appearance and voidness in terms of our conviction in this subtlest primordial mind's lack of an inherently findable nature, we come, I believe, to the same essential point at which we arrive through dzogchen meditation.

Some of the most difficult points in dzogchen that make it so profound and extensive are its methods for recognizing and experiencing clear light mind, which has as its nature mere clarity and awareness. We do this without need to block and dissolve the cognitions of the six collections of coarse levels of consciousness — visual, auditory, olfactory, gustatory, tactile or bodily, and mental. In the mahamudra presentation of the path for practitioners who progress in stages, we must block and dissolve these coarser levels of mind in order to make manifest subtlest clear light mind.

## THE COARSE AND SUBTLE PRIMORDIAL MINDS

The anuttarayoga tantra systems of Kalachakra and Guhyasamaja, taken in general, have a way of explaining how clear light mind arises that differs slightly from that found in dzogchen. One of Aku Sherab-gyatso's teachers, Gyelrong Tsültrim-nyima, in *A Last Testament Letter Cast to the Wind*, a commentary on the First Panchen Lama's mahamudra text, has differentiated between coarse and subtle primordial minds. When we consider that our coarse levels of mind are fleeting, we cannot possibly call them primordial. In general, "primordial" signifies something that has never been and can never be fleetingly contaminated due to causes and circumstances. Normally, we refer to primordial mind as the clear light mind that arises after the unconscious, most subtle conceptual appearance-making minds of appearance-congealment, light-diffusion and threshold have ceased. Therefore, the word "coarse" in the term "coarse primordial mind" cannot refer to fleeting levels of mind such as clear light mind when it is together with these three subtlest conceptual appearance-making minds, since primordial and that sense of coarse are mutually exclusive.

Gyelrong Tsültrim-nyima has explained coarse and subtle primordial minds in the context of the mahamudra system. According to his presentation, the unique feature of mahamudra is its use of a decisive understanding of the devoid nature of coarse primordial mind as a special, uncommon aid for manifesting subtle primordial mind. This gives much to think about in terms of the First Panchen Lama's presentation of the mahamudra technique of recognizing first the conventional nature of clear light primordial mind as its mere clarity and awareness — which is undoubtedly coarse primordial mind — and then coming to recognize the deepest nature of that clear light mind — its voidness of existing in any fantasized and impossible ways. For example, seeing that the conventional nature of mere clarity and awareness applies to all states of mind, like the nature of water remaining the same in both murky and pure bodies of water, helps us to see that voidness as the deepest nature is also the case with respect to all states of mind. This also gives us much to think about in terms of the differentiation made in dzogchen between effulgent pure awareness and foundational pure awareness, and the dzogchen technique of first recognizing the former in order to recognize the latter.

## THE DZOGCHEN TRADITION IN BÖN

The dzogchen tradition is found not only in the Nyingma tradition of Tibetan Buddhism, but also in the Bön tradition as well. These two lineages of dzogchen are extremely similar. Bön is the ancient religion of Tibet, present there before the spread of Buddhism. However, it is not clear how widespread it was in ancient times and whether, before the advent of Buddhism, it had a full system of a view of reality, meditation and modes of behavior. But after the coming of Buddhism to Tibet, the Bön tradition became more extensive. For example, Bön has equivalents not only of dzogchen but also of the Buddhist *Kagyur* canon, including hundred-thousand-stanza and eight-thousand-stanza Prajnaparamita sutras. There are also Bön equivalents of *pramana*, or valid cognition, with full systems of epistemology, logic and debate, as well as of madhyamaka, the middle way view of voidness.

The question arises, Was Buddhism modeled on Bön, or Bön on Buddhism? Buddhism flourished in India for over a thousand years before it came to Tibet, and its scriptures were translated from Indian languages into Tibetan. Since we can certainly say with decisiveness that Buddhism in India was not modeled on Bön, we can say with equal decisiveness that the features of Bön in Tibet that are similar to those found in Buddhism were modeled on Buddhism. But, if we look from the point of view of the original stock of teachings that are at its core, we have to say that Bön is a separate tradition from Buddhism. We can not consider it one of the Buddhist traditions since then it would need a traceable Buddhist source. Nevertheless, externally it transmits many practices that are modeled after Buddhist ones. Since these practices contain mixed with them ultimate guidelines concerning the correct view of reality, anyone properly practicing them is doing what I think amounts to Buddhist practice, whether or not they call it that.

For example, if we look at the Bön tradition of dzogchen, it has many similarities with the Nyingma presentation. But, for the same reasons as above, we cannot say that the Buddhist tradition of dzogchen is modeled on the Bön tradition. The Nyingma tradition of tantra flourished in Tibet for a long time before the new translation period began and, during that old translation period, the Bön and Buddhist traditions had intimate contact. During that period, then, Bön undoubtedly adopted many dzogchen techniques from Nyingma Buddhist tantra. After all, it was during this time that Bön adopted the Nyingma classification system of nine vehicles to structure its own teachings into nine vehicles.

Concerning Bön dzogchen, the terminology is different from that used in Nyingma dzogchen, but the meaning of its terms undoubtedly follows the Nyingma guideline instructions they borrowed. Thus in general, Bön is not a Buddhist system, but regarding specific practices, some seem to be Buddhist, while others seem not. Moreover, there are some Buddhist practitioners who perform certain ceremonies according to Bön ritual procedures, for example propitiating local deities, extending life span and so on, and there is nothing inappropriate with that. Thus both the Tibetan Buddhist and the Bön traditions contain practices that originated in the other.

## SUMMARY OF THE ANUTTARAYOGA TANTRA TRADITION OF MAHAMUDRA

Our text now continues with a summary of the anuttarayoga tantra approach to mahamudra from the new translation period. "First, we receive the four empowerments purely and keep all the vows and close bonds with the practice in the proper manner. Then, when our familiarity with the generation stage has stabilized, we use various external and internal methods to penetrate vital points of the vajra-body and so on, causing all energy-winds to enter, abide and dissolve in the central energy-channel. With the deep awareness that is a greatly blissful, simultaneously arising awareness that comes from this" — namely, that arises after the dissolution of the three unconscious, most subtle conceptual appearance-making minds — "we first gain a conceptual understanding of voidness through an accurate idea of it based on its meaning. This is known as the illustrative or approximating clear light. When this deep awareness has straightforward, non-conceptual perception of voidness, it is the actual or ultimate clear light. The illustrative and actual clear light states of deep awareness are the great seal of mahamudra.

"Different traditions use different technical terms to refer to the mind that has become of the nature of these two levels of clear light, for instance the definitive level short syllable 'A,' the non-dissipating drop, non-contriving mind, the normative way to be aware, primordial mind and so on." We can include here, from yet other great texts, terms such as "the diamond-strong scepter of mind" and "the holder of the diamond-strong scepter of space, pervasive with space," and so on.

"Many great masters of India, such as Mahasukha — also known as Padmavajra — and likewise Saraha, Nagarjuna, Shabari, Tilopa, Naropa, Maitripa and others, as well as numerous great Kagyü masters of old, such as Marpa, Milarepa, Gampopa, Pagmo-drupa and so forth, have all concurred that the ultimate mahamudra is the greatly blissful clear light mind manifested after causing the energy-winds to enter, abide and dissolve in the central energy-channel"— and dissolving there as well the three unconscious, most subtle conceptual appearance-making minds.

## THE APPROPRIATENESS OF THIS SYSTEM OF MAHAMUDRA BEING CALLED "GELUG/KAGYÜ"

It is clear from the above lines from his auto-commentary that when the First Panchen Lama discusses the Gelug/Kagyü tradition of mahamudra, he is referring to a tradition that takes as its basis the oral guidelines of the great Kagyü masters of the past and supplements it with the profound techniques for gaining a decisive understanding of voidness that Tsongkapa has uniquely presented in his great texts concerning the madhyamaka view. Thus this tradition seems, I believe, to be a synthesis of Kagyü and Gelug approaches. Although at various points in his auto-commentary, the Panchen Lama quotes several texts from the Sakya tradition, he specifically mentions here a list of Kagyü masters of old, not Sakya ones, who have concurred on this anuttarayoga tantra level of mahamudra. Furthermore, the Sakya tradition asserts only a tantra level of mahamudra, whereas both the Kagyü and the Gelug/Kagyü traditions assert both sutra and tantra levels. Therefore I think that the First Panchen Lama had something specific in mind when he used the term "Gelug/Kagyü tradition of mahamudra."

We find evidence for Tsongkapa himself being the source of this Gelug/Kagyü synthesis in Gungtangzang's *Notes from a Discourse on the Gelug Tradition of Mahamudra* and Aku Sherab-gyatso's two *Notes from a Discourse on "A Ritual to Honor the Spiritual Master" Interspersed with Mahamudra*. Gungtangzang's notes were based on a discourse by his teacher Yongdzin Yeshey-gyeltsen, a disciple of the Third Panchen Lama and the first to comment on the First Panchen Lama's mahamudra texts in conjunction with *A Ritual to Honor the Spiritual Master*. Aku Sherab-gyatso's two works are notes on discourses by two more of his teachers, Detri Jamyang-tubten-nyima and Welmang Könchog-gyeltsen, both of whom were disciples of Gungtangzang. All these masters have concurred that Tsongkapa had given a restricted discourse on mahamudra to Gungru Gyeltsen-zangpo and some others at Gaden Jangtsey Monastery. This is only reasonable since Tsongkapa himself had received numerous mahamudra teachings, for example from Lama Umapa, one of his Karma Kagyü teachers, following the tradition of the latter's Drugpa Kagyü master Barawa Gyeltsen-zangpo, disciple of the Third Karmapa, Rangjung-dorjey. Yongdzin Yeshey-gyeltsen had mentioned, as recorded by Gungtangzang, that Tsongkapa had told another of his teachers, Rendawa, that he had an uncommon guideline teaching based on the mahamudra explanations of maha-madhyamaka, or great madhyamaka, but it was not yet time to progagate them widely. Furthermore, another of Tsongkapa's disciples, Kaydrubjey, has written that the explanation of voidness, the non-affirming nullification that refutes what is to be refuted, that is found in some of Gungru Gyeltsen-zangpo's writings, is not Tsongkapa's manner of explanation, but is merely Gungru Gyeltsen-zangpo's own style of explication. I think Kaydrubjey's point is relevant and adds further evidence supporting our conclusion.

Likewise, the Second Changkya, Rölpay-dorjey, the teacher of most of Gungtangzang's teachers, has written, in the collection of his *Answers to Questions*, that a geshey from Mongolia or Amdo, I don't remember which, had reported to him that these days there was a lineage called the Gelug tradition of mahamudra that transmitted an uncommon presentation of a correct view of reality that was slightly different from Tsongkapa's usual manner of explication. He wanted to know whether or not this was something important. Changkya Rölpay-dorjey answered that this was in fact Tsongkapa's special way of explaining the correct view that was different from his usual manner.

We have further evidence for this from an incident in the life of the Second Chankya's first teacher, the omniscient First Jamyang-zheypa, Ngawang-tsöndrü, a great being beyond imagination, who expanded on the meanings of all eighteen volumes of Tsongkapa's works in an immaculate manner. He, the Mongolian Lama Mergen Lozang-tsültrim, and the First Changkya, Ngawang-chöden, had heard of a special near lineage of the Say and Ensa oral lineages of Tsongkapa's guideline instructions that existed to the west of where they were living in Amdo. They thought that they must take interest in this special near lineage and go to receive it. They then added it to the rest of their lineages of Tsongkapa that they held.

Previously, they had felt that whatever guideline instructions there were in the Ensa oral lineage — deriving from Ensapa, the teacher of the First Panchen Lama's root guru, Sanggyay-yeshey — had all been transmitted from the First Panchen Lama to his disciple Dorjey-dzinpa Könchog-gyeltsen and were to be heard from him, and that the complete Say lineage — deriving from the founder of Gyümay (Lower Tantric College), Sherab-senggey, a disciple of Tsongkapa — were to be heard from Saygyü Könchog-yarpel. The first Changkya and the others had received these two lineages from these two teachers and had previously combined them.

The First Jamyang-zhepa, for example, had gone to Saygyü Könchog-yarpel and requested the empowerments and discourses of Guhyasamaja, Chakrasamvara and Vajrabhairava. When he was told he could not receive all three, only one, he requested Guhyasamaja. Saygyü Könchog-yarpel was very pleased and transmitted to him everything. There is an account of this. In such ways as this, these great masters received the guideline teachings of the Ensa and Say lineages of Tsongkapa from Dorjey-dzinpa Könchog-gyeltsen and Saygyü Könchog-yarpel, and then combined their points.

Yet despite there already being a tradition of explanation according to the Say lineage, the omniscient First Jamyang-zheypa composed *An Interlinear Commentary on "A Ritual to Honor the Spiritual Master"* — starting from "Within a state of inseparable bliss and voidness..." — to transmit an explanation based on the discourse he had heard on the extra teachings he had added to the previously combined lineage. He himself was extremely learned and accomplished in the Guhyasamaja system. There was not much concerning tantra in general that he left unexplained in his writings. He was extremely erudite and vastly skilled in all aspects of sutra, tantra and the various fields of knowledge. He was able to explain all the contents of tantra within the context of the points of the Guhyasamaja path, and he based his word-for-word commentary on *A Ritual to Honor the Spiritual Master* on Guhyasamaja. Yet, he did not base this commentary on the discourses he had heard of the familiar lineage of the text, but on the special unfamiliar one he had received. This is very clear. I find that quite remarkable and noteworthy, and have often wondered why.

The lineage of his discourse tradition continued in eastern Tibet to the next generation of great masters: the Second Jamyang-zheypa Könchog-jigmey-wangpo, the Third Panchen Lama Pelden-yeshey and Purchog Ngawang-jampa — fully qualified upholders of the teachings, the cream of the Gelug scholar/practitioners. I think this lineage, then, is one that has many special and important features. The great Fifth Dalai Lama, however, the main disciple of the First Panchen Lama, had stated that it was not necessary to add the word "Kagyü" to the name of this lineage and that it was sufficient to call it merely the "Gelug tradition of mahamudra." Among others, the Third Panchen Lama's disciple Yongdzin Yeshey-gyeltsen and his disciple Gungtangzang, followed his advice in the titles of their commentaries on the subject. The Fifth Dalai Lama was not just giving this tradition this title for no reason at all. He must have had some important reason in mind. To say that it is totally within the sphere of Gelug and there-fore there is no need to also say it is a Gelug/Kagyü hybrid still leaves the question unsettled of why the First Panchen Lama gave it the title he did.

When I look at it, it seems as though this tradition has as its foun-dation the presentation of mahamudra according to the manner of explanation of the Kagyü masters of old. It then adds, on top of that, Tsongkapa's manner of explanation of the madhyamaka texts of Nagarjuna and his spiritual sons, as found in *An Ocean of Reason [Commentary on Nagarjuna's "Root Stanzas on the Middle Way"]* and *Totally Clarifying the Intentions [of Chandrakirti's "Supplement to (Nagarjuna's 'Root Stanzas on) the Middle Way'"]* and reflected in his disciple Gyeltsabjey's *The Heart of Excellent Explanation [Commentary on Aryadeva's "Four Hundred Stanzas"]*. Tsongkapa never left any texts, especially on the madhyamaka view, with even a single syllable that he did not fully understand. He took special interest in the most diffi-cult points that the previous learned scholars had not taken interest to explain, whether because they did not know what they meant or had not fully realized them, or for whatever reason they might have had. Relying on the Buddha-form Manjushri, he explained each and every word and line.

No one else had ever done what Tsongkapa did. These are not words of sectarianism, but are the fact. The special, unique talent of Tsongkapa was his ability to explain every word and line of the most difficult sections of the texts in a totally clear and decisive manner. If we com-pare the collected works of Tsongkapa with those of some of his pre-decessors, for example the great Sakya encyclopedist Bodong Choglay-namgyel, the works of the latter were certainly more extensive. He knew and explained each and every text there was on each and every topic. But except for mostly giving a general overview and collecting and abbreviating the major issues, he rarely explained the difficult points concerning each word and line by presenting all the previous interpretations, giving the logical objections to them and, through a process of reason, coming to a decisive conclusion about their mean-ing. Although Tsongkapa's works cannot compare with Bodong Choglay-namgyel's in extensiveness and breadth, he treated all the difficult points that the latter glossed over.

Let me cite the example of another encyclopedist, the omniscient Butön. This prolific Sakya master has written *An Explanatory Discourse on [Chandrakirti's] "An Illuminating Lamp [for 'The Guhyasamaja Root*

*Tantra']"* and *An Extensive Commentary on [Nagarjuna's "A Method to Actualize Guhyasamaja] Made in Brief."* His explanations flow well, are easy to read and are very extensive, but have considerable trouble making the difficult points intelligible. Tsongkapa's writings, on the other hand, are unlike anyone else's.

Having come to a decisive understanding of the madhyamaka view of reality, Tsongkapa was able to gather together the opinions stated in a wide variety of texts and decisively settle the most difficult issues and make them uncommonly easy to understand. This is his special manner of explication which makes him so excellent. Since the First Panchen Lama presents a tradition that sets out the Kagyü manner of explaining mahamudra supplemented with a discussion of voidness in the style of Tsongkapa, I think that undoubtedly there is a valid point in his calling it a Gelug/Kagyü tradition that combines into one features and manners of approach from both lineages.

## OTHER-VOIDNESS AND SELF-VOIDNESS

There are two manners of explaining the correct view of reality, then, attributed to Tsongkapa. One is his unique manner of explanation according to the madhyamaka view, as found in the eighteen volumes of his collected works. The other, whether it is different or not, is his manner of explaining the view according to mahamudra. Let us leave aside, for a moment, the question concerning the authenticity of ascribing two views to Tsongkapa and speak more in general about different ways of expressing a correct view of reality.

The main teacher with whom Tsongkapa studied and debated the madhyamaka view of reality was the Sakya master Rendawa. Manjushri himself had told Tsongkapa, "The best lama who can clear away your doubts concerning madhyamaka is Rendawa. But you will not gain a decisive understanding on the basis of this. Rather, if you continually study and meditate on the great texts yourself, relying on me, step by step, as your bedrock and standard, you will definitely gain an unmistaken madhyamaka view."

Thus, in that situation, regarding the topic of madhyamaka, the great Rendawa was the best of all learned, erudite masters with whom Tsongkapa could have a direct relationship. On the face value of Rendawa's writings, however, concerning the decisive understanding of the madhyamaka view, we would have to say that he does not assert voidness as a non-affirming nullification. But Kaydrubjey, in his *Miscellaneous Writings,* has asserted that although Rendawa's and Tsongkapa's writings on the topic have different manners of expression, they come down to the same thing. This is one point, and I wonder if this is not also the case regarding the manner of meditating on a correct view that derives from Gungru Gyeltsen-zangpo.

Concerning the statement by the First Panchen Lama Lozang-chökyi-gyeltsen in the root text, "Nevertheless, when examined by a yogi learned in scripture and logic and experienced [in meditation], their definitive meanings are all seen to come to the same intended point," some later Gelug masters have said that except for when the First Panchen Lama himself was alive and could explain himself, how can we understand that a view that relies on an affirming nullification and one that relies on a non-affirming nullification come to the same intended point? The Third Panchen Lama Pelden-yeshey had asked that when delivering a discourse on mahamudra at Kumbum.

First of all, there must undoubtedly have been a special, uncommon tradition of discourse, transmitted from learned practitioners of the past, explaining their method of meditating on voidness in connection with their practice of anuttarayoga tantra, that asserted and described like this, based on personal experience. Secondly, as we were discussing in terms of dzogchen, we can speak of the nature of reality in terms of either devoid nature itself or that which has voidness as its nature. If we speak in terms of the latter, we arrive at an affirming nullification. Thus we can present primordial, simultaneously arising clear light mind as "other-voidness" — it is devoid of everything other, namely it is devoid of all fabricating levels of mind and their mental fabrications, from the three unconscious, most subtle conceptual appearance-making minds of threshold, light-diffusion and appearance-congealment onwards. Primordial, simultaneously arising clear light mind of deep awareness, the foundation responsible for the appearance-making and appearance of everything of samsara and nirvana, is devoid in the sense of not being any of the coarser, fleeting levels, starting from the three most subtle conceptual minds. In the terminology of Nagarjuna's and Aryadeva's commentaries to Guhyasamaja, clear light mind is all-void. Since the fact that clear light mind is a level of mind that is devoid of all fleeting levels, or devoid of being them, affirms that clear light mind is something else or something other than this, clear light mind, as an other-voidness, is an affirming nullification.

When we speak of clear light mind as primally pure, we are referring to its devoid nature — its nature of being devoid of all fantasized and impossible ways of existing. Something's being devoid, from the depths, of any fantasized and impossible manner of existence as its nature fulfills the definition of being a self-voidness — a voidness of a self-nature. When we go on to speak of clear light mind as also spontaneously establishing the appearance-making and appearance of all phenomena, we understand a type of other-voidness that is based on this. But since this understanding of other-voidness is based on clear light mind's being primally pure, it combines the essence of the second and third rounds of transmission of Buddha's teachings — respectively, the teachings on discriminating awareness from the Prajnaparamita sutras and Buddha-nature from *The Sutra on the Essential Factors for Accordant Progress*. And because such presentation combines the second and third rounds of transmission, it has no fault.

We must note that this other-voidness position which combines the second and third rounds of transmission defines the third round in a manner quite different from that of Tsongkapa. According to Tsongkapa's usage of terms, Buddha presented the madhyamaka view that all phenomena lack true unimputed existence in the second round of his Dharma transmission, while in the third he explained the chittamatra view that only some things lack such existence, while others in fact do exist unimputedly. Those who assert other-voidness do not consider the teachings of the third round to concern the chittamatra view, but only Buddha-nature understood within a madhyamaka context. Moreover, they consider the Buddha-nature teachings to imply the anuttarayoga tantra presentation in terms of clear light mind.

Some systems asserting other-voidness, however, do not combine Buddha's second and third rounds of transmission defined in this manner. Although they consider the Prajnaparamita sutras to comprise the second round, they say that the main purpose of these sutras is to help people overcome intellectual formulations about reality. Since they say that these sutras do not give any presentation of how phenomena in fact do exist, they take the second round to be interpretable. It is intended to lead disciples deeper, namely to the third round explanation of how everything exists in terms of clear light mind. They teach that the third round propagates what comes from meditation, while the second round clears away what comes from intellectual fabrication. They identify the position of the second round, defined in this manner, as prasangika-madhyamaka, while they ascribe the name "maha-madhyamaka," or great madhyamaka, to the third-round teachings of other-voidness.

Although this other-voidness position is not at all the same as the chittamatra view, it uses much of the same terminology but with different definitions. Of the three types of phenomena each having their own defining characteristics, dependent, or "other-powered," and imputed, or "totally imaginary" phenomena constitute the conventional level and are devoid of a self-nature. They arise dependently on unawareness as the first of the twelve factors that dependently arise. Thoroughly established phenomena, referring to clear light minds, are devoid in the sense of their being devoid of dependent and imputed phenomena, or devoid of being either of those two. They are an other-voidness. Since they do not arise from unawareness, they are beyond dependent arising.

Among those who define the two rounds of transmission in this way, there are some who totally denigrate the second round and take the third round to teach, in addition to Buddha-nature, that some phenomena do not exist at all, whereas others do. They take the lack of self-existence, or self-voidness, taught in the Prajnaparamita sutras to be equivalent to total non-existence — the position of nihilism. Consequently, dependent and imputed phenomena, being self-void, are totally non-existent. Ultimately, the impure conventional level that they constitute does not exist at all. Thoroughly established phenomena, on the other hand, being devoid of the other two types of phenomena, are likewise devoid of their mode of existence. Therefore, thoroughly established phenomena — referring to clear light minds — are transcendent phenomena forming an ultimate level of reality, or deepest level of truth, that is not devoid of a self-nature. Other-void phenomena, then, are also devoid being self-void.

This is the inferior view of other-voidness. Even though it is called other-voidness, it is an extremely deficient and faulty assertion of other-voidness. Many learned and experienced masters from the Sakya, Kagyü, Gelug and Nyingma traditions have refuted it. In taking voidness of a self-nature to be equivalent to total non-existence and dependent arising to mean arising dependently on unawareness, and asserting thoroughly established clear light mind as an other-voidness devoid of non-self-existence and this type of dependent arising, they are left with no alternative but that clear light mind is truly and inherently existent, existing through its own power, by virtue of itself. It is devoid not only of arising dependently on unawareness, but also of arising dependently by virtue simply of mental labeling.

Such assertion is clearly in total contradiction with what Nagarjuna has expounded. It basically contradicts the sutras. If we accept as the authentic words of Buddha the expanded, intermediate and brief recensions of the Prajnaparamita sutras and take them as valid, this type of other-voidness view becomes untenable. The frequent presentation in these sutras of sixteen or eighteen types of voidness always includes the ultimate or deepest level of truth as a basis that is characterized by voidness of a self-nature in exactly the same way as all other bases. This is why these other-voidness proponents are logically forced to assert the second round of transmission as interpretable, not definitive. But even if we explain exclusively in terms of Maitreya's *The Furthest Everlasting Stream*, which they take as a source for their view, we find it difficult to be comfortable with their interpretation of how the ultimate or deepest level exists. How can truly and inherently existent thoroughly established phenomena be the source of non-existent impure phenomena that they are totally devoid of?

Those who accept only the third round of transmission as definitive explain that the source of impure phenomena is alayavijnana — foundational mind — while clear light mind, as foundational deep awareness, is the source of only pure phenomena. Thoroughly established clear light mind dependently gives rise only to pure appearances — but not in the sense of the process arising dependently on unawareness. For those among them who assert self-voidness to be equivalent to total non-existence, however, they are forced to conclude that non-existent foundational mind gives rise to non-existent impure appearances, while truly and inherently existent clear light mind gives rise to truly and inherently existent pure appearances. The question still remains how either totally non-existent or truly and inherently existent phenomena can give rise to anything.

Moreover, if (1) they explain that prasangika-madhyamaka asserts only non-self-existence — and they take this as equivalent to total non-existence — while maha-madhyamaka asserts other-voidness which is devoid of non-self-existence in this nihilistic sense, and (2) at the same time, they identify what they call the prasangika-madhyamaka position with Nagarjuna and Chandrakirti, and denigrate them as arrogantly naive madhyamikas, they have even more problems with their view. In repudiating the ability of madhyamaka lines of reasoning to establish and confirm the functioning of any type of conventional level and dismissing as interpretable and inferior the texts that propound these logical arguments, they deny themselves a stable basis for understanding how even pure phenomena can arise dependently. Even if, based on meditation on clear light mind, they should experience a pure appearance of dependent arising, if they continue to repudiate the Prajnaparamita texts, they have difficulty correctly apprehending and understanding what they experience — specifically,

difficulty in correlating dependent arising with, for example, voidness of inherent, findable existence in the sense in which Tsongkapa
defines it, or with primal purity as presented in dzogchen. Therefore
great care is needed when formulating a correct view that uses the
term "non-self-existence" to mean total non-existence. Of course it is
necessary to refute total non-existence, but we must take care not to
limit ourselves by our definition of terms from deriving the full benefit of the Prajanaparamita teachings.

The other-voidness tradition that accepts as equally valid the second and third rounds of transmission, on the other hand, and which
understands non-self-existence to mean dependently arising by virtue simply of mental labeling and therefore not equivalent to total
non-existence, has its special, unique presentation of the two levels of
truth. What is primordial and spontaneously establishes is the deepest level of true or actual phenomena, while what is coarse and fleeting, both impure and pure, is the conventional level of true or actual
phenomena. Both levels actually exist. What is primordial and spontaneously establishes is devoid of existing truly and inherently, but at
the same time is devoid of what is coarse and fleeting and devoid of
being itself coarse and fleeting. This explanation of other-voidness that
accepts a deepest level of actual phenomena that is both self-void and
other-void — a deepest level that is primally pure by nature, and yet
also has the feature of spontaneously establishing the conventional
level of actual phenomena — combines the essence of the second and
third rounds of transmission of Buddha's teachings, and is perfectly
acceptable.

Primordial clear light mind which spontaneously establishes all
phenomena that exist and can thus appear is primally pure by nature.
From its depths, it is devoid of being a concrete reality. When we meditate single-pointedly on such a clear light mind as a special basis characterized by voidness of self-nature, we are meditating on what
amounts to an affirming nullification. This type of meditation on an
affirming nullification, however, comes to the same essential point as
meditation on a non-affirming nullification. But its manner of explanation and the technique it employs at the start for direct meditation
are slightly different. As there is a difference of opinion among various lamas within the Gelug tradition concerning mahamudra as explained in the discourse lineage of *A Ritual to Honor the Spiritual Master*, it is important to examine this issue from both historical and theoretical points of view.

# Session Four

## THE AUTHENTICITY OF THE TRADITIONS OF THE DOHAS AND DZOGCHEN

In the root text, the First Panchen Lama states that the explanation of anuttarayoga tantra's complete stage level of mahamudra practice is in accordance with *"The [Seven Texts of the] Mahasiddhas* and *The [Three] Core Volumes."* The seven texts are *Establishing the Hidden Factors* by Mahasukha, *Establishing Method and Discriminating Awareness* by Anangavajra, *Establishing Deep Awareness* by Indrabhuti, *Establishing Non-discordance* by Lashmikara, *Establishing What Simultaneously Arises* by Dombi Heruka, *Establishing the Very Nature of the Reality of the Great Hidden Factors* by Darika, and *Establishing the Very Nature of the Reality of What Follows from Becoming Clear about Functional Phenomena* by Yogini Chintta. Some of these are still extant in the original Indian languages. *The Three Core Volumes* refer to the three collections of Saraha's *dohas,* songs recounting his meditational experience. These are *The King Dohas, The Queen Dohas* and *The Commoner Dohas.*

In the auto-commentary, the Panchen Lama raises a query which we can paraphrase as follows. Some may object that since the techniques of mahamudra meditation outlined in these texts are not homogenous with those described by Nagarjuna in *The Five Stages [of the Guhyasamaja Complete Stage],* they are incorrect. After all, the method presented in Saraha's doha collections is one of here-and-now, non-contriving meditation and is intended for the practice of those of sharpest faculties for whom everything happens at once. The five stages system, on the other hand, as presented by fatherly Nagarjuna and his spiritual sons, is to be followed like climbing the rungs of a ladder.

The conclusion that the mahamudra system of the dohas is fallacious, however, is erroneous. The doha collections indicate a gateway
for practice that is harmonious with the complete stage. Even though
they contain certain differences in practice from the graduated path of
the five stages, there are no contradictions. The First Panchen Lama
decisively states, "They are in no way incorrect texts."

A similar question arose with regard to dzogchen in the collection
of Kaydrubjey's *Answers to Questions* in his *Miscellaneous Writings.*
Someone had remarked that certain people at that time were denigrating practitioners of dzogchen, and had asked whether the
dzogchen teachings were pure. Kaydrubjey has answered, "The
dzogchen teachings are definitely pure. The criticism of dzogchen practitioners is because there are certain individuals among them who
practice a contrived version of dzogchen that they have made up from
their misunderstanding. Basically, however, dzogchen presents a path
that is harmonious with that of anuttarayoga tantra."

A certain Indian translator in Tibet at that time, Kaydrubjey continues, "had seen certain dzogchen texts in Magadha in the possession
of some learned Indian masters there. Furthermore, many excellent
practitioners in Tibet have achieved advanced pathway minds and
bodhisattva levels based on dzogchen practice. Therefore repudiation
of these teachings is an appropriate cause for a fall to rebirth in one of
the three worse forms of life."

Despite such a statement, Kaydrubjey himself, in several of his
works, has refuted certain aspects of dzogchen, such as the oral guidelines of Aro, using very strong language. In those texts, however, he is
clearly using the name "dzogchen" to refer to certain specific cases
and not to all of dzogchen in general. He is faulting and refuting the
manner of explaining dzogchen used by certain specific dzogchen
practitioners. But concerning the dzogchen teachings in general, he
has said very decisively in his *Miscellaneous Writings,* "The dzogchen
teachings are definitely pure... Repudiation of these teachings is an
appropriate cause for a fall to rebirth in one of the three worse forms
of life." The same thing applies to the mahamudra teachings of the
dohas. They present a practice harmonious with anuttarayoga tantra's
complete stage. It would be totally wrong for a beginner to attempt to
practice them, but basically they are completely pure teachings. It is
the same situation, then, as dzogchen.

Dzogchen teaches that practice conducted with contriving, rough
fleeting minds cannot bring enlightenment. Only practice with the deep
awareness of non-contriving rigpa, pure awareness, can bring us to

the state of a Buddha. We can understand this in the same way as we do the statement that practice of the yoga class of tantras and below cannot bring us enlightenment by itself. The ultimate, deepest reason why it cannot is that the pathways of practice of these levels of teaching cannot by themselves make manifest the deep awareness of subtlest clear light mind. Without the manifestation of the deep awareness of clear light mind, we do not have the perpetrating causes for an enlightening body and enlightening mind of a Buddha — causes that are in the same uncommon category of phenomena as a Buddha's body and mind. Therefore, no matter how much we practice with pathway minds of yoga tantra and below, we are never able to attain to enlightenment on their basis alone.

This is exactly the same as the dzogchen assertion that we cannot attain enlightenment with any practices conducted with contriving minds. If we try to use a coarse level of mind — the level of mental cognition included in the six collections of coarse levels of consciousness — as the mind that would actualize and meditate further on the pathway minds, it can never become the perpetrating cause for an omniscient mind. Such a cause would have to be in the same category of phenomena as such a mind. Similarly, when we make clear light mind of deep awareness prominent or enhanced through techniques presented in the anuttarayoga tantra texts, and then transform it into the nature of being a pathway mind, only then do we have what can actualize an enlightening body and enlightening mind of a Buddha. Thus the statement in dzogchen that we cannot attain enlightenment with any contriving level of mind, and the statement in anuttarayoga tantra that we cannot attain enlightenment by relying on pathway minds of yoga tantra and below by themselves, have exactly the same meaning.

## DIVISION SCHEMES OF MAHA-, ANU- AND ATIYOGA, AND FATHER, MOTHER AND NON-DUAL TANTRA

Dzogchen is by no means intended for just anyone to practice in just any fashion. It is definitely only for those who have built up an enormous store of positive potential and have extremely sharp faculties. For such persons, it offers special, uncommon techniques for making clear light mind prominent and enhancing it. Its way of proceeding can be understood in terms of equivalent parallels in the new translation anuttarayoga tantra system.

If we look at the Nyingma texts from the point of view of a practitioner who has studied and trained in the Gelug tradition regarding the tantras of the new translation period, we can easily understand the classification scheme of maha-, anu- and atiyoga that appears in the context of the nine vehicles. Mahayoga emphasizes the material of the generation stage of anuttarayoga tantra at which we practice on the basis of imagination and fervent regard. Anuyoga emphasizes primarily the complete stage practices with energy-winds and energy-channels, such as tummo. Atiyoga, or dzogchen, emphasizes methods for making arise the object sensed by reflexive pure awareness that go beyond the maha- and anuyoga methods for making it arise.

If we apply these to the new translation traditions of anuttarayoga tantra, then, I believe according to Sakya Pandita's *Differentiating the Three Levels of Vowed Restraints*, we have generation stage practice, then complete stage practice up to and including the mind isolation stage, and then, by relying on external and internal methods for penetrating vital points of the vajra-body, the manifestation of clear light deep awareness as the result. Making manifested clear light deep awareness into a pathway mind is the lower boundary of what is included in dzogchen practice. There are great similarities between the two systems, despite slight differences in terminology and manner of explanation.

The way in which old translation dzogchen and new translation anuttarayoga tantra offer equivalent paths that can bring the practitioner to the same resultant state of Buddhahood is parallel to the way in which father and mother tantra lead to the same goal within the fold of new translation anuttarayoga tantra. According to the Gelug presentation, father tantra emphasizes and offers more detail on the practices of illusory body, while mother tantra emphasizes clear light practice. Tsongkapa rejected the criteria of earlier Sakya masters, also accepted by Kagyü scholars, that father tantra emphasizes the practices of blissful awareness, mother tantra the practices of voidness, and non-dual tantra the combined practice of both. His reason is that the defining characteristic of all anuttarayoga tantras is their emphasis on inseparable bliss and voidness. Therefore the category of non-dual tantra is redundant and unnecessary.

In *An Ocean of Teachings on the General Meaning of Kalachakra*, however, the post-Tsongkapa Sakya scholar Tagtsang Lotsawa has asserted a different criterion for differentiating father, mother and non-dual anuttarayoga tantras. Of the four anuttarayoga empowerments, father tantra emphasizes the secret or hidden empowerment, which plants seeds for achieving an illusory body on the basis of practices with the subtle energy-system. Mother tantra emphasizes the deep awareness empowerment, which plants seeds for achieving a clear light mind of inseparable bliss and voidness. Non-dual tantra emphasizes the fourth or word empowerment which plants seeds for achieving the state of unity of the two levels of true or actual phenomena. Such a presentation of non-dual tantra and the defining characteristics of these three divisions of anuttarayoga tantra is perfectly acceptable.

There is no need, however, to practice both father and mother tantra, or all three — father, mother and non-dual tantra — just as there is no need to practice both anuttarayoga tantra and dzogchen. Just practicing one of them is sufficient. Each provides a full path leading to enlightenment on its own. The enlightenment gained through one is never superior or inferior to that which is gained through any of the others. Within the context of anuttarayoga tantra, however, if we wish to engage in a really splendid practice, we can train ourselves by practicing both a father and a mother tantra.

For example, the Gelug tradition teaches special methods for the combined practice of Guhyasamaja, Chakrasamvara and Vajrabhairava. Since each of these anuttarayoga systems has its own speciality for which it provides the most extensive explanations and techniques, their combined practice provides the most splendid accumulation of comprehensive causes for enlightenment. But such extensive practice is not suited to everyone, and is certainly not required. In Tibet we have a saying, "The great practitioners of India practiced one Buddha-form and were able to actualize hundreds, while the practitioners of Tibet practice hundreds of Buddha-forms and are not able to actualize even one!"

Within the Nyingma system, practitioners for whom everything happens at once have no need to practice all three classes — maha-, anu- and atiyoga. They simply practice dzogchen alone. Those who progress through graded stages, however, usually practice at least mahayoga tantra before proceeding to dzogchen. Thus we commonly refer to dzogchen practice not only as atiyoga, but also maha-atiyoga.

## UNCONVENTIONAL BEHAVIOR OF THE MOST HIGHLY REALIZED PRACTITIONERS

In certain ways, the behavior of the most advanced practitioners of new translation anuttarayoga tantra and dzogchen may seem similar, but there are certain theoretical differences. According to the new translation tantra system, practitioners of varying levels of dull and sharp faculties progress through the stages of the anuttarayoga path by relying on behavior with or without varying degrees of elaboration. Thus, after realizing actual clear light mind, some yogi practitioners continue their path by engaging in behavior with elaboration, especially with what is technically called "adding the lord of the Buddha-family trait."

In anuttarayoga tantra in general, behavior with elaboration takes as its basis the sexual organs, purified of their ordinary state and transformed by crowning them with the lord of the practitioner's Buddha-family trait, or "Buddha-family." It uses them for enhancing the practice of clear light deep awareness of bliss and voidness by helping intensify blissful awareness as much as possible. This is the reason explained in the texts. Thus it seems that this could even apply to the generation stage on which the visualizations of adding the lord of the Buddha-family trait can serve, through a process of dependent arising, as causes for later full attainment of blissful deep awareness of voidness with subtlest clear light mind.

It is relatively easy to visualize our organs crowned with the lord of our Buddha-family trait in some manner or another that would facilitate our mind's giving rise, more conveniently, to a pure appearance of them. The texts speak of such behavior in order to enhance and deepen our practice. There is no other special reason for it than what is explained in terms of the path of using desirable sensory objects. This is easy to understand. On the most advanced levels, however, although manifested, actual clear light deep awareness cannot be improved, yet there is the explanation of adding to it the lord of the Buddha-family trait. The importance and necessity for doing so at this stage of practice is not so obvious.

Let us look, by way of comparison, at the behavior of dzogchen practitioners on an equivalent level. If we were to try to progress along the stages of the spiritual path and, throughout the entire process, try to actualize all the pathway minds and bodhisattva levels on the basis of coarse mental cognition included in the six collections of coarse levels of consciousness, but transformed into constructive or virtuous states of mind, we would still commit many positive or negative actions mixed with confusion when we were not totally absorbed on voidness. This is because we would still be under the influence of coarse levels of mind. We need to properly safeguard ourselves from positive or negative actions mixed with confusion, otherwise we experience their results in terms of uncontrollably recurring rebirth in either better or worse conditions.

The presentation of positive or negative pertains to states of mind within the set of coarse mental or sensory cognitions. But once we have crossed the threshold at which the three unconscious, most subtle conceptual appearance-making levels of mind of appearance-congealment, light-diffusion and threshold have ceased, and the clear light subtlest level of mind has manifested, at that point we are beyond the realm of positive or negative and we remain there so long as we maintain that level of mind. We have crossed the border marking the boundary of what we consider positive or negative for beginners in general.

Thus yogi practitioners taking as their basis their practice of pure awareness or clear light have overcome all conceptual, judgmental levels of mind. They have gone beyond the boundary of "good" or "bad." I think that their practice on this level also has a relation with that. Sometimes we hear that even if persons at this stage commit actions that conventionally would build up negative potentials because they are destructive, they build up no such potentials. But this is extremely difficult to understand and I cannot make a decisive statement on all levels of its meaning. It certainly does not mean that the realization of such persons invalidates the conventional operation of the karmic laws of behavioral cause and effect. Nor does it mean that the level of realization of such persons releases them from all responsibility for their actions and behavior, and allows them to act in a manner that is harmful to others.

When we look from the point of view of such persons, it seems as though since they have gone beyond the level of conceptual minds that are constructive or destructive, and since only those or more coarse levels of mind would build up positive or negative karmic potentials, their actions do not accumulate karmic potentials. Being not far from the ultimate state of enlightenment endowed with seven facets, this ultimate, final level of mind on which they rely as a method — the manifested, non-contriving clear light mind of deep awareness — is far beyond the manner of thinking of our coarse level of mind mixed with confusion. Like the sutra presentation of "contaminated" and "uncontaminated" actions — in other words, karmic actions mixed with confusion about voidness, or pure, non-karmic actions unmixed with such lack of awareness — all their actions serve as pure causes for their enlightenment. They meditate on and continually remain mindful of the clear light mind that is known as the most constructive phenomenon of all that is constructive.

It is in this context that we can perhaps understand the statement that persons who practice with such a mind totally absorbed on the nature of all phenomena do not need to make prostration or circumambulation, or recite mantras or any recitation-style meditational text. It is perfect for such persons to meditate on clear light alone. This indicates perhaps one level of meaning of the statement that the actions of such practitioners are beyond "good" or "bad." Thus we find mention in the dzogchen texts concerning the close bonding practices for atiyoga dzogchen that "being without safeguards is the best safeguard." The behavior of such practitioners must be understood within the context of conventional appearances reflexively emanating and automatically releasing themselves or disappearing. This is an important point.

Another point is that when yogi practitioners at such a level of attainment enhance their clear light practice, they gain control over their internal elements. Then, just as they are able to bring their internal elements under control, they are able to bring under control as well the external elements around them. Concerning the actions of such yogis with others, from the side of other sentient beings — literally, others operating on the level of limited awareness — there would be karmic actions, mixed with confusion, and the experience of their results. But from the side of the yogi practitioners themselves, they can take others' lives and then revive them because they have control over the elements.

In *A Treasure-house of Special Topics of Knowledge*, Vasubandhu has differentiated three types of constructive phenomena — those constructive by concomitance, by motivation and by nature. The same threefold division equally applies to destructive phenomena. Consider the case of a bodhisattva, motivated by compassion and the wish to be helpful, who takes someone's life. According to this abhidharma system, that act of mercy killing ripens into something unpleasant to be later experienced by that bodhisattva. It is considered a destructive act, not something constructive. But what makes it destructive?

According to Vasubandhu, physical and verbal actions have two stages of motivation — causal and contemporaneous. A causal motivation draws us toward an action, while a contemporaneous one, occurring at the moment of the action, subsequently brings us into the specific activity of that action. The contemporaneous motivation, not the causal one, determines whether an action is destructive or constructive.

Compassion and the wish to help are certainly the causal motivations for a bodhisattva's act of mercy killing. But we cannot say that the contemporaneous motivation in this example is a destructive disturbing emotion such as repulsion or aggression — as when an ordinary person squashes a cockroach that is half-crushed and squirming on the ground — and that is what renders the act destructive. Only anuttarayoga tantra systems, such as Kalachakra, assert taking disturbing emotions, such as repulsion or aggression, as a pathway of mind. This is a special feature unique to anuttarayoga tantra. Therefore only from the point of view of such a system can a bodhisattva's act of mercy killing be contemporaneously motivated by repulsion or aggression, because only such systems assert bodhisattvas who do not rid themselves of disturbing emotions. The perfection vehicle systems hardly assert at all taking disturbing emotions or attitudes as a pathway of mind. Therefore, from the point of view of such systems, bodhisattvas do not rely on repulsion or aggression as the contemporaneous motivation for any of their actions. In *Notes on the Five Stages [of the Guhyasamaja Complete Stage]*, Sershül has cited many quotations to the effect that when practicing the path of the perfection vehicle, there seem to be no occasions when one purposely acts with repulsion or aggression.

Whether or not this is totally the case with practitioners emphasizing the perfection vehicle, consider the case of a yogi practitioner of anuttarayoga tantra, for instance one on the generation stage. Suppose such a practitioner were to let repulsion or aggression arise and, with this as contemporaneous motivation, commit a mercy killing. This yogi's action still could not be considered constructive. It still undoubtedly ripens into an unpleasant experience for the yogi in the future.

The ethical status and results that ripen from the actions of bodhisattvas on the five stages of the anuttarayoga complete stage, however, depend on which of the five stages they are included within. Bodhisattvas who have manifested actual clear light and are practicing on the stage of unity still with further training left have rid themselves totally of all disturbing emotions and attitudes. Any mercy killing that they might commit would be beyond the fence of what is either destructive or constructive. In general, however, if a bodhisattva commits a mercy killing motivated by bodhichitta, it is beneficial for the other being and contributes to the bodhisattva's build-up of positive potential. But, be that as it may, it is undoubtedly certain that the potential built up by the act ripens in the form of a future unpleasant experience for that bodhisattva. I think we can decide that this is so. To argue whether a bodhisattva's act of mercy killing is destructive or constructive, then, is just quibbling with words.

Thus, the behavior described in the context of the atiyoga dzogchen presentation of view, meditation and behavior is on the one hand rather awkward to explain, and yet on the other extremely deep and profound. I think this is slightly different from the behavior of adding the lord of the Buddha-family trait explained in the new translation tantras.

## COMPASSION AND WISDOM WITHIN THE CONTEXT OF ANUTTARAYOGA TANTRA

The First Panchen Lama summarizes the meaning of the dohas by explaining that it is necessary to combine compassion — which in this context means a clear light mind simultaneously arising each moment with greatly blissful awareness — together with voidness, in the manner of the former being the mind that apprehends the latter. Meditation on voidness alone, lacking the compassion that is a greatly blissful deep awareness and that blocks bliss in general or the bliss of orgasmic emission, is not the supreme pathway of mind that can bring us full enlightenment in one lifetime. On the other hand, a blissful awareness by itself, which lacks the practice of voidness and thus arises on the basis of the craving that apprehends everything as having true and inherent existence, can only keep us in uncontrollably recurring situations, samsara. It cannot bring us liberation from them. Only the power of a union of method and wisdom — namely the union of compassion, as a greatly blissful awareness, and the discriminating awareness of voidness — allows us to attain the total release of supreme nirvana, namely enlightenment. Thus it enables us to overcome the extremes of compulsive samsaric existence as well as the inertia of remaining at rest with an arhat's nirvana.

The Sanskrit word for compassion, "karuna," has the implication of "that which blocks or prevents bliss." In general, when we develop compassion, we develop very strongly the attitude that cannot bear the suffering of other beings. We wish for it to end and for them to become free. Although we do not actually experience others' suffering at that time, the strength of the attitude that cannot bear their suffering causes our mind also to become unhappy. This is the general sense in which compassion blocks bliss.

Moreover, greatly blissful deep awareness arises only on the basis of blocking the bliss of orgasmic emission — either male or female. More specifically, it arises from binding the subtle energy-drops or energy-sparks so that we do not emit and lose them, as happens with orgasm. This is why such a blissful awareness is also called "karuna," compassion — that which blocks bliss. Furthermore, greatly blissful deep awareness enables us to free others from their suffering. Thus another reason for calling greatly blissful awareness "compassion" is that it acts as a cause for success in the practice of compassion.

## HOW CHITTAMATRA PRACTITIONERS OF TANTRA GAIN A MADHYAMAKA VIEW

The First Panchen Lama goes on to discuss a point that comes out most clearly in the collection of the Third Panchen Lama Pelden-yeshey's *Answers to Questions*. There were certain masters in India who held the chittamatra view, such as the learned scholars Shantipa and Bhairava, who later became yogi practitioners of tantra. The latter, when he had previously been a pandit, was called Dharmapala, the elder mentioned by Chandrakirti in *An Auto-commentary on "A Supplement to [Nagarjuna's 'Root Stanzas on] the Middle Way.'"* Someone had asked the Third Panchen Lama what were the circumstances leading such chittamatra practitioners of tantra as these to upgrade their view of reality to a more subtle one of madhyamaka.

Panchen Pelden-yeshey has explained that some practitioners among them were unable to upgrade their realization and gain a decisive understanding of the prasangika-madhyamaka refutation of the apprehension of true, inherent existence solely on the basis of external study. Although of course they had to rely on an external circumstance such as pondering the correct understanding concerning the apprehension of true, inherent existence, they relied primarily on internal methods.

When, through the methods of anuttarayoga tantra concerning the complete stage practice with the energy-channels and energy-winds, chittamatra practitioners are able to make their coarse level of cognition increasingly more subtle, they make manifest the most subtle clear light level of mind. As their experience of this clear light mind becomes increasingly more profound and subtle, the mass of discordant appearance-making minds and discordant appearances of true, inherent existence automatically dissipates and ceases by the strength of their focus on clear light. As this ceasing or stopping becomes total and they reach the full, complete experience of primordial simultaneously arising clear light, they directly experience their clear light mind automatically giving rise to an aspect that has the appearance of the object the mind gives rise to when it has straightforward, non-conceptual perception of voidness — a total absence of fantasized, impossible ways of existing in general. By means of their experience of the dissolution of the most subtle level of discordant appearance-making minds and the most subtle level of discordant appearances, they consequently gain a decisive understanding that the fantasized, impossible mode of existence that is totally absent from the appearance of voidness their mind gives rise to is, in fact, the true and inherent existence of even an atom or micro-moment of any phenomenon whatsoever, established from its own side. In this way, they gain conviction in the non-affirming refutation and nullification of true, inherent, findable existence — the prasangika-madhyamaka view.

The Third Panchen Lama has summarized this by stating that, "The boundary line marking when yogi practitioners holding a chittamatra view gain a decisive understanding of the prasangika-madhyamaka view, with nothing incorrect, is when they practice the mind isolation stage of anuttarayoga tantra's complete stage. At that stage, their inner experience induces exceptional conviction in the correct madhyamaka view."

This indicates a very important point, I believe. In general, when we manifest clear light mind, as I just explained, that mind gives rise to an appearance of the object that also arises when there is a straightforward, non-conceptual perception of voidness. Kaydrub Norzang-gyatso, a great Kalachakra master, for example, has similarly explained in *An Ornament for "The Stainless Light" [Commentary on "The Abbreviated Kalachakra Tantra"]*, that at the time of the clear light of death, clear light mind gives rise to an appearance of voidness. This is what allows for an upgrade in our view of reality. When primordial simultaneously arising clear light mind becomes manifest through the power of meditation, this experience can, in certain cases, bring conviction in the fact that all phenomena, except for existing as what the names or words for them refer to, do not exist from their own side.

When we experience death, although the primordial clear light mind manifests, we are normally unable to become aware of the nature of that clear light mind. Under the influence of deceptive states of mind, those experiencing death have fallacious perception of the appearance their clear light mind of death gives rise to. But when yogis have realization of the straightforward, non-conceptual experience of primordial mind, they see that all phenomena, in a cognitive sense, are emanations of that primordial mind.

## ALL PHENOMENA AS THE PLAY OF PRIMORDIAL CLEAR LIGHT MIND

What the First Panchen Lama explains here is the same as what Tsongkapa has noted in *Precious Sprout, Deciding the Difficult Points of [Chandrakirti's] "An Illuminating Lamp [for 'The Guhyasamaja Root Tantra']."* In his explanation of the prologue of *The Guhyasamaja Root Tantra*, in the section concerning the activity of illusory body, commenting on a line from Nagarjuna's *The Five Stages [of the Guhyasamaja Complete Stage]*, Tsongkapa has explained that yogis abiding in a state of absorbed concentration on all phenomena being like illusion see that all appearances that mind produces of what exists — either of the inanimate environment or the animate beings within it — are the play or in the nature of subtlest energy-wind and subtlest mind.

Since, in general, the ultimate or deepest basis for labeling beings is the continuity of their individual stream of subtlest energy-wind and subtlest mind, then in this sense all animate beings are the play of subtlest energy-wind and mind. As for the external, inanimate environment, such as mountains, valleys and so on, although it does not directly have subtlest energy-wind and mind as its basis for labeling in the same way as do the beings within it, nevertheless it comes about by the power of karma or impulses, with the provisions we discussed before, that affect this primordial level. Being that which karma makes appear, both in a material and cognitive sense, external phenomena arise by virtue of their being devoid of existing by means of an inherently findable nature. These external phenomena that mind gives rise to an appearance of, because of being devoid by nature, arise in our experience on the crest of the three unconscious, most subtle, conceptual appearance-making minds of threshold, light-diffusion and appearance-congealment. In other words, when the subtlest energy-wind causes movement from the sphere of clear light, the coarser levels of mind that emerge, from the three most subtle, conceptual appearance-making minds onwards, produce the appearances of all phenomena of the environment. In this sense, these phenomena arise as the play or emanation of this primordial level though the power of karma.

In short, all appearances mind produces of what exists are the play of primordial mind. Although this primordial mind always becomes manifest at the time of death, we normally never recognize its nature. This is because we are unable to remain in the experience of the clear light of death with an intelligent, perceptive mind. Thus although we experience clear light mind, we are unable to be aware of it. Once we are able to recognize clear light mind, however, we arrive at a very great stage. We gain an exceptional realization of the most subtle abiding nature of all phenomena. To be able to do this, however, we must rely on a guru as our spiritual guide.

As the dohas explain, simultaneously arising clear light mind of deep awareness functions as the basis for all phenomena of samsara and nirvana. It is like the ultimate or deepest creator of all samsara and nirvana. Is primordial clear light mind something established as truly and inherently existing? No, it definitely is not. This clear light mind, however, as a non-inherently existent phenomenon, is not totally non-existent either. It functions as the basis for all samsara and nirvana, being neither totally non-existent nor truly and inherently existent. This is the Buddhist explanation for what is called the creator in other traditions. Perhaps this is what is meant by the Holy Ghost!

## PRIMORDIAL CLEAR LIGHT MIND AS BUDDHA-NATURE

A primordial clear light mind is something that we all have within us. It is not something external to us. It is on this basis that we can attain enlightenment. When we can see, straightforwardly and non-conceptually, the nature of our clear light mind and remain totally absorbed on this nature without ever regressing from it, we have become a Buddha. That being the case, Buddhahood is not something that can be given to us by someone else. If we think in this way, we must conclude that we all have Buddha-nature — the factors that allow us to become a Buddha. This is the ultimate, deepest point that we come to in meditation on the essential factors for blissful progress discussed in Maitreya's *The Furthest Everlasting Stream.*

Primordial simultaneously arising clear light subtlest mind, which we all have had without beginning and which becomes manifest each time we die, is the basis dharmakaya — a body encompassing everything, which forever abides as a basis. Since basis dharmakaya continues each moment after the next, when we transform it, with skillful means, into having the nature of a pathway mind, it functions as a pathway dharmakaya. When we cultivate pathway dharmakaya, continually making it more and more excellent, so that it becomes totally purified of all obstacles regarding knowables together with their instincts — or, if we describe it from another point of view, when we reach the state at which we forever remain totally absorbed on clear light mind without ever being parted from a correct view of reality — clear light mind becomes the resultant dharmakaya.

## RELYING ON A SEALING PARTNER

In order to make primordial simultaneously arising clear light mind fully and completely manifest, we must totally stop or cease all coarser levels of energy-wind and mind. In order to stop the coarser levels of energy-wind and mind from predominating, we need to generate a greatly blissful deep awareness. To generate a blissful awareness that is sufficiently intense and powerful to accomplish these aims, it is necessary for most persons to rely on a mudra, a sealing physical partner. The reason why the central Buddha-forms in the mandalas or symbolic universes of the anuttarayoga tantra class are mostly in the aspect of a father and mother couple is to indicate this necessity.

There is a great difference between relying on a sealing partner with full awareness that doing so is solely to provide the circumstance and source for developing a greatly blissful awareness to be used for the above purposes, and relying on one as a pathway of practice in the manner of a trespasser. Therefore, only especially well-qualified practitioners well-advanced on anuttarayoga tantra's complete stage, who have trained in the practices of the subtle energy-channels and winds and who have gained mastery over them, are permitted to practice with an actual, physical karmamudra, a sealing partner for their behavior. Because they have gained full mastery over their energy-winds and channels, such practitioners never have the danger of experiencing the ordinary bliss of orgasmic emission that would either prevent or destroy their generation of a greatly blissful deep awareness. They are merely using their external and vajra-bodies as a mechanical device to intensify the blissful awareness of voidness they have already achieved.

Before we have reached this advanced level of accomplishment, we are permitted to practice only with a visualized jnanamudra, a sealing partner for deep awareness. In *An Ornament for "The Stainless Light" [Commentary on "The Abbreviated Kalachakra Tantra"]* Kaydrub Norzang-gyatso has explained that, for practitioners of especially sharp faculties, relying on a visualized jnanamudra partner can also serve as a method for generating a greatly blissful awareness strong enough to dissolve at the center of the heart chakra all the energy-winds that are the most difficult to dissolve so that the clear light mind becomes totally and completely manifest. Thus it is not absolutely mandatory to rely on a physical karmamudra partner.

But regardless of our level of realization, and whether we are practicing with a visualized jnanamudra partner or a physical karmamudra one, it is extremely essential to keep the purpose in mind and never practice without the three types of discernment or recognition. In order to block the mind's ordinary appearance-making and apprehension of true and inherent existence, we visualize ourselves and our partner in the aspect of Buddha-forms made to appear by a mind that is blissfully aware of voidness. We discern our speech as the expression of clear light mind of inseparable bliss and voidness, symbolized by the seed syllables from which the appearance of our sexual organs arises in a purified form and with which they are "crowned" or marked. Furthermore, we understand our mind as always being a primordial clear light mind that arises simultaneously with each moment as a blissful awareness that is inseparable from also being a discriminating awareness of voidness. These are extremely important points that render reliance on a visualized or physical sealing partner into a skillful method on the path. Such reliance generates a deeply blissful awareness that acts as a circumstance for blocking the coarser levels of energy-wind and mind and making manifest clear light mind so that this clear light mind can be generated as a greatly blissful deep awareness of voidness. Only such awareness can eliminate the obstacles preventing liberation all at once and only such awareness can remove the obstacles preventing omniscience. To rely on a sealing partner as a method of practice without these three types of discernment is a transgression of the tantric vows.

## SUMMARY OF THE TANTRA LEVEL OF MAHAMUDRA PRACTICE

Those who have trained thoroughly through intensive practice either in previous lives or in the earlier part of this life are able to recognize mahamudra by the force of one concerted effort. They are able to cultivate their practice in the manner of those for whom everything happens at once. Beginners, however, must train in stages. We need to manifest mahamudra by practicing tummo and so forth step by step. All great masters of the past, such as Milarepa and Gampopa, have proclaimed this with a single voice.

This concludes the First Panchen Lama's presentation of the tantra tradition of mahamudra. Because he has explained it more briefly, he has placed it first in his text. He now explains the sutra level of mahamudra, placing it second because there are more texts explicating this level of practice and also because he will explain it much more extensively.

## THE DIFFERENCES BETWEEN THE SUTRA AND TANTRA LEVELS OF MAHAMUDRA

The sutra tradition of mahamudra, as the First Panchen Lama states in his root text, entails "the ways of meditating on voidness as directly indicated in the expanded, intermediate and brief [Prajnaparamita sutras]." The special feature of the mahamudra presentation of voidness meditation is that such meditation is focused primarily on the nature of the reality of mind. Although the object having this nature upon which we focus and the manner of explanation are slightly different, the actual body of practice for gaining a decisive understanding of voidness is the same as that which the Prajnaparamita sutras present.

In *Differentiating the Three Levels of Vowed Restraints*, Sakya Pandita has stated there is no difference in the correct view of reality according to sutra or tantra. Dzogchen and similar systems, on the other hand, assert a great difference between the two. I think, however, there is simply a difference in the manner of meditation on a correct view between the sutra and tantra traditions, but the meaning at which they both arrive is the same.

In order to understand the assertion by the masters of the Sakya and Gelug traditions, such as Sakya Pandita and Tsongkapa, that there is no difference between the sutra and tantra views of reality, we must differentiate between two senses of the word "view." Just as we can use the word "aim" in either a verbal or substantive way to mean either "aim at something" or the "aim at which we focus," likewise we can use the word "view" in the same two ways. We can "view reality" or focus on a "view of reality." Those who assert no difference between the sutra and tantra views are using the word "view" in its substantive sense to mean the object, namely voidness, on which we meditate. Voidness, as the absence of true and inherent existence, is exactly the same in both the sutra and tantra traditions. But from the point of view of the mind that does the correct viewing of reality, there is a great difference.

All the great Gelug commentaries on tantra, such as Tsongkapa's *A Lamp for Clarifying the Five Stages [of the Guhyasamaja Complete Stage]*, also assert that although there is no difference here in the object upon which we meditate, there is a great difference in the mind that does the meditating. In *A Root Text on the Tenet Systems*, the omniscient First Jamyang-zheypa has also asserted that the sutra tradition teaches primarily voidness as an object, but keeps hidden and does not teach the

special mind of greatly blissful deep awareness with which to apprehend it as its object. This clearly shows the widespread acceptance in
the Gelug tradition of a difference between sutra and tantra concerning the mind with which to understand voidness.

We find this in the Sakya tradition as well. While declaring in *Differentiating the Three Levels of Vowed Restraints* no difference in view
between sutra and tantra, Sakya Pandita in the very same text has
explained four types of view, correlated with the four anuttarayoga
tantra empowerments. One of his distinctive teachings explains the
four empowerments in terms of four views and four tenet systems.

The tenet system associated with the vase empowerment is that of
the inseparability of samsara and nirvana. Its view is seeing the nature of everything to be of the same entity or in the same package as
three things — appearance, voidness and the unity of the two. The
tenet system correlated with the hidden or secret empowerment is
that of the total completeness of that which is unadulterated, namely
clear light mind. Its view is to see, with the four types of deep awareness, that which automatically occurs — namely, to see with absorbed
concentration that disturbing emotions and attitudes, conceptual
minds, the turning around and stilling of both, and clarity and illumination each occur automatically from clear light mind. The tenet system of the deep discriminating awareness empowerment is called
modestly expansive blissful awareness and voidness. Its view is seeing voidness with the four levels of simultaneously arising joyous
awareness — joy, supreme joy, separated joy and simultaneously arising joy — that occur when subtle energy-drops descend through the
four chakras, starting from the top of the central energy-channel in
the subtle vajra-body. The tenet system associated with the fourth empowerment is vastly expansive blissful awareness and voidness. Its
view is seeing voidness with the four levels of joyous awareness that
stabilize when the subtle energy drops re-ascend through the four
chakras, starting from the bottom of the central energy-channel, bringing realization of the very nature of total purity of all phenomena.

Commenting on Sakya Pandita's *Differentiating the Three Levels of
Vowed Restraints*, Ngari Panchen Pema-wanggyel, a Nyingma master
from the northern treasure-text lineage, has written in *Ascertaining the
Three Levels of Vowed Restraints*, "If there were no difference in view
between sutra and tantra, then doesn't the Sakya tradition teach four
different views, one each in relation to each of the four empowerments?
Surely this indicates a difference in view." This is certainly true. In

sutra practice, we use simply a single view. Thus there is a great difference between sutra and tantra concerning the mind that aims at voidness, while the voidness of true and inherent existence aimed at by both is the same.

Concerning the difference in mind that meditates on voidness, in the sutra tradition we employ an individualizing discriminating awareness for meditation to gain a correct view. For achieving vipashyana, an exceptionally perceptive state of mind, we need scrutinizing or "analytical" meditation. We use individualizing discriminating awareness in meditation to scrutinize intelligently in order to discern voidness. In the anuttarayoga tantra system, on the other hand, the mind that recognizes voidness engages only in absorptive or "formal" meditation with placement on certain vital points in the subtle vajra-body that are more special and more powerful than others. This is a great difference. By the force of there being a special mind that is aimed at voidness, there is the circumstance for attaining together, at the same occasion, both serenely stilled and settled as well as exceptionally perceptive states of mind. Thus, by relying on special methods, we attain shamata and vipashyana simultaneously with anuttarayoga tantra meditation, whereas with the sutra techniques we first achieve shamata by itself and then combine it with vipashyana. In either case, however, as our foundation we must meditate on a correct view of reality as explained by Nagarjuna and Chandrakirti. Therefore the First Panchen Lama bases his presentation of voidness meditation on the teachings of Nagarjuna.

In short, what does "mahamudra" mean in this context? Because voidness is the actual nature of all phenomena, or the manner in which all things exist, voidness is a "mudra" or seal. Voidness, as the manner in which everything exists, is the seal that guarantees the nature of all things in the sense that there is nothing that can go beyond this. Everything has voidness as its nature. Furthermore, because the realization of voidness liberates us from all the fetters of suffering and their causes, it is "maha" or great.

# Session Five

## THE WAY TO LISTEN TO TEACHINGS

We have all come to listen to teachings on mahamudra, the great seal. But whenever we listen to teachings, we need a proper motivation. No matter how profound or excellent a teaching may be, if we do not listen to it with proper motivation, this will not do. Therefore we need to set the proper, full motivation of wishing, by means of hearing, practicing and realizing these teachings, to attain the enlightened state of a Buddha in order to be able to benefit all beings. We need to set this motivation very deeply and sincerely from the depths of our hearts.

Not only must we have a proper motivation when listening to teachings, we must have no mental wandering. Otherwise, we miss certain points and become lost. Since we must listen attentively, if some extraneous thought or image comes to mind we must pay it no heed. We need to listen single-pointedly and not let our minds be distracted by anything extraneous.

Furthermore, it is very important not only to listen attentively, but also to retain what we hear and not forget it. When listening to teachings or reading a written version of them, it is helpful to take notes. If in the future we refer back to these notes and study them, we gain great benefit in our practice. Therefore we need to listen to these teachings with proper motivation and single-pointed attentiveness, not letting ourselves forget anything.

## NON-SECTARIANISM

In *Four Hundred Stanzas,* Aryadeva has defined a disciple who is fit for receiving Dharma teachings as one who is "impartial, has common sense and takes interest." The first of these qualities, impartiality, means that disciples must not be attached to their own tradition and hostile toward others. They must not hold their own views as being the only ones proper and everything else as being at fault. Being impartial, they need to be open-minded about others' views. There are many religious traditions in the world and, among them, many national traditions of Buddhism. All of them are beneficial. Anyone who practices any of them sincerely and looks to their essence learns about training in ethics and other beneficial practices. Therefore, it is very important not to be sectarian. Without partiality or bias, we need to regard all religious and spiritual traditions with great respect.

Even within the folds of the Tibetan lineages of Buddhism, we have several traditions — Nyingma, Sakya, Kagyü and Gelug. As disciples of the Tibetan form of Buddhism, we must especially not have sectarian regard toward any of these. If we hold a sectarian, prejudiced attitude toward these traditions, with hard feelings toward some, and create or further disharmony among them, we disable ourselves from building up positive potential from our Dharma practice. There is great danger of a serious downfall. We must take care about our attitudes.

There are two different ways of looking with a discriminating eye at the various traditions. One is to examine each of them closely based on a sincere interest to know the distinctive features of each. We examine the assertions and practices of the various traditions with a critical eye, trying to establish the scriptural authority and logical basis for each. We undertake this so as to be able to understand and appreciate the grounds and sources that have given rise to the different traditions. The other way of looking with a critical eye is to judge them with an ordinary mind of attachment, hostility and closed-minded, foolish confusion. This latter manner of looking is the defining characteristic of sectarianism.

There were many realized beings in India as well as Tibet who debated in order to refute various interpretations and views. When great learned masters debate with each other, in an impartial manner, in order to determine which positions are valid and which are either illogical, self-contradictory or in contradiction to the scriptures, they are motivated by the sincere wish to benefit practitioners. But when others who are not especially learned, experienced or mature imitate this with a motivating basis of attachment and hostility, they simply argue and call each other nasty names. This type of endeavor is pathetic and misses the point of debate. Therefore, it is very important not to entertain a sectarian view toward the various traditions and systems, but rather to remain always impartial and have equal respect for all.

I myself have great respect for all the Buddhist lineages of Tibet — Sakya, Kagyü, Nyingma and Gelug — and likewise respect for Bön and all the other religions and spiritual traditions we find in the world. If we look in an unbiased manner, we see that each of them has its own good points. Each is suited to a particular type of individual with a particular type of disposition and needs. As each is beneficial for the people it suits, it is totally appropriate to maintain respectful belief in the value of this wide variety of traditions, both within and beyond the Buddhist fold.

As for our own study and practice of Buddhism, depending on the direction of our interests and our capacity, we should try to study as widely as possible, and with sincere respect, as many of its traditions as we can. This helps us broaden and deepen our understanding and practice of whatever is our main tradition. For example, if Gelug practitioners study a dzogchen text, they gain a special and unique understanding of the Nyingma teachings on the basis of their Gelug training that can further enhance their Gelug studies and practice. The same is true of dzogchen practitioners who study a Gelug text, and so forth. Thus we must try to have a very broad and open attitude, and, based on respect and interest, study and practice as widely as we can the various traditions of Buddhism. The First Panchen Lama's approach in this text comes to the same point.

BRIEF RÉSUMÉ OF THE TEXT

The outline for this text divides it into three sections: the preliminary discussion, actual explanation and dedication of positive potential. It then divides the actual explanation into discussion of the preparations, actual techniques and concluding procedures. The actual techniques involve the tantra and sutra traditions of mahamudra. For the tantra methods, we need to follow the procedures in their proper order. First we establish a firm foundation for practice by training ourselves with the common and uncommon preliminaries. Then, on the basis of this preparation, we receive a full set of empowerments, from a properly qualified master, that plant the seeds for being able to attain the four bodies of a Buddha. Strictly keeping to all the vows and close bonds that we have received at the time of empowerment, we then enter into the practices. The main point of practice is, through various techniques, to make manifest the simultaneously arising primordial clear light of deep awareness. The sutra tradition of mahamudra is to gain a decisive understanding of the correct view of reality as presented in the three major recensions of the Prajnaparamita sutras, known in Tibetan as *The Three Mothers*.

The First Panchen Lama next lists a number of teaching traditions that have appeared in Tibet. Among them are several mahamudra traditions from various Kagyü lineages. There are basically two Kagyü lineages: Shangpa Kagyü from Kaydrub Kyungpo and Dagpo Kagyü, which traces itself from Tilopa through Naropa, Marpa and Milarepa to Gampopa from Dagpo, who combined the Kadam and mahamudra traditions. Twelve Dagpo Kagyü lineages derive from Gampopa's disciples. The four primary ones — Karma Kamtsang or simply Karma, Barom, Pagdru and Tselpa — trace from direct disciples of Gampopa himself. The eight secondary ones — Drigung, Drugpa, Taglung, Shugseb, Yelpa, Marpa, Yazang and Tropu — trace themselves from disciples of Gampopa's disciple Pagmo-drupa. From among these various Kagyü traditions, the First Panchen Lama mentions "simultaneously arising as merged," deriving from Gampopa and found in Karma Kagyü; the "amulet box" from Kaydrub Kyungpo in Shangpa Kagyü; and "possessing five" from Jigten-gönpo in Drigung Kagyü. The "six spheres of equal taste" derives from a work buried as a treasure-text by Milarepa's disciple Rechungpa, recovered by Tsangpa Gyaray and passed on to his disciple Götsangpa, in Drugpa Kagyü; while the "four syllables" from Saraha's disciple Maitripa, another of Marpa's Indian masters, is found in the various Dagpo Kagyü lineages. Outside these Kagyü lines, the Panchen Lama also mentions the "pacifier" tradition from another of Maitripa's disciples, Pa Dampa-sanggyay, in which "the pure Dharma pacifies suffering," and also the "object to be cut off," tracing from Pa Dampa-sanggyay's disciple Machig Labkyi-drölma. Furthermore, there is dzogchen in Nyingma and the discursive madhyamaka view in Gelug.

The First Panchen Lama concludes his list with the word "and so on." Included in "and so on" are the traditions of the Sakya lineage. Although Sakya discusses the view of reality in the context of pathway appearance-making of those who strive, presented as one of the three stages of appearance-making, the Panchen Lama is undoubtedly referring here to its view of the inseparability of samsara and nirvana discussed in the context of the causal everlasting stream of the alaya, the all-encompassing foundation, presented as one of the three everlasting streams.

All these traditions have individual, different names. But if we, as Dharma practitioners, examine them from the point of view of scriptural quotation from Buddha's sutras of definitive meaning, as well as with lines of reasoning that establish what is of definitive meaning, and, not leaving that merely on the level of words, combine our thorough understanding of both with personal meditational experience, we see that despite their differences in name, they each come to the same meaning and point.

## THE SIMULTANEOUSLY ARISING AS MERGED TRADITION OF KARMA KAGYÜ

The main point of the simultaneously arising as merged tradition is, as our auto-commentary quotes, "The simultaneously arising mind itself is dharmakaya, a body encompassing everything." This tradition, speaking primarily from the point of view of tantra, correlates primordial simultaneously arising clear light mind with dharmakaya. "Simultaneously arising conceptual minds are the waves of dharmakaya." In other words, the arising of our numerous conceptual minds or thoughts of "good" or "bad" are like waves of that primordial simultaneously arising clear light dharmakaya mind. Here, dharmakaya clear light mind is likened to the ocean, while conceptual minds that think "good" or "bad" are likened to waves that arise from the ocean.

Furthermore, "Simultaneously arising appearances are the luster or brilliance of dharmakaya." In other words, the root of the various appearances of "good" or "bad" to which our various conceptual thoughts give rise is the sphere of simultaneously arising clear light. Thus both appearances and the conceptual minds that give rise to them do not go beyond having clear light mind as their nature.

The quotation ends, "Appearance and mind simultaneously arise, inseparably." This is not asserting, as with the chittamatra view, that external appearances and the internal minds that cognize them exist truly and unimputedly as being substantially one by nature. But rather this view asserts that all pure and impure emanated appearances can be presented in terms of the sphere of clear light. It is in this sense that the Karma Kagyü tradition speaks of inseparable appearance and mind.

Once, when Changkya Rölpay-dorjey was staying in China at Wutaishan, the holy five-peaked mountain plateau of Manjushri, he received in a dream a hidden vision of an emanation of the Buddha-form Manjushri himself. In this vision, Manjushri gave him very clear guidelines for understanding the madhyamaka view starting on the basis of the chittamatra subject matter of the fourth chapter of Dharma-kirti's *A Commentary on [Dignaga's "Compendium of] Validly Cognizing Minds."* Although it was a vision that appeared in a dream, it amounted to what we call a pure vision. Similarly, there have been many great realized masters of India and Tibet who trained themselves first with a chittamatra view of reality and, in the end, were led by it to a madhyamaka view. For example, Kagyü masters of old had the saying, "Decisively understand that appearances are the vitality of mind. Decisively understand that mind itself is devoid. Decisively understand appearance and voidness as a unity." There is also the similar expression among Sakya masters, "Remain within the sphere of clarity and voidness not apprehended apart."

These are both examples of traditions indicating a view of reality based on experience. Because they are views based on experience, sometimes they have and sometimes they lack the fault of contradicting the scriptural texts. They do not take as primary what follows from words, but rather they look for the exact, appropriate occasions to touch the minds of suitable disciples with guidelines that follow from their personal meditational experience. Thus this tradition of simultaneously arising as merged, which is expressed in terms reminiscent of a chittamatra view, is an example of a tradition indicating a view of reality based on meditational experience.

## THE AMULET BOX TRADITION OF SHANGPA KAGYÜ

The amulet box tradition of the Shangpa Kagyü lineage from Kaydrub Kyungpo teaches, "The preliminary basis is [mind's] automatically coming to its own level in its three aspects. The actual method is [mind's] automatically releasing into itself the three faults. The result is [mind's] automatically giving rise to the three bodies of a Buddha. The actual method is also called 'recognizing the thieves.' The main guideline instruction of the Shangpa Kagyü line is that of the six practices or 'yogas' of Niguma."

The three aspects are mind's essence, nature and defining characteristic, namely its voidness, clear light lucidity and appearance-making. The three faults are becoming attached to the boon experiences of stark non-conceptuality, clarity and bliss based on the three aspects, which can lead to rebirth in, respectively, the realms of formless beings, ethereal forms or desirable sensory objects. Likewise, the three bodies of a Buddha automatically arise from the three aspects of mind — from its voidness, a body encompassing everything; from its clear light lucidity, a body of forms of full use; and from its appearance-making, a body of emanations.

The auto-commentary continues, "Of these six practices of Niguma, those of tummo are for inducing the many realizations of the pathway minds. The illusory body ones are for the automatic release of attachment and hostility." The illusory body here seems to be slightly different from that presented in the Guhyasamaja system. In this context, illusory body seems to refer to the practices for seeing everything to be like illusion, as explained in the madhyamaka texts. By training our mind to see that, like illusions, everything that appears to the mind does so on the basis of being devoid of true and inherent existence, we are able to experience attachment and hostility automatically releasing themselves.

Furthermore, "The dream practices entail deceptive appearances within what is already deceptive automatically clearing away. Clear light practice is for eliminating the darkness of ignorance. Transference of consciousness is for attaining Buddhahood without meditation. Bardo practice, during the period between death and rebirth, is for achieving a triumphant Buddha's body of full use. Of these six practices of Niguma, the amulet box tradition takes as primary the practice of clear light." This involves anuttarayoga tantra methods of meditation for penetrating vital points of the vajra-body in order to make manifest clear light mind.

Kaydrub Kyungpo was a great yogi meditator. In his text *Hundreds of Verses for Auspiciousness*, which contains verses for all to be auspicious for meditation, he wrote, "May everything be auspicious for the mahamudra of great bliss — the sphere of voidness, clarity and appearance — [seen] when purified down to the depths. Any appearance to which mind gives rise of anything that exists automatically emanates like a dream or illusion — a tone of uninterrupted great bliss."

This is Kaydrub Kyungpo's description of the mahamudra that is the greatly blissful simultaneously arising clear light mind of deep awareness. His point that it can only be seen "when purified down to the depths" implies that it cannot be apprehended by coarser levels of mind. Therefore, to see it we must stop taking things to mind on the coarser levels. This, then, is not the Hoshang position of blank-mindedness in which we do not take anything to mind at all, although the manner of expression may lead us to consider it the same. This is similarly the case with the line, "If it is apprehended, it is not the view."

We should note that there were undoubtedly two Hoshangs in the history of Buddhism in Tibet. "Hoshang" is simply the Chinese word for "monk." The first hoshangs in Tibet were masters of the Chan tradition — called "Zen" in Japan — who translated Chinese texts into Tibetan at Samyay Monastery at the time of Shantarakshita. If they had been advocates of blank-minded meditation and had repudiated the value of constructive deeds, Shantarakshita himself would have refuted them in debate. There would have been no need to invite his disciple Kamalashila to come to Tibet from India in the future to refute the Hoshang who would teach distorted, antagonistic views. The Hoshang whom Kamalashila defeated at the Samyay debates, then, was another Chinese hoshang or monk who advocated a degenerate, incorrect view of Chan.

The next line of Kaydrub Kyungpo's verse, "Any appearance to which mind gives rise of anything that exists automatically emanates...," refers to the fact that since all phenomena, from their depths, are devoid of being concretely real, anything having a devoid nature automatically establishes its existence. It "automatically emanates" in the sense that, by virtue of being devoid of a true and inherent nature, it is able to arise, able to exist. Thus when we say, as in *The Heart Sutra*, "Voidness is form; form is voidness," we mean "Voidness, therefore form; form, therefore voidness."

Because anything, such as forms of physical phenomena, automatically establishes its existence by virtue of its having a devoid nature, and is thus devoid of being a concrete reality, it is not the case that originally phenomena had a truly and inherently existing nature and then had that nature removed from them as their basis. From the start, everything, primordially from its depths, has been devoid of existing as a concrete reality. Thus the line, "Not being [truly and inherently existent], they appear like an illusion," is extremely powerful. This is the meaning of the term "automatically emanates" in Kaydrub Kyungpo's verse.

"Uninterrupted great bliss" in the phrase "a tone of uninterrupted great bliss" refers to a greatly blissful awareness that is generated into a deep awareness of voidness and is thus inseparably in the same package as the void abiding nature of all objects that automatically emanate. Just as anything that exists, and can thus appear, is an automatic emanation of voidness, likewise any appearance of what exists is an automatic emanation or "tone" of the greatly blissful clear light deep awareness of that voidness which, simultaneously arising with each moment, is "uninterrupted." When this type of greatly blissful deep awareness has manifested — in other words when the deep awareness arises that is an individualizing, reflexive pure awareness of itself as a unity of blissful awareness and its emanations and that is the stable foundational basis for any appearance that emanates — we have purified down to the depths.

This is "the sphere of voidness, clarity and appearance," in the sense that while appearing, things are devoid of concrete reality, and while being devoid of impossible modes of existence, things clearly arise. Thus the unity of appearance and voidness, of emanation and blissful awareness, is like space — a lack of anything tangible or physically obstructive. This tradition, then, ascribes the name "mahamudra" to such greatly blissful deep awareness.

## THE POSSESSING FIVE TRADITION OF DRIGUNG KAGYÜ

The possessing five tradition, according to the auto-commentary, "asserts in songs of meditational experience that the enlightening influence of the Dagpo Kagyü lineage masters is great and that of Jigten-gönpo is the root." Jigten-gönpo, as the paramount guru, is the founder of the Drigung school. In a short conversation I once had with Kyungka Rinpochey, this late Ladhaki Drigung Kagyü lama affirmed to me that the root of the possessing five tradition is indeed fervent regard and respect for the gurus. Thus there is a great emphasis on guru-yoga and practices of collecting and cleansing.

The first of the five features of this tradition is, "If you fail to direct the racehorse of bodhichitta to the racetrack of benefiting others, you miss outstripping in radiance worldly gods and men. Therefore, exert effort in this dedicated heart as preliminary." Thus the first point is bodhichitta meditation as preliminary. All practices of the perfection vehicle are included in the practices of bodhichitta and the six far-reaching attitudes. Since we must hold the rest of the pathway minds within the context of a dedicated heart of bodhichitta, if we lack it, we are unable to stabilize all that follows. "Therefore, exert effort in this dedicated heart as preliminary."

As for the second feature, "If you fail to take, as an unchanging basis, your body generated in the aspect of a kingly Buddha-form, you miss gathering together an attendant circle of dakinis — female forces of unimpeded action. Therefore, exert effort in your body as a divine yidam — a Buddha-form with which to bond." We must stop our mind's producing an appearance of our body in its ordinary fashion and implying its true inherent existence, and generate instead, in a stable and enduring manner, a pure appearance of it as a Buddha-form and apprehend it as such. If we do not do this in a stable fashion so that it does not alter, we lack a basis for gathering together, on vital points of our subtle vajra-body, dakinis to help develop and enhance in us a joyful state of awareness. "Therefore exert effort in your body as a divine yidam." The second feature of the five, then, is visualizing our body in the aspect of a Buddha-form.

The third feature is, "If you fail to shine the sun of fervent regard and respect on the snow mountain of your guru, who possesses the four Buddha-bodies, you miss having a stream of waters of inspiration flow forth. Therefore exert effort in this mind of fervent regard and respect." The root of all actual attainments through the tantra path is our guru as a Buddha-form with which to bond. Moreover, the root for all inspiration to achieve these attainments is the guru. Thus if we lack the sun of a mind of fervent regard and respect for our guru, we are unable to experience a flow of inspiration cascading into our mind like the rushing of a mountain stream. "Therefore exert effort in this mind of fervent regard and respect."

As for the fourth feature, "If you fail to purify the mass of clouds of conceptual thoughts from the expanse of space of mind itself, you miss having the planets and stars of twofold omniscient awareness sparkle forth. Therefore, exert effort in this non-conceptual mind." In order to come to the deep awareness of an omniscient mind of a Buddha that straightforwardly and non-conceptually omnisciently knows simultaneously the extent of all phenomena and how they exist, we must accustom ourselves to the primordial, simultaneously arising clear light mind of deep awareness on its full and complete level. In order to do this, we must dissipate the mass of clouds of our conceptual minds. "Therefore exert effort in this non-conceptual mind."

The fifth and final feature of the possessing five tradition is, "If you fail to polish with prayers the wish-granting gem of your two bountiful stores, you miss having flow forth the enlightening influence needed and desired. Therefore, exert effort in this dedication at the end." The two bountiful stores of positive potential and deep awareness are likened here to a wish-granting gem. We must enhance them properly with our repeated prayers and dedications. If we do not properly dedicate these bountiful stores we have built up so that they serve as causes for our attainment to the enlightened state of a Buddha, we miss receiving the enlightening influence of the Three Precious Gems. "Therefore exert effort in this dedication at the end."


## THE DRUGPA KAGYÜ TRADITION OF THE SIX SPHERES OF EQUAL TASTE

The tradition of the six spheres of equal taste transmits "eight great discourses, six spheres of equal taste, and seven measures to practice and hold tightly. The eight great discourses concern the guru's three Buddha-bodies, love and compassion, the dependent arising of cause and effect, the dripping of nectars possessing five, simultaneously arising as merged, the six practices of Naropa, equalizing the mind toward the eight transitory things in life, and meditating on turning away interferences with hidden behavior." The six practices or "yogas" of Naropa are tummo, illusory body, clear light, bardo, transference of consciousness and entering the citadel. Dream practices are included among those of illusory body. The eight transitory things in life are praise, blame, good news, bad news, gains, losses, things going well and things going poorly.

"The six spheres of equal taste" — meaning an equal taste on the conventional and deepest levels — "are taking conceptual minds, disturbing emotions and attitudes, massive sicknesses, demonic curses, sufferings and death each as a pathway." It teaches various attitudes to develop with regard to the conventional and deepest levels for equalizing our attitudes toward each of these six.

"The seven measures are the four ornaments for the profound Dharma and the ornaments of guidelines for the three spheres. The four ornaments for the profound Dharma are the source of good qualities — namely, engaging in the preliminary practices for tantra — receiving empowerments, practicing the two stages based on hidden explanation of the subtle vajra-body, and engaging in the bardo practices in between rebirths for enhancing our progress. The ornaments of guidelines for the three spheres concern eliminating interfering spirits, registering the hundreds of thousands of songs of meditational experience, and detailing the collection of fine points." These are all transmitted by the Drugpa Kagyü tradition.

In the writings on the dependent arising tradition in the works of the Drugpa Kagyü founder, Tsangpa Gyaray, we find ample explanation of realizing the unity of inseparable dependent arising and voidness. He explains that the main point of the correct view of reality is to see the unity of these two in the sense that dependent arising helps establish voidness, and voidness helps establish dependent arising. Except for a difference in manner of expression, his presentation comes to exactly the same point as we find in other traditions.

## THE FOUR SYLLABLES TRADITION COMMON TO ALL DAGPO KAGYÜ LINEAGES

The four syllables tradition, deriving from Maitripa, expounds on the four syllables "a-ma-na-si," which comprise the Sanskrit word "not to take to mind." "A" is the Sanskrit prefix for negation, while "manasi" means "to take to mind." As for the deeper significance of the four syllables, the auto-commentary explains, "The first refers to cutting down to the foundational root state, the second shows the methods for settling the mind, the third cuts mind off from points where it can deviate, and the fourth demonstrates how to take mind as a pathway." This tradition teaches methods for mahamudra meditation in terms of these four points.

## THE PACIFIER TRADITION OF PA DAMPA-SANGGYAY

Next is the pacifier tradition of fatherly Pa Dampa-sanggyay, deriving from the scriptural line, "The pure view pacifies all suffering." We pacify all sickness, suffering, interferences, problems from harmful spirits, and so forth, into the pure sphere of clear light mind. We do this by looking barely and starkly at this basic primordial mind and train ourselves to see that all appearances arise from it like an illusory body, or illusion in general. In meditation, we overcome mental dullness by exclaiming loudly and forcefully the syllable "pay" (phat), while imagining our mind shooting out the top of the crown of our head and mixing with space. To overcome flightiness of mind, we cut down to the root, in other words we cut away the level of mind that goes toward appealing distractions. If our mind wanders after various objects of attachment or desire, we focus on the underlying nature or basis for these objects. In this way, a correct view of reality in terms of clear light mind pacifies all suffering and problems.

This is a very profound system of practice. When our mind gives rise to any bad omens, we transform our experience of them into a pathway of practice by seeing them to be in the nature of conceptual mind. When our body gives rise to sicknesses, we see them as what dependently arises from a disturbance of the four elements. Thus, we take as our main practice *lojong*, cleansing our attitudes, accomplished through *tonglen*, taking on and giving. We take on or accept whatever experiences of difficulties or hardships arise and give them a beneficial function by transforming them into pathway minds through seeing their clear light nature. Thus even when we experience death, we continue our practice by transforming it into the perfect opportunity for realizing the mother clear light mind. Thus our "pure view pacifies all suffering."

## THE OBJECT TO BE CUT OFF, DZOGCHEN AND MADHYAMAKA DISCURSIVE VIEW TRADITIONS

The object to be cut off tradition, deriving from the One Mother of All, Machig Labkyi-drölma, transmits *chöd*, the cutting-off rite, as found in all subsequent traditions in Tibet. The auto-commentary does not elaborate further. The dzogchen tradition derives from the heart essence of the mind of Padmasambhava, Guru Rinpochey. It has three divisions or lineages, known as the mind, open expanse and oral guideline divisions. Although each transmits the full dzogchen teachings, the mind division emphasizes primal purity, the open expanse stresses spontaneously establishing; while the oral guideline underscores the unity of the two. Finally, the First Panchen Lama lists the tradition of the discursive view of madhyamaka transmitted by the Gelug lineage, followed by "and so on," without further comment.

The First Panchen Lama concludes by stating that all these traditions come, in the end, to the same intended point. He supports this in the auto-commentary with an example deriving from *The Stainless Light*, a commentary by Pundarika on *The Abbreviated Kalachakra Tantra*. The example is that of a precious gem. Although different languages may have different names for this object, it is still the same gem no matter what we call it. Likewise these different traditions use different names and words for the deepest points, but their meaning is the same.

# Session Six

## THE BASIC PREREQUISITES FOR ACHIEVING SHAMATHA

Having presented the various traditions that transmit methods for meditating on mahamudra, the First Panchen Lama now begins his discussion of the actual techniques for mahamudra practice. He explains that there are two approaches. Those of sharpest faculties seek first an understanding of the correct view and, once that understanding has become decisive, pursue afterwards the methods for meditating single-pointedly on it. The other approach follows a quotation from Shantideva's *Engaging in a Bodhisattva's Deeds* that first we pursue meditation for achieving shamata and then, once we have a significant level of success in that, we apply that mind single-pointedly to scrutinizing or "analytical" meditation on the correct view. Here, the First Panchen Lama explains Shantideva's tradition of seeking the meditative state first, and then, on top of that, the view of reality. Therefore he now presents the techniques for achieving shamata. For this, he divides his presentation into a discussion of the preliminaries, actual techniques and concluding procedures.

The preliminaries are the prerequisites described in the texts of Maitreya. First, we need a proper place for meditation practice, one with easy access to various necessities such as food and water, where the conditions are not harmful to health. In other words, we need a place where everything is conducive and nothing detrimental for intensive practice. Furthermore, if the site has been blessed by the presence of a great practitioner in the past, the enduring impression of his or her inspiration will render the place particularly conducive for gaining absorbed concentration. Then we must establish, as the stable foundation for practice of shamata, our training in ethical self-discipline. As Tsongkapa has explained clearly in *A Grand* and *A Short Presentation of the Graded Stages of the Path*, training in higher concentration is founded on prior training in ethical self-discipline.

To gain a concentrated state of shamata, it is necessary to stop the mind from all flightiness and dullness. The main tools to accomplish this are mindfulness or remembering, and alertness. To gain the skill and strength to apply these two to bringing our state of mind under control, we cultivate them through training in ethical self-discipline. As the foundation, then, for our practice of shamata, we uphold purely whatever level of vowed restraints we have accepted, appropriate to our status — either those of a lay person, or those of a novice or fully ordained monk or nun. With mindfulness, we always keep in mind or remember, "If I act like this, it is totally improper. If I act like that, it is perfectly proper." With alertness, we keep constant watch on our actions and whenever necessary apply self-control and restraint. By strengthening our mindfulness and alertness in this way, we build the foundation for being able to apply these faculties for restraining our mind from subtle deviations of distraction and so forth during meditation. This is extremely important.

Next, for achieving shamata it is necessary to practice in a disciplined fashion. Even if we are practicing many short sessions a day to cultivate absorbed concentration, we must keep to a strict schedule and hold the sessions at the same place, at their proper times, focusing on the same object. If we are nervous, frightened, restless, preoccupied with busywork or have many things to do or think about, we will never be able to become focused. Therefore we must keep our tasks and purposes to a minimum. For this reason, it is quite impossible to attain a state of shamata while actively working and living in society. We have to remain in an isolated, quiet place and devote our time and energies exclusively to this. Although the scriptural texts claim that we can achieve a state of shamata within a mere six months of practice, that is extremely rare and difficult. We must be prepared for several years of intensive work in a completely isolated location.

Contentment is also an important adjunct for achieving a serenely stilled and settled mind. If we are dissatisfied with our situation and always thinking about finding a better place for meditating or better conditions, we never settle down to concentrating our mind. We are constantly distracted, always thinking about one thing or another extraneous to our object of focus. We must be content with what we have and get down to our purpose.

## CLEANING THE PLACE OF PRACTICE, PREPARING THE SEAT AND ASSUMING THE PROPER POSTURE

Every day we need to perform the six basic preliminaries before beginning our meditation practice. This pertains not only to developing shamata, but to any meditation in general. First is tidying, sweeping and dusting our place of practice. We do not do this in just a perfunctory manner, but conscientiously and carefully. If the environment around us is neat, clean and orderly, this makes a significant difference in our meditative state of mind. Secondly, we arrange representations of the enlightening body, speech and mind of the Buddhas. These can be either elaborate or modest, it makes no difference. But they should be as handsome as possible, and placed on an altar in the proper manner and order. Before them, we lay out actual offerings, the best we can afford, arranging them also in the proper way.

The third basic preliminary begins with making three prostrations and taking our seat. Our seat should be one conducive for gaining mental stability and absorbed concentration. Thus its back needs to be raised a few finger widths higher than the front so that it is easier to sit with our back straight. This can be accomplished by sitting on a cushion of comfortable thickness and hardness.

When we sit and study, our posture is not especially critical. But here, for meditation, it is important. We need optimally to sit in the sevenfold posture of Vairochana, with legs crossed in the full vajra position, more popularly known by its name in hatha yoga, the full lotus position. The back is straight, shoulders even and held slightly back, head slightly bent forward, eyes loosely focused in the direction of the tip of the nose, and teeth and lips not clenched but with the tip of the tongue touching the upper palate. The hands are resting in the lap in the pose of total absorption, with palms up, the right hand on top of the left, and thumbs touching each other to form a triangle, with their tips placed at or slightly below the navel. The elbows are not locked making the arms stiff, but are bent and held slightly away from the body.

If we cannot sit in the full vajra position, it is fine to sit in the half vajra posture, or just in the usual way in which you sit cross-legged. But it is auspicious at least to start the session by sitting, even for a very short while, in the full vajra posture. You can then shift to a more comfortable position. It is very important, however, no matter which way you sit, for your back to be straight and not to sway back and forth or up and down. For those unaccustomed from childhood to sitting cross-legged, it is possible to sit on a chair. But you must sit up, with your back straight and not leaning against the backrest.

## GENERATING AN INITIAL NEUTRAL STATE OF MIND WITH THE NINE TASTES OF BREATH

Next we perform a round of the nine tastes of breath. In the preliminary practices for developing tummo, we start these nine by first breathing in through the left nostril in accordance with the customs of mother tantra. But here, there is no need for that. We begin instead by inhaling first through the right nostril. Thus we block the left nostril with the forefinger and breathe in through the right nostril. Then blocking the right nostril with that same finger, we exhale through the left. We repeat this cycle three times. Then we reverse this procedure, blocking the right nostril with the forefinger and inhaling through the left. Then blocking the left nostril, we breathe out our right. We repeat this cycle also three times. We then inhale and exhale three times evenly through both nostrils at once. While doing this, we focus solely on the breath coming in and going out, without thinking about anything else. There is no need to visualize the various energy-channels and chakras as we would do when performing these nine rounds as a preliminary for anuttarayoga tantra's complete stage practice.

When we focus our attention on the passage of breath, we break the usually continuous flow of thoughts of attachment, hostility and so forth, whatever they might be. This causes such thoughts to subside for the moment. Thus, by occupying the mind with our breath, we cleanse it of all positive and negative conceptual thoughts and thus remain in a neutral state of mind unspecified as either constructive or destructive. This is the meaning of the line in the root text, "Thoroughly clean out your state of awareness." This unspecified or neutral state of mind, cleaned out of all positive and negative conceptual thoughts, is the most conducive one to work with. Because an unspecified state of mind like this is unburdened and supple, it is relatively easy to generate it into a constructive state.

## GENERATING A CONSTRUCTIVE STATE OF MIND

We generate this constructive state purely by working ourselves up to feeling a proper motivation. To do this, we think thoroughly about turning the mind away from its obsession with this lifetime and then away from its obsession with future lives. Subsequently, we generate the excellent state of mind that thinks, "May I be able to bring deep and everlasting happiness and its causes to all beings and free them completely from all sufferings and their causes." On this basis, we then take safe direction and dedicate our hearts with bodhichitta.

As the fourth preliminary, we visualize a field for building up positive potential and, as our fifth, perform a seven-part practice and offer a mandala. Finally, the sixth preliminary is guru-yoga. For these last preliminaries, once we have performed a round of the nine tastes of breath, we usually recite *A Ritual to Honor the Spiritual Master*, starting from "Within a state of indivisible bliss and voidness...." We recite it while thinking very carefully about each point in accordance with a discourse that we have received separately on the text and practice. If we cannot do that, we can perform any other guru-yoga, either elaborate or brief. We regard our guru as incorporating all gurus, Buddha-forms, Buddhas, dharma-protectors, dakinis, Sangha and all holy Dharma teachings. In other words, we regard our guru as having a nature that incorporates all precious objects of safe direction. We think, "No matter what situation or circumstance may arise, I set my hopes on and take safe direction from no one but you." Thus from the depths of our heart, with total sincerity, we take safe direction and make requests for inspiration while repeating the mantra of our guru's name.

If we are practicing guru-yoga on the basis of *A Ritual to Honor the Spiritual Master* and are visualizing the tree of assembled gurus as our field for building up positive potential, we imagine at the end of our recitation that this field dissolves in stages into the central figure, Lama Lozang Tubwang Dorjeychang. He then comes to the top of our head. We make even stronger, special requests for inspiration while imagining a flow of purifying nectars entering us from him, and, in the end, imagine that our guru, in the form of this composite figure, dissolves into us. Then, imagining that our faculties of body, speech and mind have integrated inseparably with those of our glorious guru's enlightening body, speech and mind, we remain in a state of faith, joy and respect. It is within the context of this state of mind that we take mind itself as our object of focus for developing shamata.

## FOCUSING ON MIND ITSELF

Having performed all these preliminaries, we proceed with the actual body of the meditation. The root text says, "Absorb for a while unwaveringly in this state in which all haphazard appearance-making and appearances have been contracted until they have disappeared. Do not contrive anything with thoughts such as expectations or worries."

In general, for accomplishing shamata, we can choose from various objects on which to focus, depending on our disposition, intelligence and capacity. Tsongkapa has discussed this thoroughly in *A Grand* and *A Short Presentation of the Graded Stages of the Path.* We can focus on a fully embraced object, either something physical like the breath or a visualized image, for instance a Buddha, with either of them entailing focus either simply on the object itself or on the object together with its qualities that we have previously inspected. Or we can focus on an object, together with its qualities that we have previously scrutinized, for cleansing our behavior from being under the influence of a specific disturbing emotion or attitude, such as focusing on a body for which we have longing desire, together with its ugly aspects. Likewise, we can focus on an object for cleansing our mind of disturbing emotions and attitudes in general, such as the trance-like absorptions associated with the realms of ethereal forms or formless beings, or the sixteen aspects of the four true facts in life. There are also objects of the learned and skilled, such as the five aggregate factors of experience or the twelve factors that dependently arise. There are so many possible objects of focus — we can focus on an external object or, within our bodies, on an energy-drop, a visualized seed-syllable or various lights. Here, on this occasion, the object of focus for developing a state of shamata is our own mind.

The samadhi or absorbed concentration that we try to achieve is a non-conceptual state that has the two features of being firmly settled and vividly clear. The actual state fulfilling the definition of shamata that we try to achieve is accomplished from a single-pointed state of this type of absorbed concentration, one that is still included within the realm of desirable sensory objects. The method for achieving this is, as outlined by Maitreya, to recognize the five deterrents to concentration, rely on the eight composing mental faculties to correct them, and progress through the nine stages for settling the mind by employing the six powers and the four types of attention. The five deterrents are laziness, forgetfulness, mental dullness and flightiness, non-application of opponents and over-application of opponents. The eight composing mental faculties are respectful belief, intention, positive enthusiasm, a sense of fitness, mindfulness, alertness, application of opponents when needed and no longer applying opponents when unnecessary. The nine stages for settling the mind are initial settling on an object of focus, settling with continuity, settling repeatedly, close settling, taming, stilling, complete stilling, single-pointedness and settling with equal ease. The six powers are listening to the instructions, pondering them, mindfulness, alertness, positive enthusiasm and complete familiarity. The four types of attention are painstaking, resetting, uninterrupted and spontaneous.

Here, the preliminary practice of guru-yoga helps to establish an extremely conducive state of mind with which to begin to focus on mind itself. When we have made sincere requests for inspiration to our guru with a great deal of feeling so that our heart is genuinely moved, we dissolve the visualization of our guru into us. We feel great inspiration by imagining our own faculties of body, speech and mind being inseparably integrated with the enlightened physical, verbal, and mental faculties of our guru. This makes our state of mind one of serene, uplifting joy, based on a deep and sincere feeling of respect and confident belief in our guru. We rest in this state for a little while.

In the process of contracting the visualization of the tree of assembled gurus into the central figure of our guru, bringing that to the top of the crown of our head and dissolving that into us so that it disappears, we have stopped our mind from its appearance-making. This procedure for temporarily stopping the mind from its usual habits functions to draw the mind in closer. As we withdraw the mind from gross external objects and gross conceptual imaginings in this manner, we automatically arrive at a more subtle state of mind. Moreover, our feelings of confident trust, respect, inspiration, and serene, uplifting joy make it a very vivid and alert state of mind with only the subtlest conceptual aspects.

In such a relatively subtle state of mind in which appearances have been contracted and appearance-making thoughts have ceased, we try not to generate any new thoughts about hopes for the future, whether that be for temporary or ultimate goals. Likewise, we try not to think of or remember what we have done in the past, or self-consciously think about what we are doing now. Rather, we simply remain within the present moment, in a non-contriving state of mind, without mentally fabricating expectations or worries, and absorb our mind in the mere clarity and awareness that is the mind.

This mere clarity and mere awareness into which we absorb is free from all conceptual thought of the past, present or future. Free from all expectations or worries, it is here-and-now, without any contriving. It is the immediate cause that, when it meets with circumstances, gives rise to all thoughts and appearance-making minds. It is in this sense that I think that the mere clarity and awareness that we focus on here in this subtle state of mind with no conceptual thoughts is the coarse primordial mind that we mentioned before.

Consider the example of water. When water is murky and dirty, it has the nature of being fluid and wet. When it is clear and clean, its nature of being fluid and wet is still the same. This is the nature of water. Whether water is clean or dirty, its nature as a liquid remains the same. Likewise, even when a disturbed state of mind such as attachment or anger is manifest, it does not discard having a nature of being a mere clarity and a mere awareness. Even when our ultimate, deepest, most subtle clear light mind is manifest, it still does not discard having this very same nature. Mere clarity and awareness is something that has been there from the depths, primally, with no beginning. In this sense, it is primordial. Thus the subtlest primordial mind of clear light, which arises simultaneously with each moment and which is this here-and-now, non-contriving mind, without any artifice of conceptual thoughts such as hopes or fears, is undoubtedly what Gyelrong Tsültrim-nyima has given the name "coarse primordial mind." This coarse primordial mind, then, comes down to being mind's mere clarity and awareness that has primordially always been the case, with no beginning. We absorb our mind into this.

## RECOGNIZING MERE CLARITY AND AWARENESS

It is quite difficult to recognize what mere clarity and mere awareness actually refer to. We all learned this definition of mind in the early stages of our Buddhist education when we studied *lorig*, ways of knowing, and *dura*, collected topics. Something rough comes to mind when we think about the division of non-static or "impermanent" phenomena into those that are forms of physical phenomena, those that are ways of being aware of something and those affecting variables that are neither — in other words, forms, minds and neither. But it is quite difficult to recognize the meaning of clarity and awareness on the basis of experience. We can easily list hundreds of examples of ways of being aware of something, but to recognize what their nature of being mere clarity and awareness is actually referring to is rather enigmatic. It is not something we can know simply from reading books. We can only recognize it by extensively investigating internally, researching our own experience of mind from many points of view.

Mere clarity and awareness refers to the fact that mind is something that, when it meets with the proper circumstances, can, without obstruction, give rise to an appearance of anything as something that is known. In this respect, mind is somewhat similar to a mirror that, on an external, non-cognitive level, unobstructively also gives rise to appearances of objects. No matter what aspect of what external object we encounter — its sight, sound, smell, taste or tactile or physical sensation — clarity is that which allows for a corresponding aspect to arise or appear unobstructedly. Awareness is an engaging with or pervading of an object in such a way as to render it something that is known, unobstructedly, in one way or another. Thus, from another point of view, clarity and awareness are absences of obstruction that would prevent anything from arising as something that is known. This is mind's nature of being mere clarity and awareness.

## FOCUSING WITH MINDFULNESS AND ALERTNESS
When we recognize this here-and-now, non-contriving mind — its primordial state of being mere clarity and awareness — we take this as the focal object of our meditation. While we are experiencing it, we must avoid falling to a withdrawn state of not having any mental activity or not being mindful of anything — as if we had fallen unconscious or asleep. Should we meditate in such a manner, then even though we may have placement on the nature of the here-and-now, non-contriving mind, we receive no benefit. This is due to the total degeneration of our mindfulness and alertness. Therefore, we must be vigilant in always accompanying our meditation with strong mindfulness and alertness. The First Panchen Lama says in the root text, "Tie [your attention] to the post of mindfulness in order not to wander, and station alertness to be aware of any mental movement."

Mindfulness is the mental faculty accompanying our meditative state that keeps our attention fixed to the object of focus so that it does not wander from it. With mindfulness, we constantly remember the object in the sense of constantly keeping it in mind without letting go. The function of alertness is to keep a continuous check for any mental wandering, in other words any movement from the object of focus, as well as any mental dullness. With alertness, we remain ever prepared to correct our meditative state if we notice any deviation or fault. This is the general presentation of mindfulness and alertness.

## DEGREES AND VARIETIES OF DISTRACTION AND DULLNESS

To correct our meditation from deviations in focus throughout the process of settling the mind, we need to identify and recognize clearly and immediately the numerous hindrances to concentration to which mind commonly gives rise. For example, there are different types of distraction. Flightiness of mind is when mind flies off to an attractive object because of attachment. When it strays to an extraneous object for any other reason in general, this is simply called mental wandering. Mental wandering is less compelling than flightiness of mind. There are two general levels of flightiness. The gross level is when mind loses the hold of its mindfulness on its focal object completely. The subtle level occurs when mind maintains its hold, but either has a subtle level of wandering beneath the surface, like the slow flow of water on the bottom of a frozen river, or is more steady but seemingly "itchy" to move.

Mental dullness has gross, middling and subtle degrees. When mind loses its focal object because it lacks all clarity, this is gross mental dullness. When this degenerates further, we experience foggy-mindedness, with which our body and mind feel very heavy, as if plunged into a darkness or a dense fog. Foggy-mindedness soon brings on sleepiness and even falling asleep. The middling degree of mental dullness is when mind has clarity on its object of focus, but no sharpness associated with the tightness of hold of its mindfulness. This happens when that tightness has become completely casual and therefore far too loose. Subtle mental dullness occurs when the mind that is single-pointedly focused on its object slightly loses the sharpness associated with the tightness of hold of its mindfulness on that object, so that such a mind loses its freshness and becomes slightly stale. This happens when the tightness in this situation has become a little too loose or relaxed. Because this is so subtle, there is a great danger of mistaking a meditative state containing subtle mental dullness for one of faultless absorbed concentration. Maintaining a check on our meditative state with alertness, we must notice all these faults to concentration as soon as the mind gives rise to any of them, so that we can eliminate them immediately.

## HOW TO CULTIVATE ALERTNESS AND ABSORBED CONCENTRATION

The most important factor, then, for achieving an unchanging state of absorbed concentration is using mindfulness and alertness in the proper manner. In A *Last Testament Letter Cast to the Wind*, Gyelrong Tsültrim-nyima has explained that if we look from the side of mind's single-pointed hold on its object of focus so that there is no wandering from it, we call it mindfulness. If we look from the side of its remaining single-pointedly placed or focused on its object so long as it is held, we call it absorbed concentration. Thus these two mental faculties are of the same entity — they come in the same package — and are, in fact, the same mind regarded from the point of view of two functions: holding its object and remaining placed on its object. By logically excluding everything that each is not, we specify two different things.

This explanation of these two mental factors comes from meditative experience and indicates a very important oral guideline. The way to achieve absorbed concentration is, in fact, the way in which we achieve mindfulness. By cultivating our hold on an object of focus so that we never lose it, we accomplish remaining single-pointedly placed on and absorbed in that object.

Shantideva has explained how to develop alertness in the chapter on this topic in *Engaging in a Bodhisattva's Deeds*, "When mental placement has been achieved in the sense that mindfulness is protecting it from [leaving] the gateway of the mind, alertness comes naturally. And even if [placement] goes, it brings it back." The actual definition of alertness appears later in that chapter, "The defining characteristic of safeguarding with alertness is, in brief, just this — inspecting, over and again, the condition of the body and mind."

In *A Grand Presentation of the Graded Stages of the Path*, Tsongkapa has differentiated two levels of alertness we need to develop. The common one is that which comes concomitant with the establishment of stable mindfulness. The uncommon one is that which later makes occasional spot-checks. Mindfulness, however, is the main mental faculty to cultivate, while alertness is secondary since it comes naturally within a state of mindfulness.

When we say that alertness is a consequence of mindfulness, we do not mean that they are related through a sequence of cause and effect like a sprout being the result of a seed. Their relation is similar to that between the sun and rays of sunlight. If there is a sun, there are automatically rays of sunlight simultaneously with it. Sunlight depends on a sun for its existence. It is a consequence of a sun, but not the sequential result of a sun in the manner of a sprout coming from a seed. Thus if we have strong mindfulness like a sun, as a consequence we have alertness as well, like rays of sunlight. This seems also to be an explanation that comes from meditational experience.

When we check the state of our concentration with alertness, we do so with just a corner of our mind. The main part of mind is placed single-pointedly on the object of focus, while just a corner of it is keeping a check. We need to discover the correct measure for this, because if we maintain this watch too strongly with alertness, we face the danger of losing our focal object. In other words, we shall be concentrating more on maintaining a watch than on our intended object of focus. Therefore we must sink our mind deeply into our focal object so that it is absorbed in it, yet still maintain a watch with a corner of our mind to check whether or not our mental placement is remaining properly.

## REDUCING CONCEPTUAL THOUGHTS

When we have decisively identified and recognized the mere clarity and awareness that is the nature of mind, we hold it tightly with mindfulness and, as the First Panchen Lama says in the root text, single-pointedly "behold it starkly." When we are meditating like this, should the mind give rise to any mental movement or conceptual thoughts, we must first recognize them. To be able to do so depends on alertness.

In *Notes from a Discourse on the Gelug Tradition of Mahamudra,* Gungtangzang has differentiated several ways of cultivating mindfulness, such as cultivating a new mindfulness, cultivating the old mindfulness, cultivating it just on the occasion, cultivating it under another name and cultivating it with a conceptual thought by itself. I am not positive whether this division applies here or not, but when, in his root text, the First Panchen Lama gives a choice of methods to use when our mind gives rise to conceptual thoughts, "...simply recognize them or, like your opponent in a duel, cut thoughts immediately as soon as they occur," it seems as though in the former case we employ the method of cultivating a new mindfulness, whereas in the second, cultivating our old mindfulness. But I am not sure. Gungtangzang associates these different ways to cultivate mindfulness with specific stages that we pass through as we progress through the nine stages for settling the mind. In their notes on our root text, however, neither Gungtangzang nor Aku Sherab-gyatso have applied this division here. They simply state the two techniques that the First Panchen Lama himself differentiates.

In any case, when, in a here-and-now, non-contriving mind we vividly and starkly behold its nature, holding this with tight mindfulness as our object of focus and maintaining a watch with alertness, should our mind all of a sudden give rise to a conceptual thought, then without purposely blocking it we recognize and focus on its nature. The here-and-now, non-contriving mind — in other words, coarse primordial mind — is like an ocean. When we consider conceptual thoughts to be like fleeting waves that rise out of the ocean without going beyond being in the nature of water, we do not experience any harm from them to our vivid placement on here-and-now, non-contriving mind. This is the special feature of the technique of recognizing the nature of conceptual thoughts — namely, recognizing conceptual minds for what they are. As we say in the Karma Kagyü tradition, "Conceptual minds are waves of dharmakaya."

For example, when we dream, if we do not recognize our dream as a dream, we experience the happenings in the dream as if they were real and they go on. But, if we recognize our dream as a dream, the dream is still happening, yet because we recognize it as a dream, our mind is more relaxed about it, even if it is a fearsome dream. We do not fall under the power of the dream even if it goes on. Like this example, when a conceptual thought arises while we are vividly focused on here-and-now, non-contriving mind, if we recognize the thought for what it is, we render it powerless.

If we recognize our dreams as dreams, then if in a dream a murderer appears, we think, "Oh, this is just a dream." We do not become frightened. The murderer cannot hit his or her target for real. If when our mind gives rise to a conceptual thought we come under its power, we experience our usual coarse levels of mind following from it. But even should our mind emanate a thought, if we recognize the nature of that thought, then because we are abiding — so long as the mind that recognizes that thought as a thought does not cease — in that which is here-and-now and non-contriving, we are not taken hold of by that thought. This is the point of the technique of recognizing thoughts for what they are. The alternative method here is when our mind gives rise to a conceptual thought, to become aware of it immediately and stop it.

If, having recognized a thought as a thought as soon as our mind gives rise to one, we follow along with it, we follow along while nevertheless abiding in the basis from which it has emerged. Or, if we use the second method and purposely stop any thought immediately once we have recognized it, we likewise return to the here-and-now, non-contriving mind itself. If we continue our practice, applying very conscientiously and continuously either of these two techniques, we experience, as a result of the habit we build up, a settling of mind on itself in which we have greatly reduced our mind's giving rise to conceptual thoughts.

## LOOSENING THE TIGHTNESS OF MINDFULNESS

When we reach the state of meditation in which our conceptual thoughts of distraction have drastically reduced, then, the First Panchen Lama writes, "Without losing your mindfulness, loosen and relax its tightness." This means that in the depth of our focus, we still maintain mindfulness strongly, but on the surface we slightly loosen and relax it. We no longer need to be so tight or insistent on the surface of our focus.

What happens is as in the two quotations that the First Panchen Lama cites. Machig Labkyi-drölma has written, "Loosen and relax its firm tightness and there is the settled state of mind." The great brahmin Saraha has similarly said, "When mind ensnared in a tangle is relaxed, it frees itself without a doubt." The example is that of a string tangled in knots. When loosened, the knots naturally become untied by virtue of the loosening itself. Thus, when we have become somewhat familiar with this level of meditation and we find our hold on the object of focus to be too strong, too tight or too heavy, if at that point we loosen and on the surface somewhat relax the hold of our mindfulness, we experience improvement in our meditation.

If the mind is too tight and tense, it becomes itchy with subtle flightiness of mind. It can even fly off and discard its object of focus completely. Thus there is danger of coarse flightiness of mind as well. This the reason why, if the hold of our mindfulness is too tight, we must loosen it slightly. If, on the other hand, we loosen its hold too much, our mind loses the freshness and perhaps even the sharpness of its focus. This amounts to subtle and middling mental dullness, out of which mind lacks the strength to uplift itself. Therefore we must take care not to loosen the hold of our mindfulness too much. We need to adjust the strength of its hold to be just right in order to cultivate absorbed concentration free from all fault.

We can also understand a different level of meaning from the quotation from Saraha, "When mind ensnared in a tangle is relaxed, it frees itself without a doubt." This level concerns practitioners with a certain degree of realization of anuttarayoga tantra's complete stage. Specifically, it refers to a guideline instruction for practitioners who have reached the stage at which, for the first time, they are able to render their subtle energy-winds and minds fit for use under their meditational control. The instruction is to relax or loosen a little and continue meditating within the context of the tantra path.

In *A Grand Presentation of the Graded Stages of the Secret Mantra Path*, Tsongkapa has explained that when we have single-pointed placement on our object of focus, then by the force of having caused the subtle energy-source of bliss in our forehead chakra to melt through the practice of tummo, we experience our focus automatically becoming more vivid. At this point in our meditation on mind, tightening our awareness, as is done when practicing the perfection vehicle in order to avoid even the slightest arising of mental dullness that could harm our concentration, is unnecessary and, in fact, is the fault of redundancy. But if instead of tightening our awareness, we loosen and relax it slightly, there is no danger.

We wish to avoid the danger of mental dullness — specifically a loss of freshness or sharpness of clarity, which on the sutra level of practice can come from keeping the hold of our mindfulness too loosely on our object of focus. On anuttarayoga tantra's complete stage, however, we avoid any danger of subtle or middling mental dullness through the circumstance of our mind giving rise to either a blissful awareness, from melting our subtle energy-source, or a stark, more subtle awareness, from gathering in our energy-winds, as with vajra-breathing. While we have another method to act as an opponent for avoiding the danger of mental dullness arising when we focus on mind, if we were especially to tighten our focus on our object as an opponent force to avoid that same danger, we would have the fault of redundancy. Therefore, in that circumstance, we must loosen or relax the tightness of the hold of our mindfulness. Relaxing slightly at this point is the best way to meditate. Thus we can explain Saraha's quotation in this manner as well, in connection with tantra practice.

## SEEING THAT THE SETTLED AND MOVING MINDS ARE MIXED TOGETHER

Eventually we reach the point in our meditation on mere clarity and awareness at which any conceptual thought that arises automatically disappears by the force of our merely looking at its nature. The strength of thoughts becomes so small that all they give rise to is the bare absence that comes from their disappearance. Likewise, if we examine at the time when we have single-pointed placement on the here-and-now, non-contriving mind that is unadulterated by any conceptual thought, we see a vivid, non-obstructing bare absence and clarity as well — a pristine clarity that cannot be touched by any form of matter and which neither obstructs nor can be obstructed by anything. As our root text says, "You see that the settled and moving minds are mixed together."

In other words, even if our mind gives rise to a conceptual thought, this thought cannot hold its ground. Once we recognize this thought's face, it cannot remain standing there, having been conceived, born and now standing on its own. Immediately, in its place, mind gives rise to an appearance of the bare absence of it — equivalent to here-and-now mind's natural bare absence of anything contrived. When mind is settled on itself, it gives rise to a similar appearance of the very same bare absence and clarity. Thus we "see that the settled and moving minds are mixed together." When mind is settled on itself, it gives rise to a bare absence and clarity. When it is moving with conceptual thought, it also immediately gives rise to a bare absence and clarity. In either case, we reach the same appearance-making and appearance in the end.

## RECOGNIZING THE NATURE OF CONCEPTUAL THOUGHT

The text now explains two methods for recognizing and then placing concentration on the nature of a conceptual thought when the mind gives rise to one, without need to stop it while mind is moving or running with it. When our mind lets loose a thought, like a bird, from its here-and-now, non-contriving state, we examine, How did it arise? To where is it rushing? When we investigate it flapping its wings, we see that the thought is powerless — it cannot go anywhere. When we see the nature of a thought that is flying off, it can only disappear.

It is like the example cited in the root text from one of Saraha's dohas. In ancient times, before there were compasses, ships voyaging on the ocean would carry a few birds. If the navigator saw in the distance what seemed like a large wave, but thought that perhaps it might be dry land instead, he would release one of them. If the bird did not return to the ship, he knew there was dry land ahead. But if it were only a wave, then since they were in the middle of the sea, there was no place for the bird to land other than back on the ship. No matter how far or for how long the bird flew, in the end it would have to return. The same is true with any conceptual thought let loose by the mind. It takes off from the here-and-now, non-contriving mind and, no matter how far it goes, can only return or disappear into the here-and-now, non-contriving mind once more. This is one method.

The second method derives from Götsangpa's disciple, the Drugpa Kagyü master Yanggönpa. "When mind gives rise to a thought, do not fault it. Do not purposely meditate on a non-conceptual state. Leave mind to its own manner and keep a distant watch. It falls into place in a meditative state of shamata."

## SIX TECHNIQUES FOR ACHIEVING SHAMATA

The First Panchen Lama now explains six techniques, current at his time among all Kagyü lineages, for bringing the mind to a state of shamata. The first is to settle the mind like the example of a sun freed from all clouds. Without purposely stopping conceptual thoughts or purposely meditating in a non-conceptual manner, we just vividly focus on coarse primordial mind — the here-and-now, non-contriving, clear light nature of mind — which, like the sun freed from all clouds, remains always shining and bright and cannot be obscured by any verbal thoughts, flightiness of mind or mental dullness. If we vividly focus on mind's shining brightness for a long time, we naturally achieve a state of shamata.

The second technique is to settle the mind like an eagle gliding in the sky. When a great eagle flies through the air, due to its strength it glides without need to flap its wings furiously like a tiny sparrow. Wherever it plans to go, it simply soars off with great strength and, without flapping its wings, remains gliding aloft in a relaxed state. Likewise, without holding the mind either too tightly or too loosely, we have it soar off into its clear light state with clarity and sharpness, and then let it glide in a relaxed manner without exercising mindfulness or alertness in any extensive, frenetic way.

The third technique is to settle the mind like a ship on the great ocean. When the wind is blowing, although small waves may rise on the surface of the waters, they are powerless to jostle a great ocean liner. Likewise, when mind is focused on its object, even if it gives rise to some subtle conceptual thoughts, it is never jostled, even slightly, such that it would churn out gross conceptual thoughts. Thus even if a thought arises, if we do not make anything special out of it but just stay placidly as we are for some time, we find we cannot become involved in a mere thought.

The fourth is settling the mind like a baby looking in a temple. When a baby looks in a temple, he or she does not inspect and scrutinize the details of the murals painted on the walls. Just seeing the rough design, the baby looks without becoming involved. Likewise, when the meditating mind is fixed on its object of focus, no matter what sensory objects appear before it — attractive or displeasing — it does not look at them with inspection or scrutiny. The mind just remains single-pointedly fixed on its object. In other words, we consider any external object before us while we are meditating to be merely a play of light and remain focused instead on our object of meditation.

The fifth technique is to settle the mind like a sparrow flying through the sky and not leaving a trace. When a tiny sparrow flies through the sky, it leaves no trace. Likewise, when we experience feelings of pleasure or pain, or neutral feelings arising during meditation, we let them pass without leaving a trace. Not coming under the power of attachment, repulsion or foolish confusion about them, we remain focused on our object of meditation.

The sixth and final technique is settling the mind like a matted piece of wool. When a matted piece of wool is placed in water, it loosens up, becoming pliable and soft. Likewise, when the mind is immersed in absorbed concentration, the manifest aspect of the three poisonous emotions and similarly flightiness of mind and mental dullness loosen and separate out from the meditating mind.

## BRINGING OUR MEDITATION FROM ABSORBED CONCENTRATION TO A STATE OF SHAMATA

Having skillfully cultivated absorbed concentration by dealing with conceptual thought in one of these ways, our consciousness now remains, in a fluid and flowing manner, in its here-and-now, non-contriving state. When we settle single-pointedly in this state, we find that our mind gives rise to an even clearer appearance of the clarity of mind. Finally, we come to recognize, starkly and distinctly, before the face of our total absorption, a crisp clarity that is immaterial, unobstructed by anything, pristine and lucid, devoid of any form of color or shape. No matter what circumstance it encounters, it allows for a cognized aspect of that object or situation to dawn without exception.

When, by following these methods, we attain a state of samadhi — absorbed concentration — if is not conjoined with the mental factor of a serenely joyous sense of physical and mental suppleness and fitness brought on by this state, it remains simply a single-pointed mind of the realm of desirable sensory objects. It does not qualify as shamata, a serenely stilled and settled mind. But once it has this factor of serenely joyous suppleness, our absorbed concentration becomes a state of shamata that is the indispensable prerequisite preliminary state for achieving a first-level stable mind — the first dhyana.

A mind of shamata is the gateway for all good qualities, such as heightened levels of extra-sensory awareness and extra-physical abilities, and all the various absorbed concentrations included as modest or vast vehicles of mind. Even more importantly, such a mind is the basis for attaining the arya pathways of mind of the three vehicles — the "noble paths" having straightforward, non-conceptual perception of voidness. The ethical status of a mind of shamata, however, is unspecified — neither constructive nor destructive — although it lies as the common, shared basis for all inner and outer good qualities. Without being inspiring or uplifting in and of itself, yet because it is the basis upon which rely so many good qualities, both mundane and transcendent, and from which they are actualized, a mind of shamata is extremely important and valuable.

When we have achieved a state of shamata focused on the here-and-now, non-contriving mind like this, what is the nature of what we have achieved? The First Panchen Lama answers unequivocally, "The great meditators of the snow mountains are practically of a single opinion in proclaiming that this is a guideline indicating how to forge a state of Buddhahood. Be that as it may, I, Chökyi-gyeltsen, say that this is a wondrous skillful means for beginners to accomplish the settling of their mind and is a way that leads you to recognize [merely] the conventional nature of mind that conceals something deeper."

If we use the terminology of Gyelrong Tsültrim-nyima, we have, at this stage, recognized coarse primordial mind and achieved a state of shamata focused on it. On this basis, we now meditate on the deepest, devoid nature of that mind. If we do so properly and successfully, then, when we manifest subtle primordial mind, we experience our meditation ripening specifically and specially into our ability to meditate on the devoid nature of mind with this subtlest, primordial clear light mind as both the meditating mind and the basis for voidness.

# Session Seven

## WORKING TO BENEFIT OTHERS

As the fully enlightened Buddha has said, "Refrain from all negativities and build up everything positive. By relying on this, one becomes enlightened." This is a fundamental point of Buddha's teachings. We all wish to be happy, and nobody wishes any suffering or pain. To bring this about, we need to know the causes for happiness and the causes that bring about suffering. On that basis, we must build up and enhance these causes for happiness, and eliminate and avoid those causes for unhappiness and problems. The true causes for unhappiness and problems are our negative, destructive actions. The proper mode of behavior, then, is to refrain from doing, saying or thinking anything negative or destructive.

What is a destructive action? It is any action that does or can bring about harm to ourselves or others. What motivates such actions? Our disturbing emotions and attitudes motivate us to act in destructive ways. Therefore we need both to refrain from all negative, destructive actions, as well as curtail all disturbed and disturbing states of mind that would motivate us to engage in them. Likewise, we need to create a splendid array of everything positive and constructive. It is not sufficient merely to restrain ourselves from negativities and refrain from harming others. We need actively to engage in what is helpful for others. To do this, we need as motivation an attitude of wishing to benefit them. We must dedicate our hearts to others and to enlightenment — in other words, develop a dedicated heart of bodhichitta. With such a dedicated heart, we are able to benefit everyone. Bodhichitta, then, is the basis for achieving all splendid and positive virtues.

We can condense Buddha's message into two lines, "Try to help others as much as you can. And if that is not possible, at least do not cause any harm." Thus, if we are followers of Buddha's teachings, we try to help others as much as we can. We try to see clearly what any situation requires, and then do what is of most benefit to others. If we are not capable of such noble action, or there is nothing we can do that would help a situation, we at least do not aggravate it by causing any harm. We exercise restraint and self-control so as not to create any trouble, problems or difficulties for others.

There are many ways to benefit others, both temporarily and in an ultimate, deepest sense. The ultimate way of benefitting others is to lead them to a state of enlightenment — the state of a Buddha in which they have eliminated all their problems and their causes, and have realized all their potentials, so that they can be of fullest benefit to themselves and others. We strive to do this for others — even just for those around us with whom we have the most contact. We try to help lead them to enlightenment. Furthermore, we try to be helpful to others on a temporary level as well, aiding and assisting them in any way that we can. In this way, we try to bring them some sort of benefit, even if it is only a temporary one.

## A LIFE OF INTENSIVE MEDITATIONAL PRACTICE VERSUS A LIFE OF SERVICE

It is difficult to work simultaneously at being beneficial to others temporarily and ultimately. Concerning this point, we need to differentiate two types of persons. There are some very special and rare individuals who, if they apply themselves single-pointedly to very intensive meditation, are able to devote all their energies to this undertaking, without major problems or blocks, and thus make rapid and significant progress on the path to enlightenment. In this way, they become able to benefit others in an ultimate sense. There are others, however, for whom it is more suitable and fitting to devote their physical, verbal and mental faculties to the immediate service of others, trying to be of help in whatever way daily situations demand. For such individuals, a life of service is a far more practical way of making progress along the spiritual path to enlightenment.

It is very important, then, to examine ourselves carefully and honestly to identify correctly which of these two types of disposition we have. Without romanticizing the spiritual path or entertaining fantasies about ourselves, we must accurately determine what our propensities are in order to know which type of lifestyle and practice best suits us. If we are really someone who is capable of intensive meditation, we can make great progress like that. Such a course of action, then, is appropriate for us. If, however, it suits us better to devote all our energies to humanitarian service, a life of such service is the appropriate choice. It is essential to have a very down-to-earth, pragmatic attitude toward this issue. We must evaluate our situation and potentials in a dispassionate, objective manner and choose a lifestyle for practice that is based on reality, not fantasy.

In *Engaging in a Bodhisattva's Deeds,* Shantideva has stressed, on many levels, basing our practice on seeing reality. From one point of view, a dedicated life of service to others cannot, by itself, bring us to enlightenment. Compassionate service alone cannot counter our apprehending everything and everyone we encounter, as well as ourselves, as existing truly and inherently, which leads to our mind giving rise to disturbing emotions and attitudes, thus creating our problems. We need to supplement our practice of compassionate methods with the wisdom, or discriminating awareness, that understands voidness — the total absence of all fantasized and impossible ways of existing.

On another level, we also need to see reality in order to determine the appropriate course of action that is of most benefit for others in a specific situation. We need to be able to discriminate, for example, between those situations that call for more generosity and less stringent ethical self-discipline, and those that call for strict ethical conduct that is less generous. For example, a monk with the vow not to touch women must know to relax that prohibition when he sees a woman drowning. On the other hand, it is necessary to refrain from adultery even if a married person constantly begs us to have a sexual affair with him or her.

In making our choice of lifestyle between intensive meditative practice and intensive service to others, we must not think that the latter is less productive and a waste of time. Take my own case. I read about the great meditators of the past who came from Amdo, the same region as I do. They practiced meditation single-mindedly and achieved wondrous states of attainment. I sometimes think how splendid it would be to follow their example. But then I look at the situation around me and the scope of my abilities and talents, and evaluate what I can do on the basis of the position in society into which I was born. I see quite clearly there is a great need for me to engage myself in service for others. Thus, without any regrets, I happily devote my time and energies in this direction.

In short, we must each examine ourselves to determine which mode of practice accords with the reality of our life, our capacities and our disposition. If we truly find that we are best suited for intensive meditational practice and we have the opportunity and ability to engage in that as our lifestyle, we should by all means go ahead with this course. For those like that, long-term, intensive meditational retreat is perfectly proper and productive. And if we are better suited to engage in some sort of humanitarian activity such as social service, if we follow that course we will also find it totally suitable and beneficial.

Engaging ourselves in serving society, trying to be of benefit to others, is not only helpful, but an excellent way to spend our life totally in accord with Dharma. Society and the environment exert a subtle influence on everyone. Therefore if we can contribute toward making either or both of these more positive, we are spending our time and effort in a very worthwhile pursuit. For those of us suited to this type of activity, it is excellent to try to contribute whatever we can toward making the world and society more positive.

## PROVIDING OURSELVES WITH STRENGTH TO MAINTAIN A LIFE OF SERVICE TO OTHERS

When serving society or others in general, it is very important to set a proper motivation at the start of each day. When we wake up each morning, we reflect, "Today I am not going to come under the power of either attachment or hostility. Today I am going to be of benefit and help to others." Thus we consciously set the tone for the entire day so that we go through it within the context of a pure, altruistic motivation and attitude. During the day if we notice our mind giving rise to any problems of selfishness, greed or anger, and if as soon as we notice them we apply opponent forces directly at that time, we are handling these problems in the best possible manner. But even if we cannot do that, we address them later, before going to sleep at night, by reviewing the activities of our day. We identify and acknowledge all the destructive things we did, said or thought — when we lost self-control — openly admitting that they were mistakes. Regretting them, we apply opponent forces to purify ourselves of their negative potentials. Then we review the constructive and positive things that we did, said or thought during the course of the day, and without pride or conceit rejoice in them. Such a daily practice gives us much strength in a life of service to others.

Sometimes, however, while living a life of service, we find our environment and situation overwhelming. We lose all energy and become depressed. At such times, it is beneficial to do a short meditational retreat to "recharge our batteries," as it were. We gain far more positive energy to revitalize our work if instead of going to the beach and lying in the sun, we retreat to a quiet place and engage in meditation.

In short, except for a very few, rare individuals, it is best to remain part of society and actively serve it, rather than withdraw — particularly if we would withdraw into a state of indifference toward others. But whether we engage in short-term or long-term intensive meditational practice, we need to focus on training the mind to change and improve its attitudes, not simply on training the body to gain physical improvement.

As for methods to tame and train the mind, we have the mahamudra techniques as shown in our text for gaining a state of mind that combines shamata and vipashyana focused on mind itself — in other words, a state of mind that is both serenely stilled and settled into its here-and-now, non-contriving state of mere clarity and awareness, and that is, at the same time, exceptionally perceptive of its deepest, devoid nature. Therefore, setting our motivation on learning a technique that allows us to become of both temporary and ultimate benefit to others, we now listen to the continuation of these mahamudra teachings.

## BROAD GUIDELINES FOR MEDITATION

There are two ways to accomplish a combined state of shamata and vipashyana. One is to first ascertain a correct view and then gain a single-pointed meditative state focused on it. The other is to gain a concentrated meditative mind first and then a correct view with that mind. Here, the First Panchen Lama explains the latter technique. He divides his discussion into the preliminaries, actual techniques and concluding procedures.

The general preliminaries to perform beforehand, on an extensive scale, are the four forward-leading practices, such as making mandala offerings and so forth. Then, for any specific meditation session for gaining shamata or vipashyana, we begin with six preliminaries, which include cleaning our place of meditation, arranging offerings, sitting on a proper seat in the sevenfold posture of Vairochana, clearing out our mind with a round of nine tastes of breath, taking safe direction, enhancing our bodhichitta motivation and then practicing guru-yoga.

In general, the best time for meditation is early in the morning, preferably when the sky is just starting to become light. This is the main time we usually reserve for meditation because our mind is especially fresh and clear at that time of morning. That clarity, however, depends very much not only on how we have slept, but also on how much food we have eaten the night before. If we go to sleep with a heavy or bloated stomach, our sleep likewise becomes heavy and we wake up with a mind still heavy and not very clear. Furthermore, if we do not eat meat but follow a vegetarian diet, we definitely feel an effect on our meditation. Thus daily behavior and habits are very important for successful meditation practice.

But, except for these being broad guidelines for meditation in general, they are not injunctions, like laws that everyone must follow. We must each examine our dispositions, preferences, metabolism, health and living situation, and adjust these guidelines accordingly. Thus within his Dharma teachings, Buddha taught techniques and methods to suit every disposition, preference, metabolism and so on. We must examine ourselves carefully and choose a style of practice that suits us properly.

Furthermore, as Tsongkapa has stressed in *A Grand* and *A Short Presentation of the Graded Stages of the Path*, before engaging in meditation it is crucial to listen to the teachings properly and think about them extensively, not only concerning the topic of meditation but also the techniques for meditating on it. We must know the faults that can arise during meditation and how to eliminate them. We learn about these faults and the various supporting mental factors to employ in meditation by reading, studying and reflecting on the great scriptural texts and their commentaries. We need to have some understanding of all these points in order even to begin meditation. As we proceed with our practice, we compare what we learned with our meditational experience in order to deepen our understanding, particularly concerning the faults that arise to prevent absorbed concentration, and the function and employment of the factors with which to counter them, namely mindfulness and alertness.

There are many different forms of guru-yoga we may perform as a preliminary to mahamudra meditation, for example *A Ritual to Honor the Spiritual Master*, *The Hundreds of Deities of Tushita* or *The Six-session Guru-yoga*. All are acceptable. But regardless of which recitation text or form we use, we must try to integrate our practice of guru-yoga with our mind-stream. When sincerely and properly done with strong feeling from the depths of our heart, guru-yoga has a very profound effect on the mind and thus on our meditation. Making heartfelt requests for inspiration, dissolving our guru into us and feeling that our faculties of body, speech and mind are inseparably integrated with those of our guru render the mind more uplifted, inspired, joyous, clear, subtle and intense than before. This is extremely helpful.

STAGES OF FOCUSING MIND ON MIND

With this state of mind, free from any expectations or fears, devoid of any thoughts concerning the past, present or future, we focus single-pointedly on mind's nature of mere clarity and awareness — the here-and-now, non-contriving mind itself. We use focusing on coarse primordial mind itself as our technique for achieving shamata. To do this, of course, requires correctly recognizing, from personal experience, the conventional nature of mind and then placing mind vividly on this. As for how to achieve a mind focused on mind, in *Notes from a Discourse on the Gelug Tradition of Mahamudra*, Gungtangzang has explained that we focus on the feeling — in the Western sense of the term — that remains from our experience of the immediately preceding moment of mind with the immediately following moment of mind. Gungtangzang's teacher, Yongdzin Yeshey-gyeltsen, on the other hand, in his own *Notes from a Discourse on the Gelug Tradition of Mahamudra*, recording the teachings of his guru, the Third Panchen Lama, and in *Clearly Indicating the Main Points from the Oral Teachings of the Gelug Tradition of Mahamudra*, has explained that we focus on mind with a mind that is within the same moment as it.

Although Gungtangzang's text is based on a discourse by Yongdzin Yeshey-gyeltsen, his explanation here probably follows a guideline from another of his teachers, the Second Jamyang-zhepa, Könchog-jigmey-wangpo. After the mind gives rise to the experience of mind as mere clarity and awareness, it apprehends or holds that experience with mindfulness — the mental factor of remembering. The next moment of mind then takes as its object of focus that experienced feeling of the previous moment of mind apprehended or held by mindfulness — in other words, it focuses on the feeling of the remembered experience of the previous moment of mind.

In either case, we now hold this mere clarity and awareness as our focal object with strong mindfulness and keep watch on our concentration with alertness. If our mind gives rise to conceptual thoughts, we apply various techniques, such as recognizing the thought for what it is so that we are not caught in it and it disappears. Or we consciously cut it off as soon as it arises. With either technique we automatically arrive back at our object of focus — the sphere of mind as mere clarity and awareness.

Eventually, the mind no longer gives rise to thoughts in meditation. We are able to focus single-pointedly on mere clarity and awareness that is mind itself. The longer we remain focused on this, the more vivid and vibrant the clarity aspect of mind becomes that appears before the face of our absorbed concentration. This is an indication that our perception of mere clarity and awareness is becoming more straightforward and non-conceptual.

It is best not to make our meditation sessions too long in the beginning, otherwise there is a greater danger of experiencing mental dullness and other difficulties. It is therefore better at first to have short but frequent sessions. As we become able, with growing facility in this practice, to have frequent short sessions that proceed very well, we gradually increase their duration. At the conclusion of each session, we dedicate the positive potential built up from the practice for all beings to attain enlightenment, crowning our dedication with whatever level of understanding we have of the correct view of voidness — the absence of true and inherent existence.

BOON EXPERIENCES

When we have achieved this level of settling our mind single-pointedly in this manner, we eventually experience the mind giving rise to a clarity before the face of absorbed concentration that is so pristinely vivid and vibrant, unobstructed by anything, that it seems as though we are seeing it as vividly as seeing a wall or something made of atoms in front of us. At this point, body and mind feel totally light, and mind gives rise to a tone of serene bliss unlike anything else. With this attainment, we achieve a state of absorbed concentration having the so-called boons of bliss, clarity and non-conceptuality or starkness.

If we have been practicing the yogic methods of anuttarayoga tantra's complete stage, we  now apply special, inspiring, skillful techniques to progress beyond this non-conceptual absorbed concentration having features of bliss, clarity and non-conceptuality. Through these techniques we are able, on the basis of absorbed concentration focused non-conceptually on coarse primordial mind, to make manifest subtle primordial mind. But, whether we apply these special techniques or not, in general if we gain a mind of shamata focused on mind — even with boon experiences of bliss, clarity and non-conceptuality — we have only achieved a fully concentrated mind, with all its attendant good qualities. This is an attainment common to both Buddhists and non-Buddhists alike. Absorbed concentration like this, with bliss, clarity and non-conceptuality cannot by itself bring liberation from samsara. Therefore, the First Panchen Lama states emphatically that this attainment has not reached a state of mahamudra focused on voidness, the deepest nature of mind, but only one focused on its conventional nature.

## THE IMPORTANCE OF REALIZING THE DEVOID NATURE OF MIND

Taking the conventional nature of mind, seen and focused upon in this way, as a basis characterized by voidness as its deepest nature, we now meditate on the devoid nature of mind. Since the First Panchen Lama presents the meditations for gaining a decisive understanding of mind's devoid nature as a separate topic in his text, he begins his discussion with another promise to compose as a way to connect it with what he has explained before. He then divides his presentation into two sections — a general explanation of the different methods for recognizing the deepest nature of reality, and a specific indication of their essence.

Citing quotations by Saraha and Drugchen Lingraypa in his auto-commentary, the First Panchen Lama stresses that whether we experience the uncontrollably recurring problems of samsara or a state of nirvana liberated from them depends on whether we are unaware or aware of the abiding nature of reality. Thus unawareness and awareness determine and create samsara and nirvana. Unawareness and awareness here refer to the abiding devoid nature, in general, of all reality, but most importantly of the mind. As we commonly say, "The root of the three realms of compulsive existence is just mind."

Chandrakirti has written as much in *A Supplement to [Nagarjuna's "Root Stanzas on] the Middle Way,"* "Through mind itself, all variety of worlds and beings inhabiting them come about. Thus [Buddha] has said that wandering beings, without exception, are born from karma. If you rid your mind [of unawareness], you no longer have any karma either." This is because karma is inseparable from the unaware mind. Nagarjuna has also said the same in his various texts on

*The Guhyasamaja Tantra,* "All depends on the diamond-strong scepter of mind." Thus the root of all impure and pure appearance-making and appearances of samsara and nirvana comes down to mind itself. Therefore, it is extremely important to gain a decisive understanding of the devoid nature of reality in general, but specifically of mind itself as a basis characterized by voidness as its nature.

## FIVE TRADITIONS FOR CUTTING DOWN TO THE DEEPEST NATURE OF MIND

The First Panchen Lama now explains five traditions of meditation that cut down to the foundational state of the deepest nature of mind. When we look at the words with which some of these techniques are expressed, we find they do not stand up to logical debate and are not readily or clearly understandable. The words of such highly accomplished meditators as the founders of these traditions, however, are unmistaken since they are based on valid meditational experience. This is despite the fact that the manner of expression of some of them opens them to the danger of misinterpretation because they are imprecise and unclear. Therefore we must take care when learning about these techniques so that we do not become confused.

There are several situations in which an imprecise manner of expression in teaching can occur. One is when a great meditational master's words are not intended primarily for critical examination with logic. Another is when, out of necessity, the master must explain in a manner that suits the capacity, disposition and preferences of the disciple. In this latter case, the master chooses words with the intention of suiting the disciple, but the master's own intended meaning is not the same. The master's intended meaning and the meaning of his or her words are different, whereas in the former case the intended meaning of both is the same. In the latter case, the master is speaking from personal meditative experience and the choice of words is intended to bring an immediate, direct understanding for that specific disciple at that specific occasion. This is often the case with traditions indicating a view of reality based on experience, as we discussed before. Therefore, just because the manner of expression of some of these following meditational traditions is imprecise and can be logically faulted, this does not render them inept instructions to be smugly dismissed. We cannot say that these highly accomplished great meditational masters did not know what they were talking about.

Once a teacher of logic and debate came to Milarepa and accused him of the faults of inattentive perception, contradiction and irrelevancy. Milarepa replied, "Sir, your mind-stream being mixed with irrelevant disturbing emotions and attitudes is your fault of irrelevancy. Your inattention to the fact that the appearances of external phenomena you see are merely appearances produced by your mind is your fault of inattentive perception. Your mind-stream being in contradiction to the Dharma is your fault of contradiction." His curt answer is really helpful for our minds. To hit on these points when we search for contradictions and irrelevancies is real Dharma practice. As Milarepa also once said, "Explaining exactly with the words of the scriptural texts, there is no hope. But explaining directly with words that suit the occasion, there is definitely hope. Decisively understand the meaning of the texts!"

The first of the five traditions is, "Within a state of absorbed concentration, to scrutinize mind to determine if it is established as external or internal, or as something that arises, abides or ceases. When one sees that it cannot be established as any of these, one has cut down to the foundational state of mind. One has recognized mind. One has reached the meaning of mahamudra. The backing support for this is a doha, 'When you search for any mind or appearance, you cannot find one. There is an absence of even anyone searching. This absence, which neither arises nor ceases in any of the three times and which never alters, is the abiding nature of natural, greatly blissful awareness. In this way, all appearance-making and appearances are dharmakaya — a body encompassing everything.'"

The second tradition is, "When one searches for mind, to look for it within the body, from the crown of one's head to the tip of one's toes. It cannot be established as any part of the body." In other words, when we search for an actual basis with the defining characteristic making it our mind, we cannot find any part of our body, from the top of our head to the tip of our toes, that satisfies that. Thus mind cannot be established as any of these. Mind, having a nature of mere clarity and awareness — a nature of being something that cognizes — is something distinct from body. Thus no part of the body can be given the name "mind" since none of them is a basis having the defining characteristic that would make it a mind.

Furthermore, because mind is not a form of physical phenomenon, it has neither shape nor color. The text therefore continues, "When one sees that it cannot be established as any form of physical phenomenon having shape or color, one sees the nature of mind. The backing support for this is a quotation from Zhang Rinpochey" — referring to Zhang Yudragpa Tsöndrü-dragpa, Gampopa's disciple who founded the Tselpa Kagyü lineage — "'The seed for everything, the nature of your mind, is inseparable from that of the minds of all Buddhas and their bodhisattva offspring. There is no difference. It appears as jnana-dharmakaya — a body of deep awareness encompassing everything.'" Here, if we take clear light mind as dharmakaya, the statement that the nature of our mind is the same as that of the minds of all Buddhas applies equally to the conventional and deepest abiding natures of mind. The quotation from Zhang Yudragpa concludes, "'Not established as anything material, it is clear and makes clear by virtue of its natural state. Not established as a functional phenomenon, it is a colorless, measureless absence or void.'"

Surely no one would consider simply mind's absence of shape or color due to its not being established as any form of physical phenomenon as mind's deepest nature. This manner of expression, then, is intended to lead us to a deeper, more profound understanding and is certainly not saying, as the words literally imply, that the deepest nature of mind is its lack of color or shape! As a root or starting place, however, for being led in stages to the understanding that mind by nature is devoid of true and inherent findable existence, we first look for where mind might be. Is it somewhere inside or outside our body? Is it any of the parts of our body from the crown of our head to the tip of our toes? Can we see anything that could be mind? These, then, are merely stages in a meditational technique that ultimately leads to understanding the abiding nature of mind to be only an extinction of concrete, findable, true and inherent existence.

The third tradition is, "Without following the track of thoughts of the past or scouting ahead to meet thoughts of the future, simply settle in the present moment of resplendent, here-and-now, non-contriving mind. This is bare, straightforward seeing of the nature of mind. With it, one has cut down to the foundational state of mind, one has recognized mind itself. The backing support for this is a quotation from Saraha, 'Settle, in a fluid and flowing manner, in the here-and-now, non-contriving state,' and one from Drugchen Lingraypa, 'Settle in the here-and-now, non-contriving state and mind gives rise to understanding and realization. Cultivate this like a flowing stream and mind gives rise to its full expansion. Yogis, always absorb your concentration fully into the state rid of all defining characteristics at which to focus.'"

The fourth tradition is, "No matter what appearances of objects such as sights or sounds mind gives rise to, and no matter what thoughts of good or bad, constructive or destructive, mind gives rise to, neither to negate nor affirm any of them, even to the slightest degree. If one looks starkly at their nature, they automatically disappear. To see and meld with the resplendent absence that comes after this and before straightforwardly seeing anything else is to understand and realize the nature of reality. It is to recognize mind. The backing support for this is a quotation from Maitripa, 'If you wish to realize the meaning that is beyond intellect, with nothing to be done, root out your limited awareness and settle starkly into pure awareness. Plunge into the waters of this pristine lucidity, unsullied by any stain of conceptual thinking. Settle in mind's own state in the space that is neither the appearance-making and appearance that have ceased nor the ones about to be established. In that which is neither what one is rid of nor what one is about to accept is mahamudra.'"

When we have seen starkly the nature of mind, then in the space in between the cessation of a previous thought and the mind giving rise to a next one, in the place of the cessation of the previous thought, our mind gives rise to the appearance of a bare absence. The mind gives rise to the appearance of a bare absence that is mere clarity and mere awareness in the space between the ceasing of one thought and its giving rise to the next. Seeing just precisely this is seeing the nature of mind. This is the meaning of Maitripa's quotation.

The fifth and final tradition is, "No matter what thought mind produces, to press on without trying to make it go away. Since stamped as a seal upon any thought is the guarantee that it automatically releases itself and disappears, its arising and releasing occur simultaneously. As many thoughts as arise are merely so many members of the ranks of dharmakaya — a body of deep awareness encompassing everything. As Zhang Yudragpa has said, 'In the sphere of being absorbed like this, if mind all of a sudden gives rise to a thought, it is from clear light dharmakaya. Do not think it is anything else. The emanation of thought is voidness emanating from voidness, dharmakaya emanating from dharmakaya, unity emanating from unity.'"

# Session Eight

## REMOVING THE OBSTACLES PREVENTING LIBERATION AND ENLIGHTENMENT

The First Panchen Lama now continues with the method for gaining a decisive understanding of the deepest devoid nature of mind in accordance with the intentions of Chandrakirti and other masters of the prasangika-madhyamaka tradition of explanation. According to them, the first of the two sets of obscurations, those that are disturbing attitudes and that prevent liberation, refer to all disturbing emotions and attitudes, including ignorance or unawareness of voidness, as well as their seeds or traces. When we have removed this entire set, we attain nirvana, total release from samsara or uncontrollably recurring rebirth filled with true suffering and true causes of suffering.

The attainment of the non-abiding nirvana of Buddhahood, however, is a much greater achievement. It requires eliminating not only the obstacles preventing liberation but also those preventing omniscience, namely the obstacles concerning all knowable phenomena. These refer to the instincts of unawareness of voidness that cause mind to make things appear as if they ultimately existed as inherently findable, which thus prevent mind from giving rise simultaneously, as its object of cognition, to the two levels of truth about anything. Because of this second, deeper set of obstacles, mind makes all phenomena appear as if existing ultimately, although they do not exist in this way. The setting, like a sun, of all discordant appearance-making like this into dharmadhatu, the sphere of devoid nature, such that it never rises again, is non-abiding nirvana.

But isn't this nihilism? When all discordant appearance-making has set into the sphere of devoid nature, doesn't this negate everything? Aren't we left with nothing at all, like seeing nothing when our eyes are closed? No, this is not at all the case. While training ourselves through a course of pathway minds, we build up bountiful stores of positive potential and deep awareness jointly. Consequently, even though the veiling mist of mental fabrication and fabricating has set forever into the sphere of devoid nature at the time of the resultant state of Buddhahood, still, by the force of compassion, prayers and altruistic acts, there is someone remaining who spontaneously and effortlessly fulfills others' purposes. There is still someone remaining who is straightforwardly and omnisciently aware of everything knowable, whatever exists, while simultaneously knowing that anything mind produces an appearance of cannot ultimately be found existing under its own power as something solid and tangible we could touch. It simultaneously knows that phenomena indeed perform functions yet cannot ultimately be touched.

This is quite extraordinary and difficult to explain. Omniscient awareness has two aspects that operate simultaneously with full understanding — one that validly apprehends the deepest level of truth about everything and the other everything's pure conventional level. It can do so because it is free of the obstacles preventing omniscience. The aspect that sees the deepest level apprehends the devoid nature of everything. This is the sphere of devoid nature upon which all appearance-making that mentally fabricates relies, and thus out of which it arises and into which it sets. Although this aspect of omniscient awareness that apprehends voidness does not make phenomena having devoid nature appear before its own face, the other aspect of an omniscient mind, valid for seeing the conventional level, makes these phenomena appear before it. Apprehending both simultaneously, omniscient awareness, as an integrated whole, starkly sees both devoid nature and phenomena having this nature, fully aware that, with an absence of true and inherent existence, these phenomena cannot ultimately be found and touched like something solid and tangible. Thus an omniscient mind has combined total absorption on voidness which is like space — the absence of anything tangible and obstructive — and subsequently attained deep awareness of appearances to be like illusion. This is very difficult to understand and explain. When we gain actual experience, we see it is unlike anything else. It is not only figuratively but literally beyond imagination.

## GENERAL DISCUSSION OF IDENTITYLESSNESS

For meditation on identitylessness, it is important to know what the nullification of a true and inherent identity means, and what is the meaning of a true and inherent identity that we focus on being absent from everything. The nullification here is not a matter of removing something that actually existed before, as in the case of eliminating suffering or disturbing emotions and attitudes. Rather, it means to eliminate and exterminate the deceived mind that apprehends things to exist in a way that is contrary to their actuality — namely, with a true and inherent identity. Such a mind is deceived with respect to its implied object — actual true and inherent identities. Therefore to eliminate such a deceived mind, we need to recognize that its implied object, which it misconceives as actually existing, is something that does not exist at all, even conventionally.

For this we must rely on reason. We need to become convinced that the implied object of the mind that apprehends a true and inherent identity of anything — namely an actual true and inherent identity — does not exist at all as that mind would imply. Only such conviction directly undermines the mind that apprehends a true and inherent identity. No other method exists that can eliminate such a deceived mind. Thus only a mind that decisively understands identitylessness — the lack or total absence of any such thing as true and inherent identities — directly undermines a mind that apprehends such an identity. In short, the true and inherent identity that is implied by a mind that apprehends such an identity has never been experienced as existing at any time. Its total non-existence is called identitylessness or "selflessness."

From the point of view of its nature as an absence, identitylessness cannot be divided into coarse and subtle. Yet from the point of view of the object that is the basis lacking a true identity, it can be divided into the identitylessness of phenomena and of persons or individuals. This is substantiated in the works of Chandrakirti. In this context, the "me" or "self" who feels or experiences things is a person or individual, while the aggregate factors felt or experienced, such as happiness or suffering, are phenomena. There is nothing that cannot be included as either someone who feels and experiences, or something that is felt or experienced. Since we are so concerned about being a person who wants to feel happy and never unhappy, and we are therefore so preoccupied with happiness and suffering as something that is experienced, we have this type of division. I think this is its significance.

According to the tradition of textual exegesis, we explain how to gain a decisive understanding of the identitylessness of phenomena first and then of persons second. But in terms of the meditation of yogis, we meditate on the identitylessness of persons first because it is easier to understand. As *The King of Absorbed Concentrations Sutra* explains, "When you have distinguished with respect to yourself, apply your understanding to all phenomena. The nature of all phenomena is that they are completely pure, just like space. If you know this on the basis of one thing, you know it on the basis of everything. If you see this on the basis of one thing, you see it on the basis of everything." In other words, since the manner in which everything is, by nature, devoid of true and inherent existence is exactly the same, if we understand voidness in terms of one basis, we understand it in terms of all bases, without need to rely on additional lines of reasoning to prove it.

## AVOIDING THE TWO EXTREMES IN RECOGNIZING THE OBJECT TO BE REFUTED

For meditating on the identitylessness of a person, we need first to recognize the object to be refuted. This is part of the procedure for achieving vipashyana focused specifically on how everything exists. In general, for gaining such an exceptionally perceptive state of mind we need to gather together the preliminaries such as building up positive potential and cleansing ourselves of negative potentials. In addition, we need specifically to study well the scriptural texts that provide a correct explanation of identitylessness and thoroughly ponder and think about their meaning.

In *Engaging in a Bodhisattva's Deeds*, Shantideva has said, "If you have not come in contact with the object that is to be refuted, you cannot gain an understanding of its refutation." As this quotation states, if we do not see the target at which we are aiming, we cannot shoot an arrow into it. If we do not recognize the thief, we cannot capture him or her. In the same way, we must recognize the true and inherent identity at which we are aiming our refutation. Although logical reason undermines its existence and establishes its non-existence, we must be clear about how to apply it. If we do not recognize the true and inherent identity at which we are aiming our refutation, then no matter how many logical reasons we cite, we cannot apply them accurately to hit the mark. If we do not recognize correctly the true and inherent identity that we are trying decisively to understand does not exist at all, we find logic and reason impotent to give us conviction in its non-existence. Thus we must be sure about what is to be refuted.

If what we recognize as the object to be refuted is over-pervasive — in other words, too extensive in scope — we consequently refute too much. Because we then also refute and nullify what is not to be refuted, we are in danger of denying everything and thus falling to a position of nihilism. If, on the other hand, what we recognize as the object to be refuted is under-pervasive — in other words, too limited in scope — we consequently refute too little. Then, because we do not refute and nullify the subtlest object to be refuted, we are in danger of neglecting it and thus falling to a position of eternalism as we still unknowingly affirm the existence of that object. Since the consequences of such mistakes are dire, we must take great care. As Nagarjuna has explained in *Root Stanzas on the Middle Way*, "Seeing that the correct view is so difficult to understand in its depths," Buddha hesitated at first to teach about the correct view of reality."

Madhyamaka is the middle way that falls to neither of two extremes — nihilism or eternalism, total non-existence or true, inherent existence. We need to recognize this middle way so as to avoid falling to either extreme. Having recognized this middle way, we train to view everything in this manner. In this way, we achieve a correct view of reality.

Falling to the extreme of denying and nullifying all manners of existence comes from being overzealous in filling the ranks of what is to be refuted. If we do not leave in the ranks of what actually exists everything that definitely does appear, we fall to the extreme of nihilism. If, on the other hand, we do not fill the ranks of total absences of impossible ways of existing with nullifications of everything to be refuted, from the final, most subtle level on up, we leave behind a basis at which our apprehension of true and inherent existence still aims and on which it still focuses. Thus we fall to the extreme of eternalism, which also will not do.

In short, if we overextend what is to be refuted and do not hold back when it is appropriate, we hurl ourselves to the extreme of nihilism in our zealous insistence. But if, on the other hand, we apply too little strength to our refutation, we neglect certain things that must be refuted. If we nullify merely the coarse levels of what is to be refuted, then no matter how much we meditate on a view of reality that goes only this far, we are only able to undermine slightly the coarse level of disturbing emotions and attitudes that arise. We lack the weapon to undermine the subtle levels of attachment and hostility brought on by the subtle levels of apprehending true and inherent existence. Therefore, Buddha and the great masters have said that a correct view of the middle way is very important, although indeed very difficult.

## THE THREE WAYS OF APPREHENDING "ME"

Having discussed this point at length, the First Panchen Lama now quotes from *The Eight Thousand Stanza Prajnaparamita Sutra.* "Apprehending 'me' and 'me as a possessor of things' binds all beings from round to round of uncontrollably recurring rebirth. The ultimate, deepest root of all faults is the apprehension of true and inherent existence that arises simultaneously with each moment of experience — the simultaneously arising self-preoccupation of apprehending everything in terms of 'me.'"

Are all moments of mind that arise thinking "me" included in the ranks of the self-preoccupation of apprehending things in terms of "me"? No, they are not. In general, there are three states of mind thinking "me." One has a manner of apprehension of "me" characterized by the apprehension of it as truly and inherently existent. Another has a manner of apprehension of "me" that thinks of "me" as lacking true and inherent existence, or as being simply what a name refers to, or simply what a mental label that can label it refers to, similar to an illusion. The third is a manner of apprehension of "me" that neither inspects nor scrutinizes it and is not accompanied by characterizing "me" as being either truly and inherently existent or devoid of such an impossible manner of existence.

Of these three, the last one that merely thinks "me" without characterizing it as existing truly and inherently or not is, as our text explains, "a mind validly cognizing the conventional level, that involves itself with the mere 'me.'" This is the "me" with which our mind normally involves itself when, without inspection or scrutiny, it perceives, "'I' am walking. 'I' am sitting. 'I' am reading. 'I' am meditating."

The middle manner of apprehending "me" does so characterizing it as lacking true and inherent existence, thinking it to be simply what a name or mental label refers to, like an illusion. Once we have refuted with logical reason what is to be refuted on the basis of "me," then, in the place of what has been nullified by reason, we are left with a "me" who exists simply as what can be labeled with a name. This is the "me" who generates the mind that thinks of "me" as being simply what a name or mental label refers to. Such manner of apprehending "me" only arises on the mind-stream of those who have gained a decisive understanding of the middle way view of reality.

The first manner of apprehension of "me" is the apprehension of a true and inherent identity of a person — in other words, the apprehension of a person, namely "me," as having the identity of being truly and inherently existent. Characterizing "me" as existing truly and inherently, it apprehends it in an insistent manner when it thinks "me." It involves itself with a "me" as if it were something standing on its own feet and holding its own — something establishing its own existence and identity independently, under its own power, by virtue of itself. This very forceful and compelling manner of being involved with "me" is the apprehension of a true and inherent identity.

## THE SIMULTANEOUSLY ARISING, INCORRECT VIEW OF A TRANSITORY COLLECTION THAT APPREHENDS EVERYTHING IN TERMS OF "ME"

Any moment of mind that takes as its focal object our own person and thinks "me," characterizing it as existing truly and inherently, is both an apprehension of a true and inherent identity of a person as well as an incorrect view of a transitory collection of aggregate factors composing our experience. Any such moment of mind that takes as its focal object another person, however, is merely the former and not the latter. Nor is it the self-preoccupation of apprehending everything in terms of "me" that arises simultaneously with each moment. Thus our text says, "The simultaneously arising self-preoccupation of apprehending everything in terms of 'me' — in other words, the incorrect view of a transitory collection that apprehends everything in terms of 'me' — is an aspect of disturbing discrimination, focused on the 'me' included on one's own mind-stream, that apprehends it as established as something inherently and findably existent." Of the two levels of incorrect view of a transitory collection — that which apprehends such a collection in terms simply of "me" and that which apprehends it in terms of "me as its possessor," usually translated as "mine" — the former is the level that arises simultaneously with each moment.

The First Panchen Lama now cites *A Precious Garland* by Nagarjuna, "As long as there is apprehension of one's aggregates [as truly and inherently existent], there is, from this, the self-preoccupation of apprehending 'me' [as also truly and inherently existent]. If there is this apprehension of 'me,' there is also karma. If there is karma, there is also rebirth." The meaning of this quotation is as follows. A simultaneously arising, incorrect view of a transitory collection that apprehends that collection in terms of "me" is a mind that gives rise to the transitory collection that constitutes the aggregate factors of some moment or episode of our own experience and apprehends it in terms of "me." For example, our mind gives rise to all the aggregate factors that constitute the experience of seeing our face in the mirror — the form of its appearance with wrinkles and grey hair, mental consciousness of it, distinguishing its appearance from that of the wall behind, attention to it, feeling unhappy about it and so forth — and apprehends it as "me." It apprehends the collection of all these factors as having the true and inherent identity of "seeing the sight of an old person" and then apprehends that transitory, impermanent collection in terms of a true and inherent identity of "me" — "I" exist with the true and inherent identity of being old. Thus the apprehension of a true and inherent identity of a person arises on the basis of apprehending the aggregates as existing truly and inherently. In other words, apprehending the continually changing phenomena on our own mindstream as having the identity of being truly and inherently existent is the basis for apprehending our own person as having such an identity.

Therefore, so long as we apprehend the ever-changing aggregate factors composing our experience as existing truly and inherently, we also maintain an incorrect view of that transitory collection of aggregates. With that incorrect view, we apprehend that collection in terms of a "me" that we apprehend as existing truly and inherently. We project and apprehend such a false "me" when we focus on the "me" that merely can be labeled simply on the basis of those aggregate factors. So long as we maintain our self-preoccupation apprehending the aggregate factors of our experience in terms of such a "me," we commit impulsive karmic actions. As a result of such actions, we experience uncontrollably recurring rebirth.

Our author next quotes both Chandrakirti and the King of Logicians, Dharmakirti, to the effect that the apprehension of true existence is the root of uncontrollably recurring existence. So long as we do not discredit the object's ordinary mode of appearance — its implied actual true existence — we are unable to rid ourselves of or "abandon" apprehending true identities.

Chandrakirti and Dharmakirti, as upholders of the prasangika-madhyamaka and chittamatra views respectively, assert different voidnesses, or total absences of fantasized and impossible ways of existing, from the point of view of the nature or manner of existence each nullifies and so forth. Thus each discusses different levels of apprehending true identities. Nevertheless, when each speaks of the discriminating awareness of identitylessness as that which discredits the apprehension of true identities, each accepts, in exactly the same fashion, the manner in which logical reason refutes the implied object of these minds that apprehend things in a manner contrary to fact.

The implied object of minds that apprehend true identities is actual true identities — in other words, identities of persons and phenomena as things existing in fantasized and impossible manners. Unless we discredit, refute and nullify these impossible identities as being actually true, we cannot rid ourselves of apprehending true identities. In short, the implied object of the apprehension of a person, or an individual, or "me," as existing truly in some impossible manner is a person, individual or "me" that can be established as actually existing truly in that impossible manner. We must discredit this implied object. The only thing that can discredit it is a correct view of the absence of true existence — the total absence of existence in truly impossible manners. Because the decisive understanding that persons totally lack existence in truly impossible manners is mutually exclusive with the apprehension of persons as having existence truly in those ways, they cannot co-exist in the same moment of mind. Therefore familiarity with the former state of mind weakens and eventually brings the latter to extinction.

The First Panchen Lama concludes this introductory discussion in his auto-commentary, "For these reasons, I shall first show, on the basis of guideline instructions and meditational experience, how to recognize the manner in which mind gives rise to an appearance of the object to be refuted and the manner in which it apprehends it."

## SCRUTINIZING THE MANNER OF APPEARANCE AND MANNER OF EXISTENCE OF "ME"

The author begins his discussion of meditation on the identitylessness of a person, "me," in the root text, "While in a state of total absorption as before, and like a tiny fish flashing about in a lucid pond and not disturbing it, intelligently inspect the self-nature of the person who is meditating." While totally absorbed into the mere clarity and awareness that is coarse primordial mind, we use a corner of that mere clarity and awareness to inspect and scrutinize carefully the nature of the person or "me" who is meditating. Without losing or disturbing our absorbed concentration on mind itself, we look closely and try to discern three things about the manner of existence of this person, this "me." We try to discern and distinguish the manner of existence our mind makes it appear to have, the manner of existence our mind apprehends it as having, and the manner of existence it actually has.

What is this thing we call "me"? Where would we say that this thing we call "me" is located? Especially when a mind that thinks "me" very strongly arises, how does that mind make that "me" appear to exist and how does that mind apprehend it as existing? When we are neither inspecting nor scrutinizing, what manner of appearance of "me" does our mind normally give rise to? What type of "me" does it imply exists? These are the issues we investigate and explore.

It is the custom to break here for the day in order to leave time for practice, specifically for pondering and thinking in order to try to recognize the "me" to be refuted. Tie a rope around its neck and drag it here to show me tomorrow! Once Milarepa asked a shepherd boy who was his disciple to make a similar investigation. The boy stayed up all night searching for this "me." He came back the next day completely upset and worried. Crying as if he had lost his sheep, he told Milarepa he could not find this "me." He had thought that since Milarepa had been so sincere in asking him to find it that it must be findable somewhere.

Whether this actually happened or not, we should investigate how this "me" arises to our mind. Especially when we are experiencing moments of greed, attachment or anger, what appearance of "me" does our mind give rise to then? Check and think about it carefully. There is no one among us who has not experienced moments of greed, attachment or anger. We experience them all the time. How does our mind at that time make this "me" appear? How does our mind make this "me" appear when we are not experiencing these strong and disturbing emotional states? Investigate thoroughly.

# Session Nine

## APPROACHING THE CHALLENGE OF TAMING THE MIND

The root for all actual attainments of good qualities is the decisive realization of renunciation, bodhichitta and a correct view of reality. At our present level, it may be difficult to have the full determination to be free that constitutes true renunciation and the totally dedicated heart that constitutes true bodhichitta. We may only have a small understanding and experience of them. Yet as beginners we need at least to appreciate how beneficial renunciation and bodhichitta are for taming the mind.

A decisive understanding of a correct view of reality in terms of voidness is also extremely difficult to gain. Without it, we are unable to undermine and eventually rid ourselves of our disturbing emotions and attitudes such as greed, attachment and anger. Firm renunciation and strong bodhichitta, however, are the foundation that supports and aids our gaining of this correct view. Therefore it is extremely important to try to develop, as much as possible, the understanding and realization of renunciation, bodhichitta and a correct view of reality. When the realization of these three is stable, it acts as a firm and reliable ground out of which success in the practice of tantra steadily grows.

The mahamudra teachings are extremely profound. Although it is very helpful and important to learn about them, just to know about them is not enough. We must try to put them into practice as much as we can. This is important. Although our minds may not be very well tamed or disciplined, and we may find it difficult to practice these teachings, we must persevere without becoming discouraged or denigrating ourselves as being inadequate. Taming the mind is a slow and arduous process that requires a great deal of time and patience. It is the ultimate challenge. If we conceive of our practice as an extremely long-term process, we do not become easily discouraged.

Continuous practice with continuing effort is essential when trying to implement Buddha's teachings. Inner development naturally takes time and cannot be achieved within a short period. It is quite normal and completely to be expected, as I have confirmed from my own limited practice, that gaining even the smallest level of actual experience of what the teachings describe requires many years of unbroken hard work. So naturally we must make effort continuously, with courage and determination.

There is no satisfactory alternative course in life than devoting ourselves to self-improvement based on teachings that are founded on reason. Leading our life along such a course benefits not only ourselves but society as a whole. Everyone wishes for world peace and happiness. If everyone strives toward this goal it is definitely achievable. Therefore it is worthwhile and reasonable to make effort in this direction. But without genuine mental peace internally, it is unrealistic to hope that we can achieve genuine world peace externally. This is completely clear. Thus it is appropriate to devote ourselves to achieving inner peace, and for this there are the profound methods of mahamudra.

## SEARCHING FOR THE "ME" TO BE REFUTED

Last night you were given the task to go home and look for the "me" to be refuted. Have you found it or not? Is it something very impressive looking or is it something pathetic looking? Most of us, when neither inspecting nor scrutinizing, possess a strong sense of "me, me, me." But if, when all of a sudden we develop a strong feeling of "me," we investigate and search for this "me," we discover that it is very elusive. It seems to have disappeared. When we search for something that we thought was there, most of us probably discover it is not there at all. Some of us, on the other hand, might feel that this "me" is somewhere in our head behind our eyes. This is because, out of our five senses, our visual perceptions are the most powerful and compelling. Sometimes others who look for this "me" come up with a blank darkness.

But when we really investigate and scrutinize how things exist, we discover that they are simply what can be labeled by names or concepts. Consider the case of a person, "me." Like a snake that can be labeled onto a striped rope in the dark without actually being that rope, a person is simply what can be labeled onto aggregate factors of experience as its basis for labeling but without actually being those aggregates. The auto-commentary cites a sutra to the effect that Buddha sees all wandering beings existing as who they are simply by virtue of their names. They exist simply as the persons to whom their names refer. And, in fact, all beings actually abide in this manner in which Buddha omnisciently sees them. All phenomena lack any existence other than one established simply in relation to names.

Although the manner in which all phenomena exist is like this, the manner in which our mind gives rise to an appearance of them is just to the contrary. They do not appear to be merely something the existence and identity of which are established by the fact that they can be labeled to be what they are simply by conceptual thought or mental labeling. They appear as if they were establishing their true existence by themselves, by their own power, from their own side. Because our mind, due to its beginningless habit of being unaware of the actual manner in which everything exists, makes things appear in this manner and, due to its continuing lack of awareness, apprehends them to exist as such, our mind implies something about these appearances. It implies actual objects existing from their own side that correspond to what it makes appear. Because of this implication, impulses of karma arise to deal with life on the basis of being deceived by our mind's discordant appearance-making. Enacting these impulses, we cause ourselves to wander through uncontrollably recurring rebirths, experiencing the suffering that our unawareness creates.

The manner in which our mind produces an appearance of things as if existing in a fashion discordant to the way in which they actually exist is the manner of appearance-making that is to be refuted, nullified and stopped. The way in which our mind implies true existence, then, is by implying that things are just as they appear. It implies this by believing that they truly exist in the manner in which it merely fabricates and projects an appearance of them as having. It believes them to exist in the manner in which it contrives.

Consider any appearance to which our mind gives rise, whether it be of mountains, fences, pastures, houses or whatever. Although our mind gives rise to an appearance of "this" or "that," it makes things appear as though, from their own side, through their own power, they were establishing their own existence and identity as "this" or "that," ultimately findable as such in the place where our mind makes them appear to be. Thus our mind does not simply give rise to an appearance of them, it makes mountains, fences, pastures, houses and so on appear as though their existence goes far beyond being merely by virtue of the conventions of the mind that has them as its object. It makes them appear to exist as these things through their own power, independently of the conventions of the mind that cognizes them. This is the manner of appearance-making that is to be refuted and stopped.

In summary, the manner in which our mind implies the actual existence of what is to be refuted is with the attitude thinking that these objects of mind, such as mountains, fences and so on, are actually those things over there, existing by virtue of their true and inherent identity as "this" or "that," just as they appear to be existing there as such, from their own side, through their own power, not relying on anything other than themselves to establish their existence and identity. Such a mind that implies the actual existence of this impossible manner of existence that is to be refuted, then, is the mind that apprehends true and inherent existence.

When we investigate and search, for example for a person, such as "me," and try to discern a "me" establishing its own existence, by itself, in some manner beyond being merely what a mind can produce a conventional appearance of, we do not find such a "me." This does not mean, however, that there is no such thing as "me." A "me" who can bring about benefit or harm definitely exists. Despite the fact that we cannot ultimately find this "me" when we search for it, nevertheless this thing in our thoughts, that we do not find when we investigate and search for it, is something that does arise when we do not inspect or scrutinize closely — we definitely find some "me" in our thoughts at that time. No matter how much we search, however, no phenomenon whatsoever remains as something that can be ultimately found when we search with a mind that is not satisfied with its being merely something that mind can give rise to an appearance of. There is a great difference, then, between searching for a truly and inherently existent "me" in or on its basis for labeling with a mind that inspects and scrutinizes on the deepest, ultimate level, and searching for a mere "me" with a mind that validly sees the conventional level. The former mind cannot find its object, whereas the latter finds it, for instance sitting in this room, here and not there.

This being the case, we can decide for sure that when we search for something with logic and reason, the conclusion we arrive at is correct that the thing we are searching for is something ultimately unfindable. Despite that fact, when our mind, in an impromptu manner, while not inspecting or scrutinizing closely, gives rise to an appearance of this thing or that, it produces an appearance of it as if ultimately findable, truly and inherently existing under its own power. When our mind gives rise to this type of discordant appearance of something, it makes it appear as though if we were to search for this or that object on its own side, there would be something findable there that would become increasingly clear, and proportionately more firm, the closer we inspect and scrutinize. This is the manner of existence with which our mind normally makes things appear and implies is real. This is to be refuted so that, through familiarity, we eventually rid ourselves of the habit of unawareness that causes our mind to fabricate, contrive and make such nonsense appear.

## RECOGNIZING THE MODE OF APPEARANCE-MAKING TO BE REFUTED

Holding with mindfulness the manner of existence that appears in our thoughts, we examine and investigate this impromptu manner of appearance. When it arises, our mind gives rise to an appearance of something existing in a manner of existence that is different from that which we come to when we examine and investigate closely. Reflecting on this, we gain a little more clarity about this deceptive appearance. It seems as though it is not just our mind that, in an impromptu manner, is making it appear as though what it is producing an appearance of were something ultimately findable, despite its not being so. It seems as though there really is an actual object ultimately findable there, standing on top of where our mind makes it appear to be, causing itself to appear findably there because it actually is so. This is nonsense. It does not correspond to reality.

Nevertheless, although truly existent phenomena, such as our person or "me," cannot ultimately be found when we search for them, still it is definite that there is someone existing who can bring about benefit or harm. When we inspect and scrutinize, however, looking for someone or something with a mode of existence that goes beyond its being merely something mind is making appear, we cannot find anything. We cannot locate the place of existence of a truly and inherently existing person or object findable in the depths of what mind is producing an appearance of. We cannot locate the place for its existence on the side of some phenomenon that we suppose this appearance to correspond to.

Therefore, phenomena do not establish their own existence. We can only ascribe existence to phenomena through the circumstances of, or in terms of, something other than themselves — for example, their names. Because there is no place for some findable, inherent self-nature on the side of phenomena establishing the existence of these phenomena through its own power, and because the existence of these phenomena can only be established in dependence on circumstances or factors other than themselves, we can correctly conclude that phenomena are not established as existing by virtue of themselves, but only by virtue of what is other than themselves. Thus we arrive at all things being existent simply imputedly. In other words, all phenomena depend simply on imputation or mental labeling in order to establish their existence and identity.

We may not, at first, be able to understand existence in terms simply of mental labeling on a subtle level. But still we use whatever level of understanding we gain of this type of existence to scrutinize the manner of appearance of things to which our mind normally gives rise. The mind does not at all give rise to appearances of things as having their existence and identity established from the side of the mental labels for them, but rather as having their existence established from their own side, unimputedly, through their own power, by virtue of themselves. We must come to recognize this with precision and clarity. Such recognition is called "recognizing starkly the manner of appearance-making that is to be refuted, nullified and stopped."

## DIFFERENTIATING THE MODE OF APPEARANCE-MAKING OF CONVENTIONAL REALITY FROM THE MODE OF APPEARANCE-MAKING TO BE REFUTED

In *A Supplement to [Nagarjuna's "Root Stanzas on] the Middle Way,"* Chandrakirti has explained seven ways to scrutinize phenomena — are they ultimately findable as being the same as, different from, the possessor of, what relies upon, what is relied upon by, the mere collection of all the parts of, or the shape or structure of their basis for labeling? When we search for phenomena in this sevenfold manner within the context of mental labeling, we cannot find conventionally existing phenomena, such as vases and so forth, established as ultimately existing in any of these impossible ways. But, when we do not inspect or

scrutinize, our mind does give rise to an appearance of conventionally existing phenomena, which are things that exist, and are what
they conventionally are, simply inasmuch as they can be mentally labeled as such by virtue of conventions. When we realize this, we gain
even stronger conviction in their total lack or voidness of being established as knowable objects that are not simply what can be mentally
labeled as what they are by virtue of conventions. In other words,
when we realize that what mind gives rise to a conventional appearance of could not arise to our mind as what it is other than by virtue of
its being merely what can be mentally labeled as that, relative to circumstances — despite our mind's making it appear discordantly as
existing otherwise — we gain even stronger conviction in its total lack
of existing as what it is by virtue of itself, not merely by virtue of what
can be designated by names.

Changkya Rölpay-dorjey has explained that some people think that
no matter what appearance our mind produces of conventional phenomena, we must preserve such minds and the appearances they give
rise to — even should our mind produce an appearance of things as if
they were something establishing their existence from somewhere ultimately findable in their depths. These people assert appearance-
making and appearance in general to be the measure of what exists
conventionally. They believe them to be what establishes conventional
existence. They regard appearance-making and appearances in general as the creator of all conventionalities. As they consider them to be
the foundation or basis for the occurrence of cause and effect, they
think they must be left alone.

On the basis of this faulty way of thinking, these people imagine
that the set of what conventionally exists is constituted exclusively by
ultimately findable appearance-making minds that establish conventionalities and objects corresponding to the appearances of ultimate
findability they produce, and assert that these are not be refuted, nullified or stopped, otherwise we are thrown to a position of nihilism. If,
accepting such an assertion, we fabricate a manner of existence and
designate it "existence established by a defining characteristic," or "by
an inherent nature," or "from its own side," in order to account for the
valid mental labeling of conventions, and, insisting it not be refuted,
designate as the "object to be refuted" existence independent of what
mind can make appear on the basis of objects having such a self-
nature, we have merely contrived an object to be refuted and given it
this name. Even if we were to refute such an object with valid lines of
reasoning, we hold nothing but a fantasized view of reality.

In fact, there are two types of conventional appearance-making minds — those that produce accurate appearances of how things exist — ultimately unfindable — corresponding to verifiable fact, and those that produce distorted appearances of how they exist — ultimately findable — not corresponding to anything real. Correspondingly, there are both accurate and distorted conventional appearances. The set of what conventionally exists is not constituted exclusively by discordant appearance-making minds and does not even include the objects implied by these discordant appearances. In refuting them, we have not emptied out the entire set of what conventionally exists.

The problem is that, at our present stage, our mind's accurate manner of appearance-making of conventional phenomena and manner of appearance-making of them that is to be refuted occur simultaneously with both mixed together. Like milk and water, it is very difficult to separate them out from each other. When our mind gives rise to an accurate appearance of conventional phenomena, it does so in no way other than also at the same time fabricating an appearance of them that is to be refuted. Thus it gives rise to the two appearances mixed together. Therefore it is very difficult to differentiate and know, "This is the manner of appearance-making and appearance of conventional phenomena as being what they are by virtue simply of mental labeling with names" and "That is the manner of appearance-making and appearance that is to be refuted." In fact, the latter obscures the former to such an extent that we are normally only aware of the latter.

But when, on the basis of inspecting and scrutinizing phenomena, we have gradually come to a nullification and stopping of what is to be refuted — true and inherent existence and minds that make things appear to exist in this purely fantasized, impossible manner — then, in the place left behind by the nullification of what is to be refuted, we are left with a mind that gives rise only to an accurate appearance, for example, of the mere conventional "me" who can bring about benefit or harm. It is only in this way, from personal experience of apprehending such a "me," that we are able to know decisively the conventional "me" that exists simply as what can be labeled by names.

## THE ANALOGY OF DREAMS AND ILLUSIONS

The auto-commentary next quotes Kaydrub Norzang-gyatso, who has cited the example of sights in dreams and of magical illusions. Except for their being something that our mind alone produces an appearance of, simply before its own face, dreams and so forth cannot be established as existing, even to the slightest extent, separately from this. Similarly, with respect to all knowable phenomena, an existence on top of, or from the depths of, any of them as something that does not rely on being simply what can be mentally labeled — an existence of any of them with an identity as "this" or "that" that is not established by virtue simply of the fact that they can be labeled as such by conventions or names — is the subtle object to be refuted. So long as we do not nullify this subtle object to be refuted, we continue to wander through uncontrollably recurring rebirths. Therefore we must familiarize ourselves with the total lack of true and inherent identities.

The Seventh Dalai Lama Kelzang-gyatso has elaborated on this example and point. When we are asleep, we experience in our dreams various appearances arising, such as of mountains, fences, pastures, livestock, houses and so on. Similarly, we experience various appearances of illusion arising through our visual perception being under the effect of a conjurer's spell. These are merely things that our mind makes appear. There are no actual objects at the basis where these appearances are arising that are establishing their existence. Their existence as appearances is established simply in terms of mind's mentally labeling or imputing them. Likewise, all phenomena — whether self or other, samsara or nirvana — are simply what can be mentally labeled by conventions and names. This is because nothing can ultimately be found existing as what can be labeled either in, on, or as, its basis for labeling. A solid mountain cannot ultimately be found in, on or as the appearance of one in a dream. Likewise a solid "me" cannot ultimately be found in, on or as the transitory collection of aggregates — a body, mind and so forth — as the basis for labeling one.

As ordinary beings, the cognitions of our six collections of consciousness — visual, mental and so on — are adulterated by our unawareness or ignorance. Thus no matter what our mind makes appear, it gives rise to an appearance of it as though it existed establishing itself as something ultimately findable on the basis that is the location of its appearing. We can see this if we look at our own mind and our personal experience of how things appear to us. The way our mind makes things appear is exactly like this. What appears to us is what our deceived mind, adulterated by unawareness, makes appear. This manner of existence of things as if they were sitting there, being what they are from their own side, is the subtle object to be refuted. This being the case, we must cut from the face of our mind all appearance-making and apprehensions of this fantasized, impossible mode of existence. We do this by refuting and nullifying it completely, without leaving even a trace of it.

## REFUTATION OF THE "ME" TO BE REFUTED

The First Panchen Lama now turns to the discussion of the refutation of the person or "me" to be refuted. If a person were to exist independently, through its own power, by virtue of itself, able to hold its own and stand on its own feet, then when we search for such an inherently findable person, we should experience one becoming increasingly clear. Therefore we must inspect and scrutinize closely.

In *A Precious Garland*, Nagarjuna has discussed this process clearly. When we search for our person or the individual who is our "self," we first inspect and scrutinize the aggregate factors of experience that are the basis in reliance upon which we, as a person, are mentally labeled or imputed, and which constitute the conventional location for our existence as a person. We cannot find a person within their "earth" or solid constituent factors, nor in their water, fire or wind constituents. Nor is a person the constituent of space that encompasses the four physical constituents. Neither is it the consciousness, nor the collection of all these constituents taken together. No matter what we bring to mind, none of these constitute, even in the slightest way, a basis with the defining characteristic making it a person.

But, then again, there is nothing separate or apart from the aggregate factors of our experience that constitutes, on its own, a basis with the defining characteristic making it "me." If there were such a thing as a "me" existing in the manner in which our mind gives rise to an appearance of one, as if it were something establishing its existence through its own power — if such a "me" actually existed — it could only exist at the location of our five aggregate factors of experience. We can decide for sure that it could not possibly exist somewhere else, away from the location of what constitutes our experience from moment to moment. But when we inspect and scrutinize the earth, water, fire, wind, space and consciousness constituents of our aggregate factors, we cannot find among them even the slightest thing that is a person. Not only that, but neither their collection, nor their continuum over time, nor anything else about them, is a basis with the defining characteristic making it "me."

Tsongkapa has explained this point in an even more potent manner in *Totally Clarifying the Intentions [of Chandrakirti's "Supplement to (Nagarjuna's 'Root Stanzas on) the Middle Way'"]*. In twilight, a thought may arise that a striped rope on the ground is a snake. But there is nothing on top of or inside this rope — none of its parts, nor their collection, nor the rope's continuum over time — to which we could possibly apply the name "snake" as a basis with the defining characteristic making it a snake. The snake is merely what can be designated by a mental label alone. As in this example, a thought of "me" may arise on the basis of the aggregate factors of our experience. But there is nothing about these aggregates as the basis for labeling — not any of their parts, nor the collection of their parts, nor their continuum over time, nor something separate and apart from them — which is a basis with the defining characteristic making it "me," to which we could possibly apply the name "me." That being the case, this "me" is nothing more than simply what can be designated by a mental label on the basis of aggregate factors of experience. This formulation is very powerful.

In the auto-commentary, the First Panchen Lama now quotes extensively from Shantideva's *Engaging in a Bodhisattva's Deeds*. Like Nagarjuna, Shantideva has surveyed all the parts of the body, not only its constituent elements, but its organs, limbs, shape and so forth, discounting each of them as possibly being a person, or a basis with the defining characteristic making it a person. Thus no aspect or part of the basis for labeling a person is a basis with the defining characteristic making it the person who is being labeled. If it were, then as Nagarjuna has noted in *Root Stanzas on the Middle Way*, the fault would arise that what is being labeled and the basis for its labeling would be identical. This would imply that what is taken, such as a body, mind and so forth of a particular rebirth, and the one who takes them are identical, as would be the parts of something and what has those parts.

Because a basis with the defining characteristic making it an individual, conventional self can be included within the set of different types of consciousness — a particular mind-stream, for example, conventionally constitutes an individual being — many people cite, in an impromptu manner, something that could be included within the set of different types of consciousness — for example, mental consciousness or alayavijnana, foundational mind — as being a basis with the defining characteristic making it an inherently existent, ultimately findable self. Or, because the aggregate factors of our experience include affecting variables that are neither forms of physical phenomena nor ways of being aware of something, and because the conventional self is included within this category of phenomena, some people believe this self included within the aggregates to be an inherently findable self.

But if a self, as what can be labeled, were also ultimately to be the basis for its labeling as part of the aggregates, then, as Nagarjuna has pointed out, there would be the fault of the whole being identical with one of its parts. On the basis of our everyday mind that arises simultaneously with each moment, the thought arises, "This is my mind. I shall use my mind." Thus, our everyday mind differentiates "me" as a user of mind, from "mind" as that which it uses. They are, conventionally, two distinct things. But if we posit the mind or some type of consciousness as the ultimately findable person, then we are positing as the whole one of its parts.

## TOTAL ABSORPTION ON VOIDNESS WHICH IS LIKE SPACE

As a result of our scrutiny and analysis, we eventually gain a decisive understanding that this "me" that our mind fabricates an appearance of as being solidly existent does not refer to anything real at all. As a result of not having found anything when we searched, we become totally convinced of this from the depths of our mind and the bottom of our heart. When a mind arises of total conviction that there is no such thing as what this appearance seems to be, it gives rise to a nonaffirming nullification. This is the bare absence that is the mere nullification, or refutation, or cessation, of the object to be refuted and nullified — this mode of appearance-making and appearance. Other than that, it gives rise to the appearance of nothing else. When we experience this, we totally absorb our concentration on this bare absence, without losing the strength of our manner of apprehension of it as being the total absence, or voidness, of true and inherent existence.

This is the way to meditate with total absorption on voidness which is like space. Just as space is the lack of anything tangible or obstructive on the side of some material object that could impede its physical existence in three dimensions, voidness is the total lack of impossible modes of existence that could impede the conventional existence of any phenomenon. When we first experience this total absence, if we have not thoroughly familiarized ourselves with a correct view, we become frightened. But if we are fully accustomed to it, we experience great relief and joy.

## SUBSEQUENTLY ATTAINED DEEP AWARENESS THAT EVERYTHING IS LIKE ILLUSION

When we rise from this total absorption, there is definitely "me" obviously sitting there who receives benefit or harm. No matter how much we insist that there is no "me" who was just meditating, in the end we have to concede, with a hundred-percent certainty, that there definitely is a "me" who was meditating, a "me" who wishes now to eat, a "me" who needs to go to sleep. We are, however, also totally convinced that there is no such thing as a "me" that exists in the way in which our mind normally gives rise to an appearance of one. We are deeply aware that what our mind makes appear as "me" is simply a "me" that exists merely as what can be labeled by virtue of names, like an illusion.

There are three criteria for establishing what actually exists on the conventional level. It must be well known to a mind that cognizes conventional phenomena, not be undermined by another mind that validly cognizes conventional phenomena, and not be undermined by a mind of awareness that scrutinizes and analyzes the deepest level. In other words, there are no phenomena that cannot be designated or categorized as what can be mentally labeled or imputed. But not everything that can be labeled necessarily corresponds to what exists. This is where we must take care. Because mind can give rise to an appearance of something totally insane, it is not sufficient for something to be well known to a conceptual mind in order for it to qualify as a conventional phenomenon. The actual thing that is well known must not be undermined by another mind that validly cognizes conventional phenomena. Because such a mind also cognizes appearances of phenomena as existing truly and inherently, however, the second criteria is also insufficient. Therefore what is well known to a mind that validly cognizes conventional phenomena must also not be undermined by a mind of awareness that scrutinizes the ultimate, deepest way in which things exist. These criteria define the borderline between what exists and what does not exist conventionally. What exists conventionally is like an illusion, not the same as illusion.

Thus, after we arise from our total absorption on voidness which is like space, we supplement our understanding with subsequently attained deep awareness that everything is like illusion. This subsequent awareness enhances our later practice of this total absorption, and that, in turn, likewise enhances our further subsequent deep awareness. Thus total absorption on voidness which is like space and subsequently attained deep awareness that everything is like illusion mutually support and enhance one another.

# Session Ten

## REALIZING THE VOIDNESS OF MIND ITSELF

Once we have gained conviction in the lack of true and inherent identity on the basis of our own "self," we turn to the basis of other persons or individuals and then to the massive collection of all other phenomena. We examine voidness itself and all pure and impure phenomena. When we investigate and search, we cannot find any of them. None of them can be established as a true and inherent reality. Everything is simply what can be dependently labeled. We need to know this well. When we see this devoid nature with respect to all phenomena, from forms of physical phenomena up to an omniscient mind — namely, this total lack of anything being established as a true and inherent reality — then as it says in a sutra, "This not finding is the supreme finding. This not seeing is the best seeing."

As part of this process, we now take mind as the basis for voidness — in other words, as the basis that is devoid of existing in any fantasized and impossible way. We scrutinize and analyze mind with a correct view to gain a decisive understanding of its devoid nature. Recognizing mind's devoid nature, while settled single-pointedly on its conventional nature through the previous guidelines, is very important because, in so doing, we gather together many special features that ripen into the clear light realizations discussed in tantra.

The commonplace nature of mind as a basis for voidness is that it is not established as being any form of physical phenomenon. It is immaterial and has no form. It is a bare absence, like an open space, that can be neither contacted nor touched. Furthermore, mind's uncontrived or primordial nature is something not obstructed by conceptual thoughts. It allows for an aspect of any object to arise as something known. Through the power of regarding and relying on an aspect of some external object, it allows for a corresponding aspect to arise within. Likewise, without obstruction, mind emanates, projects, or gives rise to various objects it cognizes. When an object, cognitive sensors and consciousness meet together, it allows for an aspect of the object to arise and be known without obstruction. Its nature is mere clarity and awareness. It cannot be extinguished like the dousing of a flame, but is an awareness and clarity that has continuity with no beginning or end. It obstructs neither liberation nor enlightenment.

When mind gives rise to cognition of clarity and awareness having these defining characteristics and appearing to our reflexive pure awareness, we inspect and scrutinize its factors and parts — its basis for labeling. Mind is something that is labeled by relying on its numerous factors and parts. But when our mind gives rise to an appearance of mind, it appears as if it were something existing through its own power, by virtue of itself, not dependent on anything other than itself, not needing to rely on any circumstances or conditions in order to establish its existence. The apprehension of it as existing in the manner in which mind fabricates an appearance of it is the apprehension of true and inherent existence focused on mind. The implied object of this apprehension of true and inherent existence — a mind that is actually established as existing as some true and solid reality — is what must be refuted and nullified.

Shantideva has explained how to refute and nullify it in *Engaging in a Bodhisattva's Deeds*. A collection and a continuum are labeled on the basis of the gathering of many parts. Because mind is something that is labeled on top of numerous former and later moments, it is like the examples of a rosary and an army that Shantideva has cited. On the basis of the gathering together of many things, we have a rosary and give it that conventional name. But if we untie it and sift through its parts, we cannot find anything of which we can say, "This is the rosary." Its impromptu manner of appearance is that it is a rosary. Even though we can distinguish the rosary beads and the rosary string, our mind still gives rise to an appearance of it as though there were a substantial rosary existing without being totally dependent on them. If, however, we dismantle it, we cannot find such a rosary. The same is true of armies and forests. They are only what can be labeled on the basis of the gathering of a large number of constituent members. This is easy to understand.

Like these examples, mind or consciousness is labeled on the basis of a continuum of moments. Because it is labeled on the basis of a collection of instances, it cannot be established as existing as something that does not depend on all its moments. Our mind is merely fabricating an appearance of it as though it could be established as existing through its own power, by virtue of itself. We need to prove, through scriptural authority and lines of reasoning, that this manner of appearance-making and appearance is false, not true. The First Panchen Lama thus identifies the task in his root text.

## CORROBORATION OF THE VOIDNESS OF MIND BY GREAT MEDITATIONAL MASTERS

Many masters and texts of scriptural authority have confirmed that the omniscient Buddhas have never seen in the past, do not see at present and will never see in the future a truly and inherently findable mind. Marpa, for example, studied in India with many great teachers, such as Naropa and Maitripa. Since the latter had been most instrumental for his gaining a correct view of reality, Marpa has written in one of his *Songs of Meditational Experience*, "I went to the banks of the River Ganges in the East. There, through the kindness of the great Maitripa, I was able to gain realization of the basic nature of reality which is unborn." As he achieved this through the yogic methods of anuttarayoga tantra, he gained decisive understanding of the devoid nature of primordial mind. His song continues, "My mind flared in voidness." Because of the special features of understanding voidness, not simply of any phenomenon, but of simultaneously arising primordial clear light mind as its basis, his subtlest clear light mind with this decisive understanding flared, like a brilliant torch, making enlightenment as easy to see and recognize as seeing one's mother. This is similar to Jamyang-zheypa's statement, "The techniques of anuttarayoga tantra are able to bring about the attainment of the three Buddha-bodies like seeing one's mother."

The quotation from Marpa continues, "As I saw the nature of the actual primordial state parted from all mental fabrication...." This can refer to the fact that the devoid nature of mind is parted from all mentally fabricated modes of existence. Or it can mean that he saw the deepest, ultimate nature of simultaneously arising primordial clear light mind that is parted from the mental fabricating of all conceptual levels of mind. Having made manifest primordial clear light mind in this fashion, the quotation concludes, "...I directly met with the three

Buddha-bodies like with my mother. From then on, I cut off my mental fabricating." This indicates a very potent technique, then, for liberating ourselves from samsara.

The next quotation in the auto-commentary is by Pagmo-drupa. This guiding light Kagyü master has explained that the root of samsara and nirvana is mind in the sense that the subtlest clear light mind that we come to through the techniques of anuttarayoga tantra is the source of all impure and pure appearance-making of samsara and nirvana. Mind itself cannot be established as existing as something inherently findable by nature. Mind itself exists simply inasmuch as it can be mentally labeled dependently. Primordially, from its depths, it is devoid and pure. Because mind, primordially from its depths, is stilled of existing as a solid reality, it has never arisen as something truly and inherently existent. Thus, primordially from its depths, it is stilled of all mentally fabricated and extreme modes of existence. All great masters have concluded, then, that the most important point when we practice anuttarayoga tantra is to come to the simultaneously arising primordial clear light mind and, on that basis, to meditate on its own devoid nature.

## RE-AFFIRMING CONVICTION IN VOIDNESS BY MERELY SEEING THE APPEARANCES TO WHICH MIND DEPENDENTLY GIVES RISE

In his promise to compose this section, the First Panchen Lama said he would explain in accordance with personal guideline instructions of his extremely kind root guru, Sanggyay-yeshey, who was both well learned and an accomplished practitioner. In the root text, therefore, he now quotes a verse indicating the correct view from his guru's *Songs of Meditational Experience*, " When, no matter what dawns in your mind, you are fully aware that what it is an appearance of exists simply as what can be apprehended by conceptual thought, you experience the deepest sphere of reality dawning without need to rely on anything else. While this is dawning, to immerse your awareness in it and totally absorb, my goodness!"

Those having considerable familiarity with a correct view of voidness have a great deal of experience in scrutinizing and analyzing things with a correct view. Through the power of their experience, no matter what phenomena their mind gives rise to an occurrence or appearance of — within the categories of apprehending minds and objects apprehended — they are fully aware that these are simply what can be apprehended or labeled by conceptual thought. By the force of this deep awareness, a decisive understanding of the devoid nature of phenomena dawns in their mind without need to rely on any other line of reasoning.

In *A Lamp to Clarify the Meaning of the Generation Stage of Guhyasamaja*, Kaydrub Norzang-gyatso has explained something quite similar with respect to those who have completed their training in scrutinizing and analyzing with a correct view and, as a result, see voidness with their conviction in it coming from understanding that things are devoid because of their arising dependently. For such well-trained persons, their understanding of dependent arising induces further conviction in voidness and their understanding of voidness induces further conviction in dependent arising. They need not rely on any other line of reasoning.

For example, consider the case of cross-eyed persons who, due to their affliction, see two moons. They can understand that there is no such thing as two moons simply for the reason that it is merely their mind that is making two moons appear. They need not rely on any other line of reasoning to realize the total absence or voidness of the moon existing as a double moon. Like this example, consider the case of someone who understands very well that all phenomena lack inherent, findable existence simply for the reason that they are established as existing as what they are dependently on mental labeling, and who understands as well that it is totally reasonable that things arise as what they are dependently on mental labeling simply because they lack findable existence with an inherent identity established by virtue of themselves. When the mind of such a person gives rise to the appearance of things as if they existed as what they are from their own side — not as what can only be designated as existing as such merely by virtue of conceptual thought — the appearance itself induces conviction that what mind is producing an appearance of does not exist inherently and findably.

Sanggyay-yeshey's verse has the same meaning as what Kaydrub Norzang-gyatso has explained. When, no matter what our mind gives rise to an appearance of, that appearance induces in us the realization that although it appears to us as if existing from its own side, it exists simply as what can be labeled by a conceptual thought, then we need not rely on any other line of reasoning. Although there are many lines of reasoning to refute inherent, findable existence, such as "neither one nor many," "arising from neither self nor other," and so on, we have no need to rely on any of them. The elimination or cessation of the mental fabrication and fabricating of inherent, findable existence naturally dawns, or occurs within the state of that realization. In other words, from merely seeing non-fallacious dependent arising, our mind's aim at the implied object of the apprehension of true and inherent existence naturally slows down and stops. When our mind gives rise to a vivid cognitive dawning of this elimination and absence of mental fabrication and fabricating, if we absorb our awareness into total concentration on this, we find it extremely wondrous.

Tsongkapa has made a similar point in *The Three Principal Aspects of the Path*, in which he has written, "When [total absorption and subsequently attained deep awareness] are joined together and do not merely alternate, so that from merely seeing non-fallacious dependent arising, your decisive understanding [of voidness] eradicates your manner of apprehension of objects [as truly and inherently existent], you have successfully completed scrutinizing with a correct view."

Pa Dampa-sanggyay has also spoken similarly in *A Hundred Verses to the People of Dingri*, "Within a state of voidness, the lance of awareness twirls around. A correct view of reality cannot be impeded by anything [ultimately] tangible or obstructive, O people of Dingri." No matter what phenomena our mind produces an appearance of at this point in our practice, we find that as soon as we scrutinize their nature, a decisive understanding of their voidness of an inherent, findable nature dawns in our mind, without need to rely on anything else. When this happens, our awareness of the devoid nature of reality neither obstructs nor can be obstructed.

When our mind is not well trained, its making voidness arise as its object of cognition obstructs, or temporarily blocks, its appearance-making, and its appearance-making obstructs its making voidness arise. It cannot give rise to both simultaneously. When we have achieved a very deep understanding of appearance and voidness, however, mere appearance itself induces conviction in voidness by nature. In this situation, the lance of awareness of voidness twirls around and is not obstructed by appearance-making.

After we have meditated on a correct view in this way for our full period of total absorption, we arise from that state of absorbed concentration. We then conclude our meditation session by dedicating the positive potential we have built up during our period of absorption on voidness toward the attainment of enlightenment for all.

## FURTHER CULTIVATION OF SUBSEQUENTLY ATTAINED DEEP AWARENESS

The First Panchen Lama now discusses how to enhance subsequently attained deep awareness after arising from absorbed concentration on voidness. He suggests that afterwards we investigate very carefully how mind makes the objects of any of our six collections of consciousness appear — sights, sounds and so forth. As a result of thorough familiarity with a correct view, we experience the mind automatically giving rise, immediately upon closer inspection, to apprehension of a bare manner of existence totally different from the manner of appearance as if truly and inherently existent from their own side. We perceive their bare manner of existence, stripped of true and inherent existence. This is called "the essential point of a correct view — recognizing whatever dawns in your mind."

Except when we are totally absorbed in straightforward, nonconceptual perception of voidness, the mind gives rise to an appearance of things as if truly and inherently existent. But even if mind makes everything appear to exist in this fantasized and impossible manner, conviction automatically arises in the fact that nothing exists in this way. This is what it means "to recognize whatever dawns in your mind."

The root text continues, "In short, always cultivate your realization by not apprehending things, such as your mind and so forth, [to exist in the manner in which] your mind gives rise to an appearance of [them]. Do this by keeping firm to their actual mode of existence." No matter what apprehending mind and apprehended object our mind produces an occurrence or appearance of, including mind itself, we do not apprehend them to exist in the manner in which they appear to exist. Their actual mode of existence is that they are devoid of existing as truly and inherently findable. We keep firm to this by always apprehending everything with mindfulness of this fact. In other words, we further cultivate and enhance our conviction in voidness by always remembering it no matter what arises in our mind.

The First Panchen Lama continues, "When you cognize [one thing] like this, [you see] the nature of all phenomena of samsara and nirvana as being uniformly the same." When we cognize things in this way, we see that all phenomena included as samsara and nirvana are of one taste in the sphere of their total lack of inherently findable existence. When our mind gains total conviction in this, we see that the nature of everything is uniformly the same. When we are able to gain decisive understanding of voidness on the basis of one phenomenon, then because the void manner of existence of everything is the same, we need not rely on many lines of reasoning in order to prove and establish voidness on the basis of other phenomena. We are able to cognize it easily.

## THE EXTINCTION OF DISCORDANT APPEARANCE-MAKING

Mind cannot give rise to the appearance of dependently arising phenomena in front of that aspect of it that decisively understands voidness. Appearances of phenomena with a devoid nature cannot hold their own before such a mind because if they were to arise before it, this aspect of mind would cease all appearance of them and apprehend merely their lack of inherent, findable existence — in the manner of a non-affirming nullification. Mind can give rise to appearances of conventional phenomena only before that aspect of it that can cognize the conventional level of things. The appearances that it normally produces, however, are a mixture of pure ones, whose manner of appearance is as what can simply be labeled by names, and impure ones with a manner of appearance discordant to that.

When we have accustomed ourselves to voidness as the object of our total absorption, we experience our discordant appearance-making and its mental fabrications decreasing steadily. In the end, our mind simply produces an appearance of conventional phenomena existing in a manner contrary to their being seemingly truly and inherently existent. It gives rise simply to an appearance of them parted from all contrived, mentally fabricated, extreme and impossible modes of existence.

## RE-AFFIRMATION OF THE CONVENTIONAL LEVEL OF TRUTH

Milarepa has raised the following query. In light of the deepest, ultimate level, phenomena of samsara and nirvana do not exist. But if this were true on all levels and there were no such thing as beings with limited minds — if there were no sentient beings — then from whom did, do and will the Buddhas of the three times arise? It is impossible for there to be a result that has no cause. If this were not the case — if the functioning of cause and effect were not the case — then the entire presentation of order in the universe would fall apart and be invalid. Having formulated the doubt, Milarepa has then explained that there are no such faults. In light of the conventional level of truth, all things of samsara and nirvana do exist.

Gungtangzang has written, "When a correct view searches for and scrutinizes an inherently findable self-nature and does not find one, it nullifies it." In other words, a correct view scrutinizes closely the impression we have of a seemingly findable self-nature on the side of the various phenomena our mind produces an appearance of. A correct view is not satisfied merely with how mind normally makes things appear, it scrutinizes the apparent mode of existence of the phenomena that mind gives rise to an appearance of. When it does so, it cannot find what it is searching for.

Except for searching for an inherently findable self-nature, however, a correct view has no wish to search for the various phenomena of the conventional level that it neither inspects nor scrutinizes. Of course, it searches for an inherently findable self-nature on the basis of these conventional phenomena, not elsewhere. But because it searches merely for this inherently findable self-nature that we feel these phenomena have, when it cannot find one, it refutes, nullifies and, in a sense, eliminates such a self-nature — although such a self-nature never actually existed there at all. Conventional phenomena, such as mind, from their depths have always been pure of an inherently findable self-nature.

If there were such a thing as an inherently findable self-nature, then when a correct view searched for one, it should find it. But when it searches for one, intent on finding it, and does not find it, it nullifies its existence. In this sense, logic, reason and close scrutiny undermine and nullify inherently findable existence. Inherently findable existence, then, means existence by virtue of an inherently findable self-nature. Because all phenomena lack an inherently findable self-nature — as proven by a correct view that searches for one with logic, reason and scrutiny — all phenomena lack true, inherently findable existence.

The quotation of Gungtangzang continues, "But, when it does not find it, it does not nullify the basis for labeling. It sees something left over, existing simply through names." When a correct view does not find an inherently findable self-nature, this means it does not find a self-nature, or characteristic mark, or defining characteristic ultimately and truly existing as findable on the side of the object rendering that object what it appears to be. It does not locate, or come in contact with a findable characteristic mark on the side of the basis for labeling that object which allows for it to be correctly labeled as what it correctly appears to be. It does not, however, in any way invalidate or nullify this basis for labeling that is the place for affixing the convention of the object's name whereby the object being labeled dependently exists by virtue simply of names and mental labeling, as what it conventionally and validly is. Thus, with a mind validly seeing conventional phenomena — not with that aspect of mind that sees only deepest level truths — we come to know and see left over the object being labeled existing simply by virtue of names — existing as what its name refers to, in dependence on this basis for labeling.

On the basis of existence and identity by virtue simply of labeling with names, we can establish, in an undisturbed and undisturbing manner, in accordance with our experience, what is a fault and a good quality, what is to be rejected and accepted, and the benefits of engaging in productive and constructive actions. Thus we are left with the presentation of cause and effect, operating in an orderly fashion on the basis of existence by virtue simply of names.

This conclusion is corroborated by Chandrakirti in *A Supplement to [Nagarjuna's "Root Stanzas on] the Middle Way,"* "Thus, although we cannot establish them in any of the seven ways on the very deepest or even worldly level, yet when we do not scrutinize in these ways, [we are left with the fact that] what things come from and what is here on the worldly level is what can be labeled dependently on its own parts." In other words, when we search with logic and reason, either on the deepest, ultimate level or on the conventional level, for phenomena existing in the manner in which the mind produces an appearance of them — which would have to be in one of the seven ways, such as being inherently findable as the same as or different from their basis for labeling, and so forth — we cannot find them. But when we do not scrutinize, then on their basis for labeling, under the power of the collection of circumstances and conditions, there exist phenomena that actually bring benefit or harm.

## CONVENTIONAL EXISTENCE BY VIRTUE SIMPLY OF NAMES

Thus all knowable phenomena exist, but exist merely inasmuch as they can be labeled by names. They cannot be found to exist in the manner in which they normally appear to the mind. The auto-commentary illustrates this with the example of universals and particulars from the presentation of metaphysics. Suppose in a hall we have four pillars. We can say there is a universal pervasive with all these pillars, which is just "pillar" itself. Although we can mentally label the universal "pillar" on the basis of these four pillars, yet if we search the four for a findable basis with the defining characteristic making it the universal pillar that renders each individual pillar a pillar, we cannot find anything corresponding to this universal pillar. None of the individual pillars nor their collection is the universal pillar. Nor can a universal pillar be found established as existing on its own, separate from any particular pillar.

Universal and particular pillars, however, do conventionally exist. In dependence on the existence of the universal, "pillar," as a convention, different kinds and instances of particular pillars exist as pillars. Likewise, because different kinds and instances of pillars exist, the universal, "pillar," does exist. A basis for sub-division into particulars and the particulars themselves both exist. But they exist merely dependently on each other — not independently on their own — simply as what can be labeled by conceptual thought and names.

The same is true of all conventional phenomena. Because they are merely what can be labeled by conceptual minds and names on a basis for labeling, they exist as what they conventionally are by virtue simply of mental labeling. Their existence as "this" or "that" is established merely by the fact that they can be mentally labeled "this" or "that." There is no findable self-nature inherently on their own side, or on the side of their basis for labeling, establishing their true existence either through its own power alone or in conjunction with mental labeling. All phenomena are totally devoid of such a self-nature. Thus we say in simple words, "the deepest nature of all phenomena is voidness."

## REFUTATION OF THE SVATANTRIKA-MADHYAMAKA POSITION

The auto-commentary now raises a possible qualm. Some people say it is improper to refute and nullify the existence of whatever our mind produces an appearance of. Therefore the object that logic, reason and scrutiny refute must be something separate, more gross, than what our mind makes appear. If we were to refute and nullify what our mind makes appear, we would fall to nihilism.

In answer to this qualm, the First Panchen Lama explains that, on the one hand, any appearance the mind of ordinary beings produces in their cognitions is nothing but an appearance of true and inherent existence — and true and inherent existence is the actual object to be refuted. After all, it is said that the cognition of ordinary beings is pervasive with deceptive cognition. If it is a cognition of an ordinary being, it is necessarily a deceptive cognition producing an appearance of seemingly true and inherent existence. The necessity for saying this is that otherwise appearances of true and inherent existence would still be left unrefuted had we scrutinized the manner of existence of phenomena with merely the above criterion that affirms the existence of anything mind gives rise to an appearance of. Furthermore, if we say that the impossible manner of existence that we need to refute must be a separate fantasized one, other than true and inherent existence — one that leaves intact the appearance of solid phenomena and mind's appearance-making of them — we have come to a similar position as that of the svatantrika-madhyamaka system of tenets.

Some learned proponents of this system assert that things, such as forms of physical phenomena and so forth, exist by virtue of unmistaken minds being able to give rise to an appearance of them that can be mentally labeled as what they conventionally are. In other words, something exists conventionally if an unmistaken mind can impute it on a basis for labeling and cognize it correctly. All things, then, are devoid of not existing in this way. They are devoid of what the svatantrika-madhyamaka system calls true, unimputed existence. Chandrakirti has refuted this position soundly as asserting an object of refutation that is under-pervasive. He has explained that it is insufficient to refute and nullify merely true, unimputed existence. The refutation and nullification of such an incomplete object to be refuted does not refute and nullify existence established through an inherently findable characteristic mark on the side of the basis for labeling this object of cognition. In fact, the svatantrika-madhyamaka position asserts such characteristic marks as what allow for such objects to be unmistakenly labeled as what they are by unmistaken, though deceived minds which make them appear. Such an insufficient refutation and nullification, then, leaves behind inherently findable characteristic marks, or defining characteristics, or self-natures, as what establish the conventional level of truth. What is being refuted is not subtle enough and thus this svatantrika-madhyamaka position does not assert the most subtle correct view of reality. Those who would raise the above qualm should think carefully, the First Panchen Lama advises, about Chandrakirti's uncommon, special manner of asserting the subtlest object to be refuted.

## THE PRASANGIKA-MADHYAMAKA POSITION

When we refute and nullify inherently findable defining characteristic marks establishing the existence of conventional phenomena, either within or independent of the context of mental labeling, we are still left with the basis upon which this refutation and nullification is made. In the place of the nullification of such defining characteristic marks supposedly establishing the conventional level of truth from the side of objects, we are left with the ground for the nullifcation — the orderly presentation of non-fallacious, dependently arising phenomena that exist by virtue simply of what can be mentally labeled with names, without such defining characteristic marks.

Thus the prasangika-madhyamaka position is very subtle and extremely difficult to understand and realize. If we cannot adeptly correlate (1) the basis upon which the nullification of an inherently findable self-nature as the object to be refuted is made and is the case, with (2) the non-fallacious operation of dependent arising that brings benefit and harm, then even if we speak of a bare, total absence that is the nullification of inherently findable existence, we have not reached the actual absence that is voidness. When a mind of decisive understanding and realization gives rise to the actual, authentic total absence that is voidness, it needs to give rise to a total absence of existence established by inherently findable self-natures such that this absence serves as sufficient basis not only for dependently arising phenomena to function to bring happiness or downfalls, but also for mind to be able to give rise to an appearance of them.

In other words, we need to have voidness dawn in our mind in the meaning of dependent arising — in both functional and cognitive contexts. Thus when we prove or establish the side of voidness through one of the sets of lines of reasoning of the madhyamaka middle way, even if we gain some level of understanding of voidness, if we cannot adeptly correlate voidness of true, inherent, findable existence with its being the foundation for the non-fallacious dependent arising of the unmistaken functioning of conventional phenomena and mind's unmistakably giving rise to appearances of them, it will not do. Thus the ground for the refutation and nullification is both appearance and voidness being the case.

## DEPENDENT ARISING — THE "KING OF LINES OF REASONING"

Among the many reasons that induce conviction in voidness, the line of reasoning of dependent arising is the most devastating and important. When we say that phenomena are not established as existing from their own side because they arise dependently, with their existence established by their reliance simply on factors other than themselves — in other words, when we say that objects, which exist inasmuch as their existence is established by their reliance on serving as a basis for their functioning, do not exist with an inherently findable self-nature, precisely because their existence is established simply by their being related to factors other than themselves — we are making a very potent statement. Therefore, dependent arising, as the "king of lines of reasoning," is called "that which eliminates at once the two extreme, impossible modes of existence."

"Relying on factors other than itself" and "not relying on anything other than itself" are mutually exclusive categories. Not only that, they are explicitly mutually exclusive, which means they form a dichotomy. Anything that exists must either rely on factors other than itself or not rely on any such factors. There is no third possibility. It is impossible for something to both rely and not rely on factors other than itself. For any phenomenon, either external or internal, to exist, it must rely on causes and conditions, or on what can label it. The fact that it must rely on the basis of something other than itself in order to establish both its functional and cognitive existence completely cancels and eliminates the only alternative possibility. This would be that it does not rely on anything other than itself to establish its own existence, but does so through its own power — for example, by virtue of its inherently findable self-nature or defining characteristic mark.

There are many songs of meditational experience by various masters in praise of dependent arising. Just by looking at the term "dependent arising," for example, we can explain the entire manner of existence of conventional phenomenon. "Dependent" means that something depends or relies on factors other than itself. When we say something relies on factors other than itself, because we understand that it is severed from any possibility of having a nature of existing under its own power without relying on anything other than itself, the word "dependent" signifies a devoid nature and eliminates the extreme of true, inherent existence. "Arising" also implies that something exists by relying on factors other than itself. Through the power of conditions and circumstances, something has arisen, or is established as existing, or has come to be. This eliminates the extreme that it does not exist at all. Since it eliminates the extreme of total non-existence, the word "arising" allows us to understand the orderly presentation of the dependently arising manner of the universe. Therefore, because simply by virtue of the term "dependent arising" we can understand fully both levels of truth, there is a manner for eliminating the two extreme, impossible modes of existence simply through understanding one term.

## SUPPLEMENTING THE UNDERSTANDING OF DZOGCHEN WITH TSONGKAPA'S PRESENTATION OF VOIDNESS AND VICE VERSA

We find the most clear, precise and detailed explanation of how voidness means dependent arising and dependent arising means voidness in the writings of Tsongkapa. Such clarity and depth of precision are, in fact, the uncommon feature of his great works. The great dzogchen texts and masters always speak about all phenomena "being primordially, from their depths, primally pure," "being, by nature, primally pure," "being stilled of solid reality," "being primordially, from their depths, devoid." For those who practice dzogchen, however, it is of no benefit to have merely a presumptive understanding of the expression "being, by nature, primally pure," or merely an idea of it that consists of the sound of the expression itself, but without any meaning. We must correctly and totally understand the meaning of "primally pure." For this, we must understand fully, with precision, depth, clarity and detail, the manner of voidness that is the primordial voidness, with respect to all phenomena, of an inherently findable nature from their depths, as we have just explained. This being so, if, as dzogchen practitioners, we supplement our efforts to come to an accurate understanding of the meaning of "primally pure" with Tsongkapa's explanation of all phenomena being devoid of an inherently findable self-nature, we find it very applicable and extremely beneficial.

Thus some great dzogchen masters from Kham, southeastern Tibet, have said that for gaining proper practice of the stage called "breakthrough to pure awareness," we need to have a sound understanding of the prasangika view. Likewise, some Gelug masters have said that to gain a proper understanding of clear light mind — especially of the coarse and subtle primordial minds — it is very helpful to study the dzogchen texts.

## VALID COGNITION OF THE CONVENTIONAL LEVEL OF TRUTH

The auto-commentary continues by drawing a fine but important distinction. The visual consciousness that apprehends a sight is a conventional mind that validly cognizes conventional sights — in other words, it is a "valid cognizer" of sights. It validly cognizes the appearance of the sight to which it gives rise as being just that — the appearance of a sight. Furthermore, it also validly cognizes the appearance of a sight existing as if with an inherently findable self-nature as being just that, the appearance of a sight as if with an inherently findable self-nature. If a mind is valid, it necessarily validly cognizes the appearances to which it gives rise. But, this conventionally valid visual consciousness is not valid for establishing the existence of this inherently findable self-nature. It is valid for cognizing the mode of appearance it produces, but deceptive for cognizing the mode of existence of that which it produces an appearance of. We need to understand this correctly and precisely.

When Gelug practitioners assert valid cognition of conventional phenomena by conventionally valid minds, this does not throw them to the extreme of eternalism. This assertion gives us one thing to think about, while the equally Gelug assertion that the total lack of existence by means of an inherently findable self-nature also applies to conventional phenomena gives us something further to think about. While asserting valid cognition of conventional phenomena by conventionally valid minds, the Gelug system at the same time asserts that all minds are deceived and deceptive other than those that straightforwardly and non-conceptually cognize voidness during an arya's total absorption.

## APPLYING THE UNDERSTANDING OF VOIDNESS TO EVERY APPEARANCE TO WHICH MIND GIVES RISE

The auto-commentary now cites several quotations stressing the importance of neither over- nor under-refuting what is to be refuted and nullified. Their essence is as follows. Some people think that if we refute and nullify our conventionally existent person, we fall to the extreme of nihilism. Taking our conventionally existent person to be an actual person who exists, in the way our mind gives rise to an appearance of it, as someone solid, able to stand on his or her feet and hold its own, they put such a person aside and do not deconstruct it. They then posit another type of imaginary person separate from this that they conjure with their mind and decisively refute and nullify that such a person, as a basis for voidness, is established as existing truly and inherently. The extensiveness of the range and scope of their refutation is not large enough, and so they fall to a view of eternalism.

Gungtangzang has explained, in one of his *Thousands of Songs of Meditative Experience*, that if we do not try to poke, with a correct view of voidness, the appearances to which our mind conventionally gives rise, we cannot come to an accurate understanding of the madhyamaka view. In other words, we must involve or engage our understanding of voidness with whatever appearances our mind normally produces of things in each moment, now, and try to dislodge them. We do this by seeing that the mode of existence mind makes appear and implies actually to exist does not exist at all. If we set that fact aside, letting these appearances stand as referring to something real, and engage our understanding of voidness with something else, we cannot come to an accurate understanding of the madhyamaka view. If we have gained an accurate understanding of the madhyamaka view that is exactly to the point, we must experience it unsettling and dislodging the appearances to which our mind normally gives rise.

## VOIDNESS AND DEPENDENTLY ARISING APPEARANCE BEING SYNONYMOUS

In another of his *Thousands of Songs of Meditative Experience*, Gungtangzang has explained how to understand the words "appearance" and "voidness." "Appearance" means "appearance-making" — mind's giving rise to appearances of things that can be labeled what they conventionally are by relying simply on factors other than themselves, namely conceptual minds and names. "Voidness" means devoid of existing in fantasized, impossible ways, for instance things existing as what they are by means of an inherent, findable nature. These do not contradict each other, but rather come to the same point. The fact that the existence of the phenomena mind produces an appearance of and their identity as "this" or "that" are established and proven simply by the fact that they can be labeled as "this" or "that" by the conventions of conceptual minds and words means that their existence is not established or proven from their own side by means of some inherently findable self-nature or characteristic mark making them exist and making them be what they conventionally are. The fact that all phenomena are devoid of existing in fantasized, impossible manners — for instance as constituting a solid reality with the existence of everything established independently from the side of each thing — means that everything exists in the only possible alternative fashion, namely as things whose existence is established by relying on factors other than themselves.

In short, appearance-making and appearances do not obstruct or impede voidness, and voidness does not obstruct or impede appearance-making and appearances. They indicate the same thing from two points of view. Thus, since the voidness or total absence of all fantasized, impossible ways of existing does not refute or nullify appearance-making and appearances, and vice versa, when our mind perceives both simultaneously, we have, as the root text says, "directly manifested the excellent pathway mind that perceives everything from the single, integrated point of voidness and dependent arising being synonymous."

The manner of apprehension of the total absence of true and inherent existence is equivalent to elimination or cessation of the manner of apprehension of true and inherent existence. Thus eventually mind, severed of its manner of apprehension of true and inherent existence, ceases its discordant appearance-making of phenomena as existing truly and inherently. Since mind's discordant appearance-making eventually ceases through its familiarity with understanding voidness, mind ceases to mix its appearance-making of phenomena as dependently arising with discordant appearance-making. In this way, the apprehension of voidness comes down to appearance-making of phenomena simply as what dependently arises.

Therefore, rather than blocking mind's unobscured appearance-making of dependently arising phenomena, mind's apprehension of voidness makes apprehension of this pure appearance-making unobscured. And because this appearance-making of dependently arising phenomena is not mixed with discordant appearance-making of phenomena as truly and inherently existent, it does not obscure apprehension of voidness. Thus, not only do we understand that voidness and appearance-making of dependently arising phenomena do not obstruct or impede each other, but eventually the two do not obscure each other. So long as we are not able straightforwardly to make rise the cognitive dawning of both voidness and dependently arising appearances simultaneously like this, but only one at a time, in an alternating fashion, we have not yet come to full realization of the madhyamaka path.

Now voidness dawns faultlessly in our mind. This has been corroborated by Chandrakirti in *A Supplement to [Nagarjuna's "Root Stanzas on] the Middle Way."* Because voidness of inherently findable existence is reasonable, dependently arising, reliant existence is also reasonable. When it is the case that existence established by relying on factors other than itself is reasonable, then the coming of various results from the gathering of various causes — in other words, existence created through the power of circumstances — is also reasonable. Through conducive circumstances, results arise. When these circumstances cease, their result ceases. Thus the absence of inherently findable existence is equivalent to existence established by reliance on circumstances. The fact of everything being devoid by nature makes the orderly presentation of how phenomena arise and cease totally reasonable. Likewise, order in the universe makes conviction in voidness also totally reasonable. With this understanding, voidness dawns faultlessly in our mind. As our guiding light, Nagarjuna, has said, "When you are able to understand the voidness of phenomena and at the same time see cause and effect as being completely reasonable, this is more wonderful than wonderful, more amazing than amazing."

## THE STAGES TO ENLIGHTENMENT THROUGH MAHAMUDRA

In the auto-commentary, the Panchen Lama now reviews the stages of pathway minds to enlightenment through the mahamudra techniques. "When mounted on the horse of shamata, your mind attains absorbed concentration focused on voidness cultivated through mahamudra meditation and conjoined with the mental factor of an additional serenely joyous sense of physical and mental suppleness and fitness brought on merely by virtue of your close scrutiny, you have attained the heat stage of an applying pathway of mind." In other words, when we realize, through the mahamudra techniques, a pathway mind of combined shamata and vipashyana — a mind that is both serenely stilled and settled as well as exceptionally perceptive — we have attained the first of the four stages of the second of the five pathway minds delineated by Maitreya. Its four stages are heat, peak, patience and the supreme measure.

Some masters of the Kagyü tradition, however, have divided the mahamudra path to enlightenment into simply four progressive pathway minds. The first is the stage of single-pointedness, when mind is single-pointedly settled on mind. It refers mostly to the meditative practices of shamata and covers the accumulating and applying pathways of mind, the first two in Maitreya's fivefold division. The second is the stage free from mental fabrication, when we reach the level of realization free from all mental fabricating. Attained with straightforward, non-conceptual perception of the deepest level of truth, it corresponds to the third of the five pathway minds, that of seeing. The third stage in the fourfold division is the single taste, when we gain realization of appearance and mind being of a single taste. In terms of the stages of the anuttarayoga tantra path, this undoubtedly refers to attainment of the state of unity. The fourth stage, that of no more meditation, is when we no longer meditate with even signs of true, inherent existence. According to Götsangpa, the stage of the single taste corresponds to the second through the seventh of the ten bodhisattva levels of mind, while that of no more meditation to the final three pure bodhisattva levels.

There are some differences of opinion, however, as to the exact correspondences. Zhang Yudragpa, for example, has said that the way in which those for whom everything happens at once progress to enlightenment does not correspond to the usual presentation of the paths and levels of mind of the sutra vehicle. Sakya Pandita has objected to this and questioned the authenticity of the mahamudra path of those for whom everything happens at once, because it does not correspond to the commonly accepted mahayana presentation of either the sutra or the anuttarayoga path to enlightenment.

The First Panchen Lama does not shy way from or deny these points of dispute and the debates that have arisen over them. But, after presenting all the difficulties clearly and acknowledging the importance of knowing about them, he gives very significant advice. He writes, "The actions of highly realized beings are completely beyond the understanding of ordinary beings, and the faults built up by negative thought and words about them are extremely heavy. Therefore, I, Lozang-chökyi-gyeltsen, appeal to everyone to leave aside the anger of partisan sectarianism. May everyone's mind give rise to pure appearances."

Thus, the First Panchen Lama stresses that, in the end, the essence of the teachings of each of the four Tibetan Buddhist traditions of Nyingma, Kagyü, Sakya and Gelug come to the same intended point. It is helpful to understand the differences among their presentations of the path to enlightenment. But rather than letting that knowledge fan sectarian hatred, we should use it to enhance our respect and admiration for Buddha's wide range of skillful means. I am in full agreement.

## DEDICATION AND CONCLUDING ADVICE

Of the three major divisions of the outline of the text — the preliminary discussion, the actual explanation and the dedication — the root text now concludes with the dedication. "These words have been written by the renounced meditator Lozang-chökyi-gyeltsen, who has heard many teachings. By its positive merit, may all beings quickly become triumphant Buddhas through this pathway of mind, apart from which there is no second gateway to a state of serenity."

Just as we have exerted great effort and attention to listen to and try to understand these mahamudra teachings, likewise we need to make a similar effort to apply them to our meditational practice and daily lives without simply forgetting about them. If we wish to engage in a separate, intensive practice of mahamudra, that is, of course, very excellent. But even if that is not possible, it is very beneficial to add a certain amount of mahamudra meditation to our daily practice, for example within the context of whatever tantric recitation or sadhana practice we might be doing each day. In an anuttarayoga sadhana, for example, we add it either at the beginning after we have dissolved our root guru into us at the end of the request to the lineage masters for inspiration, or when we have dissolved all appearances into voidness before arising as a Buddha-form, or as a concluding step in the process of supplementing the sadhana with subtle generation stage practices of minute visualized drops multiplying from and contracting back into the upper or lower end of the central energy-channel. At any of these points, we focus on the nature of mind and try to develop shamata on that basis.

As for our daily lives, no matter what type of difficult situation may arise, we try to see it as not having any true and inherent existence from its own side. Although conventionally it is true that the situation may be difficult, if it were intrinsically difficult from its own side, there would be nothing we could do to remove or avoid the difficulty. On the other hand, when we see that the situation exists as difficult in reliance on the conceptual mind that can label it "difficult," then we see that the situation has arisen dependently on many factors. This allows us, in a dispassionate manner, to try to change and eliminate the causes and circumstances upon which the conventionally difficult situation depends for establishing its existence. In this way, we eliminate the problem.

As beginners we may find such an advanced technique beyond our current level of training. We may strongly identify with the conventional level, firmly believing in the solidity of inherently findable benefit or harm that an inherently findable "me" can experience. But if our heart is dedicated with bodhichitta to helping others and achieving enlightenment in order to be able to accomplish that aim as fully as possible, we find that this helps us break through the self-imposed constrictions of our solid view of ourselves and of everything and everyone around us.

It is very helpful at all stages of our practice to implement lojong, the techniques for cleansing our attitudes. For example, rather than looking at a difficult situation in which we are unhappy as very terrible and becoming further depressed about it, we cleanse ourselves of this negative attitude and look at the situation from a more positive point of view. If our life is going too smoothly and well, there is the possible danger of becoming smug, complacent and insensitive to the sufferings of others. If we are in the midst of facing difficult situations, however, we are much more sober. There is a far better opportunity to appreciate and sympathize with others facing similar situations, and we are more motivated to train ourselves with spiritual techniques. If we are praised, we may become proud and not think about further improving ourselves, whereas if we are faulted and criticized, we are motivated to try to correct our mistakes and shortcomings. Therefore, lojong practice allows us to be happy when we might normally be unhappy because it provides techniques for transforming our experience of difficult situations by cleansing our attitudes. For more detail on this topic, it is best to study Shantideva's *Engaging in a Bodhisattva's Deeds*, especially the chapters on patience and mental stability.

Then if, on top of this, we try as best as we can to apply some understanding of voidness to the difficult situations we encounter, we experience a further weakening of our disturbing emotions and attitudes and eventually their elimination and extinction. For example, if we become angry with someone we try to recognize this anger as soon as our mind gives rise to it. We then inspect and scrutinize closely the appearance of this annoying person that our mind produces accompanied with anger. We try to locate a findable person who truly and inherently exists from his or her own side as a solid object against whom we direct our anger. Is that person his or her body, mind or words? Inspecting and scrutinizing closely in this way helps us dissipate our anger. Our anger, after all, has arisen because of our mind's producing an appearance of this person as if he or she were not only truly and inherently existent, but truly and inherently existent as an annoying person, and because of our mind's apprehension of him or her actually to exist in this impossible manner. The more we undermine our belief in this appearance, the less our anger has any foundation upon which to stand. We must never be lax in our efforts to understand this and implement it in our daily lives.

Let us end by dedicating the positive potential built up toward the attainment of enlightenment by everyone, for the benefit of all. By such methods as mahamudra, may everyone overcome all his or her sufferings, and attain all good qualities, so that we bring about deep and lasting happiness for all.

# THE TIBETAN TEXT

*A ROOT TEXT FOR THE PRECIOUS*
*GELUG/KAGYÜ TRADITION OF MAHAMUDRA:*
*The Main Road of the Triumphant Ones*

*by*

The First Panchen Lama

*from the Collected Works of*
*Paṇ-chen Blo-bzang chos-kyi rgyal-mtshan*

*reproduced from prints of the bKra-shis lhun-po blocks*
*by Mongolian Lama Gurudeva*
*New Delhi, 1973*

81

82

83

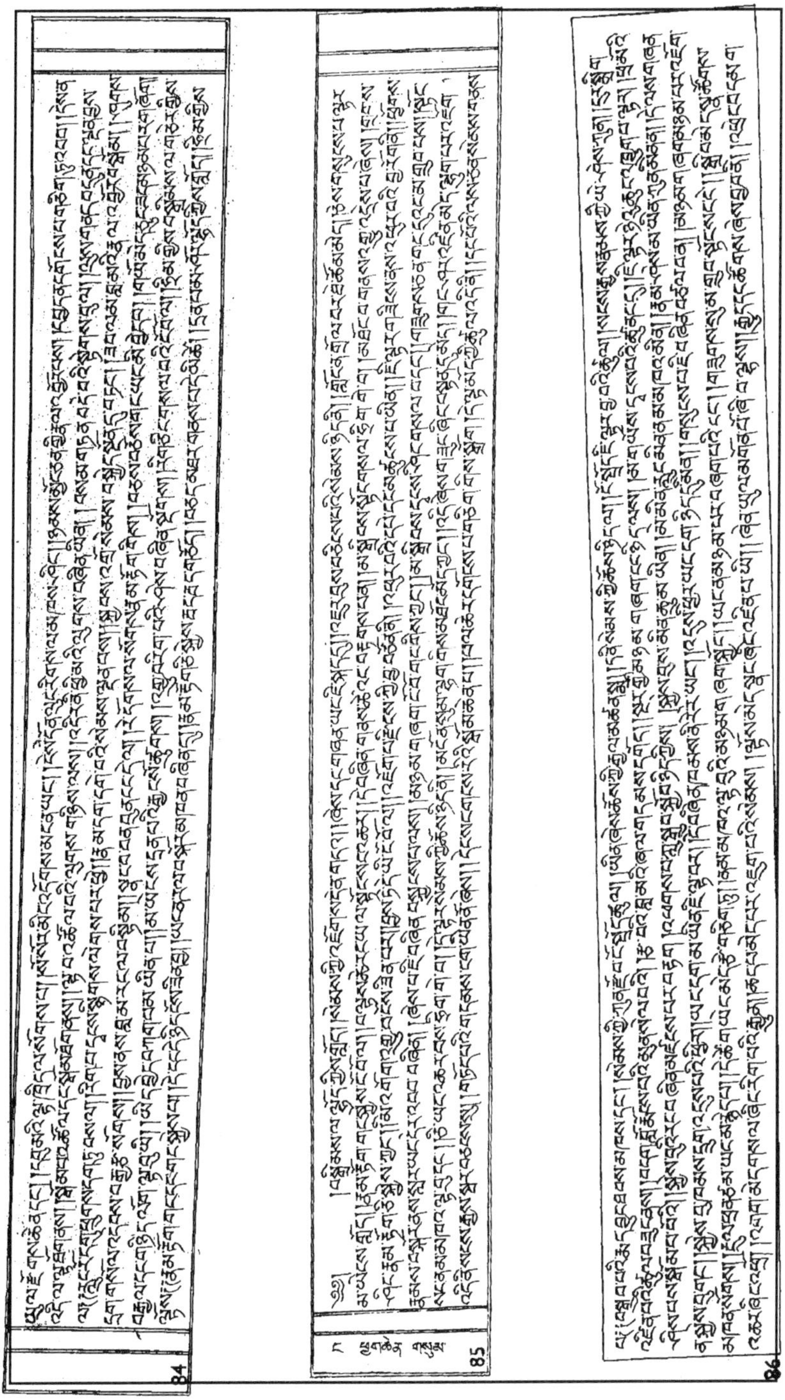
84
85
86

# Glossary

abiding nature of reality (*gnas-lugs, sdod-lugs*)
able to hold its own (*rang-tshugs thub-pa*)
absence of impossible ways of existing (*śūnyatā; stong-pa-nyid*) (voidness, emptiness)
absorbed concentration (*samādhi; ting-nge-'dzin*) (single-minded concentration, meditative absorbtion)
action tantra (*kriyātantra, bya-rgyud*)
actual attainments (*siddha; dngos-grub*) (feats)
actualizing the descendents of the vidyadharas (*rig-'dzin gdung-sgrub*) (actualizing through the descendents)
actualizing the guru (*bla-sgrub*) (actualizing throught the guru)
actualizing the mind of the vidya-dharas (*rig-'dzin thugs-sgrub*) (actualizing throught the mind)
adding the lord of a Buddha-family trait (*rigs-bdag rgyas-gdab*) (adding a crown ornament of the lord of a Buddha-family)
adulterated by conceptual thought (*rtog-pas bslad-pa*)
affected phenomena (*saṃskṛtadharma; 'dus-byas-kyi chos*) (conditioned phenomena)
affecting variables (*saṃskāra; 'du-byed*) (volition)
affecting variables that are neither (*rūpacittaviprayuktasaṃskāra; ldan-min 'du-byed*)
affirming nullification (*paryudāsapratiṣedha; ma-yin dgag*) (affirming negation)
aim (*dmigs-pa*)
alertness (*samprajanya; shes-bzhin*)
all-encompassing foundation (*ālaya; kun-gzhi*)
    for various instincts of karma (*bag-chags sna-tshogs-kyi kun-gzhi*)
    primordially there from the depths (*ye-don-gyi kun-gzhi*)
amulet box tradition (*ga'u-ma*)
anger (*pratigha; khong-'khro*) (repulsion, aggression)
appearance (*āloka; snang-ba*)
    accurate and distorted (*yang-dag-pa'i dang log-pa'i*)
    impure (*ma-dag*)
    pure (*dag*)

appearance-congealing conceptual mind (*snang-ba*) (mind of white appearance)
appearing object (*snang-yul*)
apprehending (*grāha; 'dzin-pa*) (grasping)
apprehending true existence (*satyagrāha; bden-'dzin*) (grasping for true existence)
apprehending true identities (*ātmagrāha; bdag-'dzin*) (grasping for a self)
arising (*shar*)
arising, abiding and ceasing (*skye-gnas-'gog gsum*)
arrogantly naïve madhyamika (*dbu-ma-par rlom-pa*)
artificial (*bcas-bcos*)
aspect (*ākāra; rnam-pa*)
attachment (*lobha; chags-pa*)
attention (*manaskāra; yid-la byed-pa*) (taking to mind)
    four types [painstaking (*bsgrims-du 'jug-pa'i*), resetting (*chad-cing 'jug-pa'i*), un-
        interrupted (*chad-pa med-par 'jug-pa'i*) and spontaneous (*lhun-gyi'grub-pa'i*)]
attitude (*mati; blo*)
automatic ceasing (*rang-'gag*)
automatic coming to its own state (*rang-babs*)
automatic clearing away (*rang-sangs*)
automatic disappearance (*rang-yal*)
automatic emanation (*rang-'phros*)
automatic giving rise (*rang-shar*) (automatic arising)
automatic occurring (*rang-'byung*)
automatic releasing (*rang-grol*) (self-liberation)
automatically establishing its own existence (*rang-nyid grub-pa*)
awareness (*rig*)

bardo (*antarabhāva, bar-do*)
bare absence (*stong-sang*)
basis for affixing a name (*'jog-gzhi*)
basis for labeling (*gdags-gzhi*)
basis of voidness (*stong-gzhi*)
basis with a defining characteristic making it what it is (*mtshan-gzhi*)
behavior tantra (*caryātantra, spyod-rgyud*)
behavioral cause and effect (*hetuphalaṃ; rgyu-'bras*)
being by nature primally pure (*ngo-bo ka-dag*)
being for absorbed concentration (*samādhisattva; ting-nge-'dzin sems-pa*) (concen-
    tration being)
being for bonding closely with (*samayasattva; dam-tshigs sems-pa*) (commitment
    being)
being for deep awareness (*jñānasattva; ye-shes sems-pa*) (wisdom being)
benefiting others (*gzhan-phan*)
    temporarily (*gnas-skabs-kyis*)
    ultimately (*mthar-thug-gis*)
better states of rebirth (*sugati; bde-'gro*) (higher rebirth)
beyond imagination (*blo-'das*)
blissful awareness (*sukha; bde-ba*)
    of orgasmic emission (*'dzag-bde*)

body encompassing everything (*dharmakāya; chos-sku*) (all-encompassing network, truth body)

body isolation (*lus-dben*)

body of deep awareness encompassing everything (*jñāna-dharmakāya*) (all-encompassing network of deep awareness, wisdom body)

body of emanations (*nirmāṇakāya; sprul-sku*) (network of emanations, emanation body)

body of forms (*rūpakāya; gzugs-sku*) (network of enlightening forms, form body)

body of forms with full use (*saṃbhogakāya; longs-sku*) (network of fully operational forms, enjoyment body)

body of self-nature encompassing everything (*svabhāvakāya; ngo-bo-nyid sku*) (all-encompassing basic network, nature body)

body, speech and mind (*lus-ngag-yid*)

boon experiences (*nyams*)

boredom (*nyob*)

bountiful store of deep awarenes (*jñānasaṃbhāra; ye-shes-kyi tshogs;*) (network of deep awareness, collection of insight, collection of wisdom)

bountiful store of positive potential (*puñyasaṃbhāra; bsod-nams-kyi tshogs*) (network of positive potential, collection of merit)

breakthrough (*khreg-chod*)

Buddha (*buddha; sangs-rgyas*) (fully awakened one)

Buddha-family trait (*buddhakūla; sangs-rgyas-kyi rigs*) (Buddha family)

Buddha-field (*buddhakṣetra; sangs-rgyas-kyi zhing*)

Buddha-form (*iṣṭadevatā; yi-dam*) (deity)

Buddha-nature (*dhātu; khams*) (factors allowing one to become a Buddha, source of Buddhahood)

causal everlasting stream of the alaya (*kun-gzhi rgyu'i rgyud*)

causes and circumstances (*rgyu-rkyen*)

causes of problems (*samudaya; kun-'byung*)

central energy-channel (*avadhūti; rtsa dbu-ma*)
   upper and lower ends (*dhūti'i yar-sne, dhūti'i mar-sne*)

cessation (*nirodha; 'gog-pa*) (ending, stopping)

chakra (*cakra; 'khor-lo*) (subtle energy-node)

changing phenomena (*anitya; mi-rtag-pa*) (impermanent phenomena, non-static phenomena)

channel-knots (*granthi; rtsa-mtud*)

chitta (*citta; mind*)

chittamatra (*cittamātra; sems-tsam*)

circumambulation (*āvartana; skor-ba*)

clarity (*gsal*)

clarity and voidness not apprehended apart (*gsal-stong 'dzin-med*)

cleansing of attitudes (*blo-sbyong*) (mind-training)

clear light (*prabhāsvara; 'od-gsal*)
   actual (*don-gi*)
   illustrative (*dpe'i*) (approximating)
   mother (*ma'i*)

object (*yul-gyi*)
of death (*'chi-ba'i*)
clear vision (*dag-snang*)
close bond (*samaya; dam-tshig*) (close bonding practice, word of honor)
cognition (*jñāna; shes-pa*)
cognitive dawning (*'char-ba*)
   in an exposing, resplendent manner (*rjen-par lhang-gis*)
cognitive sensor (*indriya; dbang-po*) (sense power)
cognitive spheres (*dhātu; khams*)
collected topics (*bsdus-grva*)
collecting and cleansing (*bsags-sbyangs*)
community (*saṅgha; dge-'dun*) (Sangha)
compassion (*karuṇa; snying-rje*)
complete stage (*sampannakrama; rdzogs-rim*) (completion stage)
comprehensive result (*adhipatiphalaṃ; bdag-po'i 'bras-bu*)
compulsive existence (*bhava; srid-pa*)
conceptual mind (*vikalpa; rtog-pa*) (concepts)
   conscious personal (*rtog-pa*)
   preconscious primitive (*rang-bzhin kun-btags*) (natural indicative)
   unconscious subtlest appearance-making (*snang-ba, snang-mched-thob gsum*)
concern for others (*gzhan-gces*) (cherishing others)
confident belief (*pratyayitā; yid-ches-pa*) (believing a fact based on reason)
confusion about reality (*avidyā; ma-rigs-pa*) (unawareness, ignorance)
constructive actions (*kuśala; dge-ba*) (virtuous actions)
constructive emotions and attitudes (*nyon-mongs ldog-phyogs*)
contentment (*chog-shes*)
contents of experience (*myong-yul*)
contriving (*bcos-pa*)
contriving mind (*bcos-pa'i sems*)
convention (*vyavahāra; tha-snyad*)
conventional level of truth (*saṃvṛtisatya; kun-rdzob bden-pa*) (conventional truth)
   corresponding to fact and not corresponding to anything real (*don-mthun dang don mi-mthun*)
conventional nature (*kun-rdzob gnas-lugs*)
corner of the mind (*sems-kyi zur-cha*)
correct view (*dṛṣti, samyagdṛṣti; lta-ba, yang-dag lta-ba*) (right view)
   in terms of devoid nature (*dharmatādṛṣti; chos-nyid lta-ba*)
   in terms of what has voidness as its nature (*dharmindṛṣti; chos-can lta-ba*)
creator (*byed-pa-po*)
crisp (*shigs-se*)

deceptive appearance and appearance-making (*'khrul-snang*)
deceptive appearances within what is already deceptive (*nying-'khrul*)
deceptive cognition (*bhrāntajñāna, 'khrul-shes*)
decisive understanding (*niścaya; nges-pa*) (ascertainment, decisive apprehension)
dedicated being (*bodhisattva; byang-chub sems-dpa'*) (bodhisattva)
dedicated heart (*bodhicitta; byang-sems*) (bodhichitta)

dedication of positive potential (*pariṇāmanā; bsgno-ba*) (dedication of merit)
deep awareness (*jñāna; ye-shes*) (wisdom)
deepest level of truth (*paramārthasatya; don-dam bden-pa*) (ultimate truth)
deepest nature (*don-dam gnas-lugs*)
defining characteristic mark (*lakṣaṇa; mtshan-nyid*)
definitive level (*neyārtha; nges-don*) (ultimate level, absolute level)
definitive level short syllable "A" (*nges-don-gyi a-thung*)
dependent arising (*pratītyasamutpāda; rten-'brel*) (interdependent origination)
dependent phenomena (*paratantra; gzhan-dbang*) (other-powered phenomena)
designation (*prajñāpti; btags-pa*) (mental label)
destructive actions (*akuśala; mi-dge-ba*) (non-virtuous actions)
determination to be free (*niḥsaraṇa; nges-'byung*) (renunciation)
devoid nature (*dharmatā; chos-nyid*) (nature of things)
Dharma (*dharma; chos*) (preventative measures)
dharma-protector (*dharmapāla; chos-skyong*)
diamond-strong scepter of mind (*sems-kyi rdo-rje*) (vajra of mind)
diamond-strong sphere of mind (*vajradhātu; rdo-rje dbyings*)
dichotomy (*dngos-'gal*)
different package (*ngo-bo tha-dad*) (different entity, different by nature)
dignity of being a Buddha-form (*lha'i nga-rgyal*) (pride of the deity)
direct apprehension (*dngos-su rtogs-pa*)
discernment (*saṃjñā; 'du-shes*) (distinguishing, recognition)
disciple (*śikṣa; slob-ma*)
discordant appearance-making (*gnyis-snang*) (dual appearances)
discourse (*khrid*)
discredit (*sun-'byin*)
discriminating awareness (*prajñā; shes-rab*) (wisdom)
  disturbing (*nyon-mongs-can*)
  incorrect (*log-pa'i*)
  individualizing (*so-sor rtogs-pa'i*)
discursive madhyamaka view (*dbu-ma'i lta-khrid*)
disposition (*dhātu; khams*)
dissolution (*thim*)
distant lineage (*ring-brgyud*)
distinguishing (*saṃjñā; 'du-shes*) (descernment, recognition)
distorted, antagonistic attitude (*mithyādṛṣṭi; log-lta*) (false view)
distraction (*'phro-ba*)
disturbing emotions and attitudes (*kleśa; nyon-mongs*) (delusions, afflictive
    emotions)
  automatically arising (*sahaja; lhan-skyes*) (intuitive)
  based on preconceptions (*parikalpita; kun-brtags*) (intellectual)
dread (*bhī; 'jigs-pa*) (fear)
dream (*svapna; rmi-lam*)
dual appearances (*gnyis-snang*) (discordant appearance-making)

effulgence (*rtsal*)
eight composing mental faculties (*'du-byed brgyad*)

eight great discourses (*'khrid-chen brgyad*)
eight transitory things in life (*'jig-rten chos-brgyad*) (eight worldly dharmas)
elder (*sthavira; gnas-brtan*)
elements (*bhūta; 'byung-ba*)
emanation (*'phro-ba*)
empowerment (*abhiṣeka; dbang*) (initiation)
   four [vase (*kalaśābhiṣeka; bum-dbang*), hidden (*guhyābhiṣeka; gsang-dbang*) (se-
      cret), deep discriminating awareness (*prajñājñānābhiṣeka; shes-rab ye-shes
      dbang*) (wisdom), word (*akṣarābhiṣeka; tshig-dbang*)]
   fourth (*caturthābhiṣeka; dbang bzhi-pa*)
energy-channels (*nāḍi; rtsa*)
energy-drops (*bindu; thig-le*)
energy-winds (*prāṇa; rlung*)
engaging (*'jug-pa*)
enlightening abilities (*śakti, nus-pa*) (powerful abilities)
enlightening body, speech and mind (*sku-gsung-thugs*)
enlightening influence (*samudācāra; 'phrin-las*) (Buddha-activity)
enlightenment (*samyaksaṃbodhi; yang-dag-par byang-chub*)
enter, abide and dissolve (*zhugs-gnas-thim gsum*)
entering the citadel (*grong-'jug*)
equanimity (*upekṣā; btang-snyoms*)
essential factors for accordant progress (*tathāgatagarbha; de-gshegs snying-po*)
      (Buddha-nature)
essential factors for blissful progress (*sugatagarbha; bde-gshegs snying-po*) (Bud-
      dha-nature)
eternalism (*nityadṛṣṭi; rtag-lta*)
ethical self-discipline (*śila; tshul-khrims*)
ever-changing phenomena (*rtag-pa shes-bya-ba'i mi-rtag-pa*)
exceptional resolve (*adhyāśaya; lhag-bsam*) (pure wish)
exceptionally perceptive state of mind (*vipaśyanā; lhag-mthong*) (penetrative in-
      sight, special insight, vipashyana)
existence as a substantial entity able to stand on its own (*rang-rkya 'dzin-thub-pa'i
      rdzas-yod*)
existence established as a solid reality (*prakṛtisiddha; ngo-bo-nyid-kyis grub-pa*)
existence established at the place where something is mentally labeled to be (*btags-
      sar grub-pa*)
existence established at the place where something seems to exist (*yod-sar grub-
      pa*)
existence established by a defining characteristic (*svalakṣaṇasiddha; rang mtshan-
      nyid-kyis grub-pa*)
existence established by an inherently findable self-nature (*satyasiddha,
      svabhāvasiddha; bden-grub, rang-bzhin-gyis grub-pa*) (true, inherent existence)
existence established by virtue of dependent arising (*rten-'brel grub-pa*)
existence established by virtue of itself (*svatantrasiddha; rang-dbang-gis grub-pa*)
      (independent existence, existence established by its own power)
existence established by virtue of something other than itself (*paratantrasiddha;
      gzhan-dbang-gis grub-pa*)

existence established by virtue simply of conceptual thought (*rtog-tsam-gyis grub-pa*)

existence established by virtue simply of conventions (*tha-snyad-tsam-gyis grub-pa*)

existence established by virtue simply of mental labeling (*prajñāptimātrasiddha; btags-pa 'dog-tsam-gyi grub-pa*)

existence established by virtue simply of names (*nāmamātrasiddha; ming-tsam-gyis grub-pa*)

existence established from its own side (*svarūpasiddha; rang-ngos-nas grub-pa*)

existence established in the place where mind makes something appear to be (*snang-sar grub-pa*)

existence established relative to conditions and factors (*rkyen-rten-nas grub-pa*)

expanse of space of mind itself (*sems-nyid-kyi nam-mkha' yangs-pa*)

expectations or worries (*re-dogs*)

experience (*pratisaṃveda; myong-ba*)

external circumstances (*phyi'i rkyen*)

extra-physical abilities (*ṛddhi; rdzu-'phrul*)

extreme of passive nirvana (*śamānta; zhi-mtha'*)

fabricating (*prapañca; spros-pa*) (mental fabrication)

face of absorbed concentration (*mnyam-gzhag ngor*)

face of the mind (*sems-ngor*)

faith (*śraddha; dad-pa*) (believing a fact)

fantasized, impossible existence (*satyasiddha; bden-grub*) (true existence)

fantasy (*prapañca; spros-pa*) (mental fabrication)

far-reaching discriminating awareness (*prajñāpāramitā; sher-phyin*) (perfection of wisdom)

father and mother couple (*yab-yum*)

faults in meditation (*sgom-skyon*)

feel and utilize things (*saṃbhoga; longs-spyod*) (enjoy)

female forces of unimpeded action (*ḍākinī; mkha'-'gro-ma*) (dakini)

fervent regard and respect (*mos-gus*) (firm conviction and appreciation)

fervent requests (*saṃcetana; gsol-'debs*)

field for building up positive potential (*tshogs-zhing*) (merit-field)

first-level stable mind (*prathamadhyāna; bsam-gtan dang-po*) (first dhyana)

five aggregate factors of experience (*pañcaskandha; phung-po lnga*) (five aggregates)

five deterrents to concentration (*nyes-pa lnga*)

five kinds of nectar-like bodily fluids (*bdud-rtsi lnga*)

five stages system (*pañcakrama; rim-lnga*)

five traditions for cutting down to the foundational state of mind (*sems gzhi-rtsa gcod-tshul lugs-lnga*)

five types of flesh (*sha-lnga*)

flash experience, flash of insight (*nyams*)

fleeting level of mind (*glo-bur-ba'i sems*)

flightiness of mind (*auddhatya; rgod-pa*) (mental agitation)

    gross (*rags-pa*)

    subtle (*phra-mo*)

focus (ārambaṇa; dmigs-pa)
    depths of (dmigs-pa'i gting)
    surface of (dmigs-pa'i ngor)
foggy-mindedness (styāna; rmugs-pa)
foolish confusion (moha; gti-mug) (naivety, closed-mindedness)
forms of physical phenomena (rūpa; gzugs) (form)
    subtle (avijñapti; rnam-par rigs-byed ma-yin-pa'i gzugs) (non-revealing forms)
forward-leading preliminaries (khrid-chen)
foundation (gzhi)
    for appearance and appearance-making (snang-gzhi)
foundational deep awareness (kun-gzhi ye-shes)
foundational mind (ālayavijñāna; kun-gzhi rnam-shes) (storehouse consciousness,
    alayavijnana)
foundational root state of the mind (gzhis-rtsa)
four bodies of a Buddha (catuḥkāya; sku-bzhi)
four continent-worlds (caturdvipa; gling-bzhi)
four levels of joy (dga'-ba bzhi) [joy (dga'-ba), supreme joy (mchog-dga'), separated
    joy (dga'-bral) and simultaneously arising joy (lhan-skyes dga'-ba)]
    descending from the top (yas-bab)
    stabilizing from the bottom (mas-brtan)
four opponent powers (gnyen-po bzhi)
four ornaments for the profound Dharma (zab-chos rgyan-bzhi)
four reliances (rten-pa bzhi)
four seals (caturmudrā; phyag-rgya bzhi) (four mudras)
four syllables tradition (yi-ge bzhi)
four true facts in life (caturāryasatya; 'phags-pa'i bden-pa bzhi) (four noble truths)
    sixteen aspects (rnam-pa bcu-drug)
four types of close mindfulness (catuḥsmṛtyupasthāna; dran-pa nyer-gzhag bzhi;
    satipattana)
four voids (catuḥśūnya; stong-pa bzhi) [void (śūnya; stong-pa), very void (atiśūnya;
    shin-tu stong-ba), greatly void (mahāśūnya; stong-pa chen-po) and all-void
    (sarvaśūnya; thams-cad stong-pa)]
free from mental fabrication and fabricating (niḥprapañca; spros-bral)
freshness (gsar-ba)
full extent of what exists and how it exists (yavād-yathā; ji-snyed-pa dang ji-lta-ba)
fully embraced object (khyab-pa'i dmigs-pa)
functional phenomena (vastu, bhāva; dngos-po)
functioning (arthakriya; don-byed)

generation stage (utpattikrama; bskyed-rim) (development stage)
    subtle (phra-mo),
ghost ('dres)
good qualities (guṇa; yon-tan)
    mundane and transcendent (lokalokottara; 'jig-rten-dang 'jig-rten-las 'das-pa)
graded stages of the path (lam-rim)
great bliss (mahāsukha; bde-ba chen-po) (greatly bissful awareness)

great completeness (*mahāsampanna; rdzogs-chen*) (dzogchen)
  mind division (*sems-sde*)
  open expanse division (*klong-sde*)
  oral guideline division (*man-ngag sde*)
great madhyamaka (*mahāmadhyamaka; dbu-ma chen-po*)
great seal (*mahāmudrā; phyag-rgya chen-po*) (mahamudra)
great spaciousness (*klong-chen*)
greatly blissful awareness (*mahāsukha; bde-ba chen-po*) (great bliss)
  uninterrupted (*rgyun-'chad med-pa*)
greed (*chags-pa*)
ground for a nullification ('*gag-sa*)
guideline instructions (*gdams-ngag*)
guru (*guru; bla-ma*) (spiritual mentor, spiritual teacher)
guru-mantra (*mtshan-sngags*)
guru-yoga (*guruyoga; bla-ma'i rnal-'byor*)
guru-yoga of three rounds of inspiration (*rlabs-gsum bla-ma'i rnal-'byor*)

habit (*vāsanā; bag-chags*) (instinct, propensity)
haphazard appearance and appearance-making (*snang-ba ban-bun*)
happiness (*sukha; bde-ba*)
heart essence of the mind (*snying-thig*)
heat stage (*uṣma; drod*)
heightened awareness (*abhijñā; mngon-shes*) (extra-sensory perception)
helpfulness (*upakāra; phan-sems*)
here-and-now (*so-ma*)
here-and-now, non-contriving mind (*so-ma ma-bcos-pa'i sems*)
here-and-now, non-contriving meditation (*so-ma ma-bcos-pa'i sgom*)
hidden (*guhya; gsang-ba*) (enigmatic, secret)
highest yoga tantra (*anuttarayoga tantra; bla-med rgyud*)
highly realized being (*ārya; 'phags-pa*) (arya, noble one)
holder of the diamond-strong scepter of space, pervasive with space (*mkha-khyab mkha'i rdo-rje-can*) (holder of the vajra of space, pervasive with space)
holding the vase-breath (*rlung bum-pa-can*)
hundred-syllable mantra (*yig-brgya*)

idea (*snang-ba*) (mental image)
  involving merely a sound (*sgra-spyi; śabdasāmānya*) (sound universal)
  of a meaning (*don-spyi; arthasāmānya*) (meaning universal)
identitylessness (*nairātmya; bdag-med*) (selflessness)
  coarse (*rags-pa*)
  of persons (*pudgalanairātmya; gang-zag-gi bdag-med*)
  of phenomena (*dharmanairātmya; chos-kyi bdag-med*)
illusion (*māyā; sgyu-ma*)
illusory body (*māyākāya; sgyu-lus*)
impermanence (*anitya; mi-rtag-pa*)
implied object (*zhen-yul*)

impromptu manner of appearance (*gnas-skabs-kyi snang-tshul*)
impulse (*karma; las*) (action, karma)
   collective (*sādhāraṇakarma; thun-mong-ba'i las*)
   individual (*asādhāraṇakarma; thun-mong ma-yin-pa'i las*)
imputation (*prajñāpti; btags-pa*) (mental label)
imputed phenomena (*parikalpita; kun-brtags*) (totally imaginary phenomena)
inanimate environment and animate beings within it (*snod-bcud*)
inattentive perception (*snang-la ma-nges-pa*)
incorrect view of a transitory collection (*satkāyadṛṣṭi; 'jig-lta*)
   simultaneously arising (*sahaja; lhan-skyes*)
independently established existence (*svatantrasiddha; rang-dbang-gis grub-pa*) (existence established by virtue of itself)
indifference (*upekṣā; btang-snyoms*)
indirect apprehension (*shugs-su rtogs-pa*)
indispensable, prerequisite preliminary state for achieving a first-level stable mind
   (*prathamadhyāna samāntakānāgamya; bsam-gtan dang-po'i nyer-bsdogs mi-lcogs-med*)
individual (*puruṣa; skyes-bu*)
infatuation (*lobha, chags-pa*) (attachment)
Infinitely Learned Scholar of the Ten Fields of Knowledge (*gnas-bcu rab-'byams-pa*)
inner flame (*gtum-mo*) (tummo, psychic heat)
inseparability (*dbyer-med*)
   of appearance and mind (*snang-stong dbyer-med*)
   of bliss and voidness (*bde-stong dbyer-med*)
   of samsara and nirvana (*'khor-'das dbyer-med*)
inspection (*vitarka; rtog-pa*)
inspiration (*adhiṣṭhāna; byin-rlabs*) (blessings)
instinct (*vāsanā; bag-chags*) (habit, propensity)
intention (*chandas; 'dun-pa*)
interpretable level (*nityartha; drang-don*) (interpretive level)

joy (*dga'-ba; prīti*)

karmic actions mixed with confusion (*sāsravakarma; zag-bcas-kyi las*) (contaminated actions)
karmic connection (*las-'brel*)
karmic obstacle (*karmāvaraṇa; las-sgrib*)
kindness (*bka'-drin*)

latent awareness (*bīja; sa-bon*) (seed)
layperson (*upāsika; dge-bnyen*)
laziness (*kauśidya; le-lo*)
liberated being (*arhat; dgra-bcom-pa*) (arhat, foe-destroyer)
liberation (*mokṣa; thar-pa*)
light-diffusion conceptual mind (*mched-pa*) (mind of red increase)
limited awareness (*sems*)

line of reasoning (*liṅga, pratipatti, hetu; rtags, rigs-pa, gtan-tshigs*)
line of reasoning of being devoid of arising from self or other (*bdag-gzhan skyes-bral-gyi rigs-pa*)
line of reasoning of being devoid of existing as one or many (*gcig-du-bral-gyi rigs-pa*)
lineage (*brgyud*)
lineage founder (*srol-'byed-pa*)
listener to the teachings (*śrāvaka; nyan-thos*) (shravaka, hearer)
listening, pondering and meditating (*thos-bsam-sgom gsum*) (hearing, thinking and meditating)
location for existence (*yod-sa*)
logic (*mtshan-nyid rigs-lam*)
logical exclusion of everything something is not (*vyāvṛtti; ldog-pa*) (double negative)
loosening focus (*lhod-kyis glod*)
love (*maitrī; byams-pa*)
lucidity (*dvangs*)
luster (*mdangs*)

madhyamaka (*madhyamaka; dbu-ma*) (middle way)
maha-, anu- and atiyoga (*mahāyoga, anuyoga, atiyoga*)
maha-atiyoga (*mahā-atiyoga*)
mahasiddha (*mahāsiddha; grub-thob*) (highly accomplished adept)
malice (*vyāpāda; gnod-sems*)
mandala offering (*maṇḍala; maṇḍal*)
manner of appearance (*snang-tshul*)
manner of apprehension (*'dzin-stangs*)
manner of existence (*yod-tshul*)
mantra (*mantra; sngags*)
mass of conceptual minds (*rtog-tshogs*)
Master of the Ten Difficult Texts (*dka'-bcu-pa*)
material cause (*upadānakaraṇam; nyer-len-gyi rgyu*) (transforming cause, perpetrating cause)
material object (*bem-po*)
"me" (*aham; nga*)
    conventional (*kun-rdzob-pa'i*)
    false (*rdzun-pa'i*)
    to be refuted (*dgag-bya'i*)
"me" as a possessor of things (*maya; nga'i-ba*) (mine)
meaning beyond intellect (*blo-'das-pa'i don*)
meaning of words (*artha; don*)
measure of what exists (*yod-tshad*)
meditation (*bhāvana; sgom*)
    absorption meditation (*'jog-sgom*) (formal meditation)
    blank-minded (*ci-yang yid-la mi-byed-pa'i sgom*)
    in a non-conceptual state (*rtog-med sgom*)
    scrutinizing meditation (*dpyad-sgom*) (analytical meditation)
meditation seat (*stan*)

meditational retreat (*las-rung; ri-khrod*)
meditative absorption (*samādhi; ting-nge-'dzin*) (single-minded concentration, absorbed concentration)
memory (*smṛti; dran-pa*)
mental abiding (*gnas-pa*)
mental block (*āvaraṇa; sgrib*) (obscuration, obstacle)
mental clarity (*gsal-cha*)
mental cognition (*manojñāna; yid-kyi shes-pa*)
mental consciousness (*manovijñāna; yid-kyi rnam-shes*)
    with a defining characteristic making it "me" (*mtshan-gzhi yid-kyi rnam-shes*)
mental dullness (*nirmagnatā; bying-ba*) (sinking)
    gross (*rags-pa*)
    middling (*'bring*)
    subtle (*phra-mo*)
mental fabrication (*prapañca; spros-pa*) (fabricating)
mental factor (*caitasika; sems-byung*) (secondary mind)
mental hold (*'dzin-cha*)
mental itchiness (*tsha-gi tshi-gi*)
mental label (*prajñāpti; btags-pa*)
mental placement (*gnas-cha*)
mental stability (*dhyāna; bsam-gtan*) (concentration)
mere (*mātra; tsam*) (simply, only)
mere clarity and awareness (*gsal-rig-tsam*)
mere "me" (*nga-tsam*)
mere nullification of the object to be refuted (*dgag-bya bkag-tsam*)
messenger (*pho-nya*) (transferring partner)
method and wisdom (*upāyaprajñā; thabs-shes*)
method of actualization (*sādhana; sgrub-thabs*) (sadhana)
mind (*citta; sems*)
    coarse (*rags-pa*)
    subtle (*phra-mo*)
    subtlest (*shin-tu phra-mo*)
mind isolation (*sems-dben*)
mind-stream (*santāna; sems-rgyud*) (mental-continuum)
mindfulness (*smṛti; dran-pa*)
    intermittent ordinary type (*re-thun*)
    special dzogchen type (*thun-mong ma-yin-pa*)
mind's own manner (*sems rang-lugs*)
mind's own state (*sems rang-sor*)
mirror (*ādarśa; me-long*)
modest vehicle (*hīnayāna; theg-dman*) (hinayana, lesser vehicle)
modestly expansive blissful awareness and voidness (*bde-stong rgya-chung*)
moment (*kṣaṇa; skad-cig*)
monastics (*pravrajita; rab-byung*)
mother tantra (*ma-rgyud*)
motivation (*samutthāna; kun-slong*)
    causal (*rgyu kun-slong*)
    contemporaneous (*dus kun-slong*)

moving mind (*'gyu-sems*)
mutually exclusive (*viruddha; 'gal-ba*) (opposite)

nature and things having this nature (*dharmatādharmin; chos-nyid chos-can*)
nature of mind (*sems-kyi ngo-bo, sems-nyid*)
nature of reality (*tathātā; de-bzhin-nyid*) (thusness)
near lineage (*nye-brgyud*)
negative potential (*pāpa; sdig-pa*) (sin)
nihilism (*ucchedadṛṣṭi; chad-mthar lta-ba*)
nine stages for settling the mind (*navacittasthita; sems-gnas dgu*) [initial settling
    (*sems-'jog-pa*), settling with continuity (*rgyun-du 'jog-pa*), settling over and
    again (*blan-te 'jog-pa*), close settling (*nye-bar 'jog-pa*), taming (*dul-bar byed-
    pa*), stilling (*zhi-bar byed-pa*), complete stilling (*rnam-par zhi-bar byed-pa*),
    single-pointedness (*rtse-gcig-tu byed-pa*) and settling with equal ease
    (*mnyam-par 'jog-pa*)]
nine tastes of breath (*rlung ro-dgu*)
nine vehicles (*theg-pa dgu*)
nirvana (*nirvāṇa; myang-'das*) (total release)
    non-abiding (*mi-gnas-pa'i myang-'das*)
    without any remainder of aggregates (*lhag-med myang-'das*)
non-affirming nullification (*prasājyapratiṣedha; med-dgag*) (non-affirming negation)
non-conceptual (*nirvikalpa; rtog-med*)
non-contriving mind (*ma-bcos-pa'i sems*)
non-dissipating drop (*ma-bshig-pa'i thig-le*)
non-duality (*advaya; gnyis-med*)
non-fraudulent (*mi-bslu-ba*)
non-karmic actions unmixed with confusion (*ansāśravakarma; zag-med pa'i las*)
non-obstructive (*anivṛta; ma-bsgribs-pa*)
non-sectarianism (*phyogs-ris med-pa*)
non-static phenomena (*anitya; mi-rtag-pa*) (impermanent phenomena)
normative way to be aware (*tha-mal-gyi shes-pa*)
northern treasure-text lineage (*byang-gter*)
not being truly and inherently existent, therefore appearing (*med-snang*)
not taking anything to mind (*amanasi; yid-la mi-byed-pa*)
nullification (*pratiṣedha; 'gag-pa*) (refutation)

object for cleansing behavior (*spyad-pa rnam-sbyong-gi dmigs-pa*)
object for cleansing the mind of disturbing emotions and attitudes in general
    (*nyon-mongs rnam-sbyong-gi dmigs-pa*)
object labeled (*btags-chos*)
object of a manner of apprehension (*'dzin-stangs yul*)
object of cognition (*viṣaya, yul*)
object of engagement (*'jug-yul*) (engaged object)
object of focus (*dmigs-yul, dmigs-rten*) (focal object)
object of the learned and skilled (*mkhas-pa'i dmigs-pa*)
object to be cut off tradition (*gcod*) (chöd)
object to be refuted (*pratiṣedhya; dgag-bya*)
objective condition (*ārambaṇapratyaya; dmigs-rkyen*)

obstacles (*āvaraṇa; sgrib*) (obscurations)

obstacles preventing liberation (*kleśāvaraṇa; nyon-sgrib*) (obstacles that are disturbing emotions and attitudes)

obstacles preventing omniscience (*jñeyāvaraṇa; shes-sgrib*) (obstacles toward all knowables)

obstruct (*gegs*) (block, occlude)

offerings (*pūja; mchod-pa*)

omniscient awareness (*rnam-mkhyen*)

one entity (*ngo-bo gcig*) (one package, same package, one by nature)

one package (*ngo-bo gcig*) (one entity, same package, one by nature)

open admission (*deśanā; bshags-pa*) (confession)

oral guidelines of Aro (*A-ro man-ngag*)

ordinary appearance and appearance-making (*tha-mal-gyi snang-ba*)

ordinary appearance-making and implying (*tha-mal snang-zhen*)

ornaments of guidelines for the three spheres (*skor-gsum zhal-gdams-kyi rgyan*)

other-voidness (*gzhan-stong*)

over-refutation (*khyab-chen*)


pacifier tradition (*zhi-byed*)

pandit (*paṇḍita; paṇ-chen*) (erudite scholar)

particular (*viśeṣa; bye-brag*)

parting from the four forms of clinging (*zhen-pa bzhi-bral*)

parts and what has parts (*cha-dang cha-can*)

paths and their result (*lam-'bras*) (lamdray)

pathway appearance-making of those who strive (*'bad-lam snang-ba*)

pathway minds and bodhisattva levels (*sa-lam*)

pathway of mind (*mārga; lam*) (path)

    accumulating (*saṃbhāramārga; tshogs-lam*) (path of accumulation)

    accustoming (*bhāvanamārga; sgom-lam*) (path of meditation)

    applying (*prayogamārga; sbyor-lam*) (path of preparation)

    arya (*āryamārga; 'phags-lam*)

    free from fabrication (*spros-bral lam*)

    needing no further training (*aśaikṣamārga; mi-slob lam*) (path of no more learning)

    no more meditation (*sgom-med lam*)

    seeing (*darśanamārga; mthong-lam*) (path of seeing)

    single-pointedness (*rtse-gcig lam*)

    single taste (*ro-gcig lam*)

penetrating vital points (*gnad-du bsnun-pa*)

perfection vehicle (*pāramitāyāna; phar-phyin theg-pa*) (paramitayana, sutrayana)

perfectly solid (*yang-dag-pa*)

perpetrating cause (*upādānakaraṇam; nyer-len-gyi rgyu*) (material cause)

person (*pudgala, gang-zag*)

phenomena of samsara or nirvana (*'khor-'das thams-cad*)

physical exercises (*'phrul-'khor*)

place left behind by a nullification (*dgag-bya bkag-pa'i shul*)

play (*lalita; rol-pa*)

pondering (*cintā; bsam-pa*) (thinking)
positive potential (*puṇya; bsod-nams*) (merit)
possessing five tradition (*lnga-ldan*)
practice with elaboration (*spros-bcas-kyi spyod-pa*)
pragmatic attitude (*kha-yod lag-yod*)
Prajnaparamita sutras (*prajñāpāramitā sūtra*)
prasangika-madhyamaka (*prāsaṅgika-madhyamaka; dbu-ma thal-'gyur-pa*)
prayer (*praṇidhana; smon-lam*) (aspirational prayer)
precious human life (*mi-lus rin-po-che*)
preliminary practices (*sngon-'gro*) (ngondro)
  .  six basic (*sbyor-chos drug*)
presumption (*manaḥparikṣā; yid-dpyod*)
preventive measures (*dharma; chos*) (Dharma)
pride (*māna; nga-rgyal*)
primal matter (*prakṛti; ngo-bo-nyid*)
primally pure (*ka-dag*)
primally pure of concrete reality (*ngo-bo ka-dag*)
primordial (*gnyug-ma*)
primordial Buddhahood (*gdod-ma'i sangs-rgyas*)
primordial clear light mind (*gnyug-ma'i 'od-gsal*)
primordial mind (*gnyug-sems*)
    coarse (*rags-pa*)
    subtle (*phra-mo*)
primordially pure (*gdod-ma-nas dag-pa*)
progressive dissolution (*rjes-gzhig-gi bsdus-pa*)
progressive sequence of dissolution (*lugs-'byung*)
projection (*zhen-pa*)
prologue section of *The Guhyasamaja Tantra* (*gleng-gzhi*)
propensity (*vāsanā; bag-chags*) (habit, instinct)
prophecy (*vyākaraṇa; lung-bstan*)
prostration (*abhivandana; phyag-'tshal-ba*)
pure awareness (*rig-pa*)
    basis (*gzhi'i rig-pa*)
    effulgent (*rtsal-gyi rig-pa*)
pure from its depths (*ye-nas dag-pa*)
pure or impure phenomena (*dag ma-dag-gi chos*)
purification (*sbyang-ba*) (cleansing)

reality (*tattvaṃ; de-nyid*) (thusness)
realization (*rtogs-pa*) (stable realization, understanding)
reason (*pratipatti; rigs-pa*)
rebirth (*punarbhava; skye-ba, yang-srid*)
recognizing the mind (*sems ngo-sprod-pa*)
recognizing the thieves (*rkun-pa'i ngo-sprod*)
re-emergent sequence (*lugs-ldog*)
reflexive awareness (*svasaṃvedana; rang-rig*)
reflexive emanation (*rang-'phros*) (automatic emanation)

reflexive luster (*rang-mdangs*)
reflexive play (*rang-rol*)
reflexive pure awareness (*svasaṃvedana; rang-rig*)
release (*nirvāṇa; myang-'das*) (nirvana)
removal (*apoha; sel-ba*)
renunciation (*niḥsaraṇa; nges-'byung*) (determination to be free)
repulsion or aggression (*pratigha; khong-'khro*) (anger)
resplendent (*lhan-ne, lhang-nge-ba, lhang-gis*)
rid oneself (*prativirati; spong-ba*) (abandon)
ritual (*cho-ga*)
rounds of transmission of the Dharma (*dharmacakra; chos-'khor*) (turning of the
    wheel of Dharma)

safe direction (*śaraṇa; skyabs*) (refuge)
sagely way of life (*drang-srong-gi spyod-tshul*) (way of life of a rishi)
same category of phenomena (*rigs-'dra-ba*)
same package (*ngo-bo gcig*) (one package, one entity, one by nature )
scrutiny (*vicāra; dpyod-pa*) (analysis)
seal of close bond (*samayamudrā; dam-tshig phyag-rgya*) (samayamudra)
seal of preventive measures (*dharmamudrā; chos-kyi phyag-rgya*) (dharmamudra)
sealing partner for deep awareness (*jñānamudrā; ye-shes phyag-rgya*) (jnanamudra,
    wisdom seal)
sealing physical partner (*karmamudrā; las-rgya*) (karmamudra, seal for behavior,
    sealing physical partner)
seed of potential (*bīja; sa-bon*)
seed-syllable (*bīja; sa-bon*)
self-evolving practitioner (*pratyekabuddha; rang-rgyal*) (solitary realizer,
    pratyekabuddha)
self-importance (*māna; nga-rgyal*) (pride)
self-nature (*svabhāva; rang-bzhin*)
self-preoccupation of apprehending everything in terms of "me" (*ahaṃkāra; ngar-'dzin*)
    simultaneously arising (*sahaja; lhan-skyes*)
self-voidness (*rang-stong*)
selfishness (*rang-gces*) (self-cherishing)
semblance (*āloka; snang-ba*) (mental image)
sensory cognition (*indriyajñāna; dbang-gi shes-pa*)
sensory consciousness (*indriyavijñāna; dbang-gi rnam-shes*)
sensory object (*indriyaviṣaya; dbang-yul*)
sentient beings (*sattva; sems-can*)
separation (*visaṃyoga; bral-ba*) (parting)
serenely joyous sense of suppleness (*pariśuddha; shin-sbyangs*)
serenely stilled and settled mind (*śamatha; zhi-gnas*) (mental quiescence, calm abid-
    ing, shamata)
setting voidness out at a distance (*stong-nyid rgyang-du gzhag-pa*)
settled and moving minds mixed together (*gnas-'gyu 'dres-pa*)
settled mind (*sthitacitta; gnas-sems*)
settling in a fluid and flowing manner (*lhug-par 'jog*)

seven facets endowing enlightenment (*byang-chub kha-sbyor yan-lag bdun*)
seven measures (*ri-chos*)
seven ways to scrutinize phenomena (*rnam-dpyad rnam-pa bdun*)
seven-fold posture (*lus-gnad bdun*)
seven-part cause and effect technique (*rgyu-'bras man-ngag-bdun*)
seven-part practice (*yan-lag bdun-pa*) (seven-limb prayer)
sexual organs (*indriya; dbang-po*)
sharpness of focus (*ngar-ba*)
simultaneously arising (*sahaja; lhan-skyes*)
simultaneously arising as merged tradition (*sahajayoga; lhan-cig skyes-sbyor*)
single-pointed focus (*rtse-gcig-pa*)
single-pointed state included within the realm of desirable sensory objects (*'dod-sems rtse-gcig-pa'i*)
six bodily constituents (*khams-drug*)
six collections of consciousness (*tshogs-drug*)
six far-reaching attitudes (*ṣadpāramitā; phar-phyin drug*) (six perfections)
six practices of Naropa (*nā-ro'i chos-drug*) (six yogas of Naropa)
six practices of Niguma (*ni-gu'i chos-drug*) (six yogas of Niguma)
six spheres of equal taste tradition (*ro-snyoms skor-drug*)
sleep (*middha; gnyid*)
small death (*'chi-ba chung-ngu*)
solid existence (*prakṛtisiddha; ngo-bo-nyid-kyis grub-pa*) (existence established as a solid reality)
solid reality (*prakṛti; ngo-bo-nyid*)
song of meditational experience (*dohā, do-ha*) (doha)
space (*ākāśa; nam-mkha'*)
special topics of knowledge (*abhidharma; chos mngon-pa*)
speech isolation (*ngag-dben*)
sphere of devoid nature (*dharmadhātu; chos-dbyings*)
sphere of reality (*dharmadhātu; chos-dbyings*)
Spiritual Leader of the Three Buddha-family Traits (*rigs-gsum mgon-po*)
spontaneously establishing (*lhun-grub*)
stable realization (*rtogs-pa*) (understanding)
stark appearance (*gcer-gyi snang-ba*) (naked appearance)
starkness (*stong-pa*)
state with nothing to be done (*byar-med*)
static phenomena (*nitya; rtag-pa*) (permanent phenomena)
statues (*rūpa; sku*)
stimulators of cognition (*āyatana; skye-mched*) (cognitive sources)
stopping (*nirodha; 'gog-pa*) (ending, cessation)
straightforward perception (*pratyakṣa; mngon-sum-pa*) (bare perception)
striped rope labeled as a snake (*thag-khra sbrul-btags-pa*)
stuffing a thought back inside (*rtog-pa tshur-bkug*)
subsequently attained deep awareness (*anuprāptajñāna; rjes-thob ye-shes*) (post-meditational wisdom)
substantially different (*nānādravya; rdzas tha-dad*)
substantially the same (*ekadravya; rdzas-gcig*)

subtle energy-source of bliss (khams)
subtle energy-system (vajrakāya; rdo-rje lus) (vajra-body)
suffering (duḥkha; sdug-bsngal)
sutra (sūtra; mdo)
svatantrika-madhyamaka (svātantrika-madhyamaka; dbu-ma rang-rgyud-pa)
syllable "pay" (phaṭ)
symbolic universe (maṇḍala; dkyil-'khor) (mandala)
synonymous (don-gcig)

taking as a pathway the result of dedicating our heart with bodhichitta (sems-
    bskyed 'bras-bu lam-khyer)
taking death as a pathway for actualizing the three bodies of a Buddha ('chi-ba
    sku-gsum lam-khyer)
taking on and giving (gtong-len) (tonglen)
tamed mind (sems dul-ba)
tangible and physically obstructive (thogs-thug)
tantra (tantra; rgyud)
    four classes (rgyud-sde bzhi)
    mother, father and non-dual (pha, ma, gnyis-med)
    three inner (nang-gsum)
    three lower classes (rgyud-sde 'og-ma gsum)
    three outer (phyi-gsum)
teachings concerning the deepest meaning to which we are led (neyārtha; nges-
    don) (definitive teachings)
teachings intended to lead us deeper (nītyartha; drang-don) (interpretable teachings)
technical terms (chos-skad)
ten bodhisattva levels of mind (daśabhūmi; sa-bcu) (ten grounds)
    seven impure (ma-dag-pa'i sa-bdun)
    three pure (dag-pa'i sa-gsum)
tenet systems (siddhānta; grub-mtha')
texts (grantha; gzhung)
that which has an object (viṣayin; yul-can)
thinking (bsam-blo sdang)
thoroughly established phenomena (pariniṣpanna; yongs-grub)
those apprehending pure awareness (vidyādhāra; rig-'dzin) (vidyadhara, knowl-
    edge-holders)
those for whom everything happens at once (cig-car-pa)
those of sharp faculties (dbang-po rnon)
those who progress through graded stages (rim-skyes-pa)
thought (vikalpa; rnam-rtog)
thousand, million, billion world systems (stong-gsum-gyi 'jig-rten) (three thou-
    sand worlds)
three aspects of mind (rnam-pa gsum)
three bodies of a Buddha (trikāya; sku-gsum)
three deepest things (triparamārtha; don-dam gsum)
three everlasting streams (rgyud-gsum)
three faults (skyon-gsum)
three higher trainings (triśikṣā; bslab-gsum)

three manners of apprehending "me" (*ngar 'dzin-stangs gsum*)

Three Precious Gems (*triratna; dkon-mchog-gsum*) (three jewels of refuge)

three realms (*tridhātu; khams-gsum*)

    of desirable sensory objects (*kāmadhātu; 'dod-khams*) (desire realm)

    of ethereal forms (*rūpadhātu; gzugs-khams*) (form realm)

    of formless beings (*arūpyadhātu; gzugs-med khams*) (formless realm)

three spheres (*skor-gsum*) (three circles)

three stages of appearance-making (*snang-gsum*) (three visions)

three ultimate things (*triparamārtha; don-dam gsum*) (three deepest things)

three vehicles (*triyāna; theg-gsum*)

threshold conceptual mind (*nyer-thob*) (mind of black near attainment)

tightening focus (*hrim-gyis bsgrims*)

tone of great bliss (*bde-chen nyams*)

total absence (*med-pa*)

total absorption (*samāhita; mnyam-bzhag*) (meditative equipoise)

total completeness of that which is unadulterated (*ma-'dres-la yongs-su rdzogs-pa*)

tradition indicating a view of reality based on experience (*nyams-myong lta-ba'i ston-pa'i lugs*)

trance-like absorption (*samāpatti; snyoms-'jug*)

transference of consciousness (*'pho-ba*)

transferring partner (*pho-nya*) (messenger)

treasure text (*gter-ma*) (terma)

tree of assembled gurus (*tshogs-shing*)

true, independent existence (*satyasiddha; bden-grub*) (true existence)

true, inherent existence (*satyasiddha, svabhāvasiddha; bden-grub, rang-bzhin-gyis grub-pa*)

true, unimputed existence (*satyasiddha; bden-grub*)

tsatsa (*tsha-tsha*)

twelve factors that dependently arise (*rten-'brel yan-lag bcu-gnyis*) (twelve links of dependent arising)

two extremes (*mtha'-gnyis*)

    of existence (*yod-mtha'*)

    of non-existence (*med-mtha'*)

two levels of true nature (*dvasatya; bden-gnyis*) (two truths)

two true facts on the side of total delusion (*kun-nas nyon-mongs-pa'i bden-pa gnyis*)

two true facts on the side of total purification (*rnam-par byang-ba'i bden-pa gnyis*)


ultimately findable (*rnyed-rgyu*)

unadulterated by stains (*dri-mas ma-bslad-pa*)

unaffected phenomena (*asaṃskṛtadharma; 'dus ma-byas-kyi chos*) (unconditioned phenomena)

unawareness (*avidyā; ma-rigs-pa*) (confusion about reality, ignorance)

unconscious awareness (*bag-la nyal*)

uncontrollably recurring rebirth (*saṃsāra; 'khor-ba*) (samsara, cyclic existence)

under-refutation (*khyab-chung*)

undercurrent of thought (*rtog-pa 'og-'gyur*)

understanding (*rtogs-pa*)

unification (*zung-'brel*)

unity (*yuganaddha; zung-'jug*)
   still with further learning (*slob-pa'i zung-'jug*)
universal (*sāmānya; spyi*)
universe (*loka; 'jig-rten*)
unmistakable (*bsnyon-med*)
unobstructed (*anivṛta; ma-bsgribs-pa*) (non-obstructive)
unspecified phenomenon (*avyākṛta; lung ma-bstan*) (neutral phenomenon)


vaibhashika (*vaibhāṣika; bye-brag smra-ba*)
vajra-body (*vajrakāya; rdo-rje-sku*)
vajra position (*vajraparyaka; rdo-rje skyil-krung*)
vajra-recitation (*rdo-rje bzlas-pa*) (vajra-breathing)
valid cognition (*pramāṇa; tshad-ma*) (valid cognizer)
vast vehicle (*mahāyāna; theg-chen*) (mahayana, great vehicle)
vastly expansive blissful awareness and voidness (*bde-stong rgya-che-ba*)
very nature of reality (*tattva; de-kho-na-nyid*) (suchness)
view (*dṛṣṭi; lta-ba*)
view, meditation and behavior (*lta-sgom-spyod gsum*)
vijnanavada (*vijñānavāda; rnam-shes-tsam smra-ba*)
vinaya (*vinaya; 'dul-ba*) (vows of monastic discipline, monastic rules)
vipashyana (*vipaśyanā; lhag-mthong*) (exceptionally perceptive mind, penetrative
      insight, special insight)
visualization (*dmigs-pa*)
visualized image (*gzugs-bsnyen*)
vitality of mind (*sems-srog*)
vivid and vibrant (*sal-le-ba*)
vividness (*gsal-ba, hrig-ge-ba*)
voidness (*śūnyatā; stong-pa-nyid*) (absence of impossible ways of existing, emptiness)
vows (*saṃvara; sdom-pa*) (vowed restraints)
   for individual liberation (*prātimokṣa; so-thar*)


wandering beings (*gati; 'gro-ba*) (sentient beings, migrators)
way of being aware of something (*citta; shes-pa*) (mental phenomena)
ways of knowing (*blo-rig*) (lorig)
what a label refers to (*btags-chos*)
what exists and can thus appear (*snang-srid*) (world of appearances)
whole-hearted commitment to a spiritual teacher (*bshes-gnyen bsten-pa*) (guru-
      devotion)
without artifice (*bcas-bcos med-pa*)
words (*vākya; tshig*)
worse states of rebirth (*durgati; ngan-'gro*) (lower rebirths)


yoga tantra (*yogatantra; rnal-'byor rgyud*)
yogi practitioner (*yogin; rnal-'byor-pa*)
youth of the mind (*sems-kyi gzhon-nu*)

# Index of Text Titles

Chandrakirti (Candrakīrti), *An Auto-commentary on "A Supplement to [Nagarjuna's 'Root Stanzas on] the Middle Way'"* (Madhyamakāvatārabhāṣya; dBu-ma-la 'jug-pa'i bshad-pa) 250

——. *An Illuminating Lamp [for "The Guhyasamaja Root Tantra"]* (Pradīpoddyatana; sGron-gsal) 123

——. *A Supplement to [Nagarjuna's "Root Stanzas on] the Middle Way"* (Madhya-makāvatāra; dBu-ma-la 'jug-pa) 202, 299, 319, 336, 345

Changkya Rölpay-dorjey (lCang-skya Rol-pa'i rdo-rje), *Answers to Questions* (Dri-len) 164, 231

*The Confession Sutra Before the Thirty-five Buddhas* (lTung-bshags lha so-lnga) See *The Admission of Downfalls* 112

Darika (Dārika), *Establishing the Very Nature of the Reality of the Great Hidden Factors* (Mahāguhyatattvasiddhi; gSang-ba chen-po'i de-kho-na-nyid grub-pa) 240

Dharmakirti (Dharmakīrti), *A Commentary on [Dignaga's "Compendium of] Validly Cognizing Minds"* (Pramāṇavārttika; Tshad-ma rnam-'grel) 264

Dharmavajra (Chos-kyi rdo-rje), *The Guru-yoga of the Foremost Three-part Composite Being* (Sems-pa-gsum rtse-mo'i bla-ma'i rnal-sbyor) 109

Dombi Heruka (Ḍombī Heruka), *Establishing What Simultaneously Arises* (Sahajāsiddhi; lHan-cig skyes-grub) 240

*The Eight Thousand Stanza Prajnaparamita Sutra* (Aṣṭasāhasrikā Prajñāpāramitā Sūtra; brGyad-stong-pa) 109, 115, 309

Gampopa (sGam-po-pa Zla-'od gzhun-nu), *A Jewel Ornament for the Path to Liberation* (Thar-pa'i lam-rgyan) 205

*The Guhyasamaja Root Tantra; see The Guhyasamaja Tantra*

*The Guhyasamaja Tantra* (Guhyasamāja Tantra; gSang-'dus rtsa-rgyud) 109, 300

Gungtangzang (Gung-thang-bzang dKon-mchog bstan-pa'i sgron-me), *Notes from a Discourse on the Gelug Tradition of Mahamudra* (dGe-ldan phyag-chen khrid-kyi zin-bris) 230, 283, 297

——. *Thousands of Songs of Meditative Experience* (sTong-mgur) 343

Gyelrong Tsültrim-nyima (rGyal-rong Tshul-khrims nyi-ma), *Last Testament Letter Cast to the Wind* (Kha-chems rlung-la bskur-ba'i 'phrin-yig) 227, 282, 290

Gyeltsabjey (rGyal-tshab-rje Dar-ma rin-chen), *The Heart of Excellent Explanation [Commentary on Aryadeva's "Four Hundred Stanzas"]* (bZhi-brgya-pa'i rnam-bshad legs-bshad snying-po) 233

*The Heart Sutra* (Prajñāpāramitā Hṛdaya; Shes-rab snying-po) 266

*The Hundred Thousand Stanza Prajnaparamita Sutra* (Śatasāhasrikā Prajñāpāramitā Sūtra; 'Bum) 109, 115

(Abhidharmakośa; mDzod) 247

Yogini Chinta (Yoginī Cintā), *Establishing the Very Nature of the Reality of What Follows from Becoming Clear about Functional Phenomena* (Vyaktabhavānugata-tattvasiddhi; dNgos-po gsal-ba'i rjes-su 'gro-ba'i de-kho-na-nyid grub-pa) 240

Yongdzin Yeshey-gyeltsen (Yongs-'dzin Ye-shes rgyal-mtshan), *Clearly Indicating the Main Points from the Oral Teachings of the Gelug Tradtion of Mahamudra* (dGa'-ldan phyag-rgya chen-po'i man ngag-gi gnad gsal-bar ston-pa) 297

——. *Notes from a Discourse on the Gelug Tradition of Mahamudra* (dGa'-ldan phyag-rgya chen-po'i khrid-yig) 297

# Index